THE FOOTPRINTS OF GOD

SUNY Series in Judaica:
Hermeneutics, Mysticism, and Religion

Michael Fishbane, Robert Goldenberg, and
Arthur Green, Editors

THE FOOTPRINTS OF GOD

Divine Accommodation
in Jewish and Christian Thought

Stephen D. Benin

State University of New York Press

BS
476
.B445
1993

Published by
State University of New York Press, Albany

© 1993 State University of New York

For information, address State University of New York
Press, State University Plaza, Albany, N.Y. 12246

Production by Diane Ganeles
Marketing by Theresa A. Swierzowski

Library of Congress Cataloging-in-Publication Data

Benin, Stephen D., 1947–
    The Footprints of God: divine accommodation in Jewish and
Christian thought / Stephen D. Benin.
        p.   cm.—(SUNY series in Judaica)
    Includes bibliographical references and index.
    ISBN 0-7914-0711-X (alk. paper).—ISBN 0-7914-0712-8 (pbk.   :
alk. paper)
    1. Bible—Hermeneutics—Comparative studies.   2. Accommodation
(Hermeneutics)—Comparative studies.   3. Bible. O.T.—Criticism,
interpretation, etc., Jewish—History.   4. Bible—Criticism,
interpretation, etc.—History.   I. Title. II. Title: Divine
accommodation in Jewish and Christian thought. III. Series.
BS476. B445   1993
231.7—dc20   90-44127
                                                         CIP

10 9 8 7 6 5 4 3 2 1

Dedicated to the memory of my parents
Ely and Helen Benin

מוקדש לזכר

אבי ואמי

אליהו בן ישעיהו הלוי ז"ל

חיה אסתר בת אברהם צבי ז"ל

DEITAS.

Nunquam Augustinus Sacrum scrutaberit altum .
quærit irrutiliter quæ fugiunt hominem .

Die Gottheit.

Augustinus wolt ergründen,
was niemand weiß aufzufinden.

Zichler. del ;

Hertel. excud .

Deitas, plate 3 in *Cesare Ripa Baroque and Rococo Pictorial Imagery* from the 1758–60
Hertel edition edited by Edward A. Maser. Courtesy of Dover Publications, Inc.

CONTENTS

PREFACE

The completion of this book provides the opportunity to acknowledge and thank so many who have helped in its preparation. This book began during a conversation one afternoon with Amos Funkenstein, who, after inquiring if I could read German and Greek, handed me a copy of one of his articles, and asked me if the few pages and footnotes he suggested I read reminded me of anything. When I told him that the material which referred to some writings of Gregory of Nazianzus brought to mind Maimonides' explanation of sacrifice in Part Three of his *Guide of the Perplexed,* Amos said, "Good, then you write the book." With that conversation the work began.

A version of this book was accepted as my dissertation by the Department of History at the University of California, Berkeley where it benefited from the comments, suggestions, and criticisms of learned and dedicated scholars. It is a pleasure to thank Amos Funkenstein not only for his initial suggestion, but also for his help at particularly trying times. I wish to acknowledge my debt to Gerard Caspary for his enormous help and the benefit of his immense erudition. For those who have had the good fortune to study with him, and to learn his approach to texts and their exegesis, more need not be said. For Greek patristics and Byzantine sources, I had a sure guide in the late Paul J. Alexander. His exemplary personal and demanding scholarly qualities remain a model and inspiration to me. It is a pleasure to thank William Brinner for his generous help in countless ways; it was he who always had time to listen and provide valued advice. Baruch M. Bokser, who tragically died so young, did not live to see the completion of a work to which, at a very early stage, he made significant contributions.

This study has undergone different incarnations, and I hope that each has been an improvement upon its predecessor. Various scholars have contributed to this process and it is with delightful debt that I thank them. Peter Brown read an earlier draft of this work and sent me detailed and lengthy comments that forced me to rethink things and look at them in new and constructive ways. He made those suggestions which he alone could have made, and as usual, he saw things which others might have missed. I spent many happy hours reading midrash and other Jewish sources with Zev Gries. As is customary in such study, we argued in the friendliest way possible, but I always came away from our meetings having learned something from him. A kind and timely invitation from Joseph Dan to participate in the Third International World Congress on the History of Jewish Mysticism in Jerusalem in February 1988, enabled me to present some of my ideas on accommodation in mystical sources to an admirable group. Edward Alexander read various drafts of this work and made numerous suggestions about style. It is with gratitude that I thank Michael Fishbane, who not only expressed an early and unswerving interest in this manuscript, has not only seen various versions of it, but has displayed great patience and forebearance.

I would be remiss if I did not thank Mary Freilich, Deborah Brackstone, and Elizabeth Buck of Brister Library who answered my seemingly endless requests for books, articles and bibliographic help with expertise, patience, and above all, good humor. And Frances Evensky cheerfully processed many changes on many floppy disks.

This book is dedicated to the memory of my parents. An additional, incalculable debt is owed to my wife Sara, who makes it all worthwhile, and to Naomi Elana, our daughter, who has taught me much about the nature of accommodation.

ἀλλ' εἰ χεῖρας ἔχον βόες ⟨ἵπποι τ'⟩ ἠὲ λέοντες
ἢ γράψαι χείρεσσι καὶ ἔργα τελεῖν ἅπερ ἄνδρες,
ἵπποι μέν θ' ἵπποισι βόες δέ τε βουσὶν ὁμοίας
καὶ ⟨κε⟩ θεῶν ἰδέας ἔγραφον καὶ σώματ' ἐποίουν
τοιαῦθ' οἷόν περ καὐτοὶ δέμας εἶχον ⟨ἕκαστοι⟩.

But if oxen (and horses) and lions had hands or could
draw with hands and create works of art like those made
by men, horses would draw pictures of gods like horses,
and oxen of gods like oxen, and they would make the bodies (of their gods) in accordance with the form that each
species itself possesses.

Xenophanes of
Colophon
Fragment 15

Es ist eine Feinheit daß Gott griechisch lernte, als er
Schriftsteller werden wollte,—und daß er nicht besser lernte.

It was subtle of God to learn Greek when he wished to
become an author—and not to learn it better.

Friedrich Nietzsche
*Beyond Good and Evil, Epigrams
and Interludes,* 121.

INTRODUCTION

"The heaven, even the heavens, are the Lord's: but the earth hath
he given to the children of men."
Psalm 115:16

The title of this book, based on Job 11:7, alludes to the discernible and tangible traces of an incorporeal and transcendent God. This enchantingly provocative phrase does not exist in the original Hebrew text—the Hebraica veritas—though references to the "footprints of God" exist in the Septuagint (LXX), and the Vulgate. If the psalmist is correct and the heavens are the Lord's, then where and how did one seek and find the "footprints of God" in the realm given to humans? The translation, or mis-translation, of Job 11:7, the uses and abuses of this provocatively anthropomorphic phrase demonstrate the issue at the heart of this study: how both Jewish and Christian thinkers attempted to discover traces of the Lord and his actions in 'the earth given to the children of men'.

The unalterable division between the human and divine realms insisted upon by the psalmist was contradicted by other scriptural texts asserting the Lord's intimate connection with his creation. Scripture indeed, on ten occasions, relates that "the Lord came down" to his creation.[1] The disparity between the deity's transcendent and absolute nature and his accessibility to humanity vexed religious and secular thinkers.

Means of resolving this seeming paradox lay in the use of diverse interpretive strategems. Studying the career of one such device— divine accommodation/condescension—which permeates Christian and Jewish thought, finds expression in exegetical, legal, homiletical, and philosophical sources from the first through the sixteenth centuries, and conceivably enters the mainstream of post-Enlightenment thought as a possibly undetected element in the rise of historicism, will enable us to follow the trail left by the "footprints of God".

Divine accommodation/condescension alleges, most simply, that divine revelation is adjusted to the disparate intellectual and spiritual level of humanity at different times in history. I use accommodation/condescension since most Latin sources refer to divine actions with the verb *accommodare,* and most Greek sources employ some form of *baínō, katabaínō,* or *sygkatabaínō.* Whatever the language or terminology, the idea remains the same. The Lord accommodates or condescends, freely and benevolently, to the human level lest his salvific message go unheard and unheeded. The Lord, as it were, had to 'come down' to earth in order to effect the proper unfolding of his universe.

Without invoking the concept of divine accommodation in her admirable study of the medieval theory of knowledge Marcia Colish observed that: "The belief that God had manifested His presence, inchoately in the history of Israel, consummately in the Incarnation of Christ, and continuously since Pentecost in His living extension in time and space, the Church, held for medieval thinkers specific epistemological consequences."[2] Whether in the Law of ancient Israel, in the Incarnation of Christ, or in the continuity of the Church, the Lord, though beyond the scope of human ken, nevertheless communicated with humankind, albeit exclusively on his own terms. That is, the divine-human relationship depended on divine intervention in his mutable creation.

It was common medieval belief "that Christ had chosen to manifest Himself under the ecclesiastical dispensation, which would endure until the end of time, for the express purpose of enabling man to know and love God and other men through an integral union with Him in the life of the Church."[3] Believers in Christ's new covenant and dispensation made manifest in the economy of divine grace had "to preach and teach the Word of God."[4] Yet as Jewish and Christian teachers of God's word well understood, their task, to express the Inexpressible, was formidable if not impossible. As Colish further points out, Christians resolved this tension by appeal to the Incarnation of Christ;[5] Jews found a solution by appeal to the Incarnation of divine teaching in the dispensation of the Mosaic Law. As a rabbinic comment on Scripture penetratingly puts it: " Turn it and turn it for all is in it."[6]

The Torah and Christ's Incarnation are both examples of divine accommodation, and since accommodation is a hermeneutical strategy that is broadly available in such a variety of contexts, its specific "meaning" may become hard to grasp. Indeed, the entire Torah, according to a passage in the Zohar, is but an accommodation to the stark fact of human existence. And in other mystical systems, the total process of the universe is an accommodation to the Absolute's desire for self-knowledge. My aim is not to speculate on the Brobdingnagian vastness of these questions, but rather to compare the career of accommodation in Jewish and Christian sources. That is, I shall focus on the use of this hermeneutical device in these two religious systems with the intent of showing how both systems employed the same idea for similar, as well as different, purposes.

Accommodation began its lengthy, distinguished, and checkered career in the theological arena, appearing prolifically in both Christian and Jewish religious traditions. It remained confined to the theological realm until the early modern conquest of the sacred by the secular, when it then was put to new uses. In attempting to trace the history of any idea, and especially one which is so pervasive, it would be wise to recall Saint-Simon's observation concerning the penetration of intellectual influences. "General ideas," he noted, "may be compared to musk. One does not have to see it or touch it in order to sense its odor." [7]

Accommodation, used interchangeably by patristic writers with divine condescension, pervades countless works. It is best elucidated within certain traditions which influenced religious scholarship from the first through the sixteenth century, if not beyond. One of these traditions held that Scripture was the very word of God; or, in Calvin's phrase, Scripture was the "school of the Holy Spirit". For Judaism, the Hebrew Bible, and for Christianity, the Hebrew Bible—the "Old Testament"—and the New Testament, told all that one needed to know about any and everything.

Once accommodation's connection with the entire ancient medical tradition was introduced into the late antique environment by Galen, and associated not only with creation but with the divine economy—that is, the regulation and management of the universe—it took root and flourished.[8] Like so much else in the patristic garden, accommodation benefited immensely from the animating influence of Philo, and while it is discernible in the philonic corpus, perhaps its most luxuriant patristic examples are displayed in the works of Philo's great student, Origen.

In its development by the Church Fathers during the patristic period, accommodation branches in two directions: I identify them as positive and negative accommodation. Chapter sixteen of Acts, which tells how Paul accommodated his teaching to his audience in order to help spread the faith, is the earliest Christian example of positive accommodation; that is, religion taught on the human level in order to spread the Christian gospel. The negative aspect of accommodation appears in most of the patristic attacks on Jews and Judaism; that is, the Law given to the Jews was not the ideal Law God wished to give humanity, but rather an accommodation to a rude and uneducated people who would not have understood or benefited from a more sublime revelation. In the words of Galatians 3:24, the law was "our pedagogue in Christ". According to this view, God dealt with his people in a merciful way and gave them, at that particular time in their development, rules and regulations, proper for their particular condition, in order to restrain them from total depravity. Christians might have grudgingly granted that Judaism was better than paganism since it directed human worship toward God and not the gods, but it fell far short of the glory of the Gospel and the truth taught by Christ. Accommodation could therefore be used either to buttress the ties between the Testaments, or sever them.

The old patristic cliché of a "New Israel" replacing the "Old Israel" could now be explained in a different way; the Church was a more developed and fuller teaching suited for a more advanced religious community. Jewish ceremonial and ritual law, including the "bloody sacrifices of old" which were necessary for a less sophisticated people, could now be jettisoned. Judaism was an *éminence grise* that could be explained away and ignored.

For Christianity, Christ's sacrifice had replaced all previous offerings, and had irreparably altered history. The irony in the entire Jewish-Christian dispute was, of course, that after the destruction of the Temple and the cessation of cultic worship, rabbinic Judaism managed to put the "bloody" sacrifices safely away in the past— replacing them with prayer—looking for their renewal only in messianic times, while Christianity built its worship and pinned its soteriological hopes upon yet another "bloody" sacrifice.

The first chapter surveys the use of accommodation in the writings of Church fathers from Justin to Athanasius. It was in this formative period that accommodation was used within nascent Christianity in debates over the form that Christian belief and worship were to take, and one of the more fascinating examples of the use of accommodation in that struggle occurs in confrontations with Gnostics. Gnostics could, and did, argue that they were more spiritual than other Christians; they were more advanced, and hence their Gospels were superior to the less developed "orthodox" gospels. The very fact that the Gnostic Gospels were not an accommodation to less enlightened beings proved their superiority. Only the spiritual elect truly knew how to read them, while other Christians, or so the Gnostics claimed, believed in a "trickle-down" Christianity. What occurs within early Christianity is the phenomenon which accommodation exhibits repeatedly; namely, its resilient and supple nature. It was a pliable and potent weapon that would be wielded deftly by disparate groups. It was in this seminal period as well that accommodation would first be exploited to develop "Christian history"; that is, to buttress arguments concerning the superiority of the "New" Israel over the "Old" Israel. From Irenaeus to Eusebius, accommodation would become a tool of Christian historical investigation focusing on the development of the divine *oikonomía*. The pedagogical aspects of accommodation were introduced into Christian exegesis by Origen, who employed accommodation dazzlingly in his remarkable oeuvre painting poignant word pictures of the Lord speaking "baby-talk" with humanity in order to reveal his grand design.

The second chapter explores the cultivation of divine accommodation in the writings of the Cappadocian Fathers and John Chrysostom, the "father of accommodation." Chrysostom ceaselessly employed this principle, not only in elaborating his ideas on virginity, but in moving from those views to an historical interpretation of Christianity. The Cappadocians relied on various uses of accommodation to shore up their theological systems, and it would impinge intermittently not only on their exegesis, but upon their ideas of time and the Incarnation. The Incarnation presented, of course, the extreme example of the divine juxtaposed with the human, and posed the greatest interpretive religious and philosophical dilemmas. Accommodation was a potent ploy to explain the mystery of the faith.

So powerful and useful was this principle that the Syriac fathers delighted in it, and the unbroken chain of polemical writing based on the doctrine of accommodation and traceable for almost the entire span of Syriac literature is examined in the third chapter. The vituperations of Ephrem, the acerbic if well-reasoned lyrics of Jacob of Sarug, and the mild polemics of Aphrahat all contribute richly to the history of accommodation.

Accommodation's Latin career is reviewed in the fourth chapter, for when Augustine tied accommodation into his theory of signs, and incorporated it into his *City of God*, its future in Latin thought was guaranteed. Augustine also employed accommodation as a means of examining and interpreting history, a task carried further in the twelfth century by Hugh of St. Victor and Anselm of Havelberg. For Hugh, accommodation unearthed reasons for the sacramental system of the Church, and in Anselm's hands accommodation defended the rise and spread of new religious orders as well as the Roman Church against doctrinal attacks from Byzantine Greeks.

Accommodation served Christian religious thought very well, explaining as it did how Christianity could be seen as a superior stage in man's religious development, and why, therefore, all of the rituals of the Hebrew Scripture no longer obtained after Christ's advent. Indeed, the new dispensation did away with the old, and the Lord's management of his divine "economy" could dispense with plans outmoded for newer purposes. And recourse to the medical tradition saved exegetes from the difficulty of explaining why God seemed to change his mind by giving the Jews one set of laws and Christians another. Did not physicians prescribe different remedies even for the same person at different times?

If accommodation was a wonderful device for Christian polemics and hermeneutics, it also became part and parcel of the Jewish intellectual heritage. Accommodation's career in Jewish thought, surveyed in chapters five and six, came to cluster around certain prominent themes which find some parallels in Christian writings. Rabbinic sources early on emphasized the pedagogical nature of revelation and the different guises in which the Lord made his law known to Israel. The classical source of this educational motif was Proverbs 22:6: "Train a child in the way he should go." This advice could be bent in many directions and could serve both Jewish and Christian uses.

The educational theme finds eloquent expression in midrashic sources, explaining the seemingly different guises the Lord adopted at different historical moments, such as the deliverance from Egypt, the splitting of the Red Sea and the theophany at Sinai. Rabbinic texts seem to stress the individuality of revelation according to individual capacities, and this approach and tradition was incorporated into medieval Jewish thought. Bahya ibn Pakuda's educational program, advanced in his ethical treatise *Duties of the Heart,* would be adapted and incorporated by Maimonides in his introduction to *Perek Helek.*[9] Maimonides' view of the world and the masses shaped his understanding of the role of Torah and commandments, and accommodation's educational allures proved irresistible to him. As we shall see, accommodation's pedagogical pedigree in Jewish sources is a long and venerable one, stretching from the midrash to modern Hasidism.

Accommodation's career in Jewish thought reached its apogee in Maimonides' writings, which form the basis for chapter six, for it enabled him to create a comprehensive explanation not only for puzzling rituals and commandments, but, more importantly, for the interaction and nexus of divine providence in history and human affairs. Using biblical sacrifice as a point of departure, he went on to produce a mesmerizing rationalization for seemingly foolish religious practices, a rationalization which reshaped the contours of Jewish thought. Posterity inherited his arguments as well as the tumultuous discords and rancor they engendered, and some of those issues as well as the use of accommodation in Jewish thought after Maimonides round out chapter six.

Once Maimonides gave accommodation a place within the Jewish tradition, and once his *Guide* reached the medieval scholastic world in a Latin rehash, a Christian response was inevitable. Christians could now point to Maimonides' views on sacrifice as proof of their arguments about all the ritual observances; who could argue with truth, especially the kind purveyed by Maimonides. Of course there was a catch; Maimonides never suggested that his rationalization of the commandments constituted sufficient cause for non-observance of them. Heaven forbid one think that way and heaven forbid one not observe divine commandments! And yet, as chapter seven shows, when scholars such as William of Auvergne and Thomas Aquinas turned to Latin versions of the *Guide,* each came to grips with Maimonides in his own and unique way. Maimonides' influence on scholasticism is well known; the use of accomodation is but one more link between them.

The seventh chapter also demonstrates that if Chrysostom used accommodation seemingly without end, his closest Christian rival in its usage is Calvin. The chapter tackles the use of accommodation in late medieval and Reformation thinkers. The use of accommodation in Calvin's thought helped interpret, if not solve, the seeming disparity between a sublime God and his mundane creatures. It showed that truth resided in Scripture and not religious institutions; and it gave nascent European science a chance to be free of the shackles forged by centuries of tradition. The Reformation embraced accommodation as heartily as Catholicism had, except now accommodation was accommodating in the opposite direction, and it was turned against its former protector. The final chapter briefly traces accommodation's transition to, and survival in, the modern world. When religious thought yielded its primacy to the secular, signifying the emancipation of the secular from the transcendent, accommodation continued to thrive. The venerable theological language, rather than being abandoned, was vacated of its contents, retained and put to new use.

As extraordinary as the story of accommodation is, perhaps equally remarkable is the almost complete lack of scholarly attention its history and career have received. The "modern" study of accommodation began with John Spencer, who in 1685 published his monumental study *De Legibus Hebraeorum Ritualibus et Earum Rationibus.*[10] Spencer studied Israelite religious practices and sought to demonstrate that they were the natural outgrowth of Israelite association with other semitic peoples. He argued that the Lord, in an effort to preserve monotheism and the observance of essential moral laws, permitted Israel to borrow certain practices from her environs.[11] With *de Legibus,* Spencer set out on a new path deserting the trails of previous scholars. "He contended that the Lord sanctioned certain practices in His Law which were appropriated from foreign people, and through divine condescension (*sygkatábāsis*) accommodated those practices to divine worship."[12] As Spencer explained it:

> God, when the law was bestowed, tolerated numerous customary antique observances and rites, (and He) made use of them in His worship, in order to accommodate (*ut . . . accommodaret*) Himself to the disposition and customs of the people.[13]

While Spencer was learned enough to appreciate that his use of accommodation was not novel, it was to find eloquent expression in his wake. For example, William Warburton's *The Divine Legation of Moses Demonstrated*[14] expresses a debt "to the learned Spencer" and his "excellent work."[15] Warburton realized that according to the theory of accommodation as set forth by Spencer, "the Ritual Law thus explained is seen to be an Institution of the most beautiful and divine Contrivance."[16] Citing Maimonides as well as Spencer, Warburton felt terribly awkward and uncomfortable about suggesting that the institution of divine law simply aped heathen practice, lest any wrongly conclude that God was not the author of Scripture.[17] However pernicious the charge that divine accommodation was simply "a most beautiful and divine contrivance" may have been, it did not stop religious thinkers from embracing and exploiting it.

Scholars such as Julius Wellhausen and C. P. Tiele merely followed the path blazed by Spencer.[18] It was in 1919, with the publication of Henry Pinard's study of divine condescension, with references to Spencer's work, that a Greek and Latin patristic map of the use of accommodation began to emerge.[19] Accommodation in the writings of John Chrysostom was explored by Fabio Fabbi in 1933.[20] In 1958, Karlfried Grunder devoted a chapter of his study of Johann Hamans to the idea of accommodation,[21] and in 1963, Johanna Kopp, explored the role of divine condescension in her examination of seventeenth-century French spirituality.[22] Seminal articles by K. Duchatelez appeared in 1970 and 1973: the former devoted to idea of divine economy, while the latter considered the role of divine condescension in the history of salvation.[23] And John H. Erickson has examined the notion of divine economy in Byzantine Law.[24]

Amos Funkenstein, who has explored this principle in various publications, has shown the presence of accommodation in Jewish thought and its similarity to Christian use. He has also examined the role of accommodation as a possible intellectual bridge between science and theology from the late Middle Ages to early modern Europe.[25] Additional contributions to diverse aspects of the history of accommodation have been made by F. Dreyfus, Hans W. Frei, John Reumann, and a very few others.[26] My intention in this book is to build on the works of these scholars and present a history of divine accommodation in Jewish and Christian thought.

CHAPTER ONE

THEY WALKED BY DAY AS IN DARKNESS

> I hate, I despise your feasts, and I take no delight in your solemn assemblies. Even though you offer me your burnt offerings and cereal offerings, I will not accept them, and the peace offerings of your fatted beasts I will not look upon.
>
> —Amos 5:21–22

With these and other words of Amos and of Isaiah, Jeremiah, and Psalms, early Christian writers attacked Jewish sacrifice. They sought to prove that the sacrifices mandated of old were ordained not as a legitimate form of worship, but rather to combat the Jew's inclination to idolatry. This argument was part of the larger debate concerning the role of the Mosaic Law in a period when Christians understood Jewish messianic hopes to have been fulfilled.

This chapter will examine the course of that debate by tracing a specific exegetical device, which may be termed divine accommodation or divine condescension.[1] Accommodation/condescension is divine revelation in human terms; that is, divinity adapting and making itself comprehensible to humanity in human terms. It is the adaptation and adjustment of the transcendent to the mundane; it is the fine tuning of divine order. Accommodation, as it is used in patristic sources, falls into two broad categories, which may be seen as "positive" and "negative" accommodation.

In patristic texts, accommodation is viewed negatively when it is applied to the Jews and Jewish ritual practice. The punitive understanding of Torah and its ritual observances is a prime example of that attitude. Yet, it must be remembered that any such negative connotation may seemingly be balanced by the preventative nature of that accommodation. That is, the Lord permitted certain ceremonies, such as sacrifices, to keep his people from becoming idolators. Negative accommodation then is both punitive and prophylactic.

Positive accommodation is used in patristic sources when the rise, spread, and triumph of Christianity is being discussed. Accom-

1

modation in the "Christian era" is a great boon, and as we shall see, the Incarnation will be interpreted as the quintessential example of divine accommodation. There is another aspect to positive accommodation; that is, the very act of God recognizing the bodily dimension of humanity—part of the creation—and thus a good in itself. The church fathers, influenced by Platonism, and occupied with polemics against Jews, pagans, and schismatics, not surprisingly tended to emphasize negative accommodation at the expense of positive accommodation. Yet as we shall observe, both explanations coexisted. One of the earliest apologists to stress negative accommodation was Justin Martyr.

Justin, a convert to Christianity, sought to explain how Christians, who, in Jewish eyes, did not observe the divine precepts—even though they were part of Scripture—hoped to merit any kindness from God and how they differed from Gentiles. Indeed, the task that Justin undertook was to compose an apologia for Christian nonobservance of Torah.[2] His project demanded a full-scale examination of the Mosaic Code: its purpose, its details, and its historical role for the Jews, Gentiles, and Christians. Justin's views may best be appreciated when set against the general background of other theories of the Mosaic Code.[3]

Perhaps the cornerstone for the essentially penal character of the Law, which often occurs in patristic literature, originated with Paul. According to the usual interpretation, Paul had viewed the Law inherently as a guardian (*paidagōgós*) to restrain humanity until the advent of Christ (Gal. 3:24). For Paul, the Law was inferior to faith; Moses inferior to Abraham. The Law in fact made transgressions possible (Rom. 3:20, 5:20, 7:13), and part of the salvific nature of Christ's advent included freedom from the Law and transgression (Gal. 3:13). Indeed, as Paul wrote to the Galatians: "Wherefore then serveth the Law? It was added because of transgressions, till the seed should come to whom the promise was made; and it was ordained by angels in the hand of a mediator" (Gal. 3:19).

Paul's view that the Law was ordained by angels in the hands of a mediator, who is understood, almost universally by modern scholarship, to be Moses, could be, and was understood, differently by other early Christian interpreters.[4] Certain Gnostics would view these angels as demons who created the world and gave it an evil law.[5] Justin had to contend with a wealth of different religious and philosophical beliefs. His wares were being hawked with a voice that had to compete with those of other Christian apologists, Jews, Gnostics, and pagans in a crowded, and noisy, theological market.

Justin's clearest and most elaborate exposition of his views is contained in his *Dialogue with Trypho,* recording a debate that supposedly took place about 135 C.E. in Ephesus between Justin and the Jew, Trypho.[6] Justin is the first Christian author to challenge the unity of Scripture by dividing the Law into three parts.:

> I mean that one commandment was appointed for piety and the practice of righteousness, and another command and action was in the same way spoken either as referring to the mystery of Christ or on account of the hardness [*sklērokardíon*] of your people's hearts.[7]

The Law then as understood by Justin contains ethical teachings, prophetic—Christological—teachings, and historical accommodations. The ethics contained in Scripture were universal in scope and application and are eternally valid. They are independent of the Mosaic Code as well as being embodied within it. They are applicable to humanity at large, and in enumerating them, Justin approaches the rabbinic concept of the "Seven commandments of the sons of Noah."[8] In his prophetic/Christological interpretation set out in chapters 40–42, Justin claims that everything established by Moses can be seen as types, symbols, and proclamations of those things that were to happen as a result of the Incarnation.[9] Justin never conflates the two interpretations save in the case of circumcision, which he interprets allegorically and eschatologically.[10]

It is the third part of the Law, the "ritual commandments"—sacrifice, Sabbath, circumcision, fasts, and so on—that Justin construes as decreed by historical necessity. These rituals were legislated for, and pertain solely to, the Jews. The Law is seen as an historical accommodation for the Jews, and Justin stresses repeatedly that the Law was mandated because of the "hardness of your hearts."[11] In contrast to the ethical teachings, which were universal, these rituals were particularly Jewish. This tension between the universality and the particularism in the Law forms a major component of Justin's exegesis.

Justin's essentially penal understanding of the Law was not the only interpretation current at the time. The Torah multiplied sin, which necessitated God's bestowal of grace. This function of the Law ended with Christ.

Paul further reflects the opinion of the LXX, Josephus and remarks in the New Testament (Acts 7:38, 53; Gal. 3:19–20) that the Law was given through a mediator, or through angels, who could, in extreme instances, be seen as demons who created the world and gave it an evil law.[12] This was not Paul's view, but it was the view that would be advanced by the Marcionites. And it was not only the Marcionites with whom Justin had to contend, but with other Gnostic groups including Valentinians, Basilidians, Satornilians, and others.[13]

Justin's emphasis upon the penal character of the Law provoked Trypho to respond. Indeed, argues Trypho, did not Christ himself observe the Law, thus, in essence validating it?[14] Christ's observance, answers Justin, is part of the divine *oikonomía*, the entire plan of salvation, and since Christ effected universal salvation, his observance of particular rituals, whose observance had nothing to do with salvation, in no way validated those particular rituals.[15] In sum, then, for Justin the Law was neither evil nor unnecessary—it was ordained for a stiff-necked, hard-hearted people. As Justin noted:

> We, too, would observe your fleshly circumcision, your Sabbaths, and in brief, all your festivals, if we did not know why they were ordained, namely because of your sins and obduracy. If we patiently bear all the evils put upon us by cruel men and demons, and yet, amid tortures and death that defy description, beseech mercy for our persecutors, and seek not the slightest retaliation, as our Lawgiver decreed, why, Trypho, do we not observe those rites which can do us no harm, such as circumcision of the flesh, the Sabbaths and festivals?[16]

Justin further elaborates how the Jews' sins and obduracy affected their history and actions. God's munificence is made manifest in contrasting Abraham and Moses:

> The same is said of Abraham and his progeny until Moses, when your people, wicked and ungrateful to God, fashioned a calf in the desert. Therefore, the Lord accommodating [*harmosámenos*] Himself to that people, commanded that sacrifices be brought in his Name lest you practice idolatry. Even then you did not obey, for you sacrificed your children to demons; Sabbath observance was instituted, in order to compel you to remember Him, as Scripture states: "That you may know that I am God your Redeemer."[17]

Justin sharply delineates the difference between the New Israel and "your people" and in so doing distinguishes the particularity and limited nature of the rituals of the Mosaic Code from the ethical teachings. The emphasis again is upon the penal character of the Code. Sacrifices were enacted to prevent idolatry, and Justin applies the same reasoning to the building of the Temple in Jerusalem. The Lord permitted the Temple to be built—not for his sake—but as a prophylactic device to restrain the inclination for idolatry.[18]

In arguing about rituals of the Mosaic Law, such as circumcision and dietary restrictions, Justin will employ lengthy citations from Isaiah, Jeremiah, Hosea, Ezekiel, Amos, and Psalms to buttress his position. His anti-Jewish use of prophecy emerges as one of his most potent weapons. The prophetic citations are employed not only to demonstrate the abrogation of an old, particular law, but to contrast it with the promulgation of a new, universal code.[19]

Justin reiterates these ideas throughout the *Dialogue,* and several of them will be more fully developed by other Christian apologists. His tripartite division of the Mosaic Code, his association of the Mosaic Code with the incident of the calf, his frequent charge of Jewish idolatry—the most common one in the *Dialogue*—and his anti-Jewish use of prophecy seem to be original contributions to Christian exposition of Scripture.

Many of the themes encountered in Justin's work appear in Irenaeus of Lyon's *Refutation of False Gnosis* (*Adversus Haereses*).[20] Irenaeus' discussion of sacrifice occurs within the larger issue of the creation of mankind. God created man because of divine philanthropy and chose the patriarchs *"propter illorum salutem."*[21] He appointed a people to teach the indocile to follow him, and prophets were sent to prepare humanity for the Holy Spirit in order to facilitate communion with God. Like an architect, the Lord sketched out the divine plan of salvation, and to the Jews, who were unruly in the desert, he bestowed a most apt Law (*aptissima lex*). The Law was appropriate to the condition of the people, and the Lord attuned humanity to his "symphony of salvation."[22] Irenaeus then focuses upon the Jews:

> Thus He also gave the people the laws relative to the construction of the Tabernacle, the building of the Temple and the choosing of the Levites, the sacrifices and oblations, the purifications and other things relevant to the cult.[23]

None of these things was needed by the Lord, who educated a people easily inclined toward idols, and the Lord employed pedagogical techniques apposite for the situation. He led them to primary matters by means of secondary ones: by the figurative to the truth, by the temporal to the eternal, by the carnal to the spiritual, and by the earthly to the celestial.[24]

Employing a similar approach to the Law as Justin, Irenaeus mentions "natural precepts" contained in the Decalogue that were universally valid and that permitted people to obey the divine decrees. There were those who did not obey, and when the Children of Israel fashioned a calf and reverted mentally to their condition in Egypt, they were placed under the yoke of servitude.[25]

Irenaeus, in launching his attack upon Jewish idolatry, uses the prophets, especially Amos and Ezekiel, to buttress his attack and assert the essentially punitive nature of the Mosaic Law. In choosing Acts 7:39–43 as a proof text, Irenaeus accuses the Jews of emotional and intellectual error:

> This man [Moses] received the living precepts of God to give us, whom your fathers did not obey, but thrust him away, and turned back in their hearts [*corde suo*] to Egypt, saying to Aaron, "Make us gods who will go before us, for Moses who led us out of Egypt, we know not what has happened to him." And they made a calf in those days, and offered sacrifices to the idol, and rejoiced in the works of their hands.[26]

The error of their ways is clarified by appeal to Amos 5:25–26 and Acts 7:39–43, which recounts Israelite worship of Moloch and the star of Rephan. Thus, the Israelites did not worship natural things, such as the sun or moon, but objects of their own creation. Irenaeus asserts that the Law was given to the Jews not by another God (as some Gnostics might believe), but by the very same God of the new dispensation. However, he adjusted it to their condition at that time. In fact, certain precepts were prescribed not because the people desired them, but because they were needed due to the hardness of their hearts.[27]

Irenaeus contends that human frailties were considered not only when the Old Law was mandated, but even governed the promulgation of the New Law:

> If, therefore, even in the New Testament, the apostles are found granting certain precepts in consideration of human infirmity, because of the incontinence of some, lest such persons, having grown obdurate, and despairing altogether of their salvation, should become apostates from God—it ought not to be wondered at, if also in the Old Testament the same God permitted similar indulgences for the benefit of his people, drawing them on by means of the ordinances already mentioned, so that they might obtain salvation through them, swallowing the saving fishhook of the Decalogue, and being restrained by Him, should not revert to idolatry, nor apostasize from God, but learn to love him with the whole heart.[28]

Irenaeus, in the issues he raises and choice of language, may be reflecting silent polemics over the essential difference in the Jewish-Christian understanding of, and attitudes toward, the Law.

Perhaps a tale about an anonymous righteous man best exemplifies the rabbinic attitude toward the Law:

It happened to a Hasid that he forgot a sheaf in his field, and was thus enabled to fulfil the commandment with regard to forgetfulness [Deut. 24:19].[29] Whereupon he bade his son go to the temple, and offer for him a burnt-offering and a peace-offering, while he also gave a great banquet to his friends in honor of the event. Thereupon his son said to him: "Father, why do you rejoice in this commandment more than in any other law prescribed in the Torah?" The Hasid answered that it was the occurrence of the rare opportunity of accomplishing the will of God, even as the result of some oversight, which caused him so much joy.[30]

The story reflects the joy with which Judaism taught that the Law must be observed. Rabbis of the Talmudic and medieval period unanimously mention joy as an ingredient necessary for the proper performance of religious obligations. God, his salvation, and his Law are three things in which Israel rejoices. Indeed, the attitude of the rabbis could hardly be in sharper contrast to the punitive theories of Justin and Irenaeus.[31]

In retelling the story of the fashioning of the Golden Calf, Irenaeus follows the account in Acts 7:39 and notes that the people "in their hearts" (corde suo) turned back to Egypt. After contrasting the Old and New Law, he affirms that God wished men to love him with the "whole heart." Perhaps Irenaeus was still "Jewish" enough to use this term most calculatedly. For him, the heart was not the seat of emotions, but the seat of the deepest, unsocialized identity (what Freud would call the id). This may not have been simply another penal interpretation of the Mosaic Code, but a challenge to nascent rabbinic views of biblical history. For rabbinic Judaism, the heart was the dwelling of man's evil inclination—the yetzer ha-rah—to which all of man's organs show obedience; obeying the yetzer ha-rah was tantamount to idolatry.[32]

Irenaeus maintains that after the giving of the Law Jews were subject to idolatrous urges. This assertion flew in the face of certain rabbinic claims to the contrary, which held that the impulse for idolatry no longer existed among Jews.[33] Whether or not Irenaeus knew of, or was responding to, such claims, his punitive view of the Law is antithetical to certain rabbinic conceptions.

The giving of the Torah at Sinai provided Israel with a unique moment and opportunity in history. A Midrashic passage explains:

When Israel (at Sinai) heard the commandment, "Thou shalt have no other gods before me" [Exod. 20:3], the evil inclination was uprooted from their hearts; but when they came to Moses and said unto him, "Our master Moses, become the messenger between us [Israel and the Lord], as it is said, 'Speak with us . . . but let not God speak with us lest we die' [Exod. 20:19), the evil inclination came back at once in its place." They came again to Moses and said, "Our master Moses, we wish that God should again reveal himself to us." He answered them, "This is impossible now (but will take place in the future)."[34]

According to this Midrash, the revelation at Sinai had eradicated the evil inclination from the hearts of Israel and would have rendered Israel immune from various sins—especially from idolatry and sexual excesses. However, the opportunity was lost.[35]

Irenaeus' insistence that the Jews were idolaters implies that the Jews had not lost this inclination, and the rabbinic Midrash may be an answer to this Christian polemic. But the attack may have been more pointed; the very value, meaning, and purpose of Torah for Judaism may have been assailed. And it is noteworthy, that certain Midrashic statements speak directly to the issue.

A Midrash on Deuteronomy 11:18—"Therefore impress— *vesamtem*—these My words upon your very heart: bind them as a sign on your hand, and let them serve as a symbol upon your forehead"—elucidated the historical and moral importance of the Torah. Interpreting the verb—*vesamtem* (impress)—as two nouns—*sam tam* ("a perfect remedy"), the Midrash continues:

> This may be compared to a man who struck his son a strong blow, and then put a poultice [*retiyyah*] on his wound, saying to him, "My son! As long as this poultice is on your wound you can eat and drink at will, and bathe in hot or cold water, without fear. But if you remove it, it will break out into sores." Even so did the Holy One, blessed be He, speak unto Israel: "My children! I created the Evil Inclination, but I (also) created the Torah, as its antidote; if you occupy yourselves with the Torah, you will not be delivered into its hand . . . but if you do not occupy yourselves with the Torah, you will be delivered into its hand. . . ."[36]

Two antithetical approaches to Torah and its value emerge quite graphically. God had created the inclination and its treatment. In *Sifre,* God says: "My sons, I created for you an evil impulse; I created for you the Law to temper it."[37] What for a Jewish author is a poultice is, for Irenaeus, a straightjacket.

Irenaeus' arguments must be seen in the context of his battle against the entire Gnostic tendency to dismiss the Law entirely as an oversight of a foolish creator. That approach would have excused the Christians from even trying to fit the problem of the Law into God's providential scheme. Yet, Irenaeus accuses the Valentinians themselves of using accommodation for their nefarious purposes:

> These most vain sophists affirm that the apostles did with hypocrisy frame their doctrine according to the capacity of their hearers . . . so that the Lord and the apostles exercised the office of teacher not to further the truth, but even in hypocrisy, and as each individual was able to receive it.[38]

Irenaeus asserts most emphatically that the glory of Christianity is its truth and that neither the message nor the messengers made any accommodation to the masses. This is in fact a positive aspect of an absolutely explicit accommodation theology, which we shall see approached in Origen's exegesis. Indeed, the author of *The Second Treatise of the Great Seth* launched the following attack on "orthodox" Christianity:

> . . .we were hated and persecuted, not only by those who are ignorant (pagans), but also by those who think they are advancing the name of Christ, since they were unknowingly empty, not knowing who they are, like dumb animals.[39]

The criticism of the orthodox for being "dumb animals" implies that they possess an accommodated gospel, while the Gnostics, who possess the "real"—that is, an unaccommodated—gospel, are the true Christians and represent the true Church. If the orthodox established objective criteria for its adherents, the Gnostics stressed spiritual maturity. *The Second Treatise of the Great Seth* claims that the true church is composed of members "united in the friendship of friends forever, who neither know any hostility, nor evil, but who are united by my gnosis. . . ."[40]

One of the contested issues was, who possessed the proper understanding of the gospel. The Gnostic critique of orthodoxy centered, not on the fact orthodoxy had a false gospel, but that it did not properly understand the gospel it had. That is, the Gnostic position excoriated the orthodox for being tied solely to the most elementary level of interpretation, which precluded the possibility of obtaining the deeper truth contained in the text. The problem was that the orthodox failed to apprehend and appreciate the deeper gnosis available to those who could dive through the various levels of Scripture and plumb the great depths.[41] All levels of Scripture contained truth, but the deeper levels were suited to the more mature; the more superficial levels to the immature. This approach led to confrontation with the orthodox positions on doctrine, ritual, and ecclesiastical hierarchy: the basic elements of church organization. The attack of Irenaeus, the orthodox bishop of Lyons, against the Valentinians was part of the ongoing process of Christian self-definition; accommodation played a role in that process.

Irenaeus employs the Gnostic understanding of scriptural accommodation when he turns to the revelation given to the Jews and conflates it with medical imagery, a turn that was to prove very popular with many later exegetes. According to Irenaeus, the Lord did not prescribe medicine according to the whim of the patient, but gave the patient what was needed. "He therefore did not address them in accordance with their pristine notions, nor did He reply to them in harmony with the opinion of His questioners, but according to the doctrine leading to salvation, without hypocrisy or respect of person"[42] Irenaeus insists that the Law was given to the Jews not by any God, but by the same one the Christians worship.[43] Thus, accommodation, as applied by Irenaeus to the Jews, was essentially negative in character; yet, the concept was an accommodating one, and was to develop remarkably.

If the initial interpretations of sacrifice led to an incipient theory of accommodation, the schools and scholars of Alexandria were to refine and embellish it. Supported by the wealth of an intellectual tradition embracing Jewish, Hellenistic, and Christian elements, Alexandrian exegetes would justify accommodation's use in Christian thought.

Perhaps it was Philo's comment on Genesis 11:5—"The lawgiver talks thus in human terms about God, even though he is not a human being, for the advantage of us who are being educated, as I have often said in other passages"—which underlay the entire edifice.[44] It fell to Philo's most creative Christian student, Origen, to give accommodation perhaps its most eloquent expression.

Origen's major theological work, *On First Principles,* is a textbook on accommodation; explaining how the divine message is to be interpreted for human salvation. Origen's allegorical system equated the tripartite division of body, soul, and spirit with three levels of interpretation and scriptural truth.[45] Each level has importance and is beneficial for the "multitudes of sincere and simple believers."[46] (This, of course, was the issue between Irenaeus and the Valentinians.) Origen views this threefold nature of Scripture as a very good thing; not only does it enable the spiritual person to attain the highest level of truth, but it shields that level from the masses.

Origen conceded that simpler minds may understand Scripture in a superstitious way, but their only error is to misunderstand the divine purpose. Yet, they may be true in their belief. As Origen observed: "We teach about God both what is true and what the multitude can understand, though intelligent Christians understand it in a different sense." But Plato himself thinks it justifiable to tell a lie to a homicidal lunatic.[47]

This entire process of education was one that accommodated itself to different stages of human development, and for the Christian teacher, the problem was compounded. He must speak without upsetting the simple, yet without boring the more intelligent. Had not Paul accommodated his teachings to the carnal Corinthians, providing milk and not meat?[48]

Origen insists repeatedly that human weakness required a poor and humble style of Scripture.[49] Scripture provided the signposts for salvation; it was a written revelation, but there was even a greater revelation, namely, the Incarnation:

> While the Incarnation is a veritable revelation of God, it is the ladder by which we are to ascend from the flesh to the spirit, from the Son of Man to the Son of God. The incarnate Lord, like the written revelation in inspired scripture, is a veil that must be penetrated. It is an accommodation to our present capacities in this life. The Church's present gospel will one day be superseded by that which the Seer of the Apocalypse calls the everlasting gospel, a heavenly comprehension of truth that will surpass our present understanding by at least as much as the new covenant surpasses the old.[50]

Nor is a superficial reading of Scripture sufficient for proper understanding, for the three levels that Origen delineates are often intermingled:

> A similar method can be discerned also in the law, where it is often possible to find a precept that is useful for its own sake, and suitable to the time when the law was given. Sometimes, however, the precept does not appear to be useful. At other times even impossibilities are recorded in the law for the sake of the more skillful and inquiring readers, in order that these, by giving themselves to the toil of examining what is written, may gain a sound conviction of the necessity of seeking in such instances a meaning worthy of God.[51]

Origen recognizes, as did Irenaeus, the historical accommodations made in Scripture, yet his interpretation differs greatly. Origen seems to understand two dimensions to positive accommodation. The first is to use scriptural style and language as a challenge, for without impossibilities being recorded in the Law the "more skillful and inquiring readers" would have little incentive to pore over the sacred page. The Lord thus spurs the more skillful student on to deeper truths. The second is the way in which Scripture stoops to accommodate the simpleminded. These dimensions of accommodation would become more prominent in later exegesis.[52]

In concluding his remarks on the proper exegetical method, Origen states his position emphatically:

> Let everyone, then, who cares for truth, care little about names and words, for different kinds of speech are customary in different nations. Let him be more anxious about the fact signified than about the words by which it is signified, and particularly in questions of . . . difficulty and importance. . . . Our aim has been to show that there are certain things, the meaning of which it is impossible adequately to explain by any human language, but which are made clear rather through simple apprehension than through any power of words.[53]

For Origen, this is the second side of positive accommodation and is expressed through the metaphor of the adult stooping to help the child. "He condescends [*sygkatábē*] and accommodates Himself to our weakness [*ásthenéia*], like a schoolmaster talking a 'little language' to his children, like a father caring for his own children and adopting their ways."[54] Was that not what Origen was doing for the simpleminded? He labored to bring higher insights to the attention of inferior capacities; to provoke and cajole so that in time they might comprehend things presently beyond their range.[55]

In replying to Celsus' critique of biblical anthropomorphisms, Origen will exploit the same metaphor, though more expansively:

> Just as when we are talking to very small children we do not assume as the object of our instruction any strong understanding in them, but say what we have to say accommodating it to the small understanding of those whom we have before us [*áll harmosámenos pròs tò ásthenès tôn hypokriménōn*], and even do what seems to us useful for the education and upbringing of children, realizing that they are children: so the Word of God seems to have disposed the things which were written, adapting the suitable parts of his message to the capacity of his hearers and to their ultimate profit.[56]

Perhaps Origen's most extended and dazzling use of the familial metaphor—which would be employed no less spectacularly by Chrysostom—

occurs in his elucidation of Jeremiah 18:6–10, which seems to describe God changing his mind and repenting of evil he contemplated. For Origen, accommodation explains how God could be said to change. After presenting biblical citations culled from both testaments, Origen writes:

> But when divine providence [*oikonomía*] is involved in human affairs, God assumes human intelligence, manners and language. When we talk to a child of two we talk "baby-talk" because he is a child, for as long as we maintain the character appropriate to an adult age, and speak to children without condescending [*mḗ sygkatabainóntas*] to their language, it is impossible for children to comprehend. Now imagine a similar situation confronting God when he deals with humans especially those who are still "babes" [*népion*]. Notice too how we adults change the names of things for children, we have a special name for bread, and we call drinking by another name without using "grown-up" language, but we use another language adapted for infants and nurselings . . . [*lézei tinì paidikḗ kaì brephódei*]. And if we name clothes to children we give the clothes other names, as if we made up a special children's language. Are we then immature because we do this? And if someone hears us speaking this way with children, would he say, "This old man is losing his mind, this man has forgotten that his beard has grown, that he is a grown-up?" Or is it permissible for the sake of accommodation [*symperiphoràn*], when we are speaking with a child not to speak the language of older and mature people [*presbūtikḗ mḗdè enteleî*], but to converse in a child's language [*paidikḗ*]? God surely speaks to children.[57]

Origen truly displays his genius in this superb description of divine accommodation. Accommodation helped him explain divine revelation, the relationship between God and man, divine providence, and other issues.[58] It provided him with a powerful tool with which he could try to teach his less gifted brethren truths that they could not, by themselves, grasp. Origen might have employed accommodation as a speculative theologian and philosopher, but as a teacher, he utilized it because it served his needs so well. His embrace of this exegetical device assured it a place in Christian thought. And it is with Eusebius of Caesarea, deeply indebted though he was to Origen for his theology, philosophy, and exegesis, that accommodation, in addition to being an exegetical and polemical device, would emerge as a tool of historical examination.[59]

Eusebius' works must be set in the context of his life. He lived in a part of the Roman Empire that had strong Christian roots. His early years saw little persecution of Christianity, and the attacks on the nascent faith that his middle years witnessed yielded to the rule of a Christian emperor. He "began as a scholar, made himself into a historian, and turned to apologetics only under the pressure of circumstances. . . . The three dominant characteristics of his thought are a continual emphasis on the Bible, an intellectual framework which derives from Origen, and the celebration of the success of Christianity in the Roman world."[60]

Eusebius began composing his two tracts on the gospel shortly after Licinius defeated Maximinus in 313 and completed them before Maximinus' fall eleven years later.[61] *The Preparation for the Gospel* (*Praeparatio Evangelica*) surveys the historical relationship between Christianity and Greco-Roman civilization, and *The Proof of the Gospel* (*Demonstratio Evangelica*) explores the relationship between Christianity and Judaism. In our examination of Eusebius, we shall focus on the latter work.

In setting forth his "proof of the gospel," Eusebius employed all of his skills and demonstrated his expertise in secular and sacred history, classical literature, philosophy, geography, exegesis, and even mathematics. He sets forth his central thesis in his *Church History*, refines it in his *Prophetic Extracts,* and displays it fully in *The Preparation for the Gospel* and *The Proof of the Gospel.*

Eusebius asserts that Christianity is nothing else than the religion taught by the prophets of Israel; that is, not only a true faith but the faith primeval. With that as his starting point, Eusebius, as we shall see, spins a web of great size and suppleness, embracing the totality of human existence. It is noteworthy that the *Prophetic Extracts* form part of his *General Elementary Introduction,*[62] a work written to convince pagans not only of the inferiority of their own tradition to the Judeo-Christian teaching but the superiority of the Christian component of the latter. Eusebius defends his position by attacking the "incorrect" Jewish interpretations and the "heretical" views of such teachers as Marcion.[63]

Eusebius well understood that his message had to be adapted to his audience:

> For who of the faithful would not confess that the stores of salvation concerning the Word of God are incomparably superior to every bodily pleasure and benefit, being suited for the acquisition of truly beneficial and healthy correctness of belief? To respect this is necessary not only for those who have made moral progress and are called "kings," but also for those who are at a lower level and are

just approaching the divine word for the first time. I think that my enterprise will be especially suitable for them, so that they may be able thereby to understand thoroughly the truth of matters about which they have been informed (Luke 1:4). Pure and simple faith possesses the firm force of conviction all the more when a man uses his reason and first lays foundations by demonstration and then receives elementary instruction in the certain apprehension and knowledge of what must be accepted on faith.[64]

Eusebius believes that God has revealed himself to man only twice in history: once to the patriarchs of Israel and again in the Incarnation of the Logos. During that long intervening period, mankind had no direct apprehension of the divine. Since the patriarchs came before the Mosaic dispensation, they were, of course, Gentiles, yet they knew the Lord. The Mosaic dispensation was geared to those who followed the patriarchs and knew of God only indirectly and through shadowy representations. The Mosaic Code fit the times in which it was given, though it did contain all the details necessary to recognize Christ when he appeared. The Mosaic Code paved the way for the Incarnation, and properly interpreted, it yielded its prophetic treasure. The Jews, not recognizing what they had been given, turned against Christ, and thus lost their political independence. The ongoing punishment of the Jews in Eusebius' own time and the great strides made by Christianity only proved Eusebius' assertions.[65]

The great discrepancies between the ill-fortune of the Jews and the good fortune of the Christians are repeated constantly in the *Prophetic Extracts* and in another of Eusebius' works, the *Second Theophany:* [66]

This was uttered before the event; the Savior foretold what would be, and it soon came about, so that fulfillment of the events was seen by men's eyes not long afterward. Since his time, throughout the whole inhabited world of man, among all races, the symbols of the kingdom of God have been visible through his churches, with myriads living in them according to the gospel of salvation and endearing to worship God like the ancient prophets and Abraham himself, Isaac, and Jacob. For they too, though they preceded in time the laws of Moses, were conspicuous for living and conducting themselves according to the gospel, since they despised the polytheistic error inherited from their fathers and received the knowledge of the supreme God. For this reason, it was said that the majority of the gentiles would come from east and west, and that they would become equal to Abraham and those other blessed men because of their equally good way of life. How the descendants and successors of those same men, called sons of the kingdom because of their forefathers (for potentially, like their forefathers, they had a share in the heavenly kingdom), have been deprived of their promised blessings is shown clearly by the sack of their city, the siege of their temple, their scattering among all the races of mankind, their enslavement to their enemies, and, in addition, their deprivation of worship according to Jewish custom, their ignorance of Christ, and their alienation from the teachings of the gospel. All these things should be manifest signs of the darkness which has enveloped them, into which they have stumbled because they oppose the light of salvation.[67]

For Eusebius, the verdict of history is final and without appeal. The Jewish people have forfeited what had been theirs; they have been supplanted and replaced by the Gentiles who recognize Christ. This entire scenario and approach are, by now, well known, and Eusebius displays his enormous creativity and exegetical skill in *The Proof of the Gospel*. Eusebius elaborates an interpretation fully consonant with that in his other works, and thus the following analysis may serve as a representation of the totality of Eusebius' thought.

As Eusebius undertakes his reconstruction of Jewish history, he notes that the righteous of old did not observe any of the ritual practices of Judaism; they were neither circumcised, nor observed dietary laws; they knew nothing of the Sabbath, but lived "according to the Gospel of Christ."[68] Eusebius weaves together passages from Job 31 and Matthew to show how the righteous who existed before Moses struggled to live a virtuous life.

He summarizes his presentation:

So and in such ways the pre-Mosaic saints [*theophílon ándrón*] (for from the record of one we may imagine the life of all), waged their renowned contests for good, and were reckoned friends [*phíloi*] of God, and prophets. What need had they of the commandments of Moses, which were given to weak and sinful men [*phaloîs ándrási kaì moxthēroîs*]? From all this it is abundantly proved that the Word of God announced to all nations the ancient form of their ancestors' religion, as the new covenant does not differ from their form of holiness, which was very ancient even in the time of Moses, so that it is at the same time both old and new [*óste homoû kaì pălaían aûtén eînai kaì neán*]. It is, as I have shown, very, very old; and, on the other hand, it is new through having been as it were hidden away from men through a long period between, and now come to life again by the Saviour's teaching.[69]

Eusebius thus advances not an antinomian theory, but an "antenomian" theory; that is, Christianity is a return to the *status quo ante*. It is not a return to an *ecclesia vera et primitiva* nor a *synagoga vera et primitiva*. It is a return to that faith, pure and true, which preceded the Mosaic Code; it applauds people who were not so much before the Law, but in the truest sense of the word, above the Law. The true Law existed and was hidden away, only to emerge once again through the message of Christ. The Law has been superseded, not by a new Law, but by an "old yet new" Law. That is, Christianity is the older, truer faith; if you will, the "old" Israel reborn. Judaism thus becomes an intruder, and Eusebius explains this intrusion:

> And it was in this intermediate period, while the ideal of the new covenant was hidden from men, and as it were asleep, that the law of Moses was interposed [*pareiselthōn*] in the interval. It was like a nurse and governess of childish and imperfect souls [*hoîá tis nēpion kaì atelôn psychôn epítropos kaì oikonómos*]. It was like a doctor to heal the whole Jewish race, worn away by the terrible disease of Egypt. As such it offered a lower and less perfect way of life to the children of Abraham. For through their long sojourn in Egypt, after the death of their godly forefathers, they adopted Egyptian customs, and, as I have said, fell into idolatrous superstition.[70]

The Old Law for Eusebius, basing himself upon Romans 5:20, was an intruder that had been stealthily inserted into history. It came as a pedagogue and physician. Eusebius interprets the Law using the metaphors of his experience; that is, the image of Roman *tutela* of minors. It came to cure the "disease of Egypt"; the idolatrous practices associated with Egypt. For Eusebius, the Jews became like the Egyptians in all respects, including idolatry. It was Moses who tore them away from their godless polytheism and led them back to God.[71]

The "disease of Egypt" was idolatry. Laws were enacted to proscribe many acts that had hitherto been freely practiced. Yet, for Eusebius, this was not the sum total of Moses' accomplishments; they were more numerous and are enumerated:

> He rescued them from their wild and savage life [*paralabòn dè ek anēmérou kaì thēriódous bíou*], and gave them a polity based on better reason and good law as the times went, and was the first lawgiver to codify his enactments in writing, a practice which was not yet known to men. He dealt with them as imperfect, and when he forbade idolatry, he commanded them to worship the One Omnipotent God by sacrifices and bodily ceremonies. He enacted that

they should conduct by certain mystic symbols the ritual that he ordained, which the Holy Spirit taught him in a wonderful way was only to be temporary: he drew a circle round one place and forbade them to celebrate their ordinances anywhere, except in one place alone, namely at the Temple in Jerusalem, and never outside it.[72]

Eusebius has presented a sweeping reinterpretation of Jewish enslavement, manumission, and revelation that reverberates with the whole mystique of the end of the "beast-like life" and raises the question of the origins of society. This was an issue explored by many classical authors and is perhaps best encapsulated in the myth of Athens. Eusebius' historical exploration fits into that tradition and anchors him firmly in the classical tradition shared by educated pagans and early Christians.

Perhaps the most famous example of this genre is the *Panathenaic Discourse* of Aelius Aristides.[73] This study of Athens and its place as the mother of civilization, composed between 165 and 170 C.E., praises the Athenians as the creators of civilized life and *paideía*.[74] Aristides took his place in a long line of authors of encomia to cities and took up the themes adumbrated by Diodoros and others. As Diodoros observed:

If it can be said of any other people, the prestige of the city of the Athenians deserves our reverences, and we may well return to them our gratitude for the benefactions they have bestowed upon man. For it is they who first gave to the Hellenes a share in a food gained by cultivation of the soil, which, though they had received it from the gods for their exclusive use, they made available to all. They it was who discovered laws, by the application of which the manner of men's living has advanced from the savage and unjust existence to a civilized and just society.[75]

A most interesting inscription at Delphi contained a decree of the Delphic Amphictyony in honor of the Athenians and likens their mission to a religious duty. The decree in part praises the Athenians for contributing laws, agriculture, tragedy, and comedy, indeed, all drama to humanity. One line in particular merits consideration. We read that the Athenians led mankind out of an animal (savage) existence (. . .*èg mén toû thēriṓdous bíou metégagen toùs ánthrṓpous eis hēmerótē*) into civilization.[76] The entire treatise, which traces Athenian history, attempts to prove that Athens attained its importance through cultural imperialism—that is, the conquest of others by means of her language, literature, and philosophy.[77] Indeed, Athens is seen as the intermediary between the human and the divine.[78]

What is at stake in this remarkable discourse is much more than simply praise of a city. In asserting that Athens was the mediator between the divine and human, Aristides was reclaiming the Logos for the pagan side. No longer was it to be thought of as the Christian Christ, nor was it the Jewish Torah, but the forces of the Logos—the men of Athens—were to lead the battle against the demonic forces of the world.[79] Aristides contrasts the noted antipathy of Christians and Jews for the rest of mankind with the *philanthrōpía* of the Athenians, and Aristides' voice harmonizes with Celsus' critique of Christianity.[80]

Aristides stressed the ethos of the Athenians, and in so doing no doubt saw Christianity more as a form of barbarism than as a simple aberrant form of Hellenism. Aristides' language, at times, assumes religious colorings and raises the vision of history suffused with additional quality and meaning. This aspect of thought is also found in Justin, repeated in the *Panathenaic,* and taken up again by Celsus. Aristides used the same language as Eusebius, though for very different purposes and with different intents. Where Aristides drew on a pagan tradition of great antiquity and wealth, Eusebius, heir to the same tradition, employed Scripture instead.

Eusebius understood the role of the Law to be a positive one in leading humanity out of its animal and savage existence into civilization. His view stands in opposition to the interpretation advanced by Justin and Irenaeus. For them, the Law was punitive in nature and was given to combat the untransformed evil inclination resident in Israel. Eusebius adopted a more progressive attitude than either of his predecessors. And where they polemicized with their view and interpretation of the Law, Eusebius' more positive view was also part of the Jewish-Christian polemic.

Perhaps Jewish-Hellenistic literature as well as rabbinic sources demonstrate the issues at stake. Various Midrashic comments uphold the opinion that all culture and civilization itself are traceable to Adam. It was he who brought blessings to humankind, but these were lost after his error in Eden. One ought not be surprised to find that Socrates was a student of Ahitophel, nor that Plato had studied with Moses.[81] Indeed, one need only recall Numenius' famous quip that Plato was simply an "Atticizing" Moses.[82]

Eusebius, in the *Preparation of the Gospel,* preserved the writings of Artapanus, a Hellenized Egyptian Jew who meticulously set out the Jewish contributions to civilization. Indeed, Abraham is praised as the father of astronomy and astrology; Joseph is thanked for introducing an orderly society into Egypt, as well as its territorial divisions; Moses is the author of writing; and of course, the Jews gave the world philosophy.[83]

Some of Eusebius' comments about Moses seem to echo Jewish claims on his behalf. For Eusebius, Moses put God's Law into a written form and presented the Israelites with a new way of life, while rescuing them from their debased life-style. Dealing with them according to their level, Moses restricted religious practices to Jerusalem. Eusebius advances his interpretation of Jewish history:

> And they have come to this impasse, although Moses himself foresaw by the Holy Spirit, that, when the new covenant was revived by Christ and preached to the nations, his own legislation would become superfluous, he rightly confined its influence to one place, so that if they were ever deprived of it, and shut out of their national freedom, it might not be possible for them to carry out the ordinances of his law in a foreign country, and as of necessity they would have to receive the new covenant announced by Christ. Moses had foretold this very thing and in due course Christ sojourned in this life, and the teaching of the new covenant was borne to all nations, and at once [*parachrêma*] the Romans besieged Jerusalem, and destroyed it and the Temple there.[84]

Moses, according to Eusebius, knew the fate of the Law even as he was proclaiming it. Its observance was purposely limited so that it might eventually pass away and allow the "return" of the new and true covenant. The Romans, acting out their role in the mystery of redemption, destroyed the Temple, immediately (*parachrêma*)[85] abolishing the Old Covenant. The Romans annulled one law and fulfilled another; Christ came to restore the Law to its pristine state. With the destruction of the city and Temple, the whole of the Mosaic Code was abolished, and those who continued to observe it were cursed, for they observed a nonexistent law (cf. Deut. 27:26). The Lord could now be worshiped anywhere (cf. John 4:23), and Eusebius is quick to point out the effect of his interpretation:

> Presently, [*parachrêma*] not long after, Jerusalem was besieged, the holy place and the altar near it and the worship conducted according to Moses' ordinances were destroyed, and the archetypal holiness of the pre-Mosaic men of God reappeared. And the blessing assured thereby to all nations came, to lead those who came to it from the first step and from the first elements [*tês prôtês stoicheiôseôs*] of the Mosaic worship to a better and more perfect life. Yes, the religion of those blessed and godly men, who did not worship in any one place exclusively, neither by symbols nor types, but as our Lord and saviour requires "in spirit and in truth," by our Saviour's ap-

pearance became the possession of all the nations [*toîs éthnésin*], as the prophets of old foresaw.[86]

Eusebius contrasts the familiar particularity and elemental character of the Mosaic Code with the universality and more advanced nature of Christ's dispensation. A flood of proof texts is cited to further the argument that all are now included in the universal covenant, including the idolatrous Egyptians. As Eusebius proudly asserts, "Yes, in our own time the knowledge of our Omnipotent God shines forth, and sets a seal of certainty on the forecasts of the prophets."[87]

Eusebius proceeds to present his summation of the pre-Mosaic, Mosaic, and Christian covenants and their historical relationship. The Old Covenant is the one given to Moses, and the New Covenant, as prophesied in Jeremiah 31:31, will be unlike the Old. Therefore, the covenant introduced at the time of the Exodus and the wandering in the desert could not be the model for the New Covenant; rather the ancient covenant that obtained under the pre-Mosaic righteous people was the model for the New Covenant. As Eusebius declares:

> And, therefore, for the future you may confidently classify the ideals of religious worshipers under three heads, not two: the completely idolatrous who have fallen into the errors of polytheism; those of the circumcision, who by the aid of Moses have reached the first step of holiness; and thirdly, those who have ascended by the stair of Gospel teaching. If you regard this as a mean between the other two, you will no longer suppose that perverts from Judaism necessarily fall into Hellenism, that those who forsake Hellenism are, therefore, Jews. Recognizing the third division in the middle, you will see it standing up on high, as if it were set on a very lofty mountain ridge, with the others left below on each side of the height. For as it has escaped Greek godlessness, error, superstition, unbridled lust and disorder, so it has left behind Jewish unprofitable observances, designed by Moses to meet the needs of those who were like infants and invalids [*kaì hoîá népioîs kaì ásthenési*].[88]

The Law and the Jews are both historical interlopers, a situation that Moses recognized. The Jews represent the "New Covenant"; the Christians are truly the "Old Covenant" come again. Indeed, Eusebius has simply inverted the covenants; Judaism replaced, for a limited time and in a limited place, the true, original covenant under which the pre-Mosaic righteous individuals flourished. The Mosaic Code was historically conditioned to childlike and weakened people and was inferior to what came before and after.

Eusebius quotes at length from Matthew 5, to bring out in sharpest relief the differences between the New Covenant of the Jews and the restored Covenant of Old. He concludes his analysis by maintaining that Christ did obey the Law of Moses, in spite of the fact that he set up a new and all-virtuous system (*ho tèn kainén tautén kaì panáreton politeían*).[89] This is all the more noteworthy, for it shows the great perspicacity of Jesus. He did this out of respect for Moses and the prophets in order to establish the validity of his mission and to render it unassailable by critics. Had Christ broken the Law of Moses, nonbelievers would have been afforded ammunition with which to attack both Christ and his teachings. Jews could have used his transgressions, were they to exist, as an attack upon him also. This is abundantly clear by the actual historical fact that the Jews did attack Christ as being a "transgressor" and "apostate" (*parabátēs kaì apostátēs toû nomoû*).[90]

The ideas expounded by Eusebius are quite novel on the one hand and, on the other, quite conventional. He presents most of the stereotypical language, but introduces some new wrinkles. Judaism and its Law are the interlopers; Scripture provides abundant proof. Jews represent the "New Covenant"; Christians the reborn "Old Covenant." The Jews are under their Law; the Christians are the righteous "antenomians," come again. The essentially negative character of God's accommodation with the Jews and the punitive interpretation of the Law favored by Justin and Irenaeus have yielded to Eusebius' more positive view of accommodation and "progressivist" theory of the Law.

More light may be shed on the comparison of the essentially punitive character of the Law favored by both Irenaeus and Justin with the more positive view of Eusebius, by a very brief glance at several Judeo-Christian sources that reflect yet another facet of opinion. The *Pseudo-Clementine Recognitions,* a theological ragbag, ought to be investigated in order to examine ideas that freely crossed the rabbinic-patristic divide. The *Pseudo-Clementine Recognitions* date from sometime in the third century.[91] The *Recognitions* in describing Israelite history tell how Abraham, who was an astrologer, came to understand the role of divine providence in the world by studying the stars.[92] Abraham's two sons, Ishmael and Heliosdros, gave rise to two nations: the barbarians, and the Persians, some of whom aped their neighbors, the Brahmans, and settled in Arabia. Those who settled in Arabia became famous in Egypt, and it was from these descendants of Abraham that some Egyptians and Indians learned circumcision and to be strict in observance.[93]

The captivity in Egypt is quickly recounted, as are the births of Isaac and Jacob and the Israelites' descent into Egypt. The themes that are developed upon are set out clearly. The Jews left Egypt by the circuitous route, rather than the shortest route, in order that the novelty of a new life might be given time to extirpate the evils that resulted from long association with Egyptian customs.[94]

Of the ten precepts given to the Israelites at Sinai, the most important was the worship of only one God. However, when Moses had been on the mountain for forty days and nights, the people became very agitated and forgot all the divine mercies they had been shown. They fashioned the Golden Calf, whose form they had seen in Egypt.[95] The *Recognitions* make very clear that the people could not cleanse themselves of this Egyptian pollution. Moses, seeing the people so frantic, permitted them to sacrifice, but only to the Lord. This was done in order to remove half of the evil, for Moses knew full well that its complete removal would have to await a future teacher.[96]

The *Recognitions* elaborate upon a theme adumbrated in Justin, namely, the role of the Temple in the Mosaic dispensation. The text warns those who sacrifice that they will be given over to captivity, their lands will be conquered, and their Temple destroyed. The Lord desires merciful and righteous acts, not sacrifices.[97] Subsequent chapters in Jewish history simply reconfirm the difficulties confronting the Jews. Moses set "Auscs" over them in the Holy Land, they triumphed, erected the Temple, but fell into baser impiety. When Christ came to end sacrifices once and for all, his teachings fell on deaf ears. Sacrifice, unable to cleanse sin, was replaced by baptism.[98]

The sacrificial cult comes in for severe condemnation in the *Recognitions,* and Jesus' abolition of the cult is of primary importance. In fact, H. J. Schoeps argues that the real point of Christ's mission was the annulment of the sacrifices combined with complete loyalty and observance of the remainder of the Code.[99] Sacrifices were instituted because of the hardness of the people's hearts (cf. the polemical intents in Irenaeus). For many Jewish-Christians of the first and second centuries, Christ's promise not to change anything in the Law did not pertain to sacrifice, which, like the monarchy, female prophecies, and other things that did not truly belong to the divine law, passed away in the debacle of 70 C.E.[100] The opposition of the *Recognitions* to the cult demonstrates most convincingly that in the period before Nicaea sacrifices were a subject under discussion and review by diverse groups; Christians, Judeo-Christians, and even the Essenes—who, according to Philo and Josephus—revered Moses, yet rejected sacrifices.[101]

The ideas contained in the *Recognitions* are representative of Judeo-Christian literature. Two additional sources, the *Didascalia Apostolorum* and the *Apostolic Constitutions,* most probably reflecting the opinions of Christian communities influenced by Jewish ideas, merit brief consideration.[102] The *Didascalia* asserts, much as Eusebius, that there were in fact two laws; the Decalogue, which represents Christ and which was the law given before the sin of the calf, and the rest of the Mosaic Code, which was given as a punishment for that very sin. Christ of course observed the true, eternal law, but ended the temporary second dispensation.[103] This is the concept of *deúterosis* as a second, inferior, more onerous law; the lighter law never mentioned sacrifices or food distinctions.[104] Sacrifices were mandated only after the Exodus, when the people forgot all that God did for them:

> Therefore the Lord was angry; and in his hot anger—(yet) with the mercy of his goodness—He bound them with the Second Legislation, and laid heavy burdens upon them, and a hard yoke upon their neck. And He says now no longer: "If thou shalt make," as formerly; but He said: "make an altar and sacrifice continually," as though He had need of these things.[105]

Because of the people's errors and stiff-necked attitude, Christ came to abolish the heavy, burdensome second legislation. The Law was given for one age; the second legislation for another. This seems to conflate the positive and negative aspects of accommodation; the true Law was viewed positively; the second legislation, being the Mosaic Code, was punitive.[106]

In the age of Christ, neither the Church nor Christians are bound by the second legislation. Anyone who strives to obey the second law is guilty of calf worship, and is thus an idolater. Christ, under Roman hegemony, fulfilled the Law and abrogated the second legislation. Sacrifice and all the ceremonial ordinances are viewed negatively; they are the fetters forged by apostasy in the desert.

The *Didascalia* as it came to be incorporated in the *Apostolic Constitutions* reveals a change in tone and emphasis. The *Constitutions* assert that the calf fashioned in the desert represented the Egyptian Apis.[107] Sacrifices and dietary restrictions were imposed in order that the people "depart from the error of polytheism."[108] The rituals of the Mosaic Code were enacted to prevent the Jews from forgetting their God:

> He bound them for the hardness of their hearts, that by sacrificing, and resting, and purifying themselves, and by similar observations,

they might come to knowledge of God, who ordained these things for them.[109]

The *Didascalia* may not have seen any pedagogical purpose in the sacrifices, but in the *Constitutions* they are a heuristic device. These three Judeo-Christian sources indicate that the issue and interpretation of the biblical sacrifices were important and widely discussed. As our later examination and analysis will show, it occupied the talents of Greek, Latin, and Syriac exegetes and was to become a staple of the thought world of Christendom. Whether these three sources influenced Eusebius or not, we cannot determine; what we can say is that they shared similar concerns with Eusebius and one last Alexandrian, Athanasius, the great champion of the faith of Nicaea.

Accommodation is secure in the writings of Athanasius, and the theory was to be of great importance in his attempt to combat Arianism.[110] It is little wonder that the proof text championed by the Arians—Proverbs 8:22—was the same text Athanasius employed in his refutation of their beliefs. Proverbs 8:22 came to be coupled with other proof texts—Hebrews 1:4 3:1–2, and Acts 2:36—to stress the character of the Arian Christ, and it was precisely that character that Athanasius and other "orthodox" writers attacked.

For Athanasius, the Incarnation was an act of condescension, not an act of promotion as he understood the Arians to assert.[111] The Arian claim that Christ was a creature—no matter how exalted a creature—brought with it the repugnant corollaries that Christ was subject to change—for better or worse—though the Arians invariably meant improvement and advancement.[112] Theirs was a Christ who struggled and could earn a reward; a thought highly repugnant to Athanasius, who claimed quite simply:

> He [Christ] was not from a lower state promoted but humbled himself. Where then is any reward of virtue, or what advancement and promotion in humiliation? For if, being God, he became man, and descending [*katabàs*] from on high, he is still said to be exalted, where is he exalted, being God?[113]

The similarity of the espoused Arian position approached certain pagan and stoic ideas of advancement and perfection. The basic Arian model of a perfected creature whose advancement culminated in the crucifixion, when he submitted to divine will, gave Athanasius the opportunity to assert his basic contention that essence precedes and interprets biblical language. That is, the Incarnation represented the quintessential example of divine accommodation to humanity, not an agreement or symphonic understanding between God and a creature—no matter how meritorious.[114]

Another issue in the dispute further involved the relationship of the Incarnate Christ to God. The Arians' understanding of "grace" implied that quality by which a creature—indeed, a servant— could call God, Father. After all, for the Arians, Christ freely chose to be a servant and claimed divine fatherhood by "grace." This position could not be tolerated by Athanasius. Grace, for him, could confer sonship on humans, but could not, and did not, permit them to adopt a parent. Grace was brought to the world through Christ and represents the accommodating nature of the divine Incarnation and revelation. Grace implies the unification of the divine Logos with humanity in the flesh; it is the appearance of the Logos in history—it is the supreme act of divine condescension to humanity.[115]

The importance of the Incarnation for Athanasius can be understood by examination of other of his works, including his *Festal Epistles, Contra Gentes,* and *De Incarnatione.*[116] The themes of divine accommodation, condescension, idolatry, and the role of the ritual laws of the Jews are woven into the fabric of Athanasius' thought, and in his hands, they become bulwarks in the battle against the Arians.

The themes are often touched upon in Athanasius' Paschal Letters, and it is not accidental that the letters for Easter—the time of the Incarnation—focus on these themes. The dating of Easter was an issue of contention in the Church from the Council of Nicaea until the Synod of Whitby. By itself it indicated the attachment to and the reliance upon Jewish tradition, while at the same time attempting to sever the very ties that held it near. It ought not be forgotten that the Arians had miscalculated the date of Easter for 339/340, an event that brought them much ridicule.[117] And as we shall see, Athanasius will compare the Jews and Arians as nonbelievers who do not observe Easter in the proper manner.

Athanasius repeatedly stresses that the rituals of Judaism were limited to the Temple in Jerusalem—a charge heard before and to be repeated later by Chrysostom.[118] These customs, which were figurative and symbolic, were limited temporally as well as spatially. For Athanasius, as for Eusebius, when Jerusalem came to an end so did the rituals.[119]

Athanasius, on several occasions, refers to the true Passover meaning the Lord's festival, not the festival the Jews observe hypocritically.[120] The time of shadows has passed, and humanity must now celebrate in a new month, a new time; the time after the Incarnation.[121] In discussing the sacrificial practices of Scripture, Athanasius points out that a law had been given to the people for their education

(... *lex horum rituum lata fuit ob populi eruditionem*), and as a figure of things to come.[122] The Jews did not understand the significance of the revelation; therefore, they walked by day as in darkness (... *in die tanquam in tenebris ambulabant*). They approached the letter but not the spirit.[123] Athanasius argues that the Jews have dealt falsely with the Law, affirming things without understanding them. He uses proof texts from Isaiah and Jeremiah to excoriate Jewish religious practice and concludes that, although the Lord did not require these acts, their souls delighted in such abominations (Isa. 66.3).[124]

In turning to an investigation of the prophetic utterances, Athanasius expounds upon his historical examination by looking at the heretics who have turned against the law (*isti haereses adversus legem meditati sint*).[125] Athanasius asserts that God ordained sacrifices, and the book of Leviticus is replete with mention of diverse offerings. Sacrifices were seemingly instituted, on the one hand, to enable the offering of the bearer to be accepted by God and, on the other, to condemn those who despise sacrifices and did not offer them, in disobedience of the law. However, the proclamations of Isaiah 1:12–13 and Jeremiah 7:21–22 seem to contradict Scripture: "I have not required these by your hands. Nor did I speak to your fathers concerning sacrifices, nor command them about burnt offerings."

In trying to reconcile the pentateuchal and prophetic attitudes toward sacrifice, Athanasius will approach the Eusebian solution. The Athanasian position asserts that at first it was not the Law and commandments concerning sacrifices that were primarily intended, but rather the things that these prefigured. The Law adumbrated those good things to come, which were appointed until the time of reformation (Heb. 9:10, 10:1).[126] Athanasius states his main point:

> Therefore, the whole law did not treat of sacrifices, though there was in the law a commandment concerning sacrifices, that by means of them it might begin to instruct men and might withdraw them from idols, and bring them nearer to God, teaching them for that present time. Therefore neither at the beginning, when God brought the people out of Egypt, did He command them concerning sacrifices or whole burnt-offerings, nor even when they came to Mount Sinai. ... but His commandment was given, that they might know Him Who is truly God, and His Word, and might despise those which are falsely called gods.[127]

Athanasius proceeds to describe the events after the theophany and alludes to issues much favored by other exegetes:

> So He made Himself known to them in that He brought them out of Egypt, and caused them to pass through the Red Sea. But when they chose to serve Baal, and dared to offer sacrifices to those that have no existence, and forgot the miracles which were wrought in their behalf in Egypt, and thought of returning thither again; then indeed after the law, that commandment concerning sacrifices was ordained as law; so that with their mind, which at one time had meditated on those which are not, they might turn to Him Who is truly God, and learn not, in the first place, to sacrifice, but to turn away their faces from idols, and conform to what God commanded.[128]

In Athanasius' account, the laws concerning sacrifice were not part of the original Mosaic dispensation; they were not cunningly inserted, but were mandated by Jewish ignorance and ingratitude. Thus, Athanasius favors the punitive over the more progressive view of Eusebius. They were not an end in themselves, but a means to an end. The laws concerning sacrifice were a prophylactic device to prevent the Israelites from reverting to idolatry and a pedagogical device to help them recognize the true God and to observe his commandments. The divine plan did restrain their desire for idolatry, for Athanasius concludes that the Jews learned to serve only the Lord.[129]

Athanasius enlarges upon these themes in the *Contra Gentes* and the *De Incarnatione*. The themes encountered in Athanasius' other works were adumbrated early in his career, and the emphasis upon the role of Christ, emerges clearly. The role of Christ which Athanasius stressed in his later struggle with the Arians, is contrasted with the foolishness of pagan worship—especially idolatry.

For Athanasius, idolatry arose from evil. The human soul regressed from bad to worse, and once humanity could imagine evil, which does not exist, it proceeded to invent nonexistent gods. The glorification of the creation instead of the creator was the great folly of the idolatrous practices that arose, and once idolatry began, it became progressively worse.[130]

The folly of idolatry is a theme Athanasius exploited. Once humanity had fallen into irrationality and sculpted gods and goddesses in the shapes of diverse animals, they came to view the true God in similar fashion. Greek philosophers claimed that these statues enabled humanity to comprehend better the divine. In fact, they likened these sculptures unto letters for humanity, by means of which an understanding of the divine might be facilitated (*kaì eînai toútous hôsper grámmata toîs anthrôpois*). As Athanasius notes, this is mythology not theology![131]

The fault with the Jews is that they have received fuller teach–
ing than pagans, and yet they fell into idolatry even though Scrip–
ture forbade it.[132] Revelation of God is understandable only through
Christ, who condescends to created beings (*hoútō kaì toîs genētoîs
sygkatabaínōn*).[133] The failure of the Jews to comprehend truth was a
common motif in Athanasius and others, and he develops it even
more fully in the *De Incarnatione*.

Several sections in this work (esp. 33–40) deal with biblical exegesis in an attempt to prove the blindness and obduracy of the Jews
in their refusal to recognize Christ. Athanasius, however, begins his
examination of the Incarnation after a brief recapitulation of human
history and its fall into idolatry. And it is important to understand the
Incarnation in terms of human history, since humans were the cause
of the Incarnation. In turning away from God, mankind brought upon
itself death, and had God not intervened, the human race and other
divine works would have perished.[134]

What should God have done in such a situation? Should he have
allowed his entire creation to have been led to destruction by the
deceit of the devil? Human repentance would not have affected God's
honor. To save humanity, God, in his benevolence, condescended and
became manifest to us (*allá paragínetai sygkatabaínōn tḕ eis hēmâs
autoû phĭlanthrōpía kaì epipháneia*).[135] Divine philanthropy took pity
on the human race, was merciful to our weakness, condescended to
our corruption, and did not endure the dominion of death (*ĕléēsas tò
génos hēmôn, kaì tḕn asthenéian hēmôn oikteirésas, kaì tḕ phthorâ
hēmôn sygkatabás, kaì tḕn toû thanátou kratēsin oŭk ĕnégkas. . . .*).[136]

God knew his creatures and their weaknesses; thus, he provided
a law and prophets to safeguard them, for men can learn more directly from other men about more advanced things.[137] The Law was
not given only to the Jews, but to all humanity; for knowledge of the
Law would have kept people away from impiety and brought them to
virtuous lives. The Law and the prophets provided sacred teaching
about divine knowledge for the whole world (*pásēs dé tês oikouménēs
ĕsan didáskalion hierón tês perí theoû gnōseōs*).[138]

Athanasius introduces the concept of the Law and prophets speaking for the entire world—the *oĭkonomía*. This term was to acquire a
venerable pedigree.[139] *Oĭkonomía* took on various meanings over the
centuries, and in the Byzantine tradition, which we shall explore in
the next chapter, it seems to have acquired two predominant meanings. The first was an imitation of the divine mercy and the second
implied accommodation, "The prudent adaptation of means to an end,
diplomacy and strategy, verging on dissimulation and the 'pious lie.' "[140]
Oĭkonomía is frequently used in biblical exegesis to describe embar-

rassing incidents such as Paul's circumcision of Timothy, and in a church frequently rent from within over theological and doctrinal matters, accommodation was to become a way of life.[141]

Before examining the further development of that and other terms in later exegetes, it would be useful to review the different emphases of accommodation that we have encountered. The essentially punitive and negative interpretation of Justin, combating schismatics and non-believers, with its anti-Jewish use of prophecy agrees well with Irenaeus' polemical attack on the residual evil inclination that dwelled in Jewish hearts even after Sinai. Irenaeus' entire experience in combating Valentinians, and other schismatics who would have exonerated Christians for even bothering to fit the Law into the divine economy—a law that was simply the oversight of a foolish creator—no doubt influenced his entire approach to the issue.

In turning to the Alexandrian tradition, it is evident that for Origen accommodation was the way in which the Lord communicated with his precious children. It became an exegetical tool for expounding the word of God in a comprehensible—and in Origen's prose, a most eloquent—manner. For Eusebius, divine philanthropy, accommodation, and Jewish religious practice were all signposts on the path of historical development. History before and after Christ simply confirmed the truth of the new dispensation, and the political catastrophes of Eusebius' Jews were simply reflections of their theological rejection. Although Eusebius displays a more progressivist approach than either Justin or Irenaeus, he nevertheless demonstrates that ideas current in early Christianity and reflected in the Judeo-Christian literature of the period contributed to the development of the use of accommodation for orthodox purposes in combating Arianism and its warped understanding of the place and function of Christ in history. The Arian Christ could not have effected the same salvation as could Athanasius' Christ, and for Athanasius, the place of the incarnate logos in history was intricately bound up with biblical interpretation, the role of Jewish ritual, and the entire ordering of the divine economy.

For these authors the notion of divine accommodation was an active, historically sensitive, accurate, and reliable hermeneutical principle that could, and did, adapt itself to a variety of intellectual and theological settings. The idea of accommodation, which was so vital and important to these authors, would take root and flourish brilliantly in the writings of Antiochene and Cappadocian fathers. It is to them that we must now turn.

CHAPTER TWO

AS INFANTS AND CHILDREN

Unto Adam also and to his wife did the Lord God make coats of
skins, and clothed them. Genesis 3:21

In the year that King Uzziah died I saw also the Lord sitting upon
a throne, high and lifted up, and his train filled the temple.

Isaiah 6:1

Alexandrian exegetes used accommodation and divine condescension so abundantly and skillfully that it became a vital part of early
Christian exegesis. This chapter will examine the impressive use of
accommodation and condescension in the works of the Cappadocian
Fathers and several representatives of the school of Antioch, especially John Chrysostom, dubbed by a modern scholar, the "father of
condescension,"[1] and Theodoret of Cyrus. The earlier themes reappear with different emphases and nuances, but despite some changes
in vocabulary, the underlying ideas remain recognizable.

It was in Cappadocia, in the middle of the fourth century, that
Athanasius' work was to be continued especially by three brilliant
disciples: Basil the Great (c. 330–379), his brother, Gregory of Nyssa
(c. 335–c.394), and his friend, Gregory of Nazianzus (c. 330–389/90).[2]
By the end of the fourth century, the victory of Nicaea over Arianism
seemed assured, and the part this triad played in that victory was not
insignificant. Life-long friends, they were remarkably different sorts.
As one scholar has noted, Basil was a man of action; Gregory of
Nazianzus, a rhetorical master; and Gregory of Nyssa, a thinker.[3]

Accommodation is employed by the Cappadocians within their
work in general. An intellectual portrait of each author will enable
the Cappadocian contributions to the history of accommodation to
emerge clearly. Information about Basil's position and the esteem he
was accorded may be gleaned from a letter of Gregory of Nazianzus,
in which he calls Basil "my guide of life and my teacher of the faith."[4]

31

This same letter, dated 372/3, also discusses Basil's teaching on the Holy Spirit, and Gregory reports that their theological opinions had been assailed by certain people. At a recent party, adds Gregory, a monk attacked Basil's teaching in respect to the Deity of God as contained in the Holy Spirit, because Gregory never explicitly refers to the Holy Spirit as God. Basil had been upbraided by monks for this reserve, and Athanasius, in supporting Basil, cautions all who attack Basil to consider his intention and purpose (*oikonomía*); "to the weak he becomes weak to gain the weak."[5] At the party Gregory employs *oikonomía* as a defense for Basil as well.[6]

It is in his funeral oration for Basil, that Gregory presents the issues most clearly:

> The enemies were on the watch for the unqualified statement "the Spirit is God," which, although it is true, they and the wicked patron of their impiety imagined to be impious; so that they might banish him and his power of theological instruction from the city and themselves be able to seize upon the Church . . . . He postponed for a time the exact term, begging as a favor from the Holy Spirit Himself and His earnest champions, that they would not be annoyed at his *oikonomía* (in refraining from the express assertion "The Holy Spirit is God") nor, by clinging to a single expression, ruin the whole cause, from an uncompromising temper, at a crisis when religion was in peril. . . . Under the pressure of the difficulties of the period, he himself undertook the *oikonomía*, while allowing freedom of speech to me . . . in order that by our united efforts our Gospel might be firmly established. I mention this not to defend his reputation . . . but to prevent men from thinking that the terms found in writings are the utmost limit of the truth, and so have their faith weakened, and consider that their own error is supported by his theology, which was the joint result of the influences of the time and of the Spirit, instead of considering the sense of his writings, and the object with which they were written. . . .[7]

This rather remarkable oration tells us much about Basil and Gregory, and more about Basil's understanding of *oikonomía*. For Basil, this term, much as for Athanasius, was vitally important and meant a variety of things, including the adaptation of means to ends.[8]

Clearly, Basil understands *oikonomía* as one form of accommodation, for when he found himself in danger of being expelled from his diocese for theological differences with some who did not accept the divinity of the Holy Spirit, he accommodated his public theological statements to fit the circumstances. He deemed it proper to use *oikonomía* for the spiritual profit of his followers, who might have suffered greatly had he been driven from his post, and his absence might have greatly hurt their faith. Also of note is the secret plan by which Basil accommodated his teachings, yet Gregory, who did not face the same dangers, was permitted to speak more frankly. Theological accommodation became a fact of life in areas torn asunder by early Christian disputes, and evidence of similar arrangements may be found in the activities of Cyril of Alexandria, Eulogos, patriarch of Alexandria (580–607), and even Athanasius.[9] Here in no uncertain terms we find accommodation applied as ecclesiastical policy in the search for church unity, something very dear to Basil.

The monk, who attacked Basil's theological position, argues for ἀκρίβειᾰ, categorical definitions, or exactness and precision, not oικονομία. For Gregory of Nyssa, both were components in the Christian life, and as one scholar has recently observed, Basil's use of oικονομία combines philanthropy and wisdom.[10] Oικονομία and ἀκρίβειᾰ also came to represent the conflict between philosophy and rhetoric. For Gregory of Nazianzus, Basil was great because he combined both qualities in his life and seemed to resolve the tension between them.[11]

At the heart of the concept of oικονομία, as we have seen, "is the notion of accommodation to circumstance, whether in the daily management of an estate, as originally, or in church affairs, or in God's providential concern for his creatures as seen in the Incarnation. It is not the imposition of a rule but the exercise of a function and has properly to do not with compromise but with adjustment."[12]

For Basil, as we shall see, as well as for the other Christian authors we have examined, oικονομία possessed diverse shades of meaning and, as a process for determining values to live by, fit humanity into sacred history. As a term for the Incarnation, it was freely interchanged in patristic writing with other terms including sygkatábāsis.[13] As one scholar has observed, the use of sygkatábāsis by the Cappadocians is rather sparse, and by the fourth century, the meanings and usages of oικονομία and sygkatábāsis, little by little, approached each other.[14] For Basil, sygkatábāsis connoted a sign of power and a working of grace by which Christ humbled himself, acted as a doctor to humanity, descended to human infirmity, and called humans his brothers. In this, Basil conformed to the traditional views we have previously encountered.[15]

The concept of oικονομία, like so much else in early Christianity, including rhetoric, was inherited from the pagan world Christianity replaced. The fourth century, still under the influence of the stylists of the Second-Sophistic, was the rhetorical century par excellence, and it must be remembered, in the words of an astute observer, that "Rhetoric in the ancient world was simultaneously a science, an art, an ideal of life, and the pillar of a classical education and culture."[16] As we shall see below, churches all but became rhetorical arenas, where lackluster Christian rhetors might be thrown to figurative Christian lions, whose zeal for rhetorical displays seemingly knew no bounds.

Thus, Basil, in his *De Spiritu Sancto,* lavishes enormous attention on the language of theological formulas and meticulously scrutinizes the use of the prepositions *sýn* and *metá*.[17] Basil's exegesis focuses mainly on two scriptural passages: I Corinthians 12:4, which treats of the diversity of gifts given by the Holy Spirit, and Matthew 28:19, "baptizing them in the name of the Father and of the Son and of the Holy Spirit."[18] In this tract, Basil attacks the Anomoeans, heretics who tried to disconnect the elements of the Trinity. Their teachings, as we shall see, were also scathingly denounced by Chrysostom.

Matthew's comments may represent the manner in which humanity ascends the divine ladder, starting with the Spirit, who, in an accommodating manner, spreads his gifts among humanity. From the Spirit, mankind progresses to the Son and advances ultimately to the Father. It is an expression of the order of divine accommodation to humanity in the world; or, divine *oikonomía* in revelation. Basil argues this position in his discussion of baptism.

He wonders why Christians exalt the Holy Spirit so far above creation, when Scripture shows that similar things were previously done for mere humans.[19] His answer suggests that the Christian faith in the Holy Spirit is the same as the faith in the Father and the Son. But the faith that others placed in Moses and the cloud (cf. Exod. 14:31 in the LXX) was faith in a shadow and type.[20] In explaining his position, Basil culls imagery from the classical reservoir of *paideía:*

> The nature of the divine is very frequently represented by the rough and shadowy outlines [*skiāgrǎphía*] of the types; but because divine things are prefigured by small and human things, it is obvious that we must not therefore conclude the divine nature to be small. The type is an exhibition of things expected, and gives an imitative anticipation of the future.[21]

The use of *skiāgrǎphía* in this passage recalls Basil's famous definition of the classics as a *skiāgrǎphía* of virtue—a shadowy sketch made by dusting charcoal through a pierced pattern.[22]

Basil presents various biblical types and shadows, including the baptismal type of the passage through the Red Sea. Indeed, the sea slew the enemy, Pharaoh, in itself, just as baptism destroys man's enmity toward God. As the Israelites emerged safely from the sea, so a Christian rises "saved by grace" from the water of baptism.[23] As important for Basil as the symbol of baptism was, water symbolism was no less significant. In fact, it is second only to medical imagery in his writings.[24]

Gregory of Nazianzus, in his funeral panegyric on Basil, mentions Basil's interest in medicine: "Medicine, the result of philosophy and laboriousness, was rendered necessary for him by his physical delicacy, and his care of the sick. From these beginnings he attained to a mastery of the art."[25] Gregory knew about medicine and doctors firsthand; his brother, Caesarius, was recognized widely for his knowledge of medicine. Indeed, in his funeral encomium for Caesarius, Gregory inquires rhetorically, "In the wonderful art of medicine . . . who is there so ignorant or contentious as to think him inferior to himself, and not to be glad to be reckoned next to him, and carry off the second prize?"[26] Indeed, Caesarius gained pride of place among physicians merely by exhibiting his abilities.[27] He was court physician at Constantinople, and it was there that Gregory, upon returning from study in Athens, met and discussed their retirement to Nazianze.[28] Caesarius left the court during the reign of Julian and returned with Gregory to Nazianze. As we shall see below, Gregory also exploited medical imagery in his works. Both writers were subject to the influence of the medical imagery associated with the second sophistic, and the revival of the cult of Asclepius coupled with the prestige of such figures as Aristides, Herodes Atticus, and above all, Galen rendered certain the future role of medical metaphors and language.[29]

For Basil, then, medical imagery was near at hand and quite easily incorporated in his writings; water imagery, springing naturally from biblical allusions and baptismal practice, instinctually found its place in his works. For Basil, water did not separate, but united disparate elements. It was an agent of unity and harmony in an unharmonious and fractured world, and for Basil, unity—especially ecclesiastical unity—was a key concept. It is not perhaps accidental that he was in the forefront of the drive for the Second Ecumenical Council of 381, which sought to achieve unity through the faith of Nicaea.[30]

Insuring harmony was part of Basil's job as bishop, and in a letter to the clergy of Colonia, who were troubled at the loss of their bishop to a neighboring town, he strives to maintain unity. Even though the orthodox clergy objected to the new bishop, Basil asks them to accept him because of *oikonomía kalé*.[31] He voiced the same quest for unity in his vision of a monastic community:

> If we are not joined together by union in the Holy Spirit in
> the harmony of one body . . . we would not serve the common
> good in the ministry [*pròs tò koinē symphéron tē oikonomía
> douleuōn*]. . . . How could we, divided and separated, preserve the
> status and the mutual service of members or our subordinate rela-
> tionship to our Head which is Christ?[32]

For Basil, *oikonomía* operated on the human and the divine planes.
Church unity could be attained through its proper use, and for Basil,
as for so many of the fathers, especially Athanasius, it signified, on
the divine plane, the Incarnation.[33] As such, it approached the idea of
accommodation, which dealt with Christ's humanity, and thus differed sharply from theology, which concerned itself mainly with the
divine and eternal natures of Christ. *Oikonomía* took on added meanings for Basil, who could use it when speaking of people advancing
spiritually, of upbuilding of the faith, of distributing alms prudently
and "economically," and on occasion comparing it to both architecture
and medicine.[34]

Basil thus combines many of the stylistic devices and images of
the second sophistic in his writings, as do Gregory of Nazianzus and
Gregory of Nyssa.[35] Basil, unlike other early fathers, did not write
explicit commentaries on Scripture, and his approach to it must be
pieced together from his other writings. In a letter to Gregory of
Nazianzus, Basil observes that study of Scripture is the means to
finding one's proper direction in life. Indeed, in a combination of
various images, Basil writes: "Hence, in whatever respect each one
feels himself deficient, devoting himself to this imitation (of the lives
of blessed men detailed in Scripture), he finds, as from some dispen-
sary, the proper medicine for his ailment" (*tó prósphoron phármăkon*).[36]
Basil, in embellishing the imagery, suggests that mankind must believe and obey God as the "true Lord, Ruler, Doctor and Teacher"
(*despótē kaì basileĭ kaì iātrô kaì didaskalō alētheías*).[37] And Basil will
refer to God as "the great doctor of souls."[38] Those are the images that
we shall encounter repeatedly in the works of the Cappadocians and
Chrysostom, and it is in the spirit of the doctor and teacher that Basil
discusses the manner of divine instruction in *De Spiritu Sancto*.

As noted above, Basil focused upon shadows and types in the
Law and upbraids those who do not understand how to read and
interpret Scripture. That is, there are some who judge the reality by
the shadow and compare the typified with the type, and thus dispar-
age the entire dispensation of the gospel.[39] In order to explain the
glory of Christian baptism fully, Basil resorts to familiar arguments:

Surely it is altogether childish, and like a babe who must needs be fed on milk [cf. Heb. 5:12], to be ignorant of the great mystery of our salvation; inasmuch as, in accordance with the gradual progress of our education, while being brought to perfection in our training for godliness [cf. I Tim. 4:7], we were first taught elementary and easier lessons, suited to our intelligence, while the Dispenser of our lots was ever leading us up, by gradually accustoming us, like eyes brought up in the dark, to the great light of truth.[40]

Basil utilizes the same vocabulary as other authors in his explication of biblical hermeneutics, though he applies the terms to types and shadows related to baptism. He elaborates upon his interpretation:

For He spares our weakness (*asthéneia*) and in the depth of the riches (cf. Rom. 11:33) of His wisdom, and the inscrutable judgements of His intelligence, used this gentle treatment, fitted for our needs, gradually accustoming us to see first the shadows of objects, and to look at the sun in water, to save us from dashing against the spectacle of pure unadulterated light, and being blinded. Just so the Law, having a shadow of things to come, and the typical teachings of the prophets, which is a dark utterance of the truth, have been devised as means to train the eyes of the heart, in that hence the transition to the wisdom hidden in mystery (I Cor. 2:7) will be made easy.[41]

Of course the wisdom hidden in mystery is revealed through the Spirit, and thus Basil, in explaining the movement from the Mosaic Code to the Christian dispensation, also explains the role of the Holy Spirit in revelation. Basil truly understood the accommodative and "economical" nature of divine pedagogy and put it to good use in his episcopal role. *Oikonomía* was Basil's chief term for accommodation, but he knew the concept well and applied it to practical as well as theoretical matters. Basil's fellow Cappadocian, Gregory of Nazianzus, displays his interpretation of accommodation in a rhetorically skillful manner.

Gregory's description of Basil as "my guide of life and my teacher of the faith"[42] indicates his indebtedness to Basil. Posterity, not without reason, has conferred unto Gregory the title, "Theologian," and in his *Five Theological Orations* and several other works, his striking talent appears. Gregory never composed biblical commentaries, nor dogmatic tracts; he, alone among the fourth-century theologians, was a poet, and he was the first of the fathers to publish a collection of his letters.[43]

In his *Oration on the Theophany,* Gregory discusses the creation
of man, noting that the Lord gave humans free will in order for the
good to belong to humanity through choice, and man was placed in
Paradise in order to till the immortal plants—which Gregory interprets as divine conceptions, both simpler and more perfect. God also
gave man a Law, which pertained to the Tree of Knowledge (*theōría*),
again as material for man's free will to act upon. Gregory is very
careful to point out that the Tree was not evil from the time it was
planted; indeed, it was the proper goal of man's legitimate desire, and
it would have been good if partaken of at the proper time. Gregory
understands the Tree as a symbol of contemplation, which is safe only
for mature people, not for the simple; "just as neither is solid food
good for those who are yet tender and have need of milk."[44] The
nakedness of man represents humanity's transparency of mind to the
contemplation of things divine.

Gregory of Nazianzus' idea of time, which, as we shall see, differs
from Gregory of Nyssa's theory, suggests a precipitous Fall. Gregory
of Nazianzus posits a two-stage cosmology that begins with God,
existing alone, three in one, and self-contemplative. The first creation
results from an "overflow of goodness," which Platonic thought makes
necessary on the part of the divine, though Gregory contradicts himself on occasion by suggesting that creation flowed from God's "spon-
taneous love." Gregory describes this creation in terms any pupil of
Origen might choose, and the first creation consists only in the invisible, immaterial world. He denies that the first creation served as the
pattern for the second creation, that of the visible world, which came
into existence by a divine gratuitous act.

Gregory, in fact, combines the positive biblical account of creation
with the contradictory negative, Gnostic account of creation; God—
the Creator-Word—mingled the two creations in the making of mankind. Humanity, thus, in good Platonic language, was alien to the
world even before creation; flesh being alien to spirit. Before incarnation, humanity is described as immature and involved in a training
program; after taking on flesh and before the Fall, the human condition is seen as a trial. As R. Ruether and Brooks Otis suggest, we
have in Gregory a conflation of various strands of thought—biblical,
early Christian, especially Irenaean and Origenistic elements, and
Platonic.[45]

Mankind's sin consisted in grasping the fruit of the tree (*theōría*)
before the proper time; it was a precipitous act. Humanity strove for
philosophical speculation and the contemplative life before the education and maturation of its spirit, and thus "fell." Man's fall injured

him neither mortally nor eternally; it did however, make the task of improving man much more difficult than it had previously been.

Through sin, humanity became coarser than it had been and acquired *dermátinous chitõnas,* "coats of skin," indicating humanity's denser nature. It is this impediment that makes man's progress so difficult; no longer being "naked," man is further removed from *theõría,* and thus must undergo an educational retraining program.[46] The idea of the "coats of skin" (Gen. 3:21), found also in a ninth-century Midrash, will become a staple of Gregory of Nyssa's exegesis.[47] Indeed, as Gregory observes, God employed various devices to bring us back to him, including the Law, the prophets, signs, natural disasters, and rewards, but since humanity's diseases were growing worse, especially that first and last of all evils—idolatry—mankind needed a stronger remedy. At the proper time, the Word became Flesh.[48]

In attempting to synthesize Christ's Incarnation with Israelite history, Gregory turns to the role of the Law in human history and acknowledges that the Holy Apostle declared the Law to be but a shadow of future things, intellectual in character (cf. Heb. 10:1). When the Lord showed Moses the design and pattern of the Tabernacle, the visible details were presented as shadows of the invisible (Exod. 25:10). All of the minute details of the Tabernacle—its measurements and materials; sacrifices, offerings, and purifications—had been given with reason and were worthy of God. To believe that all who served there and all their actions were meaningless is also unfounded.[49]

Only Moses, or those who approach him in virtue and education, may comprehend those actions. "For in that Mount itself God is seen by men; on the one hand through His own descent (*katabaínõn*) from His lofty abode, on the other through His drawing us up from our abasement on earth."[50] God does this in order to allow mortal nature the chance to comprehend the Incomprehensible. All men are not equal, and only with divine aid may somatic creatures with imprisoned minds become conscious of God. Divine help is, of course, necessitated by man's fall.

Identifying himself as one who is neither totally dense nor totally contemplative, Gregory wishes to express his opinion about the human condition neither absurdly nor ridiculously:

> Our belief is that since it was needful that we, who had fallen in consequence of the original sin, and had been led away by pleasure, even as far as idolatry and unlawful bloodshed, should be recalled and raised up again to our original position through the tender mercy of God our Father, Who could not endure that such a noble work of His own hands as Man should be lost to Him; the method of

our new creation, and of what should be done, was this:—that all
violent remedies were disapproved, as not likely to persuade us,
and as quite possibly tending to add to the plague, through our
chronic pride; but that God disposed things to our restoration by a
gentle and kindly method of cure [*tǭ dè émérǭ kaì philanthôpǭ tês
therapeías oikonomēthênai pròs epanórthōsin*].[51]

Thus Gregory more fully develops a theory adumbrated above; that
is, after the fall of mankind, the Lord chose different therapies to
effect a cure. He settled upon divine economy and divine philanthropy. In a strikingly apt and artistic metaphor, Gregory presents
the divine plan:

> For a crooked sapling will not bear a sudden bending the other way,
> or violence from the hand that would straighten it, but will be more
> quickly broken than straightened; and a horse of a hot temper and
> above a certain age will not endure the tyranny of the bit without
> some coaxing and encouragement. Therefore the Law is given to us
> as an assistance [*boétheian*],[52] like a boundary wall between God
> and idols, drawing us away from one and to the Other. And it
> concedes [*sugxōreî*] a little at first, that it may receive that which is
> greater. It concedes [*sugxōreî*] the Sacrifices for a time, that it may
> establish God in us, and then when the fitting time shall come may
> abolish Sacrifices also; thus wisely changing our minds by gradual
> removals, and bringing us over to the Gospel when we have already
> been trained to a prompt obedience.[53]

In Gregory's exegesis, the written Law existed in order to gather
humanity together in Christ, who fulfilled what the Sacrifices of Old
prefigured. The sin-offerings enacted in the Mosaic dispensation could
atone for, but not remove, sin. Even though the shadows were inferior
to the reality, Gregory still opts for a positive view of the Law, since it
directed man away from idols and toward the Lord; although this is
an example of positive accommodation, Gregory provides a more elaborate illustration in his theological orations.

These orations were delivered in Constantinople in 380 C.E. They
not only defend and protect the faith of Nicaea, but present a cogent
statement of Gregory's trinitarian theology.[54] Gregory explains the
function of the Holy Spirit in much the same way as Basil did in his
exegesis of Matthew 28:19, and Gregory exploits the interpretation of
biblical, divinely conceded practices to bolster his understanding of
the accommodative nature of the Holy Spirit. He accomplishes his
objective within an expanded exegetical excursus on universal history
and biblical sacrifice. In unambiguous terms, Gregory unveils his
profoundly historical view:

There have been in the whole period of the duration of the world two conspicuous changes of men's lives, which are also called two Testaments, or, on account of the wide fame of the matter, two earthquakes; the one from idols to the Law, the other from the Law to the Gospel. And we are taught in the Gospel of a third earthquake, namely, from this Earth to that which cannot be shaken or moved.[55]

The two earthquakes are those at the theophany at Sinai and Haggai's prophecy (Hag. 2:6). Of course, Gregory contrasts the giving of the law in Exodus 19 with the call to faith in Hebrews 12, and understands Haggai's words as a reference to Christ's incarnation. The third earthquake refers to Hebrews 12:26, and not surprisingly leads to a discussion of a new kingdom of grace, which will not be moved. The three earthquakes are thus the Law, the Gospel, and Grace, or the gifts of the Father, Son, and Holy Spirit. Gregory scrupulously maintains his tone in commenting upon the nature of these events:

Now the two Testaments are alike in this respect, that the change was not made on a sudden, nor at the first moment of the endeavor. Why not (for this is a point on which we must have information)? That no violence might be done to us, but that we might be moved by persuasion. For nothing that is involuntary is durable; like streams or trees which are kept back by force. But that which is voluntary is more durable and safe. The former is due to one who uses force, the latter is ours; the one is due to the gentleness of God, the other to a tyrannical authority. Wherefore God did not think it behooved Him to benefit the unwilling, but to do good to the willing.[56]

The shift from one testament or covenant to the other was gradual lest humanity suffer violent harm. The choice had to be voluntary in order for it to be durable and salvific; the Lord exercised gentleness rather than compulsion. For Gregory, these divine actions were elaborated with utter clarity and precision:

And therefore like a tutor or physician [dià toúto paidăgōgikós tȇ kaì iātrikós] He partly removes and partly condones ancestral habits, conceding some little of what tended to pleasure, just as medical men do with their patients, that their medicine may be taken, being artfully blended with what is nice. For it is no easy matter to change from those habits which custom and use have made honorable. For instance, the first cut off the idol, but left the sacrifices; the second, while it destroyed the sacrifices did not forbid circumcision. Then, when once men had submitted to the curtailment, they also yielded that which had been conceded to them; in the first

instance the sacrifices, in the second circumcision; and became instead of Gentiles, Jews, and instead of Jews, Christians, being beguiled into the Gospel by gradual changes. Paul is proof of this; for
having at one time administered circumcision, and submitted to
ritual purity, he advanced till he could say, "and I, brethren, if I yet
preach circumcision, why do I suffer persecution?" (cf. Gal. 5). His
former conduct belonged to the temporary dispensation, his latter
to maturity.[57]

The thrust of Gregory's argument is quite clear and compelling; it
exploits historical changes in custom and belief to vindicate the divinity of the Holy Spirit. For just as mankind has progressed from an
idolatrous to a divinely ordained religious system, only to move on to
a more mature religious system without cutting all ties to the past, so
God has aided, and not violated, the natural process. It is Gregory
who advances the theological theory of "procession" as the relationship that obtains among the three elements of the Trinity, and this
theory is crucially intertwined with his view of historically accommodated revelation.

Gregory presents the relationship by describing their characters
as *àgennēsía, génnesis,* and *ékpoeúsis* or *'ékpempsis;* that is, there is a
procession and complete identity, save for the question of origins. As
Gregory explains the relationship: "The proper name of the Unoriginate
is Father, and that of the unoriginately Begotten is Son, and that of
the unbegottenly Proceeding or Going Forth is the Holy Spirit."[58]
Indeed, Gregory is the first to identify the relationship in the Trinity
by the term "procession" because "I must coin a word for the sake of
clearness."[59] We shall see the importance of this idea for the theory of
time and accommodation developed by Gregory of Nyssa.

In the bishop of Nazianzus' view, the Father was proclaimed
openly in the Hebrew Scripture, the Son more dimly. The Christian
Testament manifestly proclaimed the Son, and hinted at the divinity
of the Spirit. Now the Spirit dwells among man and provides certain
proof of itself. The process of revelation is likened to the process of
biblical practices:

> For it was not safe, when the Godhead of the Father was not yet
> acknowledged, plainly to proclaim the Son; nor when that of the
> Son was not yet received to burden us further (if I may use so bold
> an expression) with the Holy Ghost; lest perhaps people might, like
> men loaded with food beyond their strength, and presenting eyes as
> yet too weak to bear it to the sun's light, risk the loss even of that
> which was within the reach of their powers; but by gradual addi-
> tions, and as David says, Goings up, and advances and progress

from glory to glory (cf. Ps. 84:7), the Light of the Trinity might
shine upon the more illuminated. For this reason it was, I think,
that He gradually came to dwell in the Disciples, measuring Himself out to them according to their capacity to receive Him. . . . [60]

Gregory has fashioned a coherent and consistent approach for
his exegetical and theological needs; that is, the manner of interpreting biblical sacrifice as a divine accommodation provided the framework for the theological defense of the divinity of the Holy Spirit and
a trinitarian theology in general. Indeed, all were medicines to treat
man after the fall, and each was good in its time. Sacrifices led
mankind, albeit imperfectly, to the Lord, and that was all humanity
could have endured at the time. Paul accommodated his message by
permitting circumcision while banning sacrifice, and he was merely
following the divine example of gradual revelation of truth to the
disciples "according to their capacity."

Gregory, following Origen's exegetical and pedagogical steps, recognized that all humanity, including the disciples, had different capacities and that the divine revelation adjusted itself to those differences. Not so different were the Gnostic claims against the orthodox.
But Gregory, as behooved a theologian, coupled this gradual revela-
tory process to a defense of the emergent orthodox trinitarian theology. Indeed, Gregory's description of the trinitarian relationship as a
"procession" together with his comments on it ring unmistakably with
accommodation, which became for Gregory an exegetical and theological *sine qua non*. Accommodation pierced the veil surrounding
ancient shadowy types and revealed more clearly perceived Christian
realities, but perhaps more importantly, it provided Gregory of
Nazianzus a pattern with which to defend orthodoxy and its trinitarian
position.

For Gregory of Nyssa, accommodation is interwoven with his
theory of time, a hypothesis that went far in explaining, not only
man's fallen state and ultimate redemption, but Gregory's views of
history, human progress, and the Incarnation. Gregory is usually
praised for his speculative theology and mystical bent; he was educated mainly by his brother Basil and under the influence of friends,
especially Gregory of Nazianzus, gave up the teaching of rhetoric and
his worldly career to retire to the monastery in Pontus, founded by
Basil. Gregory became bishop of Nyssa in about 371, and his stormy
occupancy need not be recounted here.[61] It should, however, be pointed
out that most of his works date from the last part of his life, beginning in about 379 and thus are contemporaneous with many of Gregory of Nazianzus' writings, considered above. Gregory, much as his

fellow Cappadocians, was influenced by the style of the second sophistic, yet, as one scholar has observed, though his writings reveal a
depth and breadth of thought surpassing Basil and Gregory of
Nazianzus, "his style remains very often without charm."[62]

In his first major exegetical work, *On the Making of Man,* written in 379, a continuation of sermons delivered by Basil two years
earlier, Gregory tried to show the internal sequence of cause and
effect in the creation. Basil set forth the facts, Gregory the *akoluthía.*[63]
His is the only systematic anthropological treatise penned by a
Cappadocian, and his view of man provides entry to his use of accommodation and condescension.[64] Gregory attempts to answer the problem of the relationship between body and soul, and for him, both are
divine creations.[65] Gregory, unlike many other church fathers, used
interchangeably, the terms "image" (*eikón*) and "likeness" (*homoíōsis*);
this, coupled with his view that all of creation was excellent, enabled
Gregory to incorporate man's bodily existence in his theology without
succumbing to Origen's overly punitive interpretation of bodily existence that all but severed the delicate combination of man's composite
nature.[66]

The work divides into three parts: chapters 1–15 praise man's
creation according to the divine model, emphasizing that human physi-
cality is a reflection of divine spirituality; chapters 16–27 contrast
man's privileged birth with his present lowly status; and the last
three chapters study the form and elements of the human body, the
union of soul and body and resurrection. The bishop of Nyssa maintains that man contains all previous stages of living beings in himself
and that the process of creation is an orderly one. Gregory distinguishes three souls in mankind, corresponding to Paul's tripartite
division of body, soul, and spirit. The first parallels the life of plants,
the middle the animal life, the last the life of the intellect. He describes in detail the reason for the limbs and organization of the body
and notes that nature makes its ascent, as it were, by steps (*dià
bathmón*) from lower to more perfect things.[67] Thus, man stands at
the apex of creation. But exactly when and how does a human become a person?

Gregory rejects the twin ideas of preexistent souls and
metempsychosis; creation occurs when the human soul is united with
a body, an act that takes place repeatedly in each person. The highest
level of soul—the rational—is the full and true soul that must go
through the other stages before reaching its full potential. Thus,
Scripture's account of creation mentions plants and animals before
man, and the union of soul—not yet rational—and body occurs at

conception.[68] Gregory posits the existence of a seminal power
(*spérmatikễ dúnămis*), not only to bridge the gap between the body
and soul, but to explain how both, being unequal, nevertheless coexist
in man. As Gregory notes, the mind reflects God as a mirror, and the
body is beautified by that reflection. Gregory of Nazianzus explains it
well: "What God is to the soul, that the soul becomes for the body: it
trains (*paidăgōgésasa*) the body's matter, which is its servant, and
adapts (*oikéōsasa*) the fellow servant to God."[69] And yet in spite of
such lofty sentiments and language, humans suffer and die.

It is the seeming contradiction between man's divine origin and
his mundane existence, his history, as it were, that occupies the middle
part of the tract. Even though Scripture tells that man was made in
the image of God, human reality does not approach divine transcen-
dence. The word of God provided Gregory with an explanation for this
seeming disparity. Following Philo's lead in *De opificio mundi*, Gregory turns to the double account of the creation of man in Genesis
1:26–27 and 2:7.[70]

For Gregory, man is a hybrid created by a God who foresaw the
fall, original sin, and humanity's history. As Gregory writes:

> [God] while looking upon the nature of man in its entirety and
> fulness, by the exercise of His foreknowledge, and bestowing upon
> it a lot exalted and equal to the angels, since He saw beforehand by
> His all-seeing power the failure of their will to keep a direct course
> to what is good, and its consequent declension from the angelic life,
> in order that the multitude of human souls might not be cut short
> by its fall from that mode by which the angels were increased and
> multiplied,—for this reason, I say, He formed for our nature that
> contrivance for increase which befits those who had fallen into sin,
> implanting in mankind, instead of the angelic majesty of nature,
> that animal and irrational mode by which they no succeed one
> another.[71]

Man's sexuality is to blame for evil in the world, since man freely
withdrew from the good that God placed before him. Gregory's theory
of time attempts not only to explain how man came to be as he now
is, but to enunciate the process by which man may return to his
status quo ante; that is, how mankind, as a whole, is to become what
it originally was, a spiritual mind in a spiritual body. Gregory does
not doubt that the divine plan—namely, the existence of a humanity
in the image and likeness of God—which but for sin would have been
realized at creation, will now have to be achieved in a circuitous,
roundabout way. The "animal and irrational mode" by which human-

ity endures will have to be purged along with other less violent passions and urges, and at the end of time, the pleroma or fullness of humanity as a true image and likeness of God will finally be realized.[72]

Gregory unfolds his redemptive strategy mainly in *De Hominis Opificio* and his *Catechetical Oration*. The Great Catechism, written about 385, presents a systematic theology of Christianity and discusses the Trinity, the creation and nature of man, original sin, the mission of Christ, redemption, and the application of the grace of redemption. Gregory's theory of the creation of man, his nature, sin, and redemption, relies heavily upon the "coats of skin" of Genesis 3:21, which were employed by Gregory of Nazianzus as well. While Gregory of Nazianzus views the "coats of skin" as man's denser nature, Gregory of Nyssa understands them as the human assumption of bodily existence.[73]

Bodily existence is man's link to the animals, which means we share: "sexual union, conception, childbirth, dirt, nursing, food, excrement, the gradual growth of the body towards maturity, adulthood, old age, sickness and death."[74] How did man, the "image of God," fall to such a state? Or as Gregory asks: "How can man, mortal, subject to passion, and short-lived, be the image of the immortal, pure and eternal nature?"[75] Gregory answers in two ways: one originates in Origen and the other in Athanasius. First, he blames human free will. He explains that freedom is a divine faculty, which was given to man, and like all created things is subject to change. Thus, free will could separate itself from God, and in turning from God, man acquired his "coats of skin," which made bodily immortality impossible. Yet, this corporeal baggage was in some respects more of a remedy than a chastisement, for it allowed man to turn freely back to God. Since bringing man back unwillingly would destroy human freedom, the Lord employed the human desire for carnality, gave man "coats of skin," and thereby caused man to detest the mundane existence and freely opt to return to his former spiritual state.[76]

Gregory's "Athanasian" explanation for the "coats of skin" asserts that man was created by God much as a potter fashions a clay vessel. Our bodies are so interlaced with evil that upon our bodily death, the body, much as a clay vessel, is returned to the earth and purged of its evil. The clay may now be refashioned into its pristine form and the evil destroyed. Of the coat, Gregory notes:

> Not that it was to last forever; for a coat is something external put
> on us, lending itself to the body for a time, but not indigenous to its

nature. This liability to death, then, taken from the brute creation, was provisionally made, to envelope the nature created for immortality. It enrapped it externally, but not internally. It grasped the sentient part of man, but laid no hold upon the Divine image.[77]

The treatment was not to endure eternally. Employing medical language, Gregory suggests that the "coats of skin" were provisionally dispensed, much as medication, in order to correct humanity's desire for evil. And Gregory cautions anyone against reproaching God, who, knowing what would evolve created man anyway, since God foresaw not only the "perversion" but also man's recall to the good.[78] In explaining the process of reparation, Gregory focuses upon the double creation story of Genesis 1:26–27 and 2:7 and on 3:21 and, as others have noted, follows Philo, but with certain distinctions.[79]

Philo understood the creation in Genesis 2:7, not as the real body, but as an earthlike mind that would be, but had not yet been, mixed with the body. Philo allegorically interprets the "coats of skin" of Genesis 3:21 as man's body.[80] Gregory also posits a twofold creation, but sees in man's creation "the preexistence of human nature in the perfection of the divine knowledge—such as it will be only at the end of time. Thus for Gregory, man created as male and female though first in the order of time is only second in the order of intention."[81] Before turning away from God, man, due to the gift of *apátheia,* would have been immune to animal passions and the natural necessities of animal life; man in his ideal state was apathetic, even with a body.

Man's existence before the Fall should have been angelic and will be after resurrection. Gregory refers to *xitônes* or *éndümata phōtoeidés* or *lamprá,* garments worn by man before he donned the "coats of skin." These luminous and aerial cloaks represent man's edenic raiment lost as a result of sin. A Christian may recover them through baptism, possess them on earth by leading a spiritual, ascetic, mystical life, and saints will certainly obtain them after bodily resurrection.[82] One way of leading a spiritual, ascetic, mystical life is outlined in Gregory's *Life of Moses,* subtitled, *Perfection in the Subject of Virtue.*[83] Moses, in the march toward the promised land, embodied the quest for perfection; striving for, yet never attaining, the final goal. The image of the runner who forgets what is behind him, but reaches out to what is before him, rushing toward the unknown depicts the quest known as *épéctasis* (cf. Phil. 3:13). This *épéctasis* forms part of Gregory's mysticism and mystical theology, which lies outside our immediate interest, but it does indicate Gregory's belief that mankind may, even in the midst of this existence, strive to regain its former condition,[84] a state that was lost and that may be restored by the Incarnation.

Gregory views the Incarnation as an example of accommodation to human faculties. He compares the process of understanding resurrection to a farmer trying to explain the virtue of seeds to someone ignorant of agriculture. The farmer could demonstrate the growth of only one seed and let that stand as an example of the rest:

> Still more, however, is this case with the experience of actual resurrection which we have learnt not so much by words as by actual facts: for as the marvel of resurrection was great and passing belief, He begins gradually by inferior instances of His miraculous power, and accustoms our faith, as it were, for the reception of the greater.[85]

Gregory asserts that the Lord acted much like a mother who, at first, breastfeeds an infant, chews and softens bread for her babe, but then accustoms the child, as it grows, to more solid nourishment. The Lord used a process of adaptation for our benefit:

> So the Lord, nourishing and fostering with miracles the weakness of the human mind, like some babe not fully grown, makes first of all a prelude of the power of the resurrection in the case of a desperate disease, which prelude, though it was great in its achievement, yet was not such a thing that the statement of it would be disbelieved.[86]

Gregory cites as proof of his thesis the examples in Luke 4:39 in which Jesus cures the fever of Simon's mother-in-law; in John 4:49, where Jesus, without being present, brought about the healing of the nobleman's son; in Luke 7:13–15, the raising of the widow's son; and in John 11, Jesus raises Lazarus after four days in the tomb. Each of these actions hinted at greater miraculous deeds in order to awaken mankind to the possibility of resurrection: "For it behooved Him, when He had accustomed men to the miracle of the resurrection in other bodies to confirm His word in His own humanity."[87]

The Incarnation was to bring about humanity's return to life, which "is achieved by the 'economy' of the Lord as man."[88] This was not simply the redemption of Adam, but that of humanity en masse. Gregory praises the faith of Mary Magdalene, the first witness of the resurrection, in speaking of what she saw; for by her faith she helped undo Eve's action.[89] Christ, who came as the shepherd, the physician, the mediator and redeemer, ransomed human nature from the devil and sought to restore it to its rightful relationship with God.[90] For

Gregory, Adam's sin did not result in the loss of anything essential to human nature, but in the acquisition of nonessentials. And for man to shed these nonessentials, he had to be redeemed from the devil. The divine manner of effecting this redemption, through the Incarnation, bothered Gregory, at least rhetorically. He asks a very perspicacious question:

> For if, as our argument has shown, there is such power in Him that both the destruction of death and the introduction of life reside in Him, why does He not effect His purpose by the mere exercise of His will, instead of working out our salvation in such a roundabout way, by being born and nurtured as a man, and even, while he was saving man, tasting death; when it was possible for Him to have saved man without subjecting Himself to such conditions?[91]

That is, why did God have to resort to such an elaborate and indirect plot, when he simply could have willed salvation? Gregory presses his case by suggesting that, since sick people do not prescribe their medicine and treatment to physicians, nor do they rebuke the healing they receive from doctors who do them good, man, since he sees only the final result, cannot comprehend the divine rationale.[92] Nor ought anyone to assume that, because we are weak, God was affected by touching our infirmity; on the contrary, God's mercy is proof of his omnipotence.

Gregory insists that in the present dispensation of things (*epì tês parousês oikonomías*), God's attributes, goodness, wisdom, power, and justice, must accord with his redemptive process. That is, God must obey his own rules, and an examination of the things accomplished in an orderly fashion reveals the wisdom and skill of the divine *oikonomía*. And in scrutinizing the divine manner of redemption, two qualities stand out: divine wisdom and divine justice.[93]

Divine wisdom recognizes that, in turning from God, man became indentured to the devil, and in order to redeem man, God had to behave justly, even with the devil. Thus, God contrived to appear as a human, and by wrapping the divine nature within an envelope of flesh, God deceived the deceiver.[94] After noting that God's descent to the humiliating level of humanity indicates his omnipotence, which is found not in the stretches of heaven, but rather in God's condescension to our weakness (*hóson hē epì tó asthenés tês phúseōs hēmón sygkatábasis deíknūsi*), Gregory expresses his ransom theory—found also in Origen and later in Augustine and Ambrose, though Gregory of Nazianzus and John of Damascus offer another view—in a striking metaphor:[95]

For since, as has been said before, it was not in the nature of the opposing power to come in contact with the undiluted presence of God, and to undergo His unclouded manifestation, therefore, in order to secure that the ransom in our behalf might be easily accepted by him who required it, the Deity was hidden under the veil of our nature, that so as with ravenous fish, the hook of the Deity might be gulped down along with the bait of flesh [*hína katá toùs líxnous tòn ixthúson tó deléati tês sarkós sunapospásthē tó 'ágkistron tês theótētos*], and thus, life being introduced into the house of death, and light shining in darkness, that which is diametrically opposed to light and life might vanish.[96]

Gregory's vivid language and imagery of light and darkness assumed prominence in his mystical thought,[97] and the graphic metaphor of the devil swallowing the fishhook of the divinity won a place in future exegesis. Rufinus would expand the image, making the devil, after swallowing the hook, become bait for others, and Augustine was to recast the metaphor in a most modern manner. After noting that Christ overcame the deceiver, he asks how it happened. The answer was quite simple. Christ built a better mousetrap! (*Ad pretium nostrum tedendit muscipulam crucem suam; posuit ibi quasi escam sanguinem suum.*)[98]

Gregory insists that God acted properly, and tempered his power with goodness and justice:

His choosing to save man is a testimony of his goodness; His making the redemption of the captive a matter of exchange exhibits his justice, while the invention whereby He enabled the Enemy to apprehend that of which he was before incapable, is a manifestation of supreme wisdom.[99]

Gregory raises yet another aspect of this method of salvation; did not God use deceit (*apátē*)? After all, the devil was confronted not with pure divinity but divinity wrapped in a human envelope; is that not fraud and deception (*apátē tís ésti trópon tína kaì paralōgismós*)?[100] Gregory's answer is that the Lord was just, in that each got his due, and wise, because justice was not perverted. Yet, he does acknowledge, rather surprisingly, that God's design (*epínoia*) did contain a certain deceptive character (*apátē*); however, it not only brought salvation to man, but benefited the devil as well, for the process leads to the ultimate eradication of evil. Gregory likens the process to patients who may be angry with their doctors for painful treatments, but are thankful after they are cured.[101]

Just as a doctor gives a patient directions suitable to his patient's comprehension, so did the Lord fashion Scripture. Gregory repeatedly returns to the point that God's written revelation was specifically tuned to the human capacity. This emerges most clearly in his attacks against the Anomoeans, who claimed that the Son and Father were absolutely unlike (*ánomoiós*) each other. Gregory rebukes them by explaining very minutely how one must understand biblical language, especially anthropomorphic expressions, lest one fall prey to error. He urges people to consider the wisdom of the merciful "economy" of the Holy Spirit in revelation and sets forth, in several places, a fully mature theory of language accommodation.[102]

Gregory speaks in a most fascinating manner about various biblical citations that may be misunderstood to mean that God actually speaks, or even troubles himself with language. He accuses his opponents of demeaning the deity by suggesting that God is little more than a grammarian or lexicographer who has nothing better to do than coin words; Gregory admits that God created men, but men create their own vocabulary. If certain scriptural expressions suggest anthropomorphic acts on the part of God, we must remember that Scripture addresses us in our language; indeed, Acts 2:8 tells how, among different people, each "received the teaching of the disciples in his own language wherein he was born, understanding the sense of the words by the language he knew."[103]

For Gregory, it is trifling and mere "Jewish folly" (*phluāría taûta kaì mataiotês 'Ioudaïkế*) to assume that God set himself up like a schoolmaster (*grammătistê*) to settle the details of biblical language and terminology. After all, we speak to deaf people through signs, not because we lack voices, but because they cannot hear. Thus, God, through prophets and in numerous other ways, accommodated his power to our lower level of comprehension (*àlla tệ braxútēti tês hēmetéras sygkatioûsan dunámeōs*).[104] Gregory enlarges his theory to include the origins of different languages and states categorically that God never spoke Hebrew. Indeed, Hebrew was not an ancient language but rather improvised for the use of the Israelites after the Exodus; proof is found in Psalm 81, for when the Israelites came out of Egypt they "heard a strange language." Indeed, for Gregory, Moses never attributed human expression to God, but spoke as he did because it was impossible to convey divine truth save through human language. Yet, one must never forget that the words do have divine and profound significance.[105]

Perhaps Gregory's clearest and most eloquent example of linguistic accommodation occurs when he takes issue with Eunomius' assertion that since God, who created everything, communes with humanity one must conclude that from the time of creation the Lord provided words suitable for all the things he created, even though the Bible clearly states that although God created animals Adam named them (Gen. 2:20). What, Gregory asks rhetorically, is our response to this?

> We account for God's willingness to admit men to communion with Himself by His love towards mankind. But since that which is by nature finite cannot rise above its prescribed limits, or lay hold of the superior nature of the Most High, on this account, He, bringing His power, so full of love for humanity, down to the level of human weakness [*hēméteron ásthenḗs*], so far as it was possible for us to receive it, bestowed on us this helpful spirit of grace. For as by Divine dispensation [*katá tḕn theîan oikonomían*] the sun, tempering the intensity of its full beams with the intervening air, pours down light as well as heat on those who receive its rays, being itself unapproachable by reason of the weakness of our nature [*òn tȩ̄ astheneía tês phúseōs*], so the divine power, after the manner of the illustration I have used, though exalted far above our nature and inaccessible to all approach, like a tender mother who joins in the inarticulate utterances of her babe, gives to our human nature what it is capable of receiving; and thus in the various manifestations of God to man He both adapts Himself to man and speaks in human language [*katá ánthropōn sxēmatízetai, kaì ánthropōpikôs phthéngetai*], and assumes wrath, and pity, and such-like emotions, so that through feelings corresponding to our own infantile life [*hē nēpiódēs hēmôn zoḕ*] might be led as by the hand, and lay hold of the Divine nature by means of words which His foresight has given.[106]

Gregory, employing the vocabulary of accommodation, has spelled out convincingly and irrefutably his theory of accommodation. The terms are all present—*oikonomía, astheneía, népios*—and Gregory adds one additional fillip of his own; he notes that God not only adapted— demeaned?—himself to the human level, but communicates through Scripture in human language. As we shall see, this idea was to acquire a lengthy pedigree, and Gregory's use of it strikingly parallels the Hebrew legal maxim, "The Torah speaks in human language"— *dibberah torah kileshon benei adam*—or *scriptura humane loquitur* as the Latin knew it.[107] Whether we have here a shared tradition or a borrowing originating with Philo, Origen, or Gregory cannot be decisively determined, but the idea was to recur continually in Christian exegesis at least until the time of Calvin. Humanity had to be led by the hand, as it were, on account of the fundamental difference between humanity and divinity that found trenchant expression in Gregory's ideas of time.

As we have seen above, Gregory of Nazianzus coined the fateful term "procession" to express the relationship among the elements of the Trinity (*ágennēsía, génnesis,* and *ékpempsis*). Gregory of Nyssa and Basil the Great employed the same vocabulary in their struggle against Eunomius and other heretics whose claim that Christ was unlike—*anómoios*—the Father clashed with the orthodox opinion, that Christ was like—*homoíosis*—the Father. Eunomius employed orthodox language, *genētós-agénetos* for his unorthodox ends.

Eunomius argued that if Christ was created—*genētós*—he differed totally from the Father, who was ungenerate—*agénētos*—and Eunomius took the next logical, if dangerous, step; if the orthodox opinion held that all the terms of the Trinity defined just one *ousía,* then either term, *genētós* or *agénētos* described that *ousía.* The former term presented no problem. One could, however, argue that since orthodoxy admitted that Christ was both *agénētos* and God was that not admitting that even God the Father was *agénētos*? If one did not go that far, one nevertheless had to admit that Christ was merely a creature (*ktísma*). To argue that *agénētos* was simply negative theology did not obviate the fact that it described a positive quality. It was Gregory of Nyssa who attempted to provide a safe exit from this theological maze.[108]

Gregory (and Basil) based his response on the idea that a creature, because of its creaturely nature and existence, cannot comprehend its creator. The creature can never cross that divide; for Gregory, that divide is marked by the *diástēma.* Humans are finite; God alone is infinite.[109] Man, existing in time, can never understand or know a God who is beyond time. As Daniélou has suggested, this relationship between man and God, between generate and ungenerate, is a mystery in which the finite continually pursues, without end, the infinite. Thus, humans can never know the true divine nature; we only perceive divine actions. This view approaches later theories concerning knowledge of God through his attributes rather than fathoming directly his nature.[110] Gregory's theory not only overturned Platonic ideas about the inferiority of *genētós* to *agénētos* and the Plotinian and Origenistic view of salvation, which would unite the infinite and the finite, but it was to fuse Platonic and biblical thought into a powerful, new salvific synthesis.

Gregory's theory finds expression in his rebuttal to Eunomius:

> The capacity for an accurate knowledge of the divine essence is not in human nature. Perhaps it is a small matter to affirm this of human capacity alone, but even if one were to say that the immaterial creation [*tēn asómáton ktísin*] was too inferior to approach and grasp by knowledge the infinite nature [*tēn aópiston phúsin*], he would not altogether err as it is possible to see from familiar

instances. . . . So the capacity of angels compared with ours, seems greatly to excel, in that, with no senses interfering, it seeks lofty things with the naked and unobstructed power of knowledge. Yet if their understanding were to be looked at in relation to the great-ness of the Really Existent [*toû óntōs óntōs*], perhaps someone who ventured to say that their capacity was not more distant from the divine knowledge than our limited one is, would not venture beyond what was reasonable. For great and impassable is the intervening space by which the uncreated nature [*hē áktistos phúsis*] is sepa-rated from the created essence. The second is limited; the first has no limit. The second is comprehended by its own measures as pleases the Wisdom of its maker; the measure of the first is infinity [*tês dè métron hē ápeiría éstín*]. The second is circumscribed [*sym-parekteínetai*] by a certain limit of extension [*diastēmatiké tiní paratásei*] and confined by space and time. The first falls beyond every conception of interval [*diastēmatos*] baffling every curious attempt to get at it. In this life one must posit a beginning and an end for beings, but that blessedness beyond Creation admits nei-ther beginning nor end but is by nature beyond what is signified by either, always remaining the same and moving of itself and not proceeding by degrees [*diastēmatikôs*] from one thing to an-other in its life. Nor does it develop (*gínetai*) as it lives, by participa-tion in another life, so that it consequently acknowledges a begin-ning and end to its participation. But it is just what it is: it is life operating in itself, becoming neither more nor less from addition or subtraction.[111]

Gregory's theory encompasses all creation save for God. Angels may be immaterial beings, yet they too are circumscribed by a *diástēma*. Theirs may differ from the human *diástēma*, but the *diástēma* is the ineradicable stamp found on all creatures. Human existence occurs in this interval, and as in the *Life of Moses*, the course for humans is one of progress from a past to a hope of some-thing better in the future. As Balthasar has argued, there is a differ-ence in the human *diastemic* existence and the angelic *diastemic* existence; one is horizontal—perseverance in change—and the other is vertical—continual improvement and striving upward by angels.[112] Yet, because mankind was created in God's image, it may strive for improvement.

For Gregory, the situation is summed up in one cogent comment: "The *diástēma* is nothing less than the Creation."[113] Very simply then, humans have a choice of progress toward the good or of progress toward nothing. Created in the image of God, man has freedom and the ability to change, and since the *diástēma* covers the span from the

Fall to the universal redemption *(ápokatastăsis)*, from donning to shedding the "coats of skin," man freely chooses the direction he wishes to take. Not seeing the past, present, and future at the same time—which God alone can do —man must choose in ignorance and thus is liable to sin. Yet, for Gregory, existence within the *diástēma* is a continual educational and spiritual process leading away from sin and toward God.

The Lord knew beforehand what the ideal state of creation was to have been, but human freedom and its by-product, sin, altered the ideal, or at least postponed its realization. The ideal included asexual beings, such as angels, who reproduced without copulation; men should ideally have reproduced the same way, but in the human *diástēma,* sex marked the difference. Humans reproduced slowly, not quickly as do angels.[114] After the Fall, a different type of human was needed, as were different types of procreation and time, because humanity's worldly existence deviates from the ideal created for it. In the period between the Fall and Resurrection, the new *diástēma* of human history is the amount of time required "for man's education and redemption, for his progress from sinful to ideal freedom, for his moral 'recreation' so to speak."[115] Gregory seems to separate two *diástēmata;* an angelic and human which exist in this less than ideal present world. After the general *ápokatastăsis,* the human *diástēma* will be no more; only the angelic (vertical) one of infinite and perpetual spiritual progress will continue to endure. As several scholars have suggested, Gregory's system is an optimistic one that runs into problems attempting to account for the role of sin; he does not seem to recognize, *en façon de parler,* that sin may possess educational qualities. Yet his notion of sin colors his conception of time, which permits him to establish a relationship between a temporal creation and an atemporal creator.[116]

Much as a guest at a banquet waits until all preparations are completed before entering, so God fashioned man last in the order of creation.[117] The material world, though not ideal, was perfect, *faute de mieux,* for fallen creatures; in a sense, God's substitution of a material world for the originally envisaged immaterial world and his creation of a human *diástēma* in which mankind, as it was, functioned, are but another accommodation with humanity.

Time gave humanity the opportunity to progress spiritually and overcome its imperfections. Rather than viewing time as something less than good, leading from bad to worse until salvation abolished it, as did his Platonic forbears, time, for Gregory, became God's highway to perfection. And yet, because man is free, he could, and would, occasionally err out of ignorance, not knowing, as God alone knows, what choices were always the correct ones. God thus brought into being a world accommodated to mankind. This divine accommodation took into account human lapses; God "set bounds to the reach of evil and changed the angelic or ideal character of time itself, so that sin could finally be overcome and creaturely instability finally made compatible with a progressive or optimistic outcome. The Creation in this later sense—as a *diástēma* that will end and be superseded—is the result of freedom and sin."[118] Gregory's optimistic view of creation and creatures set him apart from most of his predecessors and contemporaries.

In Gregory, we find a positive view of the material world and material beings; the *genētós* was good and existed within a time that was also good. Unlike others who viewed time as something that had to be overcome and would be ultimately eliminated, Gregory promulgated a doctrine that saw humanity being saved within, and not outside of or beyond, time. As man was fashioned in the image of God, so was the temporal universe fashioned in the image of the atemporal; thus, by definition, it is a created good in which man's existence is recognized and given room to exercise its freedom. God established his redemptive system for humanity with judicious economy; through accommodation in creation, in biblical language, in the Incarnation, and in time, the Lord prepared a smooth road wherein mankind would not stumble.

Accommodation thus occupies a central role in, and operates on all levels of, Cappadocian thought. From Basil's political and theological difficulties with heretics and schismatics, to Gregory of Nazianzus' historical interpretation of biblical laws and the role of the Holy Spirit in trinitarian theology, to Gregory of Nyssa's philosophical and mystical teachings on human nature, creation, and the role and function of time, accommodation is heard, in one way or another, as the preeminent tone in the Cappadocian exegetical and theological compositions. Their use and development of the doctrine of accommodation made it an exegetical and theological cornerstone that subsequent builders of interpretation would not reject.

In turning from the Cappadocians to John Chrysostom, we shall see the concept of accommodation and condescension acquire a role almost unequaled among the other fathers. An examination of John's prodigious exegetical outpouring will help illumine, not only his historical outlook, but also his truly remarkable exegetical and rhetorical skills.

Chrysostom, perhaps the most eloquent of the fathers, had eminent pagan teachers, Andragathous for philosophy and Libanius for rhetoric.[119] Another of his teachers, Diodoros of Tarsus, was one of the leading members of the Antiochene school of thought. Julian reportedly said that Diodoros "had equipped his malevolent tongue against the ancient gods with the wisdom of Athens herself."[120] Diodoros and Theodore of Mopsuestia, a fellow student and lifelong friend of John's, enjoyed great praise for learning, and especially for their expositions on Scripture. Diodoros, described as a "reliable arbiter of orthodoxy" in 381, was condemned as the originator of Nestorianism at Constantinople in 499; and his pupil, Theodore, was condemned at the Fifth Ecumenical Council in 553.[121]

As leaders of the Antiochene literal reaction to Alexandrian allegory, both Diodoros and Theodore emphasized the historical narrative of Scripture at the expense of the allegorical. As Diodoros succinctly phrased it: "We prefer the literal to the allegorical method" (toû àllēgorikoû tón historikón pleîston hóson protīmômen).[122]

In discussing the sacrifice of Noah, Diodoros asserts that the Lord made concessions and accepted the sacrifices of Abel and those of Noah because of the deluge, and that the Lord also accepted the sacrifices of the patriarchs. This was done because the Lord realized a time would come when he would require sacrifices from his worshipers. God tolerated sacrifices in order to prevent the Israelites from worshiping idols.[123] Diodoros may have preferred the historical to the allegorical method, but he, and the Antiochene school of exegesis, freely employed allegory in the form of accommodation and condescension.[124] Perhaps it would find its most graphic treatment in the works of John Chrysostom.

As Robert Wilken has so clearly shown, Chrysostom's vehement excoriations of Jews, Judaism, and Jewish ritual practice did not take place in a vacuum; rather, they resulted from the continued vibrancy, attractive character, and seeming eternity of Judaism to his parishioners.[125] Indeed, the issue seems to have been that to the average person in Antioch—and for that matter the empire as a whole— Judaism enjoyed a huge advantage over Christianity by displaying, as Mr. Gladstone did at the end of his career, an "old age verging on the supernatural." It is against this Jewish, Christian, Hellenistic background that Chrysostom presented his message and in so doing drew upon a vast reservoir of associations common to a man of his education, ability, and time. As we have seen, ideas from this "association reservoir" were also used by other writers, notably Basil the Great.[126]

In examining Chrysostom's use of divine accommodation and condescension, one must remember that Christian homiletics blossomed and flourished brilliantly in the fourth century; indeed, the three

Cappadocians and Chrysostom had to entertain to packed houses demanding stellar performances. Chrysostom complained bitterly about the Antiochene crowds, yet to no avail. Describing the appetite of the congregation, he noted:

> If his sermon does not match the great expectation formed of the speaker, he will leave the pulpit the victim of countless jeers and complaints. No one ever takes into consideration that a fit of depression may cloud the clarity of his mind, and prevent his production from coming forth unalloyed. . . . Being a man he cannot invariably reach the same standard or always be successful but will naturally make many mistakes and obviously fall below the standards of his real ability. People are unwilling to allow for any of these factors . . . but criticize him as if they were sitting in judgement on an angel. [127]

Gregory of Nazianzus succinctly summed up the situation in 381 in his farewell to Constantinople: "It is orators they want, not priests!"[128]

Our examination of Chrysostom will focus upon several of his works: *On Vainglory and the Right Way for Parents to Bring Up Their Children,*[129] *On Virginity,*[130] and *On the Incomprehensible Nature of God.*[131] Chrysostom employs the ideas, if not the words, accommodation and condescension, in each of those works and in fact defines accommodation in the last. These works, together with his *Discourses Against Judaizing Christians,*[132] so skillfully mined by Robert L. Wilken, will present an excellent inquiry into Chrysostom's use of accommodation and condescension.

Chrysostom's address *On Vainglory* follows the homiletical style, and it is conceivable that the homily may in fact have been delivered sometime between 387 and 398.[133] The address commences with a hyperbolic attack and description of vainglory and its dangers to a virtuous Christian life. For John, true glory consists in fair dealing, disdain of money and fame, disregard of human values, poverty, and virtue, which will overcome human nature.[134] John discusses the education of children and asks what will become of children who lack teachers? The goal of education is to "raise up an athlete for Christ."[135]

The use of this traditional phrase, popular since Paul, appears in other of Chrysostom's works to indicate that a Christian battles in the world much as an athlete in the arena. Indeed, Christians who have two roles—being parents and raising their children piously— obtain a large, not a small, reward for raising "athletes in Christ."[136] Comparing a child to soft wax, to a pearl, to a painting, to a statue, and lastly to a city, Chrysostom cautions parents to take utmost care in fashioning their children. Chrysostom expands the final metaphor and likens the child's body to the walls of the city and the senses to gates.[137]

Chrysostom analyzes each of the sense organs, and in discussing the importance of the ears, he notes that children should hear nothing harmful from house servants, teachers, or nursemaids (*méte parà oiketôn méte parà paidagōgoû méte parà trophéōn*).[138] Chrysostom, as we shall see, favors familial and educational language, especially when he turns to the Jews, for he saw them as childlike in all their ways.[139]

Just as plants need the greatest care when they are young, warns Chrysostom, so do children. And to prevent children from hearing risqué tales, it is best to read them biblical stories.[140] The younger children should hear stories of Cain and Abel, Jacob and Esau; older children may learn of more advanced stories, until children are mature enough to hear stories of grace and hell from the Gospels. It is very much the sort of argument made by Origen and Gnostics concerning not only the levels of Scripture, but also the manner of dealing in general with the Hebrew Bible and the New Testament.[141] Indeed, Chrysostom cautions parents not to impose too great a burden upon tender understanding; education must be geared to the pupil.[142] The education of a Christian child is serious business concerned, as it is, with the origin and rhythmical education of the whole of the world—the *oikouménē* (*allà tês oikouménēs pásēs, estìn hē hypóstasis kaì hē paídeusis kaì ho hruthmós, ei taûta égineto*).[143] Education was a major component of Christianity in Chrysostom's view, for Christianity had to embrace the entire *oikouménē*.

In discussing the eyes of the child, Chrysostom warns parents that the eyes are the most difficult gate to guard. The child's teacher (*paidagōgós*) and attendant (*akólouthos*) must continually watch him.[144] To avoid the wiles of women, Chrysostom, in his usual manner, urges young men to study the story of Joseph.[145] His instructions for the education of young women are contained in the last section of the work and he adjures mothers to guide their daughters away from extravagance, personal adornment, and other vanities that mark prostitutes.[146]

Chrysostom's address was one of countless guides to educating Christians in a world dominated by classical pagan education. From Clement of Alexandria and Gregory of Nyssa to Augustine, Ambrose, and Jerome, instructions for Christians—newly converted or otherwise—are a staple of early Christian writing.[147] That the Church tolerated the use of the classics in Christian education was of course only one accommodation that it had to make. Indeed, Basil of Caesarea, in his *Exhortations to Youths as to How They Shall Best Profit by the Writings of Pagan Authors,* advised Christians to be as "bees" regarding pagan literature; they were not to approach all flowers equally, nor attempt to carry off all the pollen, but take only what was needed for their work and shun the remainder.[148]

John complained about Christians who named their children after deceased non-Christian forebears rather than after righteous individuals and saints. As an examination of his other works will clearly show, Chrysostom well understood that Christianity had to accommodate itself to its classical heritage, and he was to play a not insignificant role in that accommodation.

In *On Virginity,* John displays not only his remarkable rhetorical skills, but an historical interpretation of no mean talent. Delivered between 382 and 392, *On Virginity* is contemporary to *On Vainglory* and *On the Incomprehensible Nature of God.*[149] Bernard Grillet has argued that *On Virginity* may be read as extended exegesis on I Corinthians 7, and on Paul's arguments that marriage, though useful as a check for sexual desires, is inferior to celibacy.[150] Indeed, *On Virginity* effusively depicts the rewards of the celibate life while focusing only on the difficulties of married life. His comparison of those two states and their relationship to history and divine pedagogy displays Chrysostom's dazzling rhetorical and exegetical talents.

John interprets virginity as a necessary stage in the historical development of the world. Adam and Eve were blissful in Eden, and the absence of cities, crafts, or houses in no way limited their happiness. The natural state that adorned them was one of virginity. When humanity rebelled and laid aside its heavenly attire, people took upon themselves ruin, death, pain, and toil. In the wake of the Fall, marriage became necessary.[151] Thus marriage originated in sin, and Adam and Eve, who were created without marriage, showed that God could have populated the world without marriage, had he so desired. Indeed, John understands the divine command in Genesis 1:28, "Be fruitful and multiply" as a prophecy, rather than a mandate encouraging marriage.[152] Indeed, for Chrysostom, Adam and Eve were ignorant of carnal knowledge before the Fall; in this he differed from other fathers, notably Augustine, who felt the first couple were submissive, before the Fall, to their physical desires.[153]

John is consistent in his view that marriage is not needed to populate the world. He states unambiguously: "For marriage will not be able to produce many men if God is unwilling, nor will virginity destroy their number if he wishes there to be many. But he desired it, according to Scripture, because of us and our disobedience" (cf. Gen. 3:14–17).[154] If this is the case, then why did marriage come to exist?

> Why did marriage not appear before the treachery? Why was there no intercourse in Paradise? Why not the pains of childbirth before the curse? Because at that time these things were superfluous. The necessity arose later because of our weakness [ástheneía], as did cities, crafts, the wearing of clothes, and all our other numerous needs. Death introduced them in its wake. Moreover, do not prefer this, a concession to your weakness [ástheneía], to virginity; or rather, do not assign marriage an equal rank. If you follow this reasoning, you will say it is better to have two wives instead of being content with only one since this had been allowed under the law of Moses.[155]

Marriage is a concession to human weakness, and thus should not be preferred to virginity. Indeed, Chrysostom continues this line of argument by terming marriage a condescension (sygkatábāsis).[156]

John asserts that the Lord permitted practices that were apt for their time (Theós gár autá synexórese kaì gégonen èn kairộ xrēsíma).[157] These laws were good for children, not adults. Christ has come to perfect humanity and has commanded mankind to leave aside children's garments, which neither fit, nor adorn adults. This is neither contradictory nor inconsistent on the part of the Lord:[158]

> Although the new commandments are superior to the old, the aim of the lawgiver is the same. What is it? To reduce the baseness of our soul and to lead it to perfect virtue. Therefore, if God had been anxious not to dictate obligations greater than the former ones but to leave things eternally the same and never to release men from that inferior state, he completely contradicted himself. If at the beginning, in fact, when the human race was more childlike [nēpiódēsteros], God had prescribed this regimented sort of life, we would never have accepted it with moderation [sýmmetron] but would have totally jeopardized our salvation through immoderation [ámetría]. Similarly, if after a long period of training under the Law, when the time called us to this heavenly philosophy, if then he had permitted us to remain on earth, we would have gained nothing much from his condescension [sygkatábāsis] since we had no part in that perfection on account of which his condescension [sygkatábāsis] occurred.[159]

For Chrysostom humanity is now living in the age of parthénia, which has replaced a more childlike age. Christ's Incarnation was a divine condescension in order to lead humanity to salvation. Contrasting humanity's moderate and immoderate behavior with historical cir-

cumstances, the roles of marriage and virginity are specifically elaborated in the divine plan of salvation. Indeed, virginity was too great a
burden to impose upon a fledgling humanity, so the Law permitted
marriage as a concession. To have imposed strict regulations on children would have worsened the situation, and the Law came to school
humanity.

In the normal rhetorical style with its lavish use of metaphors,
John compares human beings to nestlings. Just as a mother bird who
has reared her young escorts them from the nest, watches over them
as they leave it, permits them to remain a bit longer if they are weak
and need a haven, she does this not to keep them in the nest forever,
but to give them time to mature so they can live on their own; thus
does God treat us. He knows that we will fall, not because he wants
us to, but because of our weakness (*àstheneía*). The Lord accordingly
permits us to remain in the nest—he permits marriage to endure in
the world for a long time.[160]

Chrysostom notes that those people who are plodding in nature
and are existing, as it were, in deep sleep cling to the darkness of the
nest and worldly things. The truly noble souls, whose wings have
sprouted and matured, quit the nest and soar. They leave far behind
all worldly conventions and possessions—marriage, money, cares, and
so forth—that normally keep humanity in the nest.[161]

According to John, Christ (cf. Matt. 19:12) wanted mankind to
leave marriage behind. In employing an expanded medical metaphor,
John asserts that the most important thing for a doctor to know is
the correct time for the appropriate precept. Just as drugs by themselves cannot heal a wound, the same obtains for laws.[162] People do
not interfere with doctors, even when they fail, all the more so should
people not interfere with God, who never fails. The commandment in
Genesis 1:28—"Be fruitful and multiply"—was required by the times
since man's nature raved and was unable to be checked.[163]

Were one to ask if God might have required people to uphold
chastity and virginity, such a commandment would have proven worse
than what was required, for it would have been untimely. Virginity,
which preceded marriage, was and is far superior to it. Had Adam
remained obedient to God, there would have been no need for marriage.[164] Just as Eusebius viewed Judaism as an intrusion in history,
so does Chrysostom view marriage. Indeed, marriage originally served
to populate the world and suppress sexual desires; now that the
world is peopled, its only purpose is to suppress debauchery and
licentiousness.[165]

John includes other parts of the Mosaic Code in addition to marriage as condescensions to human frailty. Christ narrowed the path Moses had paved; vengeance, answering an insult with an insult, handling money, swearing, taking an eye for an eye, hating one's enemy, were all permitted by Moses. Even divorce and bigamous marriages were legal; each was a condescension (*sygkatábāsis*).[166]

In a quite extraordinary display of rhetorical argument, John harmoniously weaves together disparate sources in an expanded exegesis of I Corinthians 7:36:

> "But if any man," says the apostle, "think that he behaveth himself uncomely toward his virgin, if she pass the flower of her age, and need so require, let him do what he will, he sinneth not; let them marry."—What do you mean, "let him do what he will?" You do not correct this mistaken idea but permit marriage instead? Why have you not said: but if he thinks he is behaving dishonourably he is a poor unfortunate to think so noble a state is ignominious? Why have you not advised him to put aside this suspicion and guide his daughter away from marriage?—Because, the apostle says, such souls belonged to the very weak, who crawl along the earth. It was impossible to uplift all at once to the argument on behalf of virginity, souls so disposed . . . . And then is it surprising if Paul has done this in the case of something that has been permitted when he does the same thing in the case of what has been forbidden and is contrary to law?[167]

Chrysostom cautions against judging the apostle too severely, since Paul was speaking to very weak individuals who could not apprehend the value of virginity nor its angelic state. Indeed, he preached to the Corinthians only after they asked his advice, for "the right attitude of one's listeners provides the appropriate frame of mind for receiving one's counsel."[168] Paul condoned marriage—a condescension or accommodation—permitted by the Law and yielded to others on matters not permitted by the Law:

> For instance: dietary laws, the acceptance of some foods while rejecting others, were a Jewish weakness [*astheneía*]. Nevertheless, there were among the Romans those who shared this weakness [*astheneía*] [cf. Rom. 14:1–3]. Paul has not only vehemently denounced them, but he does something more than this. He disregards the wrong-doers and censures those who attempted to prevent them with the words: "But why dost thou judge thy brother?" [Rom. 14:10] Yet he did not do this when he wrote the Colossians;

rather, with great authority he upbraids them and treats the matter philosophically. . . .[169]

Why did Paul upbraid the Romans yet speak philosophically with the Colossians?

> Because the Colossians were strong but the Romans still required much accommodation [*sygkatábāsis*]. Paul was waiting for faith to be first of all fixed in their hearts. He feared that he would prematurely and too quickly pull up the weeds and along with them the plants of sound instruction. [Matt. 13:29].[170]

Thus, Paul accommodated his message—or condescended—to different audiences depending on their strength or weakness. The contrast of strength and weakness occurs in Romans 14:1 and 15:1, and John will argue that a different standard of behavior obtains today, that people ought to be stronger than their forebears. John refers to Abraham, who married, had children, owned flocks and herds, and so on, and yet John the Baptist, Peter, and Paul all prayed to depart into his bosom. Does that make marriage superior to virginity? Chrysostom answers with a resounding "no," claiming marriage did not make Abraham what he was.[171] His situation differed from ours:

> Today it is not possible to be perfect without selling everything, without renouncing everything, not just possessions and a house, but even one's own life. In the past there was not yet an example of such great moral strictness.—Well then, do we live more strictly than the patriarch?—We ought to, and we have accepted this precept but we do not live according to it, and so fall far short of the proper goal. For it is clear to all that the trials set forth for us are greater. This is why Scripture when it admires Noah does not simply offer words of praise for him but adds: "Noah was a just man and perfect in his generation, and Noah walked with God" [Gen. 6:9]. Noah was not simply "perfect," but perfect in *his* generation. For there are many kinds of perfection that have been defined differently at different times, and with the advance of time, what was once perfect becomes imperfect later.[172]

John insists that different times demand different observances. Living according to the Mosaic Code was perfect once, but Christ demonstrated that perfection was imperfect.[173] Chrysostom uses the same argument when he turns to biblical sacrifice and employs the identical metaphors—especially the medical metaphors—and key vocabulary terms—*sygkatábāsis* (accommodation/condescension) and *astheneía* (human weakness) are present.[174] Sacrifices for John were mandated to draw men away from polytheism and propel them toward God; they were fit for the Jews of that time.[175] As indicated above, one of John's favorite descriptions of Jews was "childlike"; they were, in their time, rowdy schoolchildren who needed to be disciplined.

And just as the Jews were like little children, God set Moses over them as a schoolteacher (*grammătisês*); and God arranged these things for them through shadowy representations (*skiăgrăphía*), as we teach children letters. As we give children coins and buy them sweets, requiring them to go to school, so did the Lord *then* give (*ho theós tóte . . . 'édōke . . .*) them wealth and luxury, requiring of them but one thing: that they heed Moses. Hence, he delivered them to a schoolmaster, that they might not despise him as a tender and loving Father.[176]

Chrysostom's view of the childishness of the Jews is elaborately set forth as he expands his metaphor. The desert was a schoolhouse for the Jews, the constant arguments and nagging in the desert reflect the fights and quarrels childen have at school. Balaam's prayers on their behalf [Numbers 22] were simply a condescension (*sygkatábāsis*) to children. As children yearn for the nursing breast, so did the children of Israel wish to return to the fleshpots of Egypt.[177]

This interpretation helped explain why the Incarnation—the supreme example of condescension and accommodation—occurred when it did. Previously, the childlike Jews, of all people, "the most envious, little-minded, and in all respects imperfect,"[178] would have learned nothing, now the times have changed. Sacrifices, mandated because of human frailty and eliminated by the physical destruction of the Temple, were no longer an option for Jews, yet marriage, mandated by the same frailty, still remained an option for less than perfect Christians. Judaism had found a replacement for sacrifice, and Christianity was searching for a replacement for marriage. And so it was that John had to confront the subject. Virginity surpassed marriage spiritually and historically, yet the majority of fourth-century Christians in Antioch and Constantinople chose the less pefect path. If the plea to his own flock fell on appreciative albeit unmoved ears, not so his attacks on schismatics. The homilies *On the Incomprehensible Nature of God* apply the same materials to fashion additional examples of divine condescension and accommodation.

In those homilies, Chrysostom unfolds additional exegetical understanding of *sygkatábāsis* and its role in history and theology. John, in combating the Anomoeans, schismatics who claimed they could know the essence of God, uses the verb *katabaínō* in confronting them: "This is the first time I have come down (*katébēn*) to meet my adversaries in the arena."[179] And in talking about the earliest followers of Christ being in Antioch, John notes: "In the time of your ancestors, men came down (*katébēsán*) here from Judea. . . ."[180] In the first four homilies alone, John utilizes forms of *sygkatábainō* or *sygkatábasis* fifteen times and *ástheneía* nine times; in the twelve homilies, some form of condescension or accommodation occurs almost fifty times and *ástheneía* more than twenty times.[181] In using these familiar terms, his interpretation of them emerges irrefutably, and since the clearest definition occurs in the third homily, it is there we shall turn.

Chrysostom uses as his basic text the words of Paul's prayer in I Timothy 6:15–16: to "the King of kings and the Lord of lords, who alone has immortality, who dwells in unapproachable light, whom no human being has ever seen nor can see. To him be honor and power forever. Amen." He notes that Paul often invokes God at the beginning of his epistles, praises him, and then proceeds to expound his teaching [cf. Gal. 1:3–5; I Tim. 1:17]. Paul employs the same style when he speaks of Christ [cf. Rom. 9:3–5]; this is done, Chrysostom assures us, so that all may honor the Son just as they do the Father [cf. John 5:23].[182]

In a meticulous explication of this prayer, Chrysostom provides his surest definition of accommodation and condescension. It is best to let John's words speak:

> "The King of kings," Paul said, "The Lord of lords, who alone has immortality, who dwells in unapproachable light." Stop the heretic and ask him what "Who dwells in unapproachable light" means. And pay heed to the accuracy with which Paul speaks. He did not say: "Who is an unapproachable light," but: "Who dwells in unapproachable light." Why? So that you may learn that if the dwelling is unapproachable, much more so is the God who dwells in it. But Paul did not say this to make you suspect that there is a house or place surrounding God. Rather, he wished you to have a deeper and superior knowledge that God is beyond our comprehension.[183]

With scrupulous attention to vocabulary, nuance, and tone, Chrysostom sets forth the apostle's intention. We know that God is unapproachable, but does that imply he is unknowable? John answers with a fastidious unraveling of Scripture:

> However, he did not say: "Who dwells in incomprehensible light," but; "in unapproachable light," and this is much stronger than "incom-

prehensible." A thing is said to be incomprehensible when those who seek after it fail to comprehend it, even after they have searched and sought to understand it. A thing is unapproachable which, from the start, cannot be investigated nor can anyone come near to it. We call the sea incomprehensible because, even when divers lower themselves into its waters and go down to a great depth they cannot find the bottom. We call that thing unapproachable which, from the start, cannot be searched out or investigated.[184]

John focuses his attack on the Anomoean claim to know the "unapproachable" and "incomprehensible." Their hubris knew no bounds. Employing *synchōrēsis,* Chrysostom momentarily concedes their point for the sake of argument, only to demolish it. John wishes to know:

How will you heretics reply to that? If anyone will say that God may be incomprehensible to men, but not to angels nor to the powers above, tell me this. Are you an angel? Are you numbered among the throng of spiritual powers? Have you forgotten what your nature is? Let us grant that God is unapproachable only to men, although Paul did not add this qualification nor did he say: "Who dwells in a light unapproachable to men but which angels can approach. "Suppose, however, we make a concession [. . . *sygxōrēsin thōmen*] and grant you this qualification. Are you yourself not a man? Suppose then that the angels can approach him. What difference does it make to you since you are the meddlesome busybody who is obstinately contending that God's essence is comprehensible to human nature?[185]

Chrysostom has set his opponents up for their fall. His argument throughout the sermons has been that even the heavenly host can neither see nor approach God. In constructing his argument, he resorts to the famous vision of Isaiah 6:1–2:

And it came to pass in the year in which King Uzziah died that I saw the Lord sitting on a high and lofty throne, and his train filled the Temple. And the Seraphim stood round about him. Each one had six wings; with two they covered their faces and with two they covered their feet and with two they flew. And one cried to another and said: "Holy, holy, holy is the Lord of hosts; the whole earth is full of his glory."

This celebrated vision provides John with material to erect his splendid conception of divine accommodation and condescension. In turning to this passage, Chrysostom asks:

Why, tell me, do they stretch forth their wings and cover their faces? For what other reason than that they cannot endure the sparkling flashes nor the lightning which shines from the throne? Yet they did not see the pure light itself nor the pure essence itself. What they saw was a condescension accommodated to their nature [. . . *'allà sygkatábāsis ên tà horómena*]. What is this condescension (*tí dé ésti sygkatábāsis*]? It is when God appears and makes himself known not as he is, but in the way one incapable of beholding him is able to look upon him. In this way God reveals himself proportionally to the weakness [*astheneía*] of those who behold him.[186]

Thus, God condescends to weaker natures, be they angelic or human. This is perhaps the clearest and broadest definition of divine condescension and accommodation yet encountered. It is proportional revelation. Isaiah's vision was a divine accommodation since God does not sit—upon a throne or anything else—and sitting is a human, not a divine, activity. The seraphim covered their eyes, for they could not endure the divine presence, and note that Isaiah does not say they were "near" God, simply "round about"; they are "nearer" to the divine essence than humans in a spiritual, not a physical, sense. And if one hears a prophet claim to have seen God, this does not mean the divine essence, but rather a manifestation achieved through divine condescension.[187]

Chrysostom, in attacking the Anomoean claim that humans may behold the divine essence, adroitly descends the hierarchical ladder of existence and asserts that creatures on the lower rungs cannot contemplate those on higher rungs. Indeed, Daniel, to whom a lion showed respect, could not behold the presence of an angel (cf. Daniel 6 and 10). Thus, his opponents, who are so removed from Christian piety, ridiculously profess to know the divine essence when Daniel could not suffer to gaze upon one angel.[188]

John returns to his exegesis of the seraphim and asserts that God cannot be seen (by heavenly Powers), even by means of condescension.[189] To prove his point, John employs Ezekiel's vision of the seraphim and cherubim (cf. Ezek. 1). Chrysostom reviews Ezekiel's vision—Ezekiel 1 describes the vision and then comments, "This was the appearance of the likeness of the glory of the Lord" (Ezek. 1:28)— and fully exploiting the biblical answer, remarks that Ezekiel's qualified response proves that neither the prophet nor the angelic host approached or beheld *the* divine essence. Equating the two theophanies, John asks: "Do you see there and here God's condescension?" (*Eîdes kàkeî kaì éntaûtha sygkatábāsin.*)[190] For Chrysostom, divine condescension was much more than a manner of prophetic revelation and a

club to ward off heretics; it was quite simply the process by which
God entered human history in the person of Jesus and through him
attempted to redeem humanity and fulfill the divine plan. Indeed, as
hinted at above, John interprets Christ's manner of speaking, of teaching, indeed, all his human actions as a result of his condescension
and attempt to implement the divine plan.

John suggested that Christ's incarnation should make mankind
marvel. "That he who is God was willing to become man, that he
mightily suffered to accommodate himself [*katabénai*] is too great to
comprehend. It makes us quake with holy fear and fills us with
amazement."[191] Chrysostom will use Christ's incarnation and minis-
try among mankind as the reason for his style of teaching and preaching. Why, John inquires, did Christ and the apostles say lowly and
abasing things about him? The primary reason was to demonstrate
that Christ was a true nature and not a shadow or apparent form.
Having dispensed with heretical assertions about Christ's nature,
John asserts that, in spite of Christ's own words and the apostolic
preaching, the devil convinced some pitiful and miserable men to
deny the divine plan (*oikonomía*) and to take away the entire basis of
Christ's humanity. Christ's preaching saved many who otherwise might
have been beguiled by the devil.[192]

Christ's incarnation—divine condescension and accommodation
to humanity—in John's exegesis becomes a weapon in the battle
against heretics. As he observes:

> Do you not still hear, even today, that Marcion, Manichaeus,
> Valentinus and many others denied the plan of redemption
> [*oikonomía*] in the flesh? This is why Christ says many things which
> are human and lowly, things which fall far short of the ineffable
> essence of his. He does so to prove and guarantee the plan of re-
> demption [*oikonomía*]. The devil has striven with all his strength to
> take this faith away from men because he knew that if he destroys
> man's belief in the plan of redemption [*oikonomía*] it would be all
> over with most of the things we hold as true.[193]

Accommodation and condescension to the human condition
through the Incarnation becomes for Chrysostom, as it was, and would
be, for other fathers, the very stuff of salvation. In addition to fleshing
out God's salvific plan, John enumerates an additional reason Christ
spoke in a human manner: the weakness of those who heard him
(*hē astheneía tón akoúōnton*).[194] Much as Origen saw Scripture being
decipherable on several levels and Gnostics argued in a similar vein,
Chrysostom asserts that Christ accommodated his style of teaching to
those who listened:

> Those who were then seeing him and hearing him for the first time could not accept the more sublime words of his teaching. What I am saying is not guesswork and I shall try to prove this to you from the Scriptures themselves. I shall also try to show that if he were ever to say anything great, sublime, and worthy of his glory—but why do I say great, sublime, and worthy of his glory?—if ever he were to have said anything beyond the grasp of human nature, the men who heard him would be upset and scandalized. But if he ever were to say something in a lowly and human fashion, they would run to him and accept what he said.[195]

Chrysostom's position is well established. Christ had to speak to humanity on its own level and terms, not only because of his human form and the weakness of those who heard him, but also to teach men to be humble in their thoughts.[196]

The same device that held that Christ took on flesh in order to put the divine plan of salvation into operation could also defend certain actions against charges of being unseemly for God. For instance, Chrysostom wished to explain why Christ prayed before raising Lazarus (John 11), when he did not pray before raising other dead people (cf. Luke 7 and Mark 5). When Martha told Christ that God would give him whatever he asked for, Christ prayed. And Chrysostom declares that Christ could have raised Lazarus without a prayer, but prayed merely as an accommodation to Martha's weakness.[197] When Christ washed the feet of the apostles and was called Lord and Teacher by Peter (John 13), Chrysostom is quick to point out that Christ acted in that manner, not out of any weakness or inferiority, nor in any way that diminished his glory, but rather out of mercy and kindness to humanity, as well as to set an example of humility for his followers:

> Do you see that he did many things so as to give an example? A teacher who is full of wisdom stammers along with his stammering young students. But the teacher's stammering does not come from a lack of learning; it is a sign of the concern he feels toward the children. In the same way, Christ did not do these things because of the lowliness of his essence, he did them as a condescension (*dià sygkatábāsin*).[198]

The true glory and mystery of the Incarnation are made manifest through *sygkatábāsis*, which allowed the divine—with no diminution—to become truly human and expedite the divine redemptive plan. After scouring these three works—and the examples could be multiplied seemingly without end—it is little wonder that Chrysostom has been dubbed *"le docteur de la condescendance"; sygkatábāsis*, the stone that others might have overlooked or rejected, became for him, as for no other, the cornerstone of a prodigious hermeneutical edifice. It harmonized well with his theological, exegetical, and historical positions. It explained how God became man without demeaning the divinity, thus permitting humanity, on its own level, to behold God. It solved the exegetical problem of the superiority of the "new" law over the Mosaic Code, be it in the practice of virginity or lack of fleshly sacrifices, and demonstrated Christianity's unrivaled prominence over both Judaism and paganism. John made excellent use of an exegetical principle that not only suited his rhetorical style, but served his pastoral needs as well. With John's imprimatur, many others would use the same device, and the last great theologian of the Antiochene school, Theodoret of Cyrus, utilized it most productively.

Theodoret, elected bishop in 423, governed his diocese for thirty-five years.[199] Indeed, in his letter to Pope Leo, Theodoret describes his energetic defense of Christianity:

> By the help of God's grace working with me more than a thousand souls did I rescue from the plague of Marcion; many others from the Arian and Eunomian factions did I bring over to our Master Christ. I have done pastoral duty in eight hundred churches, for so many parishes does Cyrus contain; and in them, through your prayers, not even one tare is left, and our flock is delivered from all heresy and error. He who sees all knows how many stones have been cast at me by evil heretics, how many conflicts in most of the cities of the East I have waged against pagans, against Jews, against every heresy.[200]

An unwavering foe of pagans, Jews, and heretical Christians, Theodoret employed the conception of divine condescension in his comments on biblical sacrifice.

In his exegesis of Leviticus, Theodoret asserts that God, as is made manifest by the prophets, never desired sacrifices. It was after their long captivity in Egypt that the Jews needed to be weaned away from the worship to which they had become enslaved. The Lord tolerated sacrifice in order to liberate Israel from Egyptian idolatry. Theodoret suggests that God prepared, as it were, a medication to keep the Jews free from idolatry. This interpretation is very similar both to the rabbinic ideas involved in the possible dispute between Justin and the Jews and to those advanced by Aphrahat.[201] Indeed, it should be pointed out that while Theodoret's Greek style may have been praised by Photius,[202] yet his native tongue was Syriac, and his affinity with both Antiochene and Syriac traditions is striking. In commenting upon Isaiah 1:11, Theodoret terms the Jewish desire for sacrifice Jewish weakness (*ástheneía*) and suggests that the Lord even permitted the use of music in his worship as a concession to the juvenile attitude and infirmity (*ástheneía*) of the Jews.[203]

In his *Graecorum Affectionum Curatio,* the last and perhaps best refutation of paganism, Theodoret, indebted as he was to both Clement's *Stromata,* and Eusebius' *Praeparatio Evangelica,* tries to prove the veracity of Christianity from pagan sources. He attacks pagan and Jewish sacrifices and insists that the Christian form of worship is supreme.[204] Theodoret repeats in the *Curatio* the charge that the Israelites became addicted to animal sacrifices in Egypt. Yet the Egyptians worshiped many deities, including, among others, cows, sheep, goats, and doves. Some of these were deemed edible; others were judged unclean.[205] Theodoret suggests that the Lord, the all-wise physician (*ho pánsophos iātrós*), conceded (*sygxōrésas*) sacrifice for their weakness (*ástheneía*), as a drug (*tò phármăkon*) for the disease of Egypt.[206]

Theodoret's use of medical imagery is in keeping with the entire tradition he was heir to, and his reference to sacrifice as a drug is much closer to the language of the Syriac fathers—especially Aphrahat and Jacob of Sarug—than it is to either the Antiochene or Alexandrian usage. What this may demonstrate is Theodoret's dual heritage, his use of Antiochene and Alexandrian materials reverberating with Syriac echoes. What is certainly clear from this account is his reliance on earlier traditions. Theodoret affirms that the Jews were commanded to sacrifice those animals that they had come to worship in Egypt in order to prove that the gods of the Egyptians were not divine. And since the Egyptians relished swine flesh, it was forbidden to the Jews. The Lord juxtaposed the superstitious and the gluttonous; he opposed one malady by another and fought belief by gluttony.[207]

Theodoret claims that, if the Israelites had been given more advanced laws upon their exodus from Egypt, they would have reverted to their condition in Egypt; it was divine planning that kept them in check. Would the same situation have obtained had they from the very start been given the philosophy of the gospel?[208] Theodoret combines the use of sacrifice with dietary laws. For him, as for Aphrahat, they were inextricably intertwined in the divine plan. Dietary laws were imposed to blot out any remnants of the Egyptian dieties that might have survived the passage through the sea.[209] These commands were apt for the time they were given, and Theodoret will argue the same point in his *De Providentia.*

Indeed, in examining the biblical account of creation and God's actions after creating humanity, there are certain obvious points to be apprehended. The first law that was enjoined upon Adam forbade him to eat of a certain tree. It would have been superfluous (*perittós*) for the Lord to have given Adam commandments about adultery, murder, or bearing false witness. After all, whom could he slay were he alone; if there was but Eve, with whom could Adam have committed adultery? Against whom could he have acted unjustly or have borne false witness? Therefore, he accepted only the commandment concerning the tree since it was apt for a newly born and childlike infant.[210] This of course was but one step on the long and hard journey that culminated with the Incarnation.[211] For Theodoret, as for his fellow Antiochenes, history overshadowed allegory. Laws were accommodated to their times; this is another idea that will recur in the Syriac fathers.

The tradition of divine accommodation appeared in Byzantine exegesis and flowered in the writings of Procopius of Gaza,[212] Anastasius Sinaites,[213] and in a polemical work of the late seventh century, *The Trophies of Damascus.*[214] The idea was not confined to the borders of Byzantium; it spread far and wide and appeared in diverse sources. For example, it is to be found in the works of an eleventh-century deacon of Hagia Sophia known as John[215] and in the writings of Theophylact of Ochrida, a real Constantinopolitan who hated being in exile in a remote bishopric.[216]

As indicated above, ideas similar to those expressed by Theodoret also took root in different soil: among the Syriac-speaking Christians of the Near East. The ideas proved tenacious and flourished in the area of the foothills of the mountains of Tur Abdin. This heuristic exegetical device, which helped shape Greek exegesis in Alexandria and Antioch, would be nurtured and sustained by the Syriac fathers. It is to Aphrahat, Ephrem, Isaac of Antioch and Jacob of Sarug that we must turn.

CHAPTER THREE

BREAD AND MILK

> Behold, the days come, saith the Lord, that I will make a new
> covenant with the House of Israel, and with the House of Judah:
> Not according to the covenant that I made with their fathers in
> the day that I brought them out of the land of Egypt; which my
> covenant they brake, although I was an husband unto them, saith
> the Lord: But this shall be the covenant that I will make with the
> House of Israel; after those days, saith the Lord, I will put my law
> in their inward parts, and write it in their hearts; and I will be
> their God, and they shall be my people.
>
> — Jeremiah 31: 31-33.

The concept of divine condescension and accommodation that
flourished in Greek exegesis found creative expression in Syriac literature as well. These Christian exegetes had close contacts with
Jewish traditions, if not with Jews themselves, and the danger that
Chrysostom guarded against, namely, Judaizing Christians, was also
a constant threat in the Persian Empire. The position the Jews had
in the Roman Empire was fairly secure until threatened by growing
Christian influence. Their position in the Persian Empire—culturally, economically, and socially—was not only more secure than in
Rome; indeed, it was most probably superior to the position of the
Christians.[1]

The theological disputes, with their attendant rancor and rise of
splinter sects, coupled with pagan attacks and the reign of Julian,
seemed to check the Christian advance in Rome, while in Persia,
Christians seemed to be a fifth column of sorts. Robert Murray has
noted that for the period until the fourth century "the Christians in
Mesopotamia lived at the door of the Jews like poor relations not on
speaking terms."[2] While J. B. Segal suggests that the "turning point
in Jewish-Christian relations at Edessa must have come with the
treaty between Byzantium and Persia in 363. By this treaty the

frontiers between the two empires were sharply defined. Edessa lay firmly in the orbit of Byzantium; Nisibis had become a Persian stronghold."[3]

It was, of course, in 388 that the synagogue at Callinicos was burned by Christians, who were ordered to rebuild it by Theodosius. Ultimately, he succumbed to pressure from Ambrose and rescinded his decree. As Segal observes, by the fifth century, "the name Jew had become a word of opprobrium."[4] It is thus against a changing background that our authors wrote, and the time and place of composition are reflected in their respective tones.

Aphrahat, the first of our authors, probably lived between 270 and 345 or later.[5] About his life little is known, yet the dates of his twenty-three "Demonstrations" are fairly well established. The first ten, 336–37; eleven through twenty-two, 344; and the last, winter, 344–45.[6] The first ten present his interpretation and understanding of Christianity, while the remaining thirteen deal with matters of the Iranian church, which contained substantial numbers of Jewish converts. The Judaism of these converts was far less sophisticated than that of the Babylonian academies and may have been that of the Adiabenian converts.[7] It is one scholar's opinion that Aphrahat may have known Jews who had little or no contact with the scholars of the rabbinic academies.[8] Yet according to Segal and Frank Gavin, Aphrahat lived near Mosul and was acquainted with the Targum and the Talmud. Segal claims that Aphrahat "employs a Jewish chronology, and even his metaphors in a few places are Jewish. It is possible that he had a knowledge of Hebrew."[9] What emerges, regardless of this difference of opinion, is the fact that Aphrahat was an eclectic author and knew some type of Jewish Midrashic teachings that differed from the church's. We shall try to focus our analysis upon those links to Jewish teachings.

Of Aphrahat's twenty-three homilies, four contain an explicit critique of Jewish ceremonial practice—including dietary laws, the Sabbath, the Paschal Sacrifice, and circumcision.[10] The *Book of the Laws of Countries* records that Jews stress observance of rituals, especially the Sabbath and circumcision, in all the lands of their dispersion.[11] Indeed, Aphrahat tells his audience that the faith of the Church of God requires that people stop observing "hours and Sabbaths and moons and seasons."[12] And Segal affirms that Aphrahat's "fellow-Christians in this area, like early Christians elsewhere, maintained Jewish practices; they avoided, for example, eating meat before the blood had been removed, and at Passover they ate unleavened bread."[13] It has been suggested by several scholars that these homilies were written to bolster Christian belief in a time of difficulty and to dissuade Judaizing Christians. In light of the evidence, that is a distinct possibility.

Aphrahat, in his demonstration "On the Distinction Among Foods," discusses the Jewish dietary laws and ties them to the origins of biblical sacrifice. Aphrahat denies that dietary laws were enacted with a view toward righteousness; on the contrary, they were instituted because of lust and avariciousness. They were part of a divine plan to withdraw Jews from their idolatry in Egypt. Aphrahat notes that from the days of yore people could eat anything, save for blood. Indeed, Noah could eat as he pleased save for the blood of animals (cf. Gen. 9:4ff); and Aphrahat wonders, if any sin or error arose from the consumption of food, why did God not enact dietary laws at the creation?[14]

Aphrahat explains the injunction of distinguishing foods very simply: the children of Israel began to worship as the Egyptians worshiped and had abandoned the God of their fathers.[15] The Egyptians worshiped oxen and calves, and the story of Joseph (Gen. 43:32) proves that Egyptians and Hebrews did not share the same table. Israelites used to eat all meats before descending into Egypt but once there, they consumed only oxen and sheep. Aphrahat further asserts that Joseph instructed his brethren to tell Pharoah that they were shepherds (Gen. 46:31ff.), since the Egyptians honored shepherds; thus, they were given Goshen and not impressed into royal service.[16]

In his exegesis of Exodus 8, Aphrahat's critical and finely honed exegetical skills emerge quite nicely. Moses, in his encounter with Pharoah, informed Pharoah that the Israelites wished to depart to the wilderness for three days in order to sacrifice to their own God. Pharoah was willing to permit them to serve their own God, but only within Egypt. Moses rejected this counteroffer. Aphrahat, in an attempt to explain Moses' refusal, posits the following theory: If the Jews had sacrificed the very animals held sacred by the Egyptians in front of them, the Egyptians would have turned upon the Jews and stoned them. Furthermore, the punishment meted out to the Egyptians by God included the decimation of their flocks (Exod. 12:29); that is, the very animals held sacred in Egypt. [17]

Having sketched the background necessary for comprehending the historical situation of the Israelites in their Egyptian pied-à-terre, Aphrahat turns to biblical sacrifice as a means of using divine accommodation in his exegesis. His treatment of sacrifice commences with a series of biblical proof texts to verify Jewish idolatry in Egypt and includes mention of the worship of calves and oxen. (Aphrahat writes in prose, employing rhythmic patterns, often with thematic parallels.)[18] The Bible twice tells of Jewish apostasy and worship of calves: first, the incident of the Golden Calf; and second, the image of the calf fashioned by Jeroboam, son of Nabat.[19] On both occasions, the only image worshiped was that which the Israelites had adored in Egypt.

Aphrahat proceeds to repeat what other exegetes had claimed and others would claim: When the Holy One saw that his people were not cleansed of Egyptian habits, Moses was commanded to distinguish between clean and unclean foods. Echoing in Aphrahat's account are the reasons advanced by Manetho in Josephus' *Against Apion* and in the *Histories* of Tacitus:

> When the Holy One saw that they were not purified from the leaven (*hmyr'*) of the Egyptians, but remained in that very opinion of paganism, then He commanded Moses to distinguish foods for them. He made unclean for them those very things which had been clean for them to eat in the land of Egypt, and He commanded them to eat those very things which they had worshiped in the land of Egypt of which they [previously] had not eaten.[20]

In addition to invoking the same mirror image of Jewish history and customs that had been popular with Greco-Roman anti-Jewish polemicists, Aphrahat's utilization of the metaphor "the leaven of the Egyptians" is of interest. It may reflect Pauline language, a common cultural idiom, or it may unveil Midrashic influence in the development of his argument.

A frequent metaphor in rabbinic texts for the evil inclination, the *yeẓer rah*, is "leaven in the dough," and one instance is attributed to R. Abahu, a contemporary of Aphrahat.[21] Perhaps Aphrahat is conflating both in this passage, which continues:

> On account of their evil impulse (*wmtl yzrhwn bysh'*), He commanded that they even bring as an offering before Him that thing which they had worshiped. They should eat the flesh of sheep and oxen, which they had not wanted to eat because they were sacrifices. And note that when He distinguished many animals of purity for them, only from the sheep and oxen did He mandate sacrifice from them. [22]

Aphrahat seems to be following the Midrashic lead by invoking the use of the evil inclination, and his shift from dietary laws to sacrifice bolsters the use of the evil inclination in his argument. It is also noteworthy that Aphrahat appears to follow a Midrashic teaching that the Lord sent fire from heaven as a sign that he not only accepted Abel's sacrifice but also those of the Tabernacle.[23] In attacking the sacrifices, Aphrahat asserts:

You should know... that because He determined concerning them that they should not worship calves, the gods of the Egyptians, He distinguished for them among foods and commanded them to sacrifice offerings of the very things they had feared in the land of Egypt. For the Lord had no need of sacrifices and offerings. But in order to restrain the Jews from sacrifices and offerings so that they should not worship the gods of the peoples—when they would enter the land and be mixed among the peoples—as they had worshiped the gods of the Egyptians when they had entered Egypt and been mixed among the Egyptians, He therefore forbade and restrained the Jews thus (saying, as it were), "before My altar they should bring their offerings and sacrifice their sacrifices."[24]

Aphrahat repeats the "inversion theory" of Jewish history, yet advances his own theory of divine accommodation. The Lord permitted Israel to keep practices acquired in Egypt, but turned them in His direction. God acted to restrain idolatry while conceding sacrifice to people accustomed to it. It is perhaps not accidental that Aphrahat connects the evil inclination to his theory of sacrifice as a curb on idolatry since in rabbinic literature the evil inclination seems to prey most upon the passion for idolatry and adultery, and the former is seen as more powerful than the latter since it may cause parents to kill their own children.[25]

This is all part of Aphrahat's attack on Jewish ritual, and very similar language is employed in his *Demonstration on Circumcision,* in which Aphrahat sets forth a plan of five covenants between man and God, which, as we shall see, was an idea that would acquire a pedigree. In assaulting circumcision, Aphrahat invokes the stock-in-trade argument that, for Abraham and others, faith preceded circumcision and that fleshly circumcision was commanded of Abraham "as a seal and sign of the covenant, so that, when his seed became many, it should be distinct from all the nations among which they lived, in order not to get involved in their impure works."[26] Indeed, Abel, Enoch, Noah, and others were uncircumcised yet pleasing before the Lord, and was not Abraham blessed by Melchizedek, the uncircumcised priest of the most High God?[27] Joshua (which in Syriac, as in Hebrew, is the same as Jesus) circumcised the people a second time (Josh. 5:2), which Aphrahat understands as circumcision of the heart in order to distinguish the Israelites from the Egyptians and Ishmaelites, who also had fleshly circumcision. Aphrahat's typological interpretation of Jewish ritual serves his exegetical and polemical intent to demonstrate the changing nature of divine commands and covenants.

Aphrahat's exegesis is consistent. The rituals of the Mosaic Code are only aspects of divine law and therefore may be changed according to the times:

> In every age, the law and the covenant has been changed. At first, then, God changed the covenant of Adam and gave another to Noah. And once again He gave (another) to Abraham. And He changed that of Abraham, and He gave another to Moses. And when that of Moses was not changed, He gave another in the last generation, a covenant that does not change.[28]

Aphrahat believed that ". . . in each generation God established laws, and they ministered to their time and then are changed" (*dbdr dr qm' 'lh' nmws': wshmshw zbn' dshpr lh w'thlpw*).[29] Only the covenant with Christ is unchanging; the laws of the old Adam were completed by the new Adam.

Aphrahat presents a clear and recognizable knowledge of the theory of accommodation and condescension. Sacrifices were permitted, but only for a limited time to a people addicted to them. The Mosaic Code marked the final step on the road to Christ, which, for Aphrahat, signified not only the triumph of the Church, but victory in the history of salvation. Accommodation, in both its negative and positive applications, well suited Aphrahat's typological interpretation of history and permitted him to assert that in the plan of salvation Christians had replaced Jews. Ephrem was to employ Aphrahat's doctrines, though not his approach.

In passing from Aphrahat to Ephrem (d. 373), we move from Persian to Roman territory and from one of the mildest to one of the most ardent disputants in the Jewish-Christian encounter. It is worth remembering that by the fifth century, the word Jew becomes one of opprobrium, and while Aphrahat never terms the Jews "crucifier" (*zlb'* or *zqp'*), Ephrem shows no such restraint.[30] As Murray has written: "It must be confessed with sorrow that Ephrem hated the Jews."[31]

In the third of his *Sermons on the Faith*, Ephrem, one of the most prolific of the Syriac fathers, vigorously advanced Aphrahat's historical conception of commandments ministering to their time and then being changed:

> For the benefit of the children of (each) generation
> Were the voices spoken in (each) generation.
> There is a voice that demands sacrifices,
> And there is a voice that rejects burnt offerings.
> There is a voice that commands us to use clean foods,

And there is a voice that commands to mix and eat.
There is a voice that commands to celebrate festivals,
And there is a voice that commands to profane festivals.
There is a voice that commands to sanctify the day,
And there is a voice to reject Sabbaths.
There is a voice to circumcise males
And there is a voice that rejects circumcision.[32]

Ephrem thus interprets the familiar Jewish ritual practices—sacrifices, dietary laws, festivals, Sabbath, and circumcision—as different commands for different times. Circumcision for him was a malady (*k'b'*) that marked off the Jews from their idolatrous neighbors. Aphrahat understood circumcision to have the same role, but never termed it a malady. This, for Ephrem, was all part of the divine plan because it preserved the Jews—the vehicle through which Christ entered history—intact. Now that Christ has come and been rejected by the Jews, circumcision has played its role and is no longer of any importance. Ephrem and Aphrahat interpreted circumcision typologically.

Ephrem, in a manner reminiscent of Eusebius, divides history into three ages: the first days, when the righteous of old, who were sound in their knowledge of God, lived; the middle days, which was the time of the Jews; and the present, latter days, when Christians, who are sound in their faith, live. The rituals of the Mosaic Code were mandated for the Jews; they were a means to combat the rampant paganism and idolatry that engulfed the world at that time. As Ephrem observes in one of his Nisibene hymns:

> The whole world like a body had fallen into heavy sickness; for in the fever of heathenism, it burned and pined and fell. The right hand of tender mercy touched it, and dealt with its soul in pity; and cut off speedily its heathenism, for that was the cause of its sickness, and it was purged and sweated and restored.[33]

The world's malady, heathenism, had to be eradicated, and the process is found in Ephrem's exegesis of Matthew 12:43–5. "The man cured by the divine Physician is Israel. The unclean spirit of idolatry was cast out and wandered in desert places, that is, among the Gentiles, but could find no rest there, because the Gentiles had heard God's voice."[34]

Israel crucified Christ on the ground that he was "seducing" people away from the one God, though it was Israel that constantly drifted toward idolatry. Recalling the incident of the Golden Calf, Ephrem notes; "For the one calf which they made in the desert, pastured on their lives as on grass in the desert."[35] The source of the idolatry is revealed:

> For that idolatry which they had stolen and brought out from Egypt in their hearts, when it was made manifest, openly slew those in whom it was dwelling secretly. For it was like fire concealed in wood which when it is gendered from within it, burns it.[36]

Ephrem, like Aphrahat and others, blames the Jews for exporting idolatry from Egypt and focuses upon the heart, which as we have seen with Irenaeus was the dwelling place of the evil inclination. Indeed, Ephrem notes that when Moses ascended the mountain to receive the Law the Israelites drew near the "heathenism of Egypt" "that they might worship it openly also; for they had been secretly worshiping it in their hearts."[37]

Ephrem juxtaposes Jewish idolatry and rejection of Christ in an attempt to show how the former has led to their misfortune. The calling of the Gentiles to be the new people of God was a common motif in early Christian writings, and for Ephrem, the history of salvation demonstrated the process of replacement.[38]

In the third *Sermon on the Faith*, Ephrem turns to Christ's advent and the light it sheds on the history of salvation:

> His entire reason for preserving the flock
> Was because of something hidden in its midst.
> The something which was hidden in it has come forth,
> And has become the Shepherd of Mankind.
> In the contemptible flock, He hid
> The Prince of the Shepherds.
> He has left the foolish flock,
> For the nations have become his pasture.[39]

Stubbornly, in Ephrem's view, do the Jews, out of foolishness, cling to ritual observances and earn divine displeasure by focusing on their particular rites while ignoring Christ's universal message:

> Wroth is the Lawgiver
> Because He untied, and you, then bind.
> The commandment which He has given to you, is invalidated,
> And that which He has untied, you observe.[40]

Ephrem assails the Jews not only because they observe invalidated commandments, but even worse, they try to convert Christians. The Jews seek to subject others to an outmoded, particular Law; to reimpose the rituals from which Christ freed humanity. Ephrem excoriates the "contemptible flock" and admonishes his flock to flee the Jews:

> After he [sc. the Jew] has tasted much blood,
> He could not be quit from killing.
> Then he killed openly.
> Now he kills secretly.
> He encompasses sea and land
> To lead an adherent into Gehenna.[41]

Ephrem's belligerence crests in another warning:

> Flee from him [sc. the Jew], O weak one.
> Your blood and death are nothing to him.
> He took the blood of God.
> Will he be terrified of your blood?[42]

Ephrem, like Aphrahat, understood the ritual observances as a divine prophylactic device; yet Aphrahat's pacific and almost hushed tone has yielded to acrimony and enmity. The Jews had a positive role to perform in the divine drama of salvation; they were the vessel through which salvation, in the person of Christ, entered the world; but: "When our Lord came, they crowned their wickedness and crucified Christ as they had killed the prophets; and therefore they were rejected like a useless vessel."[43] Ephrem seems to be caught between the Scylla of divine planning—which included a major role for the Jews and the Mosaic rituals—and the Charybdis of his hatred for the Jews. They have served their purpose and now are useless.

The "malady" of circumcision was in effect a different "mark of Cain" because it separated the Jews from all others. The severity of Ephrem's opinion may be born of that historical ambiguity: The Jews, given the divine role of preparing the way for the Lord in the wilderness of heathenism, succeeded, only to fail all the more miserably in not recognizing their mission and what they had accomplished. As Ephrem intoned:

> At the present time, the commandments
> Of Sabbath, of circumcision, and of purification, are invalid.
> They are superfluous for those of the latter days,
> But for those of the middle days they were necessary.
> For those of the first days they were unnecessary,
> Because they were sound in knowledge.
> Neither are they necessary for those of the latter days,

Because they are sound in faith.
They ministered to those of the middle days alone,
Because they were struggling with paganism.[44]

The Mosaic Code was given to a particular people for a particular purpose in a particular age. The particularity of Judaism could not be more strongly contrasted with the universality of Christ's teachings. That Israel's time has past is expressed in an address to the room of the Last Supper in the *Hymns on the Crucifixion:*

> Blessed art thou, O place! For in thee the scales
>   of truth were set up for the two sides.
> There were two Passovers and two lambs,
>   two nations and two deliverances.
> The Nation was like its Passover, a lamb for a time;
>   and like its time it departed and failed.[45]

Ephrem treats the history of salvation and its unfolding in history in a manner consistent with Aphrahat's exegesis: similar images, style, and approach; what is strikingly different is the language, temper, and tone. While Aphrahat could refer to ideas he heard from a man "called a sage among the Jews," Ephrem rebuked the "tasters of blood" and "crucifiers."[46] Both fought the Jews with their words: Aphrahat indulged his disputants; Ephrem hated his.

Isaac of Antioch (d. 459) and Jacob of Sarug (d. 521) were to follow the trail Ephrem blazed.[47] Isaac, an "intellectual grandson" of Ephrem, wrote with the vehemence and animosity of his forebear, who taught Zenobius, Isaac's teacher. In "Homily Two Against the Jews," Isaac asserts that the Law given at Sinai was punitive.[48] In responding to his Jewish interlocutor, Isaac tells why the Law was bestowed:

> And I answered and said to him
> Against the perversity of his saying:
> "That it should be a fetter for your servitude,
> (Similar to) that which you served in Egypt."[49]

The Jew wonders if, indeed, the Law is a fetter, and Isaac answers in no uncertain terms:

> Then I clarified my words and said to him:
> "I am not the cause of your rebuke."
>
> Is it not after you turned astray
> From the Lord after the calf (*'gl'*)

(That) there came down to you from Mt. Sinai
A chain for your bonds,

A heavy yoke which was cast
As if upon your rebellious neck.
And a bond and a shackle it was to you,
That you should not leave your God.[50]

Isaac, punning on Exodus 19:20 (And the Lord came down from Sinai), tells how the shackles of the Law came down. Again the punitive nature of the Law is stressed, and again the homily, following Ephrem's example, tells how the Jews were the vessel through which Christ entered history; when they rejected him, they were, in turn, rejected.[51]

In his attack on ritual observance, Isaac concentrates on circumcision and repeats the standard charges that the righteous of old were not circumcised. Since the Law itself speaks at length about those who lived without it, according to Isaac, the Law proclaims its own invalidation.[52]

Isaac notes that changes have occurred in Israelite history and cites Reuben, Jacob, and Moses as examples. He concludes that the Lord's command may not be changed and His decree is everlasting (*l'lm*).[53] Yet for him the great problem with Jewish rituals was their singular ineffectiveness. Isaac contrasts the particular character of Jewish sacrifice with the universal quality of Christ's sacrifice:

He guards the vine of the nations,
And lays waste the vineyard of Israel
And he cleanses his garments in wine,
And his vestures in the blood of grapes.

Not with the blood of sacrifice does He make
The Offering, but rather with wine
He cleanses His cloak which has become red
With the blood of grapes, not with sacrifices.[54]

The offerings, so widely attacked and so often condemned as a sign of idolatry that led Israel away from her God, are roundly denounced by Isaac. As we have seen above, for Isaac as for so many other early Christian exegetes, the Law was imposed as a penalty after Israel's idolatry at Horeb (Exod. 32). Perhaps the Syriac fathers knew even better than Irenaeus rabbinic teachings concerning the evil inclination. It was the "strange god" within mankind (cf. Ps. 81:9–10), and the gravest threat of the evil impulse was to make mankind idolatrous: "For this is the art of evil impulse. Today it says to a man, Do this! and tomorrow, Do that! until at last it says, Worship other Gods, and he goes and does it."[55] Indeed, a Midrash makes it clear that angels differ from humans in several ways: They are immortal and do not propogate their species, and they have no evil inclination.[56]

The incident of the calf loomed large in rabbinic literature, and as a Midrash teaches: "All shofars [cattle horns] are valid save that of a cow" (*M. Rosh ha-Shanah* 3, 2), because it is the horn of a calf, and it is written, "They have made them a molten calf," for Scripture declares, "and it shall be no more the confidence of the house of Israel, bringing iniquity to remembrance"[57] Jewish law singles out idolatry, adultery, and the shedding of blood as "cardinal" sins and maintains that a Jew must die rather than submit to their performance. Rabbinic literature deals forthrightly with the incident of the calf, which for the rabbis became the archetypal sin. Indeed, it is recorded in rabbinic sources that "No retribution whatsoever comes upon the world [of the Jew] which does not contain a light fraction [of the sin] of the calf."[58] The Christian attack on the calf hit hard and penetrated deeply; it did not end with Isaac.

Known as "The flute of the Holy Spirit and the harp of the believing Church," Jacob of Sarug (d. 521), "one of the most illustrious and learned writers of the Syriac-speaking Church" richly improved his literary inheritance.[59] Jacob was trained in the school at Edessa founded by Ephrem, and Jacob's homilies, composed about 500, take up familiar themes: the Trinity and Incarnation, circumcision, the Sabbath, the advent of the messiah, the passion of Christ, a debate between the Church and synagogue, and sacrifices as a prefiguration of Christ's unique immolation.[60]

Jacob, in his homily "On the Trinity and the Incarnation" emphasizes that certain biblical verses (Gen. 1:26; Deut. 4:28; Isa. 6:3) allude to the Trinity and that certain natural phenomena, such as fire, which consists of three elements, flame, heat, and light, also assist in comprehending the Trinity.[61] Jacob compares the life of Jesus with those of Moses and Jacob, claiming that Jesus "bound and sealed prophecy."[62]

In "On Circumcision," Jacob asserts, as did other Syriac exegetes, that the Jews do not understand the value of faith, righteousness, and the true circumcision, that of the heart. Rather, they prize their fleshly sign as though it were a crown of gold.[63] Jacob employs Ephrem's simile of Melchizedek, the uncircumcised, blessing Abraham, the circumcised, and Ephrem's historical divisions: the first generations, the middle generations, and the latter generations. The Jews, living in the middle generations, needed a sign to mark them off from the idolators, who, at that time, filled the world:

> In the youth of the world He bound up their limbs
> Which was unnecessary in its childhood and in its old age.
> In the beginning, when the world was a child, it did not exist.
> And in the end, since it has grown up, it is not needed.
> In its youth, when it was raging with the love of images,
> The Lord cast the painful circumcision on its limbs.[64]

Faith has superseded ritual observance, and the advent of Christ has rendered circumcision invalid. Jacob's historical understanding of ritual is unmistakable; the Law was promulgated, inter alia, to eradicate idolatry.[65]

In "On the Sabbath and Its Observance," Jacob turns to the differences that obtain between Jewish and Christian exegesis. He maintains that Jews read Genesis 2:2 literally, while the truth emerges only spiritually. After all, wonders Jacob, since God created the world by an utterance—"One word, spoken one whole day"—what could have exhausted him? And what sense does it make to insist that God rested? From what did he rest? Jacob advances the spiritual interpretation of the verse, which yields the knowledge that the rest of the Sabbath refers to the day when Christ obtained relief from his suffering on the cross.[66] Jacob's language recalls statements in rabbinic literature concerning creation, but interprets them in a completely different way.[67]

The major purpose of the homily lies in its analysis of the Law and the role of the Law in history. The Sabbath was a divine lesson to teach humanity of God's existence. Abraham and other worthy ancients did not observe the Sabbath and did not need to, because they were righteous "antenomians"—before the Law—but by the time of Moses idolatry held sway over the earth. Jacob declares the reason for the Law:

> And by all means He called mankind toward Him,
> At the time of Moses, powerful was the voice of idolatry;
> The earth was full of assemblies of empty feasts.
> To Moses, the Lord bestowed the Law, as a medicinal herb ('qr').
> To battle the immense wound of that impiety.[68]

Jacob's metaphor of the Law as a medicinal herb ('qr') is strikingly similar to a Midrashic comment encountered above, where the Law is identified as poultice to combat the evil inclination. Also of note is the implication drawn in rabbinic literature about the "poultice." The Law is a poultice and a life-giving medicine if obeyed and used properly (cf. Prov. 3:18, 8:35), as the rabbinic idiom puts it, *lishmah,* for its own sake and not for ulterior motives. If the Law is abused, then the rabbis, continuing the medical imagery, conclude that the life-giving potion will become a deadly poison.[69] The rabbinic sources are all Babylonian, and their redaction is contemporaneous with Jacob; perhaps it is more than coincidence that the imagery is so similar.

For Jacob, the medicinal herb was proper in its time, and the idea of the Law being conditioned historically, serving its purpose and being changed, which was voiced by Aphrahat and Ephrem, also finds expression in Jacob. It is richly and skillfully developed in "The Sacrifices Prefigure the Unique Immolation of Christ." Jacob likens the Law, which provided nourishment not found in idolatrous practices, to a nursemaid, much as Eusebius viewed it as a Roman *tutela,* who may be needed only for a certain time.[70] In a lengthy and elaborate section of this homily, Jacob relates how the Law was given out of pity and how, like a nursemaid, it nourished Israel like mother's milk.[71] Jacob seems to reflect the rabbinic idea that all other nations took their knowledge from the Jews [cf. p. 19] when he writes: "Among all people, the Law was considered (as a) mother."[72] Thus, the Law truly was a nursemaid to the world; it nourished and sustained all people with its milk. But while children grow up and pass from liquid to solid food, which the world has done, the Jews unnaturally kept to their diet of milk and refused to advance to solid food. Behind Jacob's exegesis lies Paul's words in I Corinthians 3:2 ("I have fed you with milk and not meat . . ."), used also by Origen. Paul claimed he gave the Corinthians milk because they were as "babes in Christ," too carnal to understand the spiritual message he brought. Jacob tells the carnal Jews:

> Christ is the bread, the Law is only milk without firmness;
> And milk alone never makes a person mature.
> The time for milk is past, and [the person] does not acquiesce,
> To be weaned from the Law, which is only milk.[73]

Elaborating the message, Jacob compares the Law to a torch, enlightening humanity, as its light dispels shadows. Again Jacob sees the Law very positively; in the early days, it was a potent weapon in the struggle against idoltary. In a rather poignant passage, Jacob reflects:

> In times primeval, the world was in darkness, removed from
> knowledge,

> It was the night of idolatry over the whole universe.
> The sculpted idols in the whole world were as obstacles.
> But because it was night one endeavored not to see them.
> And the Law descended from Mount Sinai
> To be in the world, as a lamp in the night, where it would advance
>   strongly
> As a column of fire in the midst of a camp,
> The Law of God found itself in the world.
> For that person stumbled neither against idols nor carved stones,
> Moses, in the night, carried the lamp, and made it apparent.[74]

The Law was needed in the early days to lead humanity out of darkness. It descended, as did the Lord, from Sinai[75] to enlighten the world. Moses helped spread light and make it apparent to other nations, yet the times have now changed, and for Jacob, the Jews present an absurd image: They walk in the bright light of Christ, carrying a small and useless lantern, because they believe it is still night.[76]

The Law was eclipsed by Christ, and former observances are but shadows and types that have departed.[77] Jerusalem was leveled to prevent the observance of certain rites, and after the One, True Sacrifice, which completely dispensed with the need for types, no other victims may be offered. The Jews just did not understand:

> Spiritual is the Lord, and spiritually did He establish the Law,
> And the people received it and read it carnally.[78]

With a basic inability to comprehend that which they beheld, neither torches nor medicinal herbs helped; the Jews did not understand because they were incapable of grasping the message. For Jacob, the Law was bestowed for a certain purpose and a specific time, and a time had now come when it was no longer necessary.

In his homily "On the Advent of the Messiah," Jacob not only develops the possibility of the Law changing, but ties that notion to his covenantal reading of history. Jacob opens with a "Jewish" question: If indeed God had a son, why did he not reveal him to the early generations? The answer is quite simple: God waited until the earth was covered with idolatry in order that his son might sweep idolatry off the earth in one comprehensive act. Jacob's answer is reminiscent of the rabbinic tradition that the messiah would come only in a totally good or totally evil generation.[79]

Jacob, like Aphrahat, maintains that there were five covenants in human history: The first with Adam concerned forbidden fruit; the second with Noah concerned the manner of killing animals; the third with Abraham concerned circumcision; the fourth with Moses concerned the Law; and the fifth, last, and most instructive covenant with Christ marked a radical break with the past. Even though the Lord enacted five covenants at different times for different purposes, the Jews stubbornly obey all save the last. For Jacob, the overriding purpose of the covenants was didactic.[80]

God uses history pedagogically:

> (As a master) does not at first grant a complete book to a youth
> To read, but first commences with the syllables;
> He starts with the letters, to write them, and show them (to the
>   youth)
> With the syllables he progresses to words and then further,
> And when he reads well, and has formed the letters fully, then he
>   gives him
> The large tome where one may find all wisdom.
> God also, Who is a good teacher for humanity
> Raises them up, little by little, to perfection.[81]

Jacob enumerates and scrutinizes the five covenants the Lord enacted, observing that God advanced the world in stages. Mankind progressed from infancy through youth and adolescence to perfection/maturity (*gmyrwt*).[82] He expands the metaphor, noting that the five covenants correspond to the five books of Moses as well as to the five human senses. Indeed, for almost five centuries, all people—save the Jews—have recognized and worshiped Christ; the reason the Jews do not is that they are immature—imperfect—creatures. Jews lack the fifth sense—they cannot see—and as Jacob observes, without it they are incapable of perceiving Christ—the Light of the World. Since they are not followers of Christ, they wander in darkness and do not have the light of life. The word for light is built on the Syriac root *nhr*, which can be read "I am the Light/Instruction of the world." Such a reading—and Jacob probably intended both—would compound the Jewish error; they neither see the light nor accept divine instruction.[83]

This homily presents a thorough analysis of the covenantal relationship between God and humanity. Covenants were given only to be superseded. They have culminated in Christ. History is therefore a pedagogical process in which mankind emerges, bit by bit, from the darkness of the early days into the full light of the "new" Adam. The covenants represent five rungs on the historical ladder of religious development. In Jacob's "Age of Enlightenment," only the Jews remain blind.

The theme of historical accommodation is a constant one in Syriac exegesis. It would reappear in the works of Dionysius bar Salibhi (d. 1171), who, as one scholar has written, "manifests remarkable affinities with the polemical writings of the tradition of Ephrem in imagery, phraseology and development of theme."[84] Dionysius confronts the Jews over circumcision, feasts, sacrifices, and the Sabbath. He embraces the metaphor of the teacher instructing a child to explain how God might grant a covenant at one time and then, at another time, invalidate it. For Dionysius, as for the others, historical accommodation serves as an explanation for the methods of divine revelation.

In summarizing the tradition, it is Aphrahat who wrote:

> We know, then, my friend, that in every generation God established laws. (And) they ministered [shmsh] to their time and they were good for it, and then, they were changed.[85]

Ephrem noted:

> And observe, the commandment
> Ministered to its time and was ministered to
> [shmsh zvn' w'shtmsh].[86]

For Jacob of Sarug, God taught in five successive stages, and Isaac of Antioch felt the final command was immutable: "His covenant does not change."[87] The tradition held that the final covenant proved conclusive and unchangeable; the fifth command was final.[88]

In addition to demonstrating convincingly the catholic appeal and tenacity of accommodation in the thought world of the Near East, these authors did much more. They expanded the range of their endeavors to embrace the development of the world and mankind; and what emerged was not only an eloquent espousal of divine accommodation, but a full-fledged theory of historical revelation, commencing with the simplest truths revealed to Adam, leading through progressive revelations, culminating in the fifth, final, and messianic dispensation of Christ. Their accomplishment raised exegesis and polemics to a more elevated plane; divine pedagogy became historical reality. Yet they were another stone in the wider mosaic of Christendom, and to view the whole picture, we must turn to their Latin brethren.

CHAPTER FOUR

THE TIMES MAY CHANGE, BUT NOT THE FAITH

> And the Lord brought us forth out of Egypt with a mighty
> hand, and with an outstretched arm,
> and with great terribleness, and with signs,
> and with wonders.
>
> —Deut. 26:8

In attempting to evaluate the position and use of divine accommodation in the Latin tradition up to the thirteenth century, an *embarras de richesses* confronts us. The breeze of accommodation and condescension blows, for more than a millenium and a half, through the nooks and crannies of almost countless works, and an examination of each work and its author would fill volumes. Indeed, the trajectory of accommodation in the Latin tradition, as we shall see, stretches from Tertullian to Dante and Thomas More and beyond. Dante, in fact, very simply remarked about biblical anthropomorphisms: *"la Scrittura condescende a vostra facultate."*[1]

Rather than examine countless Latin authors—many of whom are very well known and have been widely studied elsewhere and many of whom simply echo ideas that became little more than clichés—this chapter will treat several authors whose use of accommodation is of signal importance and abiding interest for the Latin tradition before the thirteenth century; after that, the influence of Maimonides must be taken into account. In this chapter, Augustine will be the patristic representative of the use of accommodation, and Hugh of Saint Victor and Anselm of Havelberg will share pride of place for the medieval period.[2]

Augustine's use of accommodation appears in many of his works, and it is closely tied, as will be seen, to his ideas of signs and symbols. Hugh employs it in his history of sacraments as a tool of historical and theological development, and Anselm uses it to develop an expla-

93

nation for the varieties of Christianity as well as in defense of new
modes of religious expression.

Accommodation appears throughout Augustine's great exegetical
corpus. In one of his earliest works, *De Magistro,* a dialogue between
himself and his son, Adeodatus, Augustine raises questions about the
meaning of vocabulary and signs.[3] The text opens: "What do you
suppose is our purpose when we speak?" The answer is either to
learn something or to remind others or ourselves of something.[4] Communication is the key for Augustine. Thus, he argues, even though
Christ taught his disciples to pray in a specific manner using specific
words, he did not simply teach them words, but taught them realities
through the words. Words therefore are signs.[5] Augustine confronts
the twin problem of signs that signify things and things that are
known without the use of signs. For Augustine, words are precious
because they entice us to ask, to inquire, to search for the things they
signify; They do not, however, openly display things to us.[6]

For pedagogical purposes, human teachers must teach through
words, but Christ, the "Interior Teacher" dwelling in our minds, provides both the appropriate vocabulary and the reality behind the
words. In his *Retractions,* Augustine made the following observation
about the *De Magistro:* "There is no teacher to teach man knowledge
but God, according to the teaching of the Gospel: 'One is your master,
Christ.'"[7] Thus, divine pedagogy and the entire educational process
were of paramount importance for Augustine, and at the conclusion of
De Magistro, he promises to take up the issue again.

The task was most probably completed in several sections of *De
Doctrina Christiana,* in which Augustine provided the definition of
sign that became definitive for the medieval period.[8] To paraphrase
Augustine's definition: A sign is an element that relates three things:
the sign itself, the object the sign stands for, and the subject to whom
the sign stands for the object signified.[9] He distinguishes two types of
signs: *signa naturalis,* those signs that make something else known
without any desire on the observer's part; for example, smoke indicates fire to people without people's desire; and *signa data,* which are
signs made by living organisms in order to indicate what they feel,
perceive, or understand. These *signa data* relay information and help
communication between people; the most important *signa data* are
words that exist solely to signify something.[10] Words for Augustine
are the chief means of human communication, and they are intrinsi-
cally superior to other kinds of signs because words can explain
(*enuntiare*) other signs, but the opposite does not obtain.[11]

Augustine's fascination with words transcended his life, and rather
appropriately, the oldest extant portrait of him depicts him sitting

and gazing at a book. For him, Scripture had become "the face of God," and one was required to study, to peruse, to contemplate, and to ponder the words of Scripture in order to fathom and drink deeply from its nourishing and refreshing depths.[12] Scripture bridged the gulf between the human and the divine, and its imagery needed interpretation. Augustine understood that Scripture also employed signs, and signs in general were needed as a result of humanity's diminished capacities after the Fall. A corollary to the Fall and the use of signs was the diversity of tongues.[13] Indeed, Augustine not only believed that Hebrew was humanity's *Ursprache,* but asserted that Hebrew was the exclusive possession of Israel: "And it is in that people that the City of God has been on pilgrimage, as well as in the person of the saints, besides having a shadowy representation, in a symbolical form, in all mankind."[14] (His views on language exercised enormous influence on early modern language theories, and the entire question of the origin of languages.)[15] Augustine provided an allegorical method to interpret signs and Scripture, a method that developed into a new *"doctrina christiana,"* in which language played a featured role.

Augustine recognized that the need for communication necessitated signs and language, and he understood viscerally, as does any good teacher, that to communicate most effectively to diverse audiences in different times one might have to alter either, or both, the signs and language. Just as some of his contemporaries in Africa looked upon the Psalms as being "better" Latin than classical literature, and because language influenced both society and culture, might it not be possible to imagine that other means of communication besides language— religion, for instance—might not also be similarly reevaluated?[16] That is, might not certain societies and cultures find more fitting means of religious expression than those old, established forms inherited from their classical past? Augustine will apply his theory of signs to this issue when he confronts the correct religious attitude one might have toward Jewish rituals, pagan idolatry, and Christian sacraments.[17]

Religion, like language, is a means of communication, and if words may be changed in order to improve communication, might not the rituals also be changed? That possibility challenged him. If, as Peter Brown shrewdly suggests,[18] Augustine was the great Christian "secularizer" of the pagan past—the man who stripped away "the traditional forms laid down by men; adjusted to the needs of human society, with which we cannot dispense in this life"[19]—and thereby rendered Roman religion "safe" for Christians, he is also the great Christian "converter" of the Jewish past. That is, Augustine for the

Latin tradition, much as did Eusebius for the Greek, converts Juda-ism into a religion adjusted to the needs of a different society and culture than the Roman one in which he found himself.

Perhaps the first inkling of this emerges in *De Vera Religione,* an early work written in 390/1. As he noted in his *Retractions:* "I pointed out how great was his (God's) mercy in granting to men by a temporal dispensation the Christian religion, which is true religion" (*per temporalem dispensationem concessa sit hominibus christiana religio, quae vera religio est*).[20] Religion was something dispensed temporally; thus, it might change over time, and in his exegesis, Augustine at-tempts to link religion, language, and signs:

> ... I said, "That is the Christian religion in our times, which to know and follow is most sure and certain salvation." I was speak-ing of the name, here, and not of the thing so named. For what is now called the Christian religion existed of old and was never ab-sent from the beginning of the human race until Christ came in the flesh. Then true religion which already existed began to be called Christian.... When I said, "This is the Christian religion in our times," I did not mean that it had not existed in former times, but that it received that name later.[21]

The name Christian is the sign signifying true religion. True religion remains true even though the sign signifying it may change. Jewish teachings could be converted to Christian use because perhaps at one time they were the sign signifying true religion. Augustine likens the gold and silver the Jews carried out of Egypt (Exod. 12:35) to true philosophical teachings and suggests that those lessons that are well accommodated (*accomodata*) to Christianity should not be dismissed out of hand, but converted to Christian use (*philosophi ... in usum nostrum vindicanda*).[22] For Augustine, the raiment the Egyptians lost represents human institutions, which are also accommodated to hu-man affairs.[23] He notes that "certain silver and gold threads were scattered throughout the pagan haystack. Indeed, one might even learn about the worship of one God from the words of the vast pagan corpus."[24] Thus, mutable creatures possess mutable signs, but the realities signified remain true. But if the signs change, how does one properly read them?

In explicating the course of true religion in history, his chief concern "is with the prophetic history of the dispensation of divine providence in time—what God has done for the salvation of the hu-man race, renewing and restoring it unto eternal life" (*caput est historia et prophetia dispensationis temporalis divinae providentiae*).[25] For Augustine, the prophetic record displayed the divine *dispensatio,* the Latin equivalent of *oikonomiá,* and provided clues to unraveling the divine plan. That record was expressed in the words of Scripture. This idea, as we shall see, was to find vivid and repeated expression, as well as to dominate the historical view of Hugh of Saint Victor. Thus, Scripture, for there was nothing else, had to be examined exhaustively in order to ferret out the divine truth. As Scripture demonstrated the divine *oikonomiá* to be a process and series of events played out in history for the Greek fathers, it became—thanks to Augustine—the same for the Latin West.

Thus armed with Scripture and the historical record—the divine dispensation—Augustine sought to affirm the veracity of the "true religion" in his time, to examine its origins and ties to Judaism, as well as to confront all heresies, especially the Manichaean variety, which arose, like all others, when humanity failed to distinguish between the creator and creatures.[26]

> If we cleave to the eternal Creator we must necessarily be somehow effected by eternity. But because the soul, implicated in and overwhelmed by its sins, cannot by itself see and grasp this truth, if in human experience there were no intermediate stage whereby man might strive to rise above his earthly life and reach likeness to God, God in his ineffable mercy by a temporal dispensation [*temporali dispensatione*] has used the mutable creation, obedient however to his eternal laws, to remind the soul of its original and perfect nature, and so has come to the aid of individual men and indeed of the whole human race.[27]

The Christian religion was not only true, but was a divine gift to humanity, which, because of sin, desperately needed aid. The divine temporal dispensation provided an intermediate period during which humanity might attempt to transcend its limitations; that is, the divine dispensation came to provide mutable creatures with a chance for religious and spiritual change.

Augustine outlines seven stages in the history of individuals that map the spiritual progress from sinfulness to perpetual blessedness; from the "old, exterior man" to the "new man." In adumbrating the themes to be developed more fully in the *City of God,* Augustine divides humanity into two classes: the impious and the pious. The former have the Old Testament and its earthly kingdom, which symbolizes the latter's New Testament and its kingdom of heaven.[28] For him, one of the most remarkable qualities of the divine dispensation is its overall symmetry and fitness. It is, in the true sense of the word, economical.

For instance, in order to heal human souls, God "adopts all kinds of means suitable to the times which are ordered by his marvellous wisdom."[29] And even

> the color black in a picture may very well be beautiful [*pulcher*] if you take the picture as a whole. So the entire contest of human life is fittingly conducted by the unchanging providence of God who allots different roles to the vanquished and the victorious, the contestants, the spectators, and the tranquil who contemplate God alone.[30]

And it is in his frontal attack on schismatics, that Augustine focuses on the fitness of divine providence:

> Whoever denies that both Testaments come from the same God for the reason that our people are not bound by the same sacraments as those by which the Jews were bound and still are bound, cannot deny that it would be perfectly just and possible for one father of a family to lay one set of commands upon those for whom he judged a harsher servitude to be useful, and a different set on those whom he deigned to adopt into the position of sons. If the trouble is that the moral precepts under the old law are lower and in the Gospel higher, and that therefore both cannot come from the same God, whoever thinks in this way may find difficulty in explaining how a single physician prescribes one medicine to weaker patients through his assistants, and another by himself to stronger patients, all to restore health.[31]

Resorting to the immensely popular medical imagery nurtured by the Second-Sophistic, Augustine attempts to convert the material of the old precepts into the new. He expands the medical metaphor and lays out his views with utmost clarity and economy:

> The art of medicine remains the same and quite unchanged, but it changes its prescriptions for the sick, since the state of their health changes. So the divine providence remains entirely without change, but comes to the aid of mutable creatures in various ways, and commands or forbids different things at different times according to the different stages of their disease. . . . [32]

Augustine invokes the interpretation favored by all of the exegetes so far considered and thus guarantees its future career in the Latin tradition. The theory that he enunciates at this early stage will, as we shall see, remain supple and vibrant throughout his career. It would become a sine qua non of his entire exegetical approach.

Augustine, in the remainder of *De Vera Religione*, considers the Fall and Redemption, stressing the roles of reason and authority in the conversion of the "old man" to the "new man." He combines the idea of change with repeated references to the proportionality of creation and culls examples from myriad areas.[33] After offering examples of this symmetry and fitness in all areas of existence, including art, time, nature, and language, Augustine remarks: "The whole rhythmic succession and gradation in space and time is judged to be beautiful not by its size or length but by its ordered fitness" (*sed ordinata convenientia pulchra iudicetur*)."[34]

This fitness, alluded to above, is found in, and may be gleaned from, Scripture. God has used the sounds and letters of Scripture to teach us and, in a way, has played with our infantile character by providing parables and similes—such as fire and smoke and the cloudy pillar, as by visible words (*quasi quaedam verba visibilia cum infantia nostra parabolis ac similitudinibus quodam modo ludere . . . non aspernata est ineffabilis misericordia dei*)—fit for our abilities.[35] Augustine paradoxically views change and ordered fitness as complimentary qualities. The idea of change—temporal, theological, personal—captivated Augustine. It should not be forgotten that his was a life filled with enormous changes—journeys, religious conversions, political and religious upheavals, ecclesiastical turmoil—and their effect upon him was profound. Augustine, within a very short time after the composition of *De Vera Religione*, would be consecrated bishop of Hippo, debate both Fortunatus and Faustus, and write his *Confessions*. It is in the examination of his own past and his defense of the faith that the many individual notes about change, order, time, religious development, and his own life would come together and resonate as a powerful and moving melody.

Order, fitness, and the harmony of creation may have been a legacy from Augustine's early days as a devotee of Manichaeanism. His work, De *Pulchro et Apto*, a product of his twenty-sixth or twenty-seventh year, was already lost by the time Augustine wrote his *Confessions*.[36] The idea for *De Pulchro et Apto* sprang from Augustine's curiosity about the relationship of God to the world. Augustine confesses that, in his struggle to make sense of the entire Christian message of salvation, he understood neither God's descent to humanity nor his ascension and return to the Father. He loved corporeal rather than spiritual beauty and wondered if humans could love anything except those things that are beautiful. And further, he asked what is beauty?

And, observing things closely, I saw that in things themselves there existed one sort of beauty [*pulchrum*] which comes from a thing being an entity, and another sort which comes from the fitting accommodation of one thing to another [*aliud autem . . . quoniam apte accommodaretur alcui*], such as one part of the body to the whole, or a shoe to the foot, etc. This idea welled up in my mind from the depths of my heart, and I wrote some books on *De Pulchro et Apto*—two or three, I think. You know, God, for I cannot recall. I no longer have them somehow or other they have vanished.[37]

Augustine invokes the same language in a further reflection on the accommodation of diverse things in the universe.

But, Almighty, I did not yet see that all this depends upon your skill, for you alone cause wonders, and my mind focused on corporeal forms. I defined and distinguished the beautiful [*pulchrum*] as that which is so in, and of, itself, and the fitting as that which is accommodated to something else [*aptum autem, quod ad aliquid accommodatum deceret*] and I used corporeal examples for my argument.[38]

Scholars have argued about the origins of the ideas in *De Pulchro et Apto,* and that is a debate I do not wish to enter.[39] What I do wish to stress, however, is that from his earliest days Augustine, even as he was changing his Manichaean views to Christian ones, held the notion of accommodation dear: "Yet, sweet Truth, I was straining the ears of my heart, to try and hear your interior melody, as I meditated upon *De Pulchro et Apto.*"[40] In his struggle to understand the Christian message, it was the interior melody to which he would respond.

In moving from Milan to Carthage, Augustine relates how he was consumed with a desire to find God and turned to Scripture to see what it was like. At that time, Augustine felt that the sacred page could not be compared to the grand style of Cicero, but that opinion was to change. Augustine confesses that he

was ignorant also of that true and inward goodness which makes its judgements not from custom [*ex consuetudine*] but from the most correct and undeviating law of God Almighty. By this law the customs of different times and places are formed for those places and times, while the law is always and in all places the same, not one thing in one place and another thing elsewhere. . . . It is as if someone who knew nothing about armor or what piece of armor was accommodated for which limb [*quid cui membro accommodatum sit*] tried to place a shin guard on his head or a helmet on his foot and then complained that they fit badly [*quod non apte conveniat*]. . . . All this is like the behaviour of those who are offended when they hear that good men were allowed to do something in former ages which good men are not allowed to do today; or that, for reasons connected with time, those things which God commanded to those in former times were not the same as his commands to men of the present; yet both in the past and in the present it is the same goodness to which obedience is due.[41]

For Augustine, divine law and justice are always and everywhere the same; although they may be made more apt in one place or time by an accommodation to circumstance. To those who were offended at the seeming changes in God's decrees, time provided the clue:

> And yet they can see in one man and one day and one household examples of different things being suited to different members, of one thing allowed at one time and not allowed an hour later, or of something permitted or commanded to be done in one corner which is forbidden under pain of punishment to be done in the next corner. Does this mean that justice is something which varies and changes? Not at all, but the times, over which Justice presides, do not pass evenly, for they are times. People, however, whose days are few upon the earth, cannot by the use of their senses find in previous ages and other peoples of which they have no experience the same relations of cause and effect which they observe in time and peoples of which they have experience. In the case of one body or one day or one house they can easily see what is proper for each particular member and time and part and person.[42]

The seeming exception to his rule, poetry, troubled Augustine, for he knew that it "did not have different principles for different occasions; it comprised all the rules together in itself."[43] Nor could he yet understand how righteousness "never varied at all, although at various times instead of prescribing everything at once, it laid down rules and principles proper for each occasion."[44] Upon reflection, Augustine felt that one could grasp differences in human customs and law, but could diversity in divine commands and law be understood?

> But when God commands that something should be done which is against the customs or institutions of any people, it must be done, even if it has never been done there before; if it is something that has fallen out of use, then it must be brought back into use, and if it was never a legal obligation, then it must be made one.[45]

Divine commands are not subject to the same foibles as human custom, and while God may seem to change his commands, they must nevertheless be obeyed. Augustine carefully sets forth how divine commands seemingly change:

> But when you [God] suddenly command that something unaccustomed and unforseen should be done—even if this is something which at one time you forbade, and however much you may hide for the time being the reason for your command and however much it may run contrary to the convention of any particular human society—no one can doubt that this command of yours must be obeyed; since the only just society of men is the society which does your will. For all the acts of your servants were done either to indicate something which needed showing in their own times [*praesens*], or else to foretell what was to come in the future [*futura*].[46]

God's commands, even if they permit something that had been forbidden, must be obeyed because all the acts of previous generations may be seen as signs that taught something in their own time—the present—or were harbingers of a future message. The main lines of Augustine's thought, which emerge clearly in the *Confessions*, had been compiled, clarified, and refined in his *Contra Faustum*. It is in his debate with "this great snare of the devil"[47] that Augustine's conceptions, formulations, and ideas flow out in a mighty rhetorical defense of Christianity.

Augustine's rejoinder to Faustus' barbs touch upon the entire gamut of issues facing early Christianity. For Augustine, as for the entire Church and late antiquity as a whole, one of the main problems was in persuading a cultured pagan to accept the Incarnation. The attack and defense focused upon the relationship between Judaism and Christianity and included detailed analyses of the religious ceremonies of each. Indeed, Faustus rejected totally the Christian claim that a connection exists between the two testaments, the two dispensations, the two laws. In place of the Christian belief, Faustus posited the existence of three laws: the law of the Hebrews, the law of the Gentiles, and the law of Truth.[48] Augustine exploits biblical rituals, especially sacrifice, his theory of signs, and historical change in fashioning his rebuttal to Faustus' arguments and in strengthening his defense of the organic link between the testaments

Faustus charged that the biblical sacrifices were idolatrous and asserted that Christians shared his opinion.[49] Augustine responds:

> While we consider it no longer a duty to offer sacrifices, we recognize sacrifices as part of the mysteries of Scripture, by which those things prophesied were foreshadowed. For they were our examples [*figurae*], and in one and various ways they all signified [*significaverunt*] the one sacrifice which we now celebrate. Now that

this sacrifice has been revealed, and has been offered in due time, those are no longer binding as an act of worship, but retain their authority as a sign [*illa ... sublata sunt, sed in significandi auctoritate manserunt*].[50]

Augustine employs allegory. The practices of the Hebrew Bible were *figurae*, which signified the ultimate sacrifice on the Cross. Christians may no longer offer oblations, nor observe other Jewish customs, but those observances are still signs and retain value as such. The same point is made regarding Cain and Abel: Abel's sacrifice was preferred to Cain's in the same way that the faith of the New Testament is dearer to God than the old observances. While Augustine admits that the Jews were right in observing biblical precepts in their time, they are guilty in not recognizing that time of faith is now at hand.[51]

For Augustine, as for the Church as a whole, the problem of continued Jewish existence after Christ remained a gnawing issue. Augustine, in his examination of Jewish history, remarks that the Jews alone, of all nations subjugated by Rome, clung to the sign of their religious code (*Gens autem Iudaea ... non amiserit signum legis suae*).[52] They were marked like Cain, and they till the fields of Scripture in a carnal manner, obtaining neither understanding nor solace.[53] In delving deeper into Jewish history and observance, Augustine returns to biblical sacrifice as a means of setting forth his reading of history.

The sacrifices of old were signs; they were mandated more out of suitability to a perverse people than out of divine necessity. Yet the sacrifices and other rituals—the Sabbath, circumcision, dietary laws—were examples and prophecies for Christians (*omnia haec figurae nostrae fuerunt et prophetiae* [I Cor. 10:6]).[54] If sacrifices were simply an accommodation to the historical condition of the Jews, then the Jews were pious in offering them; but if the sacrifices were not pleasing to God, why were they mandated? Did they have any value beyond the figurative? Those were questions and challenges Augustine tackled.

In order to maintain his theological and exegetical position, Augustine resorted to his theory of signs and invoked the patristic concept of *similitudo*, which held that some semblance must exist between a sign and that which is spoken of by the sign.[55] In commenting on the value of biblical sacrifices, Augustine explicitly states that the symbolic value of sacrifices was never far from the surface, and in converting Jewish practice to Christian usage, he extols the divine power that prescribed sacrifice to be offered to God alone. He then suggests the rationale behind those ceremonies:

There are some who suppose that these visible sacrifices are suitable for other gods, but that for the one God, as he is invisible, greatest and best, only the invisible, the greatest and best sacrifices are proper; and such sacrifices are the services of a pure mind and a good will. But such people evidently do not realize that the visible sacrifices are symbols of the invisible offerings, just as spoken words are the symbols of things.[56]

If in fact the visible sacrifices are symbols, might not they be changed to effect greater communication? Augustine answers: It is God who

defines in advance the periods in which these sacrifices will be changed for something better through the action of a better priest, and by this he makes it clear that he does not himself desire such sacrifices but uses them to point to things of greater worth.[57]

Augustine simply reads Jewish history symbolically and converts the Jewish past into a Christian prologue. The sacrifices were used to point to something better and to convey a more profound, hence hidden, truth. After the advent of Christ, the truth is no longer concealed:

Hence it is that the true Mediator . . . receives the sacrifice "in the form of God," in union with the Father, with whom he is one God. And yet "in the form of a servant" he preferred to be himself the sacrifice than to receive it, to prevent anyone from supposing that sacrifice, even in this circumstance, should be offered to any created being. Thus he is both priest, himself making the offering, and the oblation. This is the reality, and he intended the daily sacrifice of the Church to be the sacramental symbol of this; for the Church, being the body of which he is the head, learns to offer itself through him. This is the true sacrifice; and the sacrifices of the saints in earlier times were many different symbols of it. This one sacrifice was prefigured by many rites, just as many words are used to refer to one thing, to emphasize a point without introducing boredom. This was the supreme sacrifice, and the true sacrifice, and all the false sacrifices yielded place to it.[58]

Christ's sacrifice supersedes and replaces all others because it was the reality suggested, only dimly and imperfectly, by all former false offerings. The true sacrifice was wisely prefigured in various ways, lest the process become tedious. And yet Augustine realized full well that, in converting Jewish customs to mere signs and symbols, he had exposed Christianity to the same vulnerability; namely, Christian customs might also be attacked as only signs and symbols and converted "for something better through the action of a better priest." Augustine never forgot that Christianity had its own sacramental—symbolical—system.

Not surprisingly, the allegorical reading of Scripture that allowed Augustine to convert Jewish custom to pre-Christian sign and symbol found no favor with the Donatists, who saw themselves as "pure," "catholic" and the "Chosen People"; they shared the same attitude as Old Israel. In Augustine's view, Israel and the Donatists acted much like old misers, jealously guarding their assets, while Christianity, much like a young entrepreneur, sought to expand its base of operations and holdings.[59] Signs and symbols, especially those associated with the sacraments, loomed large and vital in Augustine's battle with Donatism. This is not the place to recount that struggle, save to note that Augustine, in attacking the Donatists, employs the same ideas and same language used to attack Jewish ceremonies.

That is, Augustine's defense of Christianity, as well as his use of *similitudo,* sprang from neo-Platonic soil. In a universe constantly struggling to become perfect, in which shadowy, imperfect material shapes contended to "realize" their ideal forms, intelligible to the intellect alone, Augustine's Church endeavored to realize its ideal form. The ideal Church is imperfectly represented in the world by shadowy representations. It is a type—a sign and symbol—whose reality will be achieved in the fullness of time. The rites of the Church nevertheless exist independently of those who administer them "in a way Augustine never claimed to understand, the physical rites of baptism and ordination 'brand' a permanent mark on the recipient, quite independent of his conscious qualities."[60] The sacraments innoculated Christians, who still had to guard their own spiritual health. While Augustine may never have claimed to understand how sacraments worked, except in the "Name of Christ," he did understand their propaedeutic nature as symbols.[61] The ceremonies that prefigured Christ did have value beyond the figurative.

Augustine, in his discussion of biblical sacrifices, occasionally stresses their positive, rather than only their punitive and prophylactic, aspects. Humanity needs visible symbols, which should not be derided.

> There can be no religious society, whether the religion be true or false, without some sacrament or visible symbol [*signaculorum vel sacramentorum visibilium*] to serve as a bond of union. The importance of these sacraments cannot be overstated, and only scoffers will treat them lightly. For if piety requires them, it must be impiety to neglect them.[62]

Humans needed and, even after Christ, still need symbols. Not only did a qualitative difference obtain between the Jewish sacrifices and ancient pagan offerings— because the Jews of old did not offer their oblations to any earthly things or to any creatures, but to the one true God[63]—but the value of symbols and signs must never be forgotten. Much as visible symbols were an accommodation to the Jews, Augustine maintains that the Church, in establishing its *disciplina christiana,* may, at times, close one eye to certain actions of its members; that is, the Church may also employ accommodation on the most practical level.

Augustine discusses the practical problem of public intoxication at the feasts of martyrs. He condemns intemperance, both public and private, and would do so, he writes, even if the same people imbibed too heavily in their own homes. He recognizes human nature for what it is and sets forth his plan of action: "But we must try to amend what is bad as well as prescribe what is good, and must of necessity bear [*tolerare conpellimur*] for a time with some things that are not according to our teaching."[64] The Church must be tolerant, while insisting "that the rules of Christian conduct are not to be taken from the indulgences of the intemperate or the infirmities of the weak."[65] Rules cannot be established according to the lowest common denominator.

If the Church had to bear for a time certain less than respectable actions on the part of its members, it also had to explain how Jewish customs were important mainly as symbols, while the Christian sacraments, symbols also, had more than mere symbolic value. After all, Christianity still used signs, admittedly different ones than those of the Jews, but signs nonetheless. Augustine addresses the issue with rhetorical mastery: "Before (*ante*) the coming of Christ, the flesh and blood of this sacrifice were foreshadowed in the animals slain (*per victimas similitudinem promittebatur*); in (*in*) the passion of Christ the types were fulfilled by the true sacrifice; after (*post*) the ascension of Christ, this sacrifice is commemorated in the sacrament (*per sacramentum*)."[66] The value of the sacrament moves from *"ante"* Christ to *"in"* Christ and then *"post"* Christ. Theology and history become intertwined in this view of sacraments as symbols and signs. Christianity must make accommodations also, and one of these was the retention of signs and symbols in its sacramental system.

This entire issue of signs and their significations is trenchantly explored by Augustine in a letter to Boniface, an episcopal colleague who wished to know how parents could proclaim their child's belief in God at the moment of baptism and yet could not utter a word about the child's character or social inclinations.[67] Boniface wondered sincerely how the sacrament could be valid if the child did not understand what was happening.

Augustine replied by recourse to signs and what they represent. He noted that on Easter Sunday one may proclaim, "This is the day the Lord rose from the dead"—even though it is not the actual day of resurrection; no one would think the statement is a lie because there exists a certain likeness (*similitudinem*) between the first Easter Sunday and all subsequent Easter Sundays.[68] In a similar vein, Christ was offered up only once as a sacrifice, yet no one doubts the validity of the countless daily sacrificial sacraments. If sacraments did not have some points of real semblance (*similitudinem*) to the things of which they are sacraments, insists Augustine, they would not be sacraments.[69] Indeed, he asserts that in a certain way "the sacrament of Christ's body is Christ's body, the sacrament of Christ's blood is Christ's blood just as the sacrament of faith is faith."[70] Thus, an infant who becomes a believer through the sacrament of faith is of the faithful; when he matures he need not repeat the sacrament, but will come to understand and appreciate its meaning.[71] *Similitudo* permitted Augustine to preserve intact the relationship between new signs and old—*ante, in, post*—without debasing the meaning or value of either.

As we have seen, Augustine suggests that the first sacraments were harbingers of Christ, who fulfilled them by his coming.[72] These first sacraments were *figurae* that have changed, as Augustine claims, much as the form of a verb may change according to its tense. And one should never forget how important words and what they represent were for Augustine. In a lovely passage, Augustine presses his case:

> For if in language the form of the verb changes in the number of letters and syllables according to the tense, as *done* signifies the past, and *to be done* the future, why should not the symbols which declare Christ's death and resurrection to be accomplished, differ from those which predicted their accomplishment, as we see a difference in the form and sound of the words, *past* and *future*, *suffered* and *suffer*, *risen* and *to rise*? For material symbols are nothing else than visible speech, which, though sacred, is changeable and transitory.[73]

The mutability and transitory nature of the *verba visibilia* provide an elegant and uncomplicated method, a most natural procedure, for converting Jewish rituals to Christian sacraments. " Corresponding to this change in words is the change which naturally [*ideo*] took place in the substitution of new sacraments instead of those of the Old Testament."[74]

History is called upon to bear witness to Augustine's theory, and he searches early Christianity to ferret out evidence. From the outset, Christianity accommodated its message to the ears of those who listened to the word of Christ. In a remarkably practical and perceptive passage, Augustine unveils the commonsense approach of early Christianity:

> In the case of the first Christians, who came to the faith as Jews, it was by degrees [*paulatim*] that they were brought to change their customs, and to have a clear perception of the truth; and permission was given them by the apostle to preserve their hereditary worship and belief [*patrium ritum traditionemque*], in which they had been born and brought up; and those who had to do with them were required to make allowance for this reluctance to accept new customs. So the apostle circumcised Timothy, the son of a Jewish mother and a Greek father, when they went among people of this kind [cf. Acts 16]; and he accommodated his practice to theirs, not hypocritically but for a wise purpose [*etiam circumcidit apostolus atque ipse inter eos morem huiusmodi custodivit non simulatione fallaci, sed consilio prudenti*]. For these practices were harmless in the case of those born and brought up in them, though they were no longer required to prefigure things to come. It would have done more harm to condemn them as hurtful in the case of those to whose time it was intended that they should continue. Christ, who came to fulfill all these prophecies, found those people trained in their own religion. But in the case of those who had no such training, but were brought to Christ, the corner-stone, from the opposite wall of circumcision, there was no obligation to adopt Jewish customs. If, indeed, like Timothy, they chose to accommodate themselves [*vellent . . . conferre congruentiam*] to the views of those of the circumcision who were still wedded to their old sacraments, they were free to do so.[75]

In a critical reading of history, Augustine posits a theory of religious conversion predicated upon accommodation to both Jews and Gentiles. Those early Christians, who came from Judaism, were brought along slowly (*paulatim*) and by degrees weaned from their ancestral faith; Christianity made allowance for their reluctance to abandon old habits and adopt new ones in their stead. Condemnation of revered customs would have been counterproductive in the case of Jewish converts. Gentiles did not need to enter Christianity through the vestibule of Judaism, but those who wished to do so were not discouraged.

The same accommodative plan was employed by Gregory the Great in the conversion of England. In one of Gregory's letters presented in Bede's *History of the English Church and People,* one learns of Gregory's reservoir of common sense and proficiency as a student of history.[76] Idolatry was a festering sore in the conversion of the English and other European nations.[77] In a letter to Abbot Mellitus, Gregory enunciates his policy:

> Since the departure of those of our fellowship who are bearing you company, we have been seriously anxious, because we have received no news of the success of your journey. Therefore, when by God's help you reach our most reverend brother, Bishop Augustine, we wish you to inform him that we have been giving careful thought to the affairs of the English, and have come to the conclusion that the temples of the idols among that people should on no account be destroyed. The idols are to be destroyed, but the temples themselves are to be aspersed with holy water, altars set up in them, and relics deposited there. For if these temples are well-built, they must be purified from the worship of demons and dedicated to the service of the true God. In this way, we hope that the people, seeing that their temples are not destroyed, may abandon their error and, flocking more readily to their accustomed resorts, may come to know and adore the true God.[78]

Gregory proposes utilizing existing facilities for different purposes. The English will come to familiar surroundings, but for a very different form of worship. The intention behind the scheme is spelled out fully:

> And since they have a custom of sacrificing many oxen to demons, let some other solemnity be substituted in its place. . . . They are no longer to sacrifice beasts to the Devil, but they may kill them for food to the praise of God, and give thanks to the Giver of all gifts for the plenty they enjoy. If the people are allowed some worldly pleasures in this way, they will more readily come to desire the joys of the spirit. For it is certainly impossible to eradicate all errors from obstinate minds at one stroke, and whoever wishes to climb to a mountain top climbs gradually step by step, and not in one leap. It was in this way that the Lord revealed Himself to the Israelite people in Egypt, permitting the sacrifices formerly offered to the Devil to be offered thenceforward to Himself instead. So He bade

them sacrifice beasts to Him, so that, once they became enlightened, they might abandon one element of sacrifice and retain another. For, while they were to offer the same beasts as before, they
were to offer them to God instead of to idols, so that they would no
longer be offering the same sacrifices.[79]

Gregory simply employed for the English the same divine ruse the
Lord concocted for the Israelites. The visible symbols remained the
same, while the internal, spiritual goals changed. Just as Paul and
Augustine slowly accommodated Christianity to disparate audiences
in different climes, so did Gregory in the conversion of Albion.

The changed meaning of old symbols was, however, part of a
larger and more irritating problem facing Augustine and the early
church. By defending the ties between the testaments, Augustine
sought to silence the schismatics. But he had not answered the pagans, who asked, quite simply and honestly: Why does God spurn
ancient offerings yet delight in new ones? Why does God change
things once commanded? Augustine, in a response to Deogratias concerning the resurrection, wrote:

> Thus religion has been outwardly expressed and carried on under
> one set of names and signs in times past and another set now. It
> was more secret then but more open now. It had fewer worshipers
> in times past but more now. Yet it is one and the same true reli-
> gion.[80]

Augustine's response again buttressed the links between the different
manifestations of the *true* religion—regardless of its name—thereby
defusing the uncomfortable problem of a seemingly fickle God; a problem raised by Marcellinus, who, in a letter to Augustine, mentioned a
certain Volusian, whose faith had been shaken by those "who defame
the dispensation of the Lord's Incarnation."[81] It was, as we have mentioned above, a common problem of late antiquity: How could a cultured pagan accept the Incarnation?

Augustine's response to Marcellinus invokes the function of change
in the course of nature and in human affairs. He suggests that if one
desired to demonstrate the regularity of change in nature and human
affairs, time rather than examples would be lacking.[82] Indeed, one
notices the change of seasons and the birth, growth, and senescence
of humans. These are obvious, regular changes. Augustine makes the
point rhetorically as well as philosophically. "All these things change,
yet the method of divine providence, by which they are made to
change, does not change" (*haec omnia mutantur nec mutatur divinae
providentiae ratio, qua fit, ut ista mutentur*).[83]

Augustine recounts the case of Vindician, a physician who would prescribe certain remedies for ailments but never the same panacea for the same patient at different times.[84] As we have seen above, medical imagery was highly favored by Augustine, who likened it to divine providence, which is unchanging but able to aid mutable creatures in various ways at diverse times. Divine providence, like medicine, displayed utility and fitness (*aptum*) within the divine dispensation. Thus, the sacrifices commanded of old were fit (*aptum*) for that time, but no longer obtain because another precept that is fit (*aptum*) for this time is now commanded. God knows much better than man what is suitably accommodative to each age (*quid cuique tempori accommodate adhibeatur*).[85] Augustine applies this principle on a much grander scale as he turns to the whole of the human experience:

> God is the unchanging Creator of all things that change. When He adds, abolishes, curtails, increases or diminishes the rites of any age, He is ordering all events according to His providence until the beauty of the complete course of time, whose parts are the dispensations suitable to each different period [*particulae . . . suis quibusque temporibus apta sunt*], shall have played itself out, like the melody of some ineffable composer.[86]

In gazing over the vast stretches of history, Augustine came to believe, even if he, together with his fellows in the early church, never completely understood, that those events—the "narrow thread of prophetic sayings and happenings"—which culminated in the Incarnation were the most significant in the inexorable march of time and change.[87] To isolate that thread from the pattern required Augustine's expanded field of view. Using the sacrifices as a springboard, Augustine jumped from the parochial Jewish customs to the broader canvas of human history. The change in sacrifices, the *verba visibilia* that all societies need, hinted at and pointed to even greater and more profound historical changes implanted by God at creation. Humanity moves, or gropes imperceptibly, following that narrow thread toward the fulfillment of the divine plan. It is in the *City of God* that Augustine tackled the issues squarely, and the ideas adumbrated throughout his career would find their fullest and perhaps most cogent expression in his masterpiece. In extricating the "City of God" from the "City of Man," Augustine scrutinized relentlessly the broad patterns in human events and humanity's basic motives. Indeed, in his chef d'oeuvre, he explained the education of humanity:

> There is a process of education, through the epochs of a people's history, as through the successive stages of a man's life, designed to

raise them from the temporal and the visible to an apprehension of the eternal and the invisible. . . . Thus it pleased divine providence to arrange the course of the ages in such a way that . . . the Law concerning the worship of the one true God was given in decrees communicated by angels. God's own substance always remains invisible to corruptible eyes: and yet in those edicts the person of God himself became manifest by unmistakable signs, through the medium of created things in subjection to the Creator. God, in his own nature, so to say, neither begins nor ceases to speak; he speaks not temporally, but eternally; not corporeally but spiritually; not to the senses but to the understanding. Yet through his created beings he spoke in successive syllables, following one another in transitory intervals of time. . . . Now in this arrangement of the successive ages, the Law was given so as to offer, to begin with, the promise of the good things of this world. But these good things were intended to stand for the eternal blessings; and this was the meaning of the outward and visible rites which were celebrated by all the people, but understood by few.[88]

The idea of change and permanence, which emerges as part of the divine plan of revelation, took on enhanced meaning in a world where Rome, the very symbol and guarantor of stability, authority, and permanence, could be sacked and put to the torch. Augustine realized all too well that he, like everyone else, was a *peregrinus* in the earthly city and that the Incarnation had raised the curtain on the final act of the divine drama, which would result in the conclusive winnowing out of the sacred wheat from the profane chaff. In Augustine's hands, the parochialism of Jewish history had yielded to Christian universalism. He did not change the rules by which history had been interpreted; he merely studied a larger field of view. Majestic and sweeping simplicity, perfect harmony, flawless utility, and total fitness marked the grand divine dispensation, and for Augustine, as for so many of his patristic peers, divine accommodation and condescension helped unravel and kept straight the skein of historical threads that made up the fabric of history. The process begun so ardently and artistically by the bishop of Hippo and copied so slavishly —and in some cases in subsequent centuries so naively— would be taken up and perhaps best elaborated by two twelfth-century authors, Hugh of Saint Victor and Anselm of Havelberg.

These two twelfth-century scholars were heirs to Augustine's ideas and language. Indeed, they, and many of their peers, cut their historical and theological teeth on his claim that "anything in the divine world that cannot properly be related to moral uprightness or the truth of faith . . . is figurative."[89] For twelfth-century authors, as for Augustine, almost everything could be seen as *figurae*. Perhaps Hugh of Saint Victor, in a phrase adopted from Augustine, best expressed the idea of that age, marked by what M.D. Chenu felicitously dubbed, "the symbolist mentality": "The entire sense-perceptible world is like some sort of book written by the finger of God."[90]

This "second Augustine," as his contemporaries called him, urged his students to use all the latest sciences in deciphering Scripture. He cautioned them to learn in a leisurely manner, to savor the text, rather than to try to read everything ever written on a subject and then attempt to swallow it whole. A beginner, according to Hugh, ought to commence with the basics: the literal and historical level of Scripture. Geographical and historical aids are useful to students, and only after being firmly grounded in the plain sense of the text did one pass to allegory. Just as the literal study of the text commenced with the historical books of the Bible—Genesis, Exodus, Joshua, Judges, Kings, Chronicles, the Gospels and Acts—so did allegorical study begin with the New Testament, books rich in doctrine—Matthew, John, the Pauline Epistle, the Apocalypse. Church doctrine was a sine qua non for the construction of any allegorical interpretation of the sacred page. Hugh viewed doctrine as the " 'second foundation' of polished stones, which rises above the first, subterranean foundation of history, to support the wall of allegory."[91] Hugh wrote his great work, *De Sacramentis Christianae Fidei,* for that very purpose; that is to buttress allegory with history.

Hugh's educational program progressed from the literal and historical to the allegorical and culminated in the tropological, or moral, level of Scripture. The first book placed in the hands of a student was a textbook of history, *De Tribus Maximis Circumstantiis Gestorum, id est Personis Locis Temporibus,* which contains, among other useful information, Augustine's historical theory of six days and ages. Copies of Hugh's work made their way very quickly to France, Germany, the Low Countries, and England. The proliferation of Hugh's work testifies to its popularity as well as to the tenacity of Augustine's ideas.[92]

In a most enlightening anonymous letter of probable Victorine origin, curricular advice is given to a novice without scholastic training in how to proceed in his biblical studies. Of course, the literal study takes pride of place, and of great value in this is Augustine's *Quaestiones.* For the allegorical level, the student should study the sacraments "which may be found at length in the book of Master Hugh." There are many books to consult for the tropological level. One should then read a manual of the liturgy, then study Augustine's *De Doctrina Christiana* and *De Civitate Dei.*[93] Hugh's interest in the literal interpretation stemmed naturally from his interest in history, an interest he acquired, no doubt, from Augustine.[94]

Hugh's philosophy of history told, as it had for his mentor, of human religious history and the struggle for salvation. As he put it in the prologue to the *De Sacramentis:*

> ... the Word Incarnate is our King, who came into the world to fight the devil; all the saints who were before his coming are as soldiers going before the royal presence; those who came after, and those to come, until the end of the world, are as soldiers following the King. And the King is in the midst of his army.[95]

If, for Hugh, the king was directing his army in this worldly city, his ultimate victory was certain. The *De Sacramentis* is constructed along historical rather than theological lines, outlining events from the creation to the eschaton. The first book scans history from the creation to the Incarnation; the second, Christ to the apocalypse, including an analysis of the Christian sacraments. In it world history and church history coincide. Scripture is the history book par excellence, and no item, however seemingly inconsequential or insignificant, could be overlooked or ignored.

In a passage reminiscent of Augustine's notion of true religion always being present in the world, Hugh claims: "Holy Church began to exist in her faithful at the beginning, and shall last to the end. We believe that, from the beginning to the end, no period lacks its faithful to Christ."[96] One had to scan and search that history in order to understand the human condition; that is, after the Fall the world is being repaired and restored seriatim, through a series of divine sacraments, the natural, the Mosaic, and finally the Christian. For Hugh, then, there was a natural operative progress that unfolded within history. As Beryl Smalley has suggested, Hugh's fascination with sacraments may have sprung from his "period which saw a great expansion of sacramental practice and definition. We hear of his own personal devotion to the sacrament of the altar from the brother who witnessed his death. This gives us a clue to his special feeling for the letter of Scripture."[97]

Hugh differentiated divine history from the study of ancient fables; however, their literary similarities could not bridge the chasm between them. Ancient fables might, as Isidore of Seville, following custom, pointed out, help cultivate one, but divine history, as we have hinted above, was truly sacramental history. That history was the sand in which the footprints of divine actions might be found; it was, quite simply, the record of events in the divine economy, which had to be read and understood, first and foremost, on the literal level. Hugh put it quite clearly: "History is the narration of events which is contained in the first or literal meaning."[98] This was history viewed through religious spectacles, but it was history nonetheless.

History was, in Hugh's opinion, a series of sacred events. And as Chenu observes, the phrase *series narrationis* was, along with *series temporum,* one of Hugh's favorite expressions. Indeed, as Hugh expressed it:

> ... and if we investigate all things carefully according to the sequence of time (*secundum seriem temporum*), the succession of generations, and the arrangement of truths taught, we can claim confidently to have reached all levels of divine scripture.[99]

The rhythmic cadence of truth reflected the divine order disclosed in the sequence of events.[100] For Hugh, the order in this restorative effort (*in operibus restaurationis*) centered about three main areas: place, time, and dignity. The order of place and time seem to parallel each other and follow the sequence of events.[101] Hugh, in his insistence upon the restorative nature of history, and the healing of human "weakness," displayed his indebtedness to Augustine.[102] Indeed, Augustine laid the foundation when he wrote:

> The key [*caput*] to this religion is the history and prophecy of the temporal dispensation of divine providence [*dispensationis temporalis divinae providentiae*] for the salvation of the human race, which had to be reformed and restored [*reformandi et reparandi*] to eternal life.[103]

As we have seen above, the "temporal dispensation of divine providence" symbolized the divine economy of salvation, and Augustine's ideas on history and theology, bringing with them the entire patristic conception of *oikonomiá,* reverberate mightily in Hugh's pages. The translation (encountered before) of *oikonomiá* by *dispensatio* occurs again in this twelfth-century scholar, who, like his forebears, understood that the concept implied the divine management of the earthly estate by its creator. As Hugh well realized, a plan contains an arranged "series of events," implemented over a "sequence of time," which began with creation—the dispensation of the creator.[104] This divine dispensation had a geographical as well as a theological component:

> ... so that those things which happened at the beginning of time should happen in the East, as at the beginning of the world; and that then as time moved on towards the end, the climax of events

should pass to the West, from which we might conclude that the
end of time [*finem saeculi*] is approaching, since the course of events
has now reached the end of the world [*finem mundi*].[105]

In a very elegant exegetical sleight of hand, Hugh combines the
history of the world with the historical progression of the aeons—
sacred and secular history become one. Thus, in order to bring about
the realization of his plans—the temporal dispensation of divine providence, the *oikonomia*—God might understandably have resorted to
accommodation; that is, fitting together the divine and human, the
saeculum and the *mundus*.
     As Hugh expressed it:

> We do not wish to make any rash assertions about this matter, yet
> it seems to us that it is in no way derogatory to the omnipotence of
> the Creator to say that His work has been brought to completion
> over periods of time [*per intervallis temporis*]. . . . For the omnipo-
> tent God . . . in making all these things must especially have ob-
> served that mode of operation better suited to the benefit and inter-
> est of the rational creature himself [*illum praecipue modum . . . qui
> ipsius rationalis creaturae commoditati ac causae magis congruus
> fuit*].[106]

If indeed there was a progressive quality to history, it was necessitated because of human nature. In no way did it diminish the almighty
majesty of the creator, but more truly reflects his omnipotence because
it comes closer to human behavior which reflects divine actions.
     Hugh thus picks up the thread of accommodation spun by the
early fathers, and he weaves it into his exegesis. Augustine had written: "The times may change, but not the faith."[107] Hugh, in disagree-
ment, asked: "Whether faith was changed according to the changes of
time?"[108] This prickly issue occupied theologians of the twelfth and
thirteenth centuries. While dialecticians and scholastics including
Abelard, Peter Lombard, Thomas Aquinas, Robert of Melun, and others[109] could divorce theological advances from historical changes, Hugh
molds his vision and interpretation according to the "temporal dispensation of divine providence."
     Hugh claims that faith increased in all through the times, "so
that it was greater but was not changed so as to be different."[110] True
faith consists in both the creator and Christ, the Redeemer, and thus
while believers believe in both, their faith is one:

> Although in the same faith, in some cognition of these things was
> greater, in others less, according to the diversity of the times, just

as at one and the same time cognition of these things is found greater in some and less in others according to the capacity of the persons. Thus although faith increased so as to be greater at some times and in some persons, yet it was not changed so as to be different.[111]

Faith thus increases and diminishes through time. And Hugh's method and argument become more sharply focused when he turns from faith to the sacraments of faith. Much as Augustine had argued for the impossibility of religion without visible signs, Hugh acknowledges

> that sacraments were instituted from the beginning for the restoration and guardianship of man, some under the natural law, some under the written law, some under grace. And among these those which have been posterior in time are always found more worthy of the effect of spiritual grace. For all, those sacraments of earlier time, whether under the natural law or under the written, were signs, as it were, and figures of this which now have been set forth under grace.[112]

Earlier sacraments were visible signs and figures and thus were inherently inferior to the reality of Christian invisible sacraments. Also, those sacraments instituted under the natural law seem to be more of will, while those mandated under the written law or under grace seem to be more of necessity. That is, the former seem to stem from vows, the latter from precepts. Hugh argues that before the written law, the Lord never imposed tithes, oblations, or sacrifices upon humanity nor punished people for not offering them as he did under the written code. The first sacraments were enjoined to exercise devotion rather than obtain salvation. Mankind made offerings out of vows rather than commands, as the case of Jacob (Gen. 28:20–22) clearly proves.[113] Certainly, God taught and schooled man in divine service, for otherwise how could man have known to offer a tenth rather than some other portion? However, man was instructed not obligated to do so until he showed disobedience.[114]

"First, therefore, before the law He nourished the young by counsel. Then He tried by precept those exercised under the law. Finally, He permitted those perfect under grace to walk in the freedom of the spirit."[115] Three differences obtained between Christian sacraments and others. First, Christian sacraments are signs of spiritual grace, which infused blessing. Second, Jewish sacraments were only signs of the Christian sacraments. None could enter heaven, even if they were imbued with sacraments, until Christ paved the way. Third, Jewish and Christian sacraments were instituted by counsel and precept, while those of the natural law were not imposed through precepts.[116] Hugh, having put forth his historical reading of sacraments, asks the salient question:

> . . . why indeed, if grace conferred the same effect of salvation through the preceding [sacrament] as through the subsequent, divine command abolished the rite of the ancient through the institution of the subsequent. For if the same virtue was in those sacraments, why was it necessary that the former cease and the latter succeed?[117]

Why indeed? This is the question that rears its troublesome head again and again throughout these pages and the pages of the scholars studied; indeed, it is the question Christianity in general had to explain, or try to explain away. Hugh's answer is not surprising, nor is it all that new.

> But it must be realized that the order and plan of the divine dispensation demanded this—that just as from the beginning with the progress of time the coming of the Saviour approached nearer and nearer, so always the effect of salvation and the knowledge of truth increased more and more, because the signs themselves of salvation had to be changed one after the other through the succession of times in order that when the effect of divine grace increased unto salvation, at the same time sanctification might appear more evident in the visible signs themselves.[118]

The signs had to be changed, in a series, through the temporal progression until the signs themselves approached, more fully and perfectly, the sanctification and salvation that they signified. In other words, signs and sacraments were accommodated to the times of their dispensation. This is clearly Hugh's understanding, as the continuation of his argument makes evident:

> There was indeed the same Saviour, the same grace, the same faith in the former in what was to come, in the latter in what was shown. But since He himself through whom salvation was given was faraway, the signs of the same salvation had to be obscure. Afterwards, indeed, as his coming gradually approached, it was necessary that in the same order both faith in cognition and grace in salvation increase and that the same grace in the sacraments outside and in its signs manifest itself more evidently.[119]

Sacraments as signs are an accommodation, and Hugh's observation on the process of mundane (in the real meaning of the word) restoration, encompassing time, place, and dignity, subjects them all to the divine dispensation. Since, as we have seen, creation itself was a dispensation of the creator, it was, by virtue of being a *dispensatio,* an accommodation and could be adjusted and fine tuned. This idea, as we shall see below, would be elaborated upon by Anselm of Havelberg.[120] For Hugh, the sacraments of the natural law were "a kind of shadow of the truth"; those under the written law "a kind of image or figure of the truth"; while those under grace were a "body of truth" decipherable by exterior motions leading to the "truth of the spirit."[121]

In passing from his consideration of faith to the written law, Hugh observes that, although the law was given through Moses, its observance commenced with circumcision in the time of Abraham. The time of natural law from Adam to Abraham had passed,

> as it were, in a kind of confusion and those who had existed as the faithful in that age, like some few grains dispersed among the human race and separated from each other, had been united by faith alone.[122]

Few were the faithful in the earliest times. As the number of faithful increased, circumcision, which was given only to Abraham's fleshly progeny, gave way to a spiritual circumcision for those who were one in faith and spirit with Abraham. Circumcision was legislated before the Law was given in order to mark the people who were to receive the Law, just as Christians are marked by baptism before being associated with the faithful.[123]

Hugh delineates three things contained in the written law: precepts, sacraments and promises. Precepts contain merit, sacraments assistance and promises rewards. The most economical implementation of salvation would have had humans move from precepts to promises; from merit to rewards.[124] However, that was not to be. Hugh explains his position with obeisance to the medical imagery so frequently encountered in the writings of other exegetes:

> But since man was weak by himself the sacraments came midway between precepts and promises, to assist him both to perform precepts and to obtain promises. Under the natural law there were few sacraments; under the written law both were multiplied, namely, the precepts and the sacraments. For when God the physician first proceeded to cure sick men, disease had seized him entirely whom health had left entirely. And He placed in the body of the human race first of all a few antidotes for few members, that is for a few

persons, in order that gradually disease might fail and health increase. Afterwards under the written law He brought together more
remedies, and He restored more.[125]

The process of healing necessitated different prescriptions, and so in
moving from natural law to the written law, more remedies were
produced. The natural law contained only two precepts, variants on
the Golden Rule, and three sacraments, tithes in portions, oblations
in things, and sacrifices of animals. The written law multiplied both.
  The historical proliferation of precepts is characterized as the
dispensation of salvation, a process in which the Jews had been chosen "as the agents through whom the dispensation of the salvation of
humanity would be activated" (*per quos dispensatio salutis omnium
ageretur*).[126] If in fact the Jews were the leaven in the story of salvation, Hugh confronted the same problem he encountered before: the
issue of the movable precepts and "those that have been superadded"[127]
  Hugh distinguishes two types of precepts under the written law:
movable and immovable. The former "are those which from dispensation are ordained for the time."[128] The latter "are those which come
from nature and are either so evil that at no time can they be performed without blame or so good that at no time can they be dismissed without blame."[129] The natural law contained only immovable
precepts: one prohibiting mankind from doing to one's neighbor what
one did not want done to oneself, and the other commanding people
to do to others what they wished others to do to them.[130] These were
of course multiplied under the written law.
  Hugh's sacramental reading of history emerges quite intelligibly,
and he attempts to use it to explain the role of movable precepts and
those "that have been superadded":

> There follows another group of precepts which are called movable,
> since they were added to the natural commands in the course of
> time according to the dispensation [*mobilia . . . quoniam naturalibus
> mandatis secundum dispensationem ad tempus superaddita sunt*].[131]

The movable precepts are subject to temporal variations; they may
also serve different functions.

> Of the precepts which were superadded and were movable certain
> ones even now in time of grace have been retained for exercise, for
> example, the observance of fasts. And certain others which were
> instituted in earlier times have, however, been reserved providen-
> tially for the instruction of the present, and those especially which

look to the exercise of spiritual zeal are reserved in a time of grace, those being abolished which pertain to carnal observances.[132]

For Hugh, the sacraments were stones paving the almost immeasurable highway of salvation, which stretched out indefinitely through time. And yet quite remarkably, various stones, some hewn anciently, others more recently, some retained, and others discarded, nevertheless fit together to form the highway's vast mosaic design. It was along this highway that Hugh of Saint Victor measured the advance of the history of the temporal dispensation of divine providence by reflecting upon worldly events in the life of Christ.[133] Hugh saw the culmination of sacred history in the Incarnation of his Savior and did not concern himself with church history or unfolding theological teachings through time; for him, sacraments sufficed to fathom the depths of the divine economy. For his contemporary, Anselm of Havelberg, the cavalcade of church history and dogmatic wrangling revealed additional evidence of the functioning and management of the divine economy.

Anselm of Havelberg, born around 1100, served in 1135 as ambassador in Constantinople and in 1147 as papal legate in the crusade against the Wends. He was caught up in, and disgraced by, political intrigues between Emperor Conrad III and Pope Eugenius III, yet recovered enough to help reconcile differences between Eugenius and Frederick Barbarossa. He died accompanying Frederick during the siege of Milan in 1158.[134] This individual and his rather remarkable career deserve more attention than either has thus far received. To paraphrase a recent editor of Anselm's *Dialogues,* Anselm is one of those medieval authors who rests in the calm of Migne's *Patrologia* and to whom interest is paid intermittently, and only by specialized researchers or students in search of thesis topics.[135] Anselm's views of history and the role of sacraments, law, and the unity of the church and the faith constitute rich contributions to the history of accommodation.

Anselm's writings concerned themselves with the religious life; whether in the relationship between Latin West and Byzantine East or in the late eleventh- and twelfth-century conflicts between the older, more established religious orders and the newer orders of Canons Regular, Carthusians, Cistercians, and Praemonstratensians. Anselm could, and did, debate myriad issues including the procession of the Holy Spirit, ecclesiastical primacy, or divergent liturgical practices—innovations?— with Greek prelates or the validity of new religious orders—innovations?—against such conservative stalwarts as

Rupert of Deutz.[136] Little wonder that innovation and change occupied pride of place in Anselm's thought and writings.

This singular scholar tried principally to show that "novelties" and new ideas that arose within Christianity occurred under the legitimate influence of the Holy Spirit. All seeming changes were part of the great redemptive divine plan—the divine economy. Christ's salvific function had been operative throughout history; it did not commence with the Incarnation but with creation. Redemption began with Abel, the first of the elect, and would continue to the last moment of history. Indeed, the first of his *Dialogues* is entitled: "On the unity of the faith and the multiple manners of life from Abel the just to the last of the elect."[137] Where Hugh of Saint Victor's historical interest seemed to wane after the Incarnation, Anselm's waxed; indeed, it was the very historical vicissitudes that seemed to capture his fancy.

In his view, the unity of the faith coexisted unparadoxically with heterogeneity of custom because the one church was governed and regulated by the one Holy Spirit. In his debates with the Byzantines over the *filioque,* —a liturgical "innovation" which the Byzantines claimed destroyed the balance between the three persons of the Trinity—Anselm, while asking for some conformity to Rome, nevertheless insisted that, although the diversity of peoples allowed for contrasting manners and ecclesiastical customs, there should be no discord over the sacraments [*et licet pro diversitate cuiusque gentis diversi mores et ecclesiastice consuetudines habeantur . . . tamen in ecclessiasticis . . . sacramentis, nulla unquam debet esse discordia*].[138]

Just as there might be diversity in unity between East and West, so might there be between old and new religious orders. Anselm and Rupert of Deutz were eloquent spokesman for the new and old. Rupert, in his attack on newfangled religious orders and, perhaps more importantly, on the possible changes they heralded, complained, in effect, to a colleague:

> I recall certain remarks you made and I don't think I like their implications. You told me that the Babylonian kingdom was established, then reached its height, and then collapsed. And that it was supplanted by the Persian kingdom which in its turn collapsed. Then came the Macedonian kingdom. And so it goes, by a similar pattern, you added with the grandeur of the monastic orders, especially Cluny (about which I have never heard a friendly word fall from your lips). They will collapse in their turn, since new, still modest institutions will rise up to take over. What an altogether wrong and insulting comparison between the monasteries of the

kingdom of God and those monstrous kingdoms destined to the fires of hell.[139]

In addition to showing the tenacity of the historical periodization of four kingdoms and ages, Rupert's comments assault the very notion of any change or evolution in religious institutions. Anselm, who as we shall see, was a leading advocate and idealogue of states of life within the church, announced his position in the first chapter of his *Dialogues:*

> Many people are amazed and create problems for themselves and others. As slanderous inquisitors they ask: Why all these novelties in the Church of God? Why these new orders? Who is not amazed at so many types of monks? Who at last would not be scandalized amidst so many different forms of religious life, so different and so opposed to each other, as not to feel repulsion and scandal? More than that, who would not scorn a Christian religion subjected to so many variations, altered by so many innovations, upset by so many new laws and by customs changed nearly every year.... All these people, because they have nothing else to do, pose such questions and disturb simple souls, saying that a religion is contemptible if it changes like this [*Tales ... dicentes omnem religionem tanto esse contemptibiliorem, quanto mobiliorem*]. For, they say, how could a wise man imitate anything so mobile, so variable, so instable? Its very instability shows there is nothing there which one can really grasp.[140]

If a religion that changes is contemptible, how can one explain the varieties that existed within Christendom? Anselm had posed the difficult, yet logical, question. He advanced a theory of progress and transformation within Christendom that could be observed in, and corresponded to, changes and succession, not as Hugh of Saint Victor claimed in the sacraments, but in institutions.

That historical evolution was indicated by the seven seals mentioned in the fifth chapter of Revelation. Each seal represented one stage in ecclesiastical history, and despite this symbolic multiformity, the church of God that is one in faith, one in hope, one in charity, is protean in its variety of manifestations. Indeed, no one ought to marvel at the manner in which God, who is unchangeable, distinguished, by a variety of laws and observances, the different states of the church; did not the church exist before the Law, under the Law, and under grace?[141]

Lest anyone rush to the wrong conclusion that diversity in religious practice reflected poorly upon the Lord, Anselm explained the ideas behind *varietas* and *mutabilitas:*

This variety [*varietas*] (of religious practices) is explained not on account of the mutability of an immutable God [*non propter invariabilis Dei . . . mutabilitatem*] who is "always the same and whose years shall have no end" [Ps. 101:28], but on account of human infirmity, which is mutable [*propter humani generis variabilem mutabilitatem infirmitatem*], and on account of temporal changes from age to age.[142]

Anselm voices the same opinion we have heard since Irenaeus: the divine must accommodate human weakness—*infirmitas, ásthéneia*. In an account that resonates more the Greek than the Latin tradition, Anselm discloses his evolutionary conjecture. It was necessary, he felt, that in the course of time, the signs of spiritual grace increased, which unveiled the truth itself more and more, and thus augmented, from age to age, knowledge of truth and its salvific effects.[143] These changes could be measured in the familiar movement from "before the Law" to "under the law" to "under grace." This wellworn, threefold elaboration of ecclesiastical change was only one side of Anselm's theory. The other side was copied almost totally from Gregory of Nazianzus, and Gregory was a rich theological and historical vein that Anselm mined rapaciously.[144]

Anselm repeats Gregory's assertion that history has been marked by two great transpositions; equated with the two testaments. The former marked the divide between idols and the Law; the latter from the Law to the Gospel. A third transposition is predicted when the world will be destroyed and is marked by the passage to realities no longer changed or altered. In these first two transpositions, divine wisdom has functioned progressively with great diversity (*divina Sapientia tanta varietate paulatim usa est*); first, it removed idols and authorized sacrifices, then it abolished sacrifices; but not circumcision. Later circumcision was abolished and baptism introduced.[145] Anslem continues:

> And thus out of the gentiles [*de gentibus*] he made Jews, and out of Jews, Christians, and gradually [*paulatim*] setting some aside and changing them, and arranging them, he led humanity, almost by stealth [*quasi furtim*], pedagogically and curatively [*pedagogice et medicinaliter*], from the worship of idols to the Law, and then away from the Law, which did not lead to perfection to the perfection of the Gospel. Once the entire dispensation [*omni dispensatione*] had been revealed, he taught them the complete perfection of the Christian law.[146]

Anselm thus presents, clearly, though by no means innovatively, ideas and modes of expression employed in Christian exegesis for more than a millenium. These signal historic transpositions were not easily achieved. In his elaboration, Anselm trod again in the well-worn paths of Gregory of Nazianzus' familiar language and sentiments.

The Hebrew Scripture told openly only of God the Father; it told of the Son indirectly. The Christian Testament revealed the divinity of the Son openly, but only suggested that of the Spirit. When the Spirit was declared, humanity required a more adequate manifestation of its divinity. As the Son could not be known before the divinity of the Father was acknowledged, so the divinity of the Spirit could not be known before the divinity of the Son was acknowledged. To have done otherwise would have taxed humanity too sorely and too heavily oppressed human souls weakened in their earthly abode under the crushing weight of sin.[147] This accommodation to the human condition succeeded:

> Nor was it easy to alter things which had come into veneration through long custom and over an immense stretch of time; hence, the salubrious remedies [*salubris pharmacia*] of the gospel were received, bit by bit [*paulatim*], as if by sick people, and mixed as medicine by the divine art for people getting better.[148]

Anselm was perhaps the quintessential spokesman for accommodation in the twelfth century. His rather astonishing sensitivity to historical mutations, religious variety, and divine adaptations "stemmed from the needs of his controversy with the Greeks, whose doctrinal and institutional immobility he could overcome only by arguing from an unfolding evolution within the transcendent unity of faith; but even more, these views stemmed from his personal and competitive participation, outside the monastic tradition, in a highly animated transformation of the various states of life in the western church."[149] For Anselm, accommodation was an indispensable device in his professional work, defending Latin Christendom from without and within.

Anselm, in the midst of problems, debates, and discord, remained an optimist and championed his view of the "youth of the church," which was continually renewed by the increase of revealed truth. "The holy church, passing through various stages which in turn gradually [*paulatim*] succeed themselves up to this present day, is renewed just as the eagle's youth is renewed; and it always will be renewed."[150] Gradual change, innovations, and variety all testified to the implementation of the divine plan through time.

If Anselm was a twelfth-century dwarf standing on the shoulders of giants, he no doubt enjoyed that image which implied historical progress together with theological tradition and progress. Moreover, if he peered far enough ahead into the next century, he no doubt smiled broadly and approvingly when he viewed some of the workings of the Fourth Lateran Council. That conclave, in dealing with the removal of certain obstacles to marriage, pointedly enunciated a broad principle of canon law whose subsequent incorporation in the decretals assured it not only a future, but also a sizable audience. The council, seeming to fathom the mysteries of the divine *oikonomiá* and its manager, declared:

> It ought not be judged reprehensible if human institutions sometimes adapt to changing times, especially when urgent necessity or obvious utility demands it. God himself often changed in the New Testament what he had established in the Old.[151]

Anselm could not have expressed it any better. Times do change, and those changes indicate the success of the progressive implementation of God's plan in history. The Fourth Lateran merely affirmed what Anselm knew to be true all the time.

Both Hugh and Anselm employed accommodation. Hugh saw accommodation in the variety of sacraments throughout history and built his system according to the plan he perceived to exist in history. Anselm, who debated Greeks in Constantinople and traditionalist religious contemporaries in Europe, employed accommodation as an all-embracing tool of historical and theological value. Both were heirs to the Latin patristic tradition of accommodation, and Anselm was well aware of some of the Greek material on the subject. They were not the only twelfth-century authors to be aware of, and to employ, accommodation, but they are two distinguished representatives of that vibrant century and are of interest because of the manner in which they reflect and refract Latin and Greek patristic thought. We shall again pick up the Christian strand after a consideration of the Jewish contribution to the history of accommodation, in the next two chapters. Without the Hebrew sources and the perspective they provide, our story would be far from complete. For, as we shall see, when the great summae of the thirteenth century came to be written, and later when Calvin produced his exegesis, the Hebrew sources were not to be ignored. It is to those sources we must now turn.

CHAPTER FIVE

THE KING'S SON

> Train up a child in the way he should go: and when he is old, he will
> not depart from it.
>
> —Proverbs 22:6

The pedagogical principle of accommodation, which was prodigious and suasive in the Christian tradition, enjoyed a meaningful role in Jewish exegesis as well. It found eloquent expression in rabbinic as well as medieval Jewish literature. Since the sages of the Talmudic period were engaged in the vital work of explaining and adapting divine legislation to new and changed historical circumstances, and while no one-sided, all-embracing hermeneutical principle encompassing all biblical commands emerged, accommodation did prove a useful tool for rabbinic interpretation.

Accommodation in Jewish thought centered around very similar interpretive strategies and themes as in Christian thought. Pedagogical practices, childhood, healing, and medicine are the most prominent images associated with accommodation and reappear continually in rabbinic sources. Of course, all of these exegetical devices were linked to the overarching issues of sacrifice and idolatry and the notation that the "Torah speaks in human language." The latter, as we shall see, would become a towering issue in medieval Jewish thought.

In turning to an examination of the use of accommodation in rabbinic discourse, one straightforward explanation for biblical sacrifice is offered in Midrashic literature in the name of R. Pinhas, in the name of R. Levi, a third-century scholar. The Midrash proffers a simile:

> ... to a prince who became deranged and who was used to eating
> carcasses and forbidden meat. Said the king, "Let these dishes be
> always on my table, and of himself he will get weaned." So also,
> since Israel were eagerly attracted to idolatry and its sacrifices in
> Egypt ... God said, "Let them always bring their sacrifices before

127

Me in the Tabernacle, and thus they will separate themselves from idolatry and be saved."[1]

Midrash Leviticus Rabbah clearly understands sacrifice as a divine concession to the polytheistic and idolatrous addiction of the Israelites. The divine mandate is enacted in order to restrain idolatry, yet acquiesces in practices it clearly condemns. This manner of expression was to be repeated almost verbatim by Aphrahat about a century later.[2] The Midrash locates sacrifice within the larger topic of food laws, and others, including Aphrahat, were to do the same. This dietary type of accommodation is a well-established notion. Indeed, only after the flood did God concede to humanity the permission to eat flesh; a right not granted in Eden. Mankind should have been vegetarian, but only due to a divine accommodation with our nature was flesh allowed as part of our diet. This idea stretches from Eden at least to R. Abraham Isaac Kook, the first chief rabbi of the State of Israel, who was himself an avowed vegetarian.[3]

It is in the *Mekhilta,* a tannaitic Midrash on the book of Exodus that we find the beginnings of a lengthy chapter in the history of accommodation in Jewish sources. There are two recensions of the text, one attributed to R. Ishmael and the other to R. Simeon bar Yoḥai.[4] In intepreting Exodus 15:3, "The Lord is a man of war, the Lord is his name," the *Mekhilta of Rabbi Ishmael* observes: "At the Red Sea the Lord appeared to the Israelites as a mighty hero doing battle, and at Sinai, when the law was given, the Lord appeared to them as an old merciful individual" [*ke-zaken malei raḥamim*].[5] That is, the Lord seemingly adjusted his appearance to Israel depending upon *their* historical circumstances: at the time of manumission at the sea they required a hero; at Sinai, amid all the wonders, the proper mode of revelation was a merciful elder who not only revealed, but also taught the Law.

In commenting upon the theophany at Sinai, amidst the thunder and lightning, the awe and majesty of the event, the text focuses on the events described in Exodus 19:19. "The voice of the Shofar grew louder and louder; Ordinarily [*minhag hediot*] the longer the sound of a voice is prolonged the weaker it becomes, here the opposite obtained. It was soft and then loud in order that the ear might accommodate itself with its capacity of hearing."[6] An elaboration on the idea of mankind receiving an accommodated revelation, which Max Kadushin connects to God's "otherness,"[7] involves comparisons between the creator and his creatures. In much the same way that the "ear could hear within its own capacity," verses such as Amos 3:8— "The lion has roared; who will not fear? The Lord has spoken; who can but prophesy?—and Ezekiel 43:2—"His voice is like the sound of many waters"—have their explications ending frequently: "But [it is only that] the ear is made to listen to what it can hear and the eye to behold what it can see."[8] In addition, the text notes that the thundering and lightning attendant upon the theophany were perceived by each individual in a unique manner; that is to say, each heard things according to his individual capacity (*lefi koho*). Therefore, the text advances the concept that at Sinai revelation was individually accommodated.

The *Mekhilta* also extends this notion when it turns to the manna that sustained the Israelites in the desert. Surmising that the people who were accustomed to the cucumbers, melons, and other choice produce of Egypt might become bored with the same food while wandering in the desert, the Lord kept his people from dietary boredom.

> R. Joshua says: "If one liked it baked, it would become baked for him; if one liked it cooked, it would become cooked for him." R. Eleazar of Modi'im says: "If one liked to eat something baked, he could taste in the manna the taste of any baked things in the world; if one liked to eat something cooked, he could taste in it the taste of any dish in the world."[9]

For Israel, then, the taste differed according to the desire of each individual. This image of adaptation to individual desire and capacity would be cultivated and amplified elaborately in subsequent Jewish thought.

The ideas advanced simply in the *Mekhilta* were enhanced in a later Midrash, the *Pesikta of Rab Kahana*.[10] The late antique setting of such discourses and homilies, as those contained in the *Pesikta*, must be understood in order to appreciate truly the text under consideration. The homilies were probably delivered in the land of Israel in the fourth or fifth century, and we should forget modern ideas of decorum one expects in a house of worship today in order to understand the preachers of late antiquity. They were showmen and showoffs. And a popular preacher at a synagogue could outdraw crowds at circuses and theaters. Indeed, in the late fourth century, John Chrysostom noted caustically, there was no difference between a synagogue and a theater; and yet, as a great performer in his own right, he well knew the difficulties of playing to, and pleasing, a crowd in church. As we have already seen he wrote of the seemingly insatiable appetite of people in late antiquity for endless oratorical tours-de-force.

And his contemporary, Gregory of Nazianzus, when leaving Constantinople in 381, put the matter succinctly: "It is orators the people want, not priests!"[12] This is very much the setting in which the homilies in the *Pesikta* would have been delivered. Homily twelve commences with a gloss of the first word of the Ten Commandments. "I [*anokhi*] am the Lord thy God." R. Neḥemiah (mid-second century), a student of R. Akiba, who, unlike his teacher, survived the Bar Kochba Revolt of 135 C.E.,[13] begins with a philology lesson and asks the crowd what this word *anokhi* is:

> It is an Egyptian word. Why did God find it necessary to use an Egyptian word? For answer, consider the story of a mortal king whose son had been captured. The son spent many years among his captors, until the king, cloaked in vengeance, went to free his son, brought him back, and then found he had to talk with him in the captors' speech. So it was with the Holy One. . . . Israel had spent all the years of their servitude in Egypt where they learned the Egyptian speech. Finally, when the Holy One redeemed them and came to give them the Torah, they could not understand it. So the Holy One said: I will speak to them in their captors' speech.[14]

The Lord accommodated his message, speaking in a language the Children of Israel would understand at that particular time. The homily then enlarges on themes presented briefly in the *Mekhilta*.

> Because the Holy One appeared to Israel at the Red Sea as a mighty man waging war [Exod. 15:3], and appeared to them at Sinai as a pedagogue who teaches the day's lesson and then again and again goes over with his pupils what they have been taught, and appeared to them in the days of Daniel as an elder [*zaken*] teaching Torah, and in the days of Solomon appeared to them as a young man, the Holy One said to Israel: Come to no false conclusions because you see Me in many guises, for I am He who was with you at the Red Sea, and I am He who was with you at Sinai: *I am the Lord thy God.* The fact is, R. Ḥiyya bar Abba said, that He appeared to them in a guise appropriate to each and every place and time. At the Red Sea He appeared to them as a mighty man waging their wars, at Sinai He appeared to them as a pedagogue [*sofer*], as one who stands upright in awe when teaching Torah; in the days of Daniel, He appeared to them as an elder [*zaken*] teaching Torah, for the Torah is at its best when it comes from the mouths of old men; in the days of Solomon he appeared to them as a young man [*baḥur*] in keeping with the youthful spirit of Solomon's

generation—"His aspect is like Lebanon, young [bahur] as the ce-
dars" [*Song of Songs* 5:15]—At Sinai, then, when he said, *I am the
Lord thy God,* appropriately He appeared to them as a pedagogue
[*sofer*] teaching Torah.[15]

This exquisite analysis, once presented anonymously and once attributed to R. Ḥiyya bar Abba, a scholar of the late third century, fur-
nishes a striking example of divine accommodation to Israel throughout her history and amplifies the comments found in the *Mekhilta.*

The sermon, having thus far established that the Lord teaches
Torah to Israel in different guises at different times, next explores the
divine pedagogical process. It advances an assessment attributed to
R. Ḥanina bar Papa, a scholar who flourished in the late third to
early fourth century and for a while taught in Caesarea.

> The Holy One appeared to Israel with a stern face, with an
> equanimous face [*beynoniyot*], with a friendly face, with a joyous
> face: with a severe face appropriate for the teaching of Scripture—
> when a man teaches Torah to his son, he must impress upon him
> his own awe of Torah; with an equanimous face appropriate for the
> teaching of Mishnah; with a friendly face appropriate for the teach-
> ing of Talmud; with a joyous face appropriate for the teaching of
> *Aggadah.* Therefore the Holy One said to them: Though you see Me
> in all these guises, [I am still one]—I am the Lord thy God.[16]

For R. Ḥanina bar Papa, then, the Lord adapts his mode of teaching
as does a father who teaches his children. Different modes of instruction are appropriate for different subjects, and one descends from the
awe for divine writ, to reverence for the Mishnah, a creation of the
tannaim, to affability when admiring the intellectual dexterity of the
Gemarah, and finally joy when encountering the phenomenal re-
sourcefulness of the Aggadah.[17] The text therefore recognizes different levels of revelation decreasing from the loftiness of Scripture to
its human interpretation, Aggadah, each requiring an apt mode of
instruction. The manner of revelation is further examined in the
name of a talented third-century rabbi, R. Levi:

> The Holy One appeared to them as though He were a statue
> [*eikonin*][18] with faces on every side, so that though a thousand men
> might be looking at the statue, they would be led to believe that it
> was looking at each one of them. So, too, when the Holy One spoke,
> each and every person in Israel could say, "The Divine Word is
> addressing me." Note that Scripture does not say "I am the Lord
> *your* God" [*eloheichem*], but I am the Lord *thy* God [thy very own
> God] [*eloheikha*]."[19]

Playing on the biblical text that reads "I am the Lord *thy* God"—in the singular, and not the plural—R. Levi explains that just as the manna tasted differently to each individual, so at Sinai did each individual receive a unique revelation. R. Levi elucidates—in a striking metaphor, very similar to certain paintings whose eyes seem to follow the viewer across a room—how each person who stood at Sinai sensed the divine appearance and received the divine word in an exclusive manner.[20]

It is yet another Palestinian exegete of the latter half of the third century, R. Yosi bar Ḥanina, who offer a most skillful exposition of the same verse:

> Moreover . . . the Divine Word spoke to each and every person according to his particular capacity [*u-lefi kokhan*]. And do not wonder at this. For when manna came down for Israel, each and every person tasted it in keeping with his own capacity [*lefi kokho*]— infants in keeping with their capacity [*lefi kokhan*], young men in keeping with their capacity [*lefi kokhan*], and old men in keeping with their capacity [*lefi kokhan*].[21]

R. Yosi continues by noting that to infants the manna tasted like their mother's milk; to young men the manna resembled bread, oil, and honey; and to old men it was like "wafers made of honey."[22] Having explained this miraculous occurrence, he concludes:

> Now if each and every person was enabled to taste the manna according to his particular capacity [*lefi kokhan*], how much more and more was each and every person enabled according to his particular capacity [*lefi kokhan*] to hear the Divine Word.[23]

The proof text is Psalm 29:4, "The voice of the Lord is in its strength" [*bekoakh*], not in his strength [*bekokho*]. "That is, in its strength to make itself heard and understood according to the capacity of each and every person who listens to the Divine Word. Therefore the Holy One said; Do not be misled because you hear many voices. Know that I am He who is one and the same: I am the Lord thy God."[24] This expansive treatment of the initial statement of the Decalogue advances the theory that the Lord, as a superb teacher, adjusts simultaneously his revelation, in style, language, difficulty, and manner according to the capacity of each recipient. It must be stressed that the divine does not undergo any change, but rather the change is perceived in the human mode of receiving the divine message. Regardless of guise, voice, location, or time, the revelation is identical; only the means of transmission and reception differ.

These sages, R. Neḥemiah, R. Ḥiyya bar Abba, R. Ḥanina bar Papa, R. Levi, and R. Yosi bar Ḥanina, represent the two major schools of rabbinic thought, those of R. Akiba and R. Ishmael. Both schools, it is believed, produced separate Halachic Midrashim, commentaries on mostly legal scriptural verses, which also contain Aggadic or narrative and homiletical passages. Of these five teachers, one could claim that R. Neḥemiah alone was a representative of the school of R. Akiba, while the others, being students of R. Yohanan, illustrate the principles of the school of R. Ishmael. The *Mekhilta* and the *Pesikta* demonstrate to some degree that both schools knew and used this interpretive principle and that accommodation was therefore a well-known and widely used hermeneutical device in the land of Israel in the first four or five centuries of the Christian era.

If that is indeed the case, then it is not perhaps without reason that accommodation appears as we have seen in the works of Origen, who lived and studied in Caesarea from about 230 to his death about a quarter of century later. This would make him a contemporary of R. Neḥemiah and most certainly of R. Yoḥanan, the teacher of R. Ḥiyya bar Abba, R. Ḥanina bar Papa, R. Levi, and R. Yosi bar Ḥanina.[25]

Our examination of several classical Midrashim has demonstrated the degree to which accommodation was part and parcel of the period of the rabbis. The motifs and impressions common to Christian exegesis are found in rabbinic literature as well. Yet in addition to the pedagogical imagery, two additional, powerful metaphors of accommodation emerge that are of great interest: first, the connection between the Lord and the world, and second, how the Lord permitted his power and glory to be contained within the physical limits of the Ark within the Tabernacle.

The homiletical materials from the *Pesikta de Rab Kahana* support the claim that just as a verse has manifold meanings so does the Lord possess diverse countenances. A further instructive example of this perception occurs in the initial interpretation of the Midrash on Genesis. In a teaching attributed to R. Hoshaya, a contemporary of R. Joshua ben Levi, who resided at Sepphoris and Caesarea, we read:

> Rabbi Hoshaya said: "I was with Him as an *amon*[26] a source of delight every day, rejoicing before Him at all times [Prov. 8:30]. The word *amon* means tutor [*pidagog*]. *Amon* means "covered"; *amon* means "hidden"; and some say it means "great."[27] Another interpretation: *amon* means an artisan. The Torah states: I was the instrument that the Holy One, blessed be He, utilized when He practiced His craft. It is customary that when a king of flesh and blood builds a palace, he does not build it on his own but hires an architect. The architect does not build it exclusively from his head, but relies on

plans and blueprints in order to know where to place the rooms and locate the doors. So the Holy One, blessed be He, peered into the Torah and created the world. And so the Torah said: "By means of the beginning, God created the heavens and the earth,"[28] and the word, "the beginning" always hints at the Torah, as Scripture says, "The Lord created me at the beginning of His way" [Prov. 8:22].

R. Hoshaya begins with the difficulty faced by all critics, what to do with *amon*, a hapax legomenon. The emphasis on *amon* being the Lord's joy and delight may be a polemical attack on Christianity's understanding of the Law, but there is more here than simple polemics. The definition of *amon* as *paidagogos* is of course, as we have seen, connected to Galatians 3:24 and Paul's formulation of the Torah as a pedagogue to restrain the Jews before the advent of Christ. We must not necessarily conclude that the Torah described here is equated with the Platonic idea, nor confused with the concept of Logos.[29] Nor must we absolutely assume that the world as it exists is an accommodation to humanity, an inferior copy of the original blueprint.

That sort of identification was precisely the type of charge orthodox Christianity claimed Gnostics leveled at the orthodox; the Gospels were accommodated to weaker people and intellects; the true Gospels were reserved exclusively to Gnostics.[30] And it is perhaps no accident that Proverbs 8:22 was a verse employed by both the Arians and Athanasius in their struggles over Arian claims that Christ could "advance" and Athanasius' adamant denials of those claims.

The chasm between the divine and human that Christianity attempted to bridge by means of Christ's incarnation was scrupulously maintained in Judaism. Indeed, in endeavoring to depict the abyss between God and the world and to stress his "otherness" attempts were made to cleanse the scriptural understanding of anthropomorphisms and anthropopathisms.[31] This, as we shall see below, would be a special issue among medieval thinkers. One bold gambit to maintain the distance between man and God occurs in the activities of the Aramaic translators of Scripture and their products, the targumim.

Specialists of targumic studies have long pointed out the various ways in which anthropomorphic and anthropopathic activities are paraphrased in the targumim and have focused on the relationship of the divine name and divine presence.[32] Targum Onkelos aims toward a transcendentalization of God and characteristically expresses great reverence for the Lord. In examining two verses (Gen. 25:22 and Exod. 18:15), which contain the phrase *lidrosh et yhwy* (to examine/ question the Lord), Onkelos employs the preposition "before" in translating the verses. That is to say, one does not question the Lord, but

seeks guidance from "before the Lord." This also obtains in activities
such as crying, praying, offering sacrifices, and ritual celebrations.[33]
Additionally, the targum scrupulously eliminates expressions that may
convey the impression that idols are real or have any potency.[34]

In Exodus 25:8, Moses is instructed to build a sanctuary so that
the Lord could dwell among the Israelites. This verse will serve as a
common meeting ground for the two issues raised above: the relationship of the Lord to the world and the way in which the infinite could
be contained in a finite world.

The targums render all usages of the verb "to dwell" as "ashrey
shekhinta," relating to God, as he resides omnipresently in the midst
of the people. This is based on Genesis 9:27, ". . . and He shall dwell/
rest in the tents of Shem . . . " translated as "He will cause his shekhinta
to dwell/rest in the tents of Shem."[35] Thus, the targum introduces the
concept of the Shekhinah, or presence of the Lord, as a euphemism
for God. Maimonides approved of Onkelos' translation and avoidance
of anthropomorphisms, arguing that Onkelos taught the philosophical truth of incorporeality.[36] Naḥmanides disagreed with this entire
approach and argued that "among the words of the Rabbis many
things demonstrate that the name Shekhinah is indeed [that of] God."[37]
Thus, the issue of anthropomorphisms in the targumim, as we shall
see, was but one bone of contention between these giants.

If in fact the targumim tried in the above manner to solve the
problem of the relationship between the Lord and the world, this
same verse—Exodus 25:8—also shows how the Midrash, without recourse to euphemistic language, sought to explain how the infinite
could be contained in this world. The command to build the Tabernacle was given to Moses as were the plans and designs for all the
furniture (Exod. 25:9). The Lord tells Moses that Bezalel will be in
charge of the project (Exod. 31:1–2), but it was only after the sin of
the Golden Calf that work was begun to hold the Tablets of the Law.
Bezalel made the Ark (Exod. 37) as the Lord had commanded. The
biblical text relates that Bezalel alone made the Ark, while the rest of
the appurtenances were a group venture. A famous statement in
Berakoth 55a tells us that Bezalel "knew the combinations of letters
with which heaven and earth were made."[38]

One Midrash wonders why Bezalel alone made the Ark. The
response is based on a pun of the name Bezalel reading it as bezal-el
(i.e., in the shadow of God), for when Bezalel made the ark with two
cherubim, "the shadow of the Lord was there, for there He contracted
[mezamzem] His Shekhinah."[39] The proof text is Exodus 25:22, where
the Lord instructs Moses, "It is there that I shall meet you . . . between

the two cherubim. . . . " Quoting Jeremiah 23:24, "Do I not fill heaven and earth?" the Midrash recognizes the obvious paradox and proffers this solution:

> Rabbi Joshua of Siknin said in the name of R. Levi: This is a parable to a cave on the shore of the sea. The sea rushed forth and flooded the cave and yet is undiminished. So it is with the Holy One, though it is written "And the glory of the Lord filled the Tabernacle" [Exod. 40:34], and "His majesty is above the earth and heaven" (Ps. 148:13) do not say that the Lord contracted [*zimzem*] his Shekhinah within the Tabernacle, rather He contracted [*zimzem*] it within the ark, as it says: "Behold the ark of the covenant of the Lord of all the earth." [Josh. 3:11].[40]

R. Levi employs a deft parable to explain how the Lord could accommodate himself within the Ark and yet in no way be diminished. The concept of the Lord contracting or reducing himself will of course become an extremely important one in subsequent Jewish thought and theology and would, perhaps, erupt and gush forth most fully and forcefully in the thought of R. Isaac Luria in the sixteenth century.[41] And yet the example of something seemingly infinite being confined appears elsewhere in Midrashic literature.

For example, when the Israelites were gathered before the rock [Num. 20:10], all Israel stood there, and each felt as if he were standing there even though there was only a tiny opening![42] Similarly, even though the court of the Tabernacle was only one hundred cubits, it was able to contain all the Israelites![43] And when Joshua (Josh. 3:9) summoned all Israel before the Ark, "He crowded them between the staves of the Ark!"[44]

Were these miraculous occurrences not enough, the very same wonder obtained in Jerusalem. Indeed, one of the ten marvels that the Mishnah records for the Temple was that while all the people entered the Temple and stood cheek by jowl yet they had room to prostrate themselves.[45] These events are of course patterned on the principle of *zimzum*, and while the homilies all record the majesty of these happenings as they relate to Israel, one rabbinic teaching, perhaps in a polemical thrust against Christianity since it mentions two-third century scholars, R. Yoḥanan and R. Ḥanina, expands the metaphor to include all humanity in the messianic era:

> R. Joḥanan went up to inquire after the well being of R. Ḥanina, and he found him sitting and expounding on the verse; "At that time they shall call Jerusalem 'The throne of the Lord,' and all the nations shall be gathered unto it" [Jer. 3:17]. Said Yoḥanan to Ḥanina;

"Can it hold them all? It is amazing!" The Holy One, blessed be He, will order it; "Lengthen your boundaries, enlarge your space, and receive your hosts," as it is written: "Enlarge the place of your tent [Isa. 54:2]."[46]

The initial Midrashic conception of the Lord reducing his power to fit within the Ark of the Covenant, a clear case of divine accommodation, is expanded in the development of the idea to include all Israel. The whole House of Israel is then made to fit before the rock in the wilderness as well as within the confines of the Tabernacle. That miraculous occurrence is enlarged to include the Temple and then all of Jerusalem. The thought moves from God to Israel to the entire human race, which, according to Jewish tradition, will be gathered together in Jerusalem in messianic times. In this messianic claim, arguing against Christian exclusivity of salvation, we have what might almost be styled Midrashic chiasma, simultaneous restraint coupled with an ever-expanding subject.

These examples of divine accommodation in revelation and method do come from rabbinic homiletical material, even though both legal and homiletical Midrashim have been considered. There is but one additional pedagogical example of accommodation from Halachah that merits brief consideration, namely, the laws pertaining to the Passover seder.

In the course of the seder, perhaps the most beloved of all Jewish traditions, children play a prominent role. And the Mishnah instructs a child to ask his father, at a certain point in the ceremony, a set of questions. The text states clearly and simply that if the child does not know how or what to ask, his father must teach him.[47] Indeed, so important did Jewish tradition deem the lessons of Passover that if no child were present, then an adult was required to ask the questions. Even someone who was observing this family feast all alone had to ask himself the questions, and in the event that two sages were celebrating with each other, then one of them had to ask the questions.[48]

If the child did not know how to ask, how should the father teach him? As we shall see below, Maimonides, in his *Code of Law*, proposes that the father must teach "according to the capacity of the son," explaining things differently to a young or unsophisticated child than to one grown and educated. Additionally, Maimonides suggests that parched grain and nuts be distributed to children at the table in order to arouse their curiosity. Here is pedagogical accommodation serving practical religious ends.[49]

Of course, when knowledge of Hebrew proved to be an impediment in learning and understanding the ritual of the seder, the

Shulkhan Arukh, the definitive code of Jewish law to this day, accommodated the people, by stating:

> It is proper to explain the contents of the Haggadah to the members of the family in a language they *understand*. If he himself (sc. the head of the household) does not understand the Holy tongue, he should recite the Haggadah together with the vernacular translation, paragraph by paragraph, particularly the section "Rabban Gamliel said. . . ."[50]

This demonstrates convincingly how pedagogical accommodation came to serve religious ends. Indeed, what remarkable comprehension of human nature and human abilities it demonstrates.

This brief survey of accommodation in rabbinic thought demonstrates the ways in which this remarkable interpretive device came to be embedded in the rabbinic corpus, both Aggadic and Halachic. For Israel, the love of God, ultimate redemption, and religious observance in practical situations could be, and were, addressed and treated with remarkable dexterity and acumen. Accommodation made the God of "our ancestors" closer and helped Israel understand the proper method of obeying his laws. It is the reception of this interpretive device in the works of the Jewish thinkers of the Middle Ages, especially those of Maimonides, that need to be considered.

CHAPTER SIX

A WISE AND UNDERSTANDING PEOPLE

> The precepts of the Lord are right, rejoicing the heart; the commandment of the Lord is pure, enlightening the eyes.
>
> —Psalm 19:8

In turning to the application of accommodation in medieval Jewish writing, several prominent themes need to be analyzed. Among these is the use of accommodation in Jewish philosophical, as opposed to its position in mystical, writings, such as the *Zohar*. Another is the major bifurcation in Jewish thought in the Middle Ages between adherents and defenders of the Talmud: the Rabbanites, with some attention to Sa'adia Gaon,[1] and those who objected to rabbinic legislation, the Karaites. We shall tackle the latter issue first, and consider some Karaite authors.

One of the leading Karaite scholars, Jacob al-Qirqisani, a native of Upper Mesopotamia, or the general vicinity of Baghdad,[2] flourished in the first half of the tenth century. al-Qirqisani had personal relations with scholars of differing viewpoints, including Jacob ben Ephraim (a Rabbanite)—that is, one who accepted the Talmud and rabbinic Judaism—and Jesus Sexa, a Christian "bishop" (perhaps a deacon).[3] al-Qirqisani had read the New Testament, the Koran, and possibly some patristic writings in addition to having a thorough acquaintance with contemporary Arabic theological, philosophical, and scientific literature. He was familiar with the Talmud and some Midrashic literature. His major work is divided into two parts: *Book of Lights and Watch-Towers* and the *Book of Gardens and Parks*. The former is a systematic code of Karaite law, and the latter is a thirteen-part commentary on the nonlegal parts of the Bible.[4]

al-Qirqisani discusses the origins of Christianity in his *Kitab al-'Anwar,* an account of Jewish sects.[5] A commentary on Genesis, penned by Da'ud Ibn Marwar al-Rakki, known as al-Muqammis, is alluded to, and al-Qirqisani relates that the text had been translated from the

Syriac. One learns that al-Muqammis was a philosopher who, though born a Jew, became a Christian in Nisibis, through the agency of a certain Nana. Nana was an accomplished philosopher and surgeon, honored greatly by the Christians. al-Muqammis studied with him for many years and learned well the origins of Christianity and "mastered" philosophy. Afterward, rejecting his friends, al-Muqammis wrote two books against Christianity.[6]

al-Qirqisani had exposure to Syriac material, although, in examining his treatment of accommodation, no direct Christian influence may be demonstrated. Yet what is of interest is the repercussion in his work of modes of thought and expression in the world of the Near East. He commences his exegesis with a discussion of hermeneutical principles and then moves to historical interpretation.

al-Qirqisani enumerates thirty-seven preliminary principles pertaining to the explication of Scripture and the interpretation of its seeming ambiguities.[7] He advocated the following principles as necessary for proper understanding of Scripture: the Mosaic authorship of the Pentateuch, the literal interpretation of Scripture—save where a literal interpretation involved something objectionable or implied a contradiction—and acknowledgment of Hebrew as the primordial tongue in which God addressed Adam. His fourth principle explained anthropomorphisms by elaborating upon the Talmudic axiom: "The Torah speaks the language of man":

> This [the anthropomorphisms of the Bible] is similar to the reply of a certain scholar who was asked: "How can the Creator address mankind seeing that His speech is of a different species from man's speech, inasmuch as it is infinitely more sublime and exalted?" To this, the scholar replied that when God created His creatures and wished to address them with commandments, prohibitions, promises, threats, and narratives, He took into consideration the fact that their constitution could not bear to hear His natural speech because of its sublimity and exaltation and its dissimilarity from their own language; and He fashioned for them a speech akin to their own, near to their comprehension, acceptable to their understanding, and bearable to their faculties.[8]

The Lord adapted his manner of communication to mankind's level of comprehension—intellectually and physically. Spiritual accommodation bonds with carnal accommodation. The Lord "spoke," physically and intellectually, in a manner akin to human speech:

> This [as above] is comparable to our own procedure with animals and similar creatures, whose constitution is different from ours, whom we must govern and manage, to whom we must communi-

cate our wishes, who do not know our speech and whose sounds and utterances are not akin to ours. . . . This scholar's explanation is of great potency and is similar to our own view that God addresses mankind in a manner adapted to their minds and accessible to their understanding.[9]

His account of divine accommodation and the reasons behind it converges with numerous other accounts. It is in his exposition of Christian teaching that the convergence with Christian ideas on the origin of certain Jewish practices becomes sharper and more striking. al-Qirqisani labels Christianity, as introduced and established by Paul, "outright heresy" and offers as proof the belief of one substance and three hypostases in the Godhead. Attacking the Christian thinkers of his own day, he writes:

> The modern Christian philosophers assert that the laws of the Torah were given to the Children of Israel only because of God's wrath; and that they have chosen these laws for themselves only on account of their resemblance to the laws of the Sabians. This was due to the fact that they became accustomed to the ways of the Egyptians during their sojourn with them, these ways being akin to the ways of the Sabians.[10]

Here, in no uncertain terms, mention is made of a group not previously encountered: the Sabians. Nowhere in the Christian sources are they mentioned, yet al-Qirqisani berates Christian philosophers of his time for claiming that Jewish customs derived ultimately from the Sabians. This is a novel departure from both the Christian and Jewish exegetical traditions. al-Qirqisani does not accept this notion since it is asserted by "modern Christian philosophers"; but it is possible, as will be seen, that al-Qirqisani may have influenced Maimonides' understanding of accommodation.[11]

For al-Qirqisani, divine accommodation could be seen in the anthropomorphisms of the Bible and in the manner of divine revelation. His use of the Sabians in his historical exegesis is most intriguing. Other Jewish exegetes never mentioned the Sabians before al-Qirqisani, and after him, they all but vanished from view, only to reappear in Maimonides' *Guide*. The connection between al-Qirqisani and Maimonides is suspected, though beyond positive proof; yet the fact that only al-Qirqisani mentions them before Maimonides hints at a possible link and awaits further investigation.

Sa'adia, a pioneer in many fields of Jewish learning, may be credited with having fought the Karaites and having engaged in earnest the continual battle against biblical anthropomorphism. The rabbinic schools had already battled excessive anthropomorphic language and ideas with various weapons. The very idea that the "Torah speaks the language of man"—*dibberah torah kileshon benei adam* or *scriptura humane loquitur*—however divorced from its original context, emerged as a powerful antianthropomorphic weapon and was used, as we have seen, even by Karaites. Indeed, among Sa'adia's aims in writing his *Book of Beliefs and Opinions* was not only to confront the Karaites' counterclaims to rabbinic tradition and, hence, authority, but to grapple with anthropomorphisms that tended, inter alia, to focus on the corporeality of God.

Among some Christian and Muslim schools, the Jews were labeled anthropomorphists par excellence,[12] and the struggle over orthodox interpretation, which was waged in Islamic thought between the literalists and the Mutazilites concerning the Koran, was echoed and had repercussions in Judaism. Sa'adia and others perceived the dangers inherent in anthropomorphizing, and he focused his attention on the problems emanating from language.[13] He sought to purify the concept of God from the layers of noncritical beliefs applied by tradition, and it was he who introduced the Islamic method of exegesis, *taw'il*—though limiting it to only four cases—into Jewish philosophical writing.[14]

The rabbinic dictum that "the Torah speaks the language of man" bolstered *ta'wil* and aided Sa'adia's antianthropomorphic campaign, as well as the efforts of Maimonides,[15] Bahya ibn-Pakuda,[16] and Judah ha-Levi.[17] For Sa'adia, the tradition could not contradict reason; and much of his and other approaches to interpretation were based on the assumption of a hierarchy of meanings in Scripture, the hidden, inner level and the literal, obvious level (*nistar* and *nigleh*). Sa'adia saw no redeeming educational value in anthropomorphisms, and he was one vital link in a chain, stretching from Onkelos and other early biblical translators, to Maimonides and beyond, who sought to extirpate them from Israel.

Sa'adia, as one scholar has suggested, believed he could achieve his goal of eliminating anthropomorphisms from Israel by "concentrating on the main types of anthropomorphisms and anthropopathisms in the frame of Aristotle's ten categories."[18] Indeed, from Onkelos to Sa'adia and Maimonides, the clash over anthropomorphism was not just a minor debate over the use or abuse of appropriate or inappropriate language. For philosophers who viewed God as totally transcendent, the anthropomorphisms of Scripture might have been understood as an accommodation with a rude and vulgar people, yet there was more to it than that.

Perhaps the real quandary had not so much to do with the "physiological" anthropomorphisms and anthropopathisms as with the "spiritual" anthropomorphisms; that is to say, not simply describing God according to his physical attributes, but rather conceptualizing the Lord, on the basis of human morals and ethics. An ideation of God originates "in man's mind, his intellectual understanding on the one hand and his moral conscience on the other."[19] Viewing God from man's perspective requires that God "act," "think," or "do" everything in accordance with human ideas and morals; in its own crafty way, "physiological" anthropomorphism does, at the very least, restrict the divine "essence" of God. The "spiritual" type of anthropomorphism more cunningly necessitates that God not only "act," but "act properly," that is, according to human standards, and therefore "do" the "right" thing in all situations. Naive expressions had shackled God with linguistic fetters that were much easier to shatter than the philosophical chains of enlightened human values. The Lord might or might not wax angry, but when he had to behave by human standards, he was in trouble. This more sophisticated type of divine incarceration was not part of Sa'adia's struggle, but it would become a major battleground for later philosophers of religion. Sa'adia not only developed these modes of thought, but integrated Islamic philosophical approaches into Jewish thought. It was his followers who would compete in the larger philosophical arena.

It was also he who, almost uniquely among medieval Jewish authors, rejected out of hand the historical-anthropological mode of interpreting the development of religious law and practices. Sa'adia responded adamantly to the habitual and protracted Christian and Muslim charge of Judaism having been superseded and the Torah being abrogated by stating, in no uncertain terms, that God would not have issued laws solely to abrogate them. For this would result in an infinite regress of laws being enacted only to be revoked, "which is, of course, nonsense."[20] For Sa'adia, then, accommodation did not suffice to explain the origins of an *urreligion,* but as we shall see below, it could and would be invoked for didactic linguistic purposes. [21]

Several Spanish Jewish scholars also employed the theory of accommodation in their works. Baḥya ben Yosef ibn-Pakuda (second half of the eleventh century) presents a notion of divine pedagogy in his philosophical treatise *Ḥovot Ha-Levavot [The Duties of the Heart].*[22] ibn-Pakuda discusses human obligations of obedience toward the Lord and human reliance upon God alone. For him, man had to be roused by the Law:

> . . . which contains rational precepts as well as those accepted on
> authority so that through these we may rise to the service of God
> which, our reason demonstrates, is man's duty. For obedience is the
> intended purpose of the human species.[23]

For ibn-Pakuda, obedience to the Law may be stimulated either by fear of punishment, or by desire for reward. Both are praiseworthy, but those who are obedient out of an intellectual persuasion are the most praiseworthy.[24] In setting forth seven reasons for obeying the divine Law, ibn-Pakuda invokes accommodation in his sixth reason, which takes cognizance of human limitations:

> ... the Torah includes certain matters whose obedience cannot be grasped by the mind, and they are the commandments imposed by revelation and certain basic understandable principles. This was mandated by the condition of the people at that time [*ba'et hahi*] when the Torah was revealed to them. Their animal appetites held sway over them, and their minds and discernments were too feeble to grasp most of the intelligible matters.[25]

The Law includes certain principles that lie beyond rational comprehension; nevertheless, these principles are incumbent upon man. The historical condition of the Jewish people "at that time" necessitated a revelation geared to their condition. In order to facilitate observance, the Law was bestowed in a comprehensible form, considering the human limitations "at that time."

The exposition comments on the disjunction between those of sufficient intellectual vigor and those lacking intellectual strength:

> So the Torah treated them in the same manner, equalizing intelligible duties and those imposed by revelation. Whoever possessed a strong enough mind and understanding was aroused by both to accept the obligation of the performance. One whose mind was too weak to understand his obligation in both ways undertook performance by way of the Law only, regarding all as duties imposed by revelation. Thus the Law was made suitable for all.[26]

The Law was promulgated "at that time" to different and differing levels of comprehension. "The pleasant ways and peaceful paths" of the Law were accommodated according to individual capacities and abilities.

ibn-Pakuda's exposition of divine pedagogy is further expanded in a discussion of reward and punishment. He notes that little has been written concerning reward and punishment in the world to come and proffers as one possible reason man's inability to conceive of a soul without a body. Yet other reasons exist:

> Another reason why the issue of reward and punishment in the world to come was not explained is that it was accepted by the

common sort [*am ha'aretz*] as a tradition of the prophets, and by the learned by way of reason. Thus there is no mention of it in Scripture, just as much of the explication of the precepts is unrecorded due to reliance on tradition.[27]

He continues his distinction between the learned and the unlettered and cuts to the very heart of the matter:

> Another reason is that the people from what is written in the Torah were in a state of ignorance and had little understanding even of things which were not mysterious. Therefore, the Creator treated the people as a merciful father would treat his young son when he wished to educate him with gentleness and patience, as in Hosea 11:1, "When Israel was a child, then I loved him, and out of Egypt I called My son."[28]

The image and language are by now familiar: divine accommodation mediates between reason and revelation. ibn-Pakuda elaborates, employing language that will reappear in Maimonides:

> When a father wishes to instruct his young son in the disciplines unknown to the child, disciplines which the child does not comprehend at that age [*ba'et hahi*], yet will raise him to the higher degrees, he cannot make the child desire them by saying: "Suffer the trouble of discipline and study so that you may ascend to desirable heights" for the child will not endure it. And due to his lack of understanding would not pay heed. But, were the father to promise the child if he study immediate pleasures such as food, drink, fine clothes, a fine chariot, or anything similar, and if the father warned the child that if he did not heed him, he would suffer immediate pain such as hunger, nakedness, a whipping or something similar while at the same time persuades him with tangible proofs and clear, truthful arguments, then it becomes easier to bear its burdens patiently.[29]

Continuing that, as the child matures and his mind comes to comprehend the purpose of discipline and study, the child will, by himself, gravitate toward the higher degrees, ibn-Pakuda likens those actions to God's treatment of Israel; threatening the nation with impending chastisements while making the nation hunger for immediate pleasures. The Lord well knew that when obedience to him became habitual the carrot of reward and the stick of punishment in the world to come would no longer be needed, and the people would obey him of their own purpose and for his sake. The same explanation obtains for all anthropomorphic usages in Scripture.[30] ibn-Pakuda

thus employs accommodation in what was to become a classic of
Jewish philosophical-ethical literature. The influence of his approach,
as we shall see, would be exploited by Maimonides and others in
Jewish educational ideas that would reverberate for centuries.[31]

ibn-Pakuda carefully sets out the disjunction between Sa'adia's
"commandments of reason" and "commandments of observance": Some
are beyond rational comprehension and were imposed by revelation
because of the people's condition "at that time." This historical approach foreshadows Maimonides' analysis. Baḥya ibn-Pakuda stated
the generic premise that the laws, as a whole, were accommodated
teleologically to historical reality; Maimonides, as we shall see, applies the generic principle to the specific use of sacrifice before em-
barking on his full-blown historical reconstruction of nascent Israel.
But before turning to Maimonides, we need to review cursorily one
additional author, Judah ha-Levi.

In his *Book of Argument and Demonstration in Aid of the Despised Faith* [*Kitab al-Khasari*],[32] ha-Levi recognized the danger of
philosophic antinomianism, as well as attempts to make the divine
Law comprehensible. In retelling the story of the "four who entered
pardes,"[33] Judah notes that it was Elisha ben Abujah, the archetypal
heretic—referred to as Aḥer (the "Other not to be named"), who noted
pointedly: "Human actions are but instruments which lead up to
spiritual heights. Having reached these, I care not for religious ceremonies."[34] This expressed the antinomian danger in the starkest
relief possible and revealed ingenuously the perils attendant upon
philosophical speculation.

In retelling the history of the Jewish people, ha-Levi speaks of
Abraham's realization of monotheism. In ha-Levi's version of history
we learn:

> All nations were given to idolatry *at that time*. Even had they been
> philosophers, discoursing on the unity and government of God, they
> would not have been able to dispense with images, and would have
> taught the masses that a divine influence hovered over this image
> which was distinguished by some miraculous feature. Some of them
> ascribed this to God, even as we today treat some particular spots
> with reverence, going so far as to believe ourselves blessed by their
> dust and stones. . . . The people did not pay so much attention to a
> single law as to a tangible image in which they believed.[35]

Conceding the value of images as books for the unlettered, ha-
Levi underscores the childish character of humanity at a certain era
in which the practice of idolatry was so natural—ha-Levi confesses
modified forms of it existed still in his own day—and the need for

images so strong that, even had people been philosophers, they would have still required them. Ha-Levi attacks the incident at Horeb as horrible since it consisted in the "manufacturing of an image of a forbidden thing, and in attributing divine power to a creation of their own."[36] This, of course, echoes Chrysostom's charge of compounding idolatry with polytheism.[37] For ha-Levi, the matter was repulsive since "*in this age* the majority of nations have abandoned the worship of images. It appeared less objectionable *at that time,* because all nations were then idolators."[38]

Ha-Levi narrates how the Law was given and the practices of the cult established; there was direct divine revelation to Moses replete with the real shape and size, lest any error creep into the Tabernacle. He concludes his explanation of the history surrounding these events to the king of the Khazars, noting: "In the service of God there is no arguing, reasoning, and debating. Had this been possible, philosophers with their wisdom and acumen would have achieved even more than Israel."[39] Reason has its uses, but not, perhaps, in the service of God.

Bahya and ha-Levi applied the principles of teleology to history. Ha-Levi and his contemporaries were much farther along the road of progress than mankind had once been; in his day people were not idolatrous or, at least, so he claimed, not in the same way. Accommodation had thus far enjoyed a lengthy, if not mesmerizing, career in Jewish sources. However, by the twelfth century, the groundwork had been prepared; the ideas had been sorted and strained through the intellectual sieve of Jewish thought, and it would take the greatest thinker of the Middle Ages to catapult accommodation to climactic repercussions in Jewish medieval thought.

Rabbi Moses ben Maimon (1135–1204),[40] probably the best-known and most influential figure in medieval Jewish thought, incorporates accommodation prominently into his entire oeuvre.[41] With Maimonides, accommodation is employed most compellingly in his celebrated historical explanation for biblical law, in general, and for sacrifice, in particular. Indeed, Maimonides makes the clearest and most trenchant use of this exegetical principle in Jewish thought. It appears in his earliest work, *Commentary on the Mishnah,* and receives its widest application in the *Guide.* It is at the center of his thought and from it emanates his philosophy of Law. His ideas concerning accommodation are not confined solely to the *Guide,* but form part of a larger effort, described keenly by I. Twersky in his magnum opus on the *Mishneh Torah.*[42] Twersky suggests that, not only is Maimonides' rationalization of the Commandments the most comprehensive and ambitious attempt in Jewish thought, but that components of the system are found in all of his works.[43] Even though his explanation found neither universal favor nor critical standing among his contemporaries and successors; it did influence and alter the entire debate within Jewish thought. What is presented here are the main lines of Maimonides' understanding and use of accommodation, as well as his place within its history.

In the *Guide*, part 3, chapters 25–56, Maimonides unfolds and develops his theory for the philosophy of the Law and presents his own *ratio praeceptorum*.[44] Of course, Maimonides knew and rejected Sa'adia's disjunction between commandments of reason and obedience. Unlike Sa'adia, he asserted forcefully that every commandment and prohibition in the Torah is consequent upon wisdom and aims at some intended goal—and is both a commandment of reason and obedience simultaneously. In fact, the Torah itself offers proof of this. The divine statutes and judgments are termed "righteous" and "just" (Deut. 4:8 and Ps. 19:8 and 19:10).

Perhaps the first indications of Maimonides' pedagogical approach to divine Law may be found in his *Commentary to the Mishnah,* where he answers his rhetorical question; why rabbinic narrative texts speak in parables rather than in explicit and literal terms:

> And they did this to marvelous issues, i.e., wrote in parables whose literal meaning may be contrary to reason; first, to awaken the understanding of students, and also to blind the eyes of fools whose hearts will never be enlightened, and even if the truth were presented before them they would turn away from it according to the deficiency of their natures, as it is [written] said regarding those like them, "One does not reveal to them the secret" [*T.B. Kedushin* 71a], for their intellect is not perfect to the extent required to receive the truth as it is. . . . And, thus, it is improper for the man of knowledge [perfect man] to publicize what he knows of the secret teachings other than to one who is greater than he or like him. Because if he would present it before a fool, if (the latter) would not deprecate it to his face, surely the matter will not find favor in his eyes. Therefore, the wise man said: "Speak not in the ears of a fool; for he will despise the wisdom of thy words" [Prov. 23:9]. And also, it is not correct to teach the public but by the way of riddle and parable in order to include women, young men, and children, so that when their intellects reach perfection they will know the meanings (matter) of those parables. To this issue Solomon alluded in his saying, "To understand a proverb, and a figure; the words of the wise, and their dark sayings" [Prov. 1:6], and because of this our Sages, peace to them, spoke about Divine matters in riddle form. Thus it is proper for a person who happens to come across one of

their statements, which he thinks is opposed to reason, not to attribute the deficiency to those statements, but to attribute the deficiency to his own intellect. And when he sees one of their parables whose literal meaning is far from his understanding, it is proper for him to be much grieved that he did not understand the issue so that all true statements became extremely distant [to his understanding]. For the intellects of men are as different as differences of temperament, and as the temperament of one man is better and closer to the mean than the temperament of another man, so too will be the intellect of another man. There is no doubt that the intellect of one who knows a sublime matter is not as the intellect of one who does not know that matter, for the one is like an intellect *in actu* and the other an intellect *in potentia*. Therefore, there are matters [issues] which to a specific person are perfectly clear and correct, while to another person they are in the domain of the impossible, according to the extent of their level of wisdom.[45]

In this singular statement, Maimonides proposes pedagogy as the reason the sages employed parables; to stimulate the wise and confound fools; a practice he would also employ in the *Guide*.[46] Additionally, a person of knowledge ought to teach his inferior according to the latter's level, otherwise the lesson would not be understood, but rather disparaged before the teacher's eyes. Human intellects differ, and those differences must be, were and are, taken into account by the sages.

Another stunning example of Maimonides' approach to teaching is contained in his introduction to *Ḥelek:*

Imagine a small child who has been brought to his teacher so that he may be taught the Torah, which is the ultimate good because it will bring him to perfection. However, beacuse he is only a child and because his understanding is deficient, he does not grasp the true value of that good, nor does he understand the perfection which he can achieve by means of Torah. Of necessity, therefore, his teacher, who has acquired greater perfection than the child, must bribe him to study by means of things which the child loves in a childish way. Thus, the teacher may say "Read, and I will give you some nuts or figs; I will give you a bit of honey." With this stimulation the child tries to read. He does not work hard for the sake of reading itself, since he does not understand its value. He reads in order to obtain the food. Eating these delicacies is far more important to him than reading, and a greater good to him. Therefore, although he thinks of study as work and effort, he is willing to do it in order to get what he wants, a nut or a piece of candy.[47]

Employing a very similar metaphor to the one invoked by Baḥya, Maimonides portrays adroitly how tricks or ruses may be valuable in educating children. Even as the child matures, some sort of lure may still be necessary:

> As the child grows and his mind improves, what was formerly important to him to know loses its importance, while other things become precious. The teacher will stimulate his desire for whatever he wants then. The teacher may say to the child, "Read and I will give you beautiful shoes or nice clothes." Now the child will apply himself to reading for the sake of new clothes and not for the sake of study itelf. He wants the garments more than the Torah. This coat will be the end which he hopes to achieve by reading. As his intelligence improves still more and these things, too, become unimportant to him, he will set his desire upon something of greater value. Then his teacher may say to him, "Learn this passage or this chapter, and I will give you a *denar* or two." Again he will try to read in order to receive the money, since money is more important to him than study. The end which he seeks to achieve through his study is to acquire the money which has been promised him. When his understanding has so improved that even this reward has ceased to be valuable to him, he will desire something more honorable. His teacher may say to him then, "Study so that you may become the president of a court, a judge, so that people will honor you and rise before you as they honor So-and-So." He will then try hard to read in order to attain his new goal. His final end then will be to achieve the honor, the exaltation, and the praise which others might confer upon him. Now all this is deplorable. However, it is unavoidable because of man's limited insight, as a result of which he makes the goal of wisdom something other than wisdom itself, and assumes that the purpose of study is the acquisition of honor, which makes a mockery of truth.[48]

Of course, this clashes profoundly with the rabbinic maxim of *Torah lishmah* "Torah for its own sake." Man is to serve God out of love, not for any type of worldly reward. Indeed, part of Abraham's greatness lay in his love of God and his acting out of that love.[49] Maimonides knows very well that the preponderance of humanity cannot rise to Abraham's level, and thus he admits:

> Therefore, in order that the masses stay faithful and do the commandments, it was permitted to tell them that they might hope for a reward and to warn them against transgressions out of fear of punishment. It was hoped that they might be urged to strengthen their intentions so that they would ultimately grasp the truth and

the way toward perfection, just like the child in the analogy which I cited above. . . . The masses, after all, lose nothing when they do the commandments out of fear of punishment and hope of reward, since they are not perfect. It is good for them insofar as it strengthens and habituates them in loyalty to what the Torah requires. Out of this effort they may be awakened to the knowledge of the truth and serve God out of love.[50]

Perhaps indicating Alfarabi's influence,[51] Maimonides indicates that for the masses certain imperfect and impaired practices were tolerated by the sages and obtain in his own time. It is the toleration of less than perfect practices, that is an accommodation with human nature as it is in this world, that will be focus of Maimonides' historical analysis.

In the introduction to his *Book of Commandments,* an independent compilation of the 613 commandments in the Torah, Maimonides allows that he does not wish to delve into the details of the commandments, but only to list them. However, in his comment on the last negative commandment, he again returns to the limitations of the masses:

> But there is not even one commandment which does not have a reason nor cause, either remote or immediate. The majority of these reasons and causes, however, lie beyond the intelligence and understanding of the masses; yet concerning all [of the commandments] the prophet utters: "The precepts of the Lord are right, rejoicing the heart; the commandment of the Lord is pure, enlightening the eyes." [Ps. 19:8].[52]

Citing rabbinic dicta, which maintain that all the commandments have reasons, Maimonides articulates his argument in the *Guide*:

> About the statutes designated as *ḥukkim*—for instance, those concerning mingled stuff [based on Deut. 22:11, prohibiting the wearing of clothing made of wool and linen], meat in milk, and the sending away of the scapegoat [Lev. 16:10 and 21]—[the Sages] make literally the following statement: "Things which I have prescribed for you, about which you have not the permission to think, which are criticized by Satan and refuted by the Gentiles" [*BT Yoma* 67b]. They are not believed by the multitude of the Sages to be things for which there is no cause at all and for which one must not seek an end. . . . On the contrary, the multitude of the Sages believes that there indubitably is a cause for them—I mean to say a useful end—but that it is hidden from us, either because of the incapacity of our intellects or the deficiency of our knowledge. Con-

sequently there is, in their opinion, a cause for all the commandments; I mean to say that any particular commandment or prohibition has a useful end. [53]

Consequently, the commandments and prohibitions do have reasons,
and it is perfectly permissible to search for and ferret out these reasons, though humans, due to our limited or deficient capacities, may
not fathom them.

Even though all commandments are reasonable, Maimonides distinguishes between *mishpatim* (judgments) and *ḥukkim* (statutes).[54]
The former are eminently reasonable; the latter appear to lie beyond
rational scrutiny, or as Maimonides explains it in terms of the masses,
mishpatim are "those commandments whose utility is clear to the
multitude"; and *ḥukkim* are "those [commandments] whose utility is
not clear to the multitude."[55] Being fully cognizant of the antinomian
danger in exposing the reasons behind the commandments,
Maimonides cautions his readers by citing the rabbinic doctrine that
God secreted the reasons for commandments, lest if the reasons were
disclosed the commandments would come to be held in little esteem—
as, Maimonides suggests happened with regard to the three commandments whose reasons were revealed uniquely to King Solomon
(Deut. 17:16–17).[56]

Maimonides distinguishes further between commandments in general and the specific details of each commandment. For example, in
exploring the reasons behind ritual slaughter, he refers to the rabbinic vexation over what possible difference it could matter to God
how an animal was slaughtered. The general commandment is beneficial to man since it provides food, yet the details of the commandment were imposed, not because of slaughter, but rather with a view
toward purifying the people. This commandment was intended to
bring about the easiest possible death for the animal and, since be-
heading could be best achieved with a very sharp instrument, the
details are given, lest any type of implement might have been used to
mangle the poor creature's throat and cause undue suffering.[57] Furthermore, in the *Mishneh Torah,* Maimonides asserts that *sheḥitah*
was ordained in Scripture without explanation, yet it must be explained in order to know the limits and extent of the Law.[58] Part of
the process involved covering the shed blood; this was not done indis-
criminately, but according to certain observances that Maimonides
clarifies:

> When one performs the commandment of covering up the blood, he
> should do it not with his foot, but with his hand, or with a knife or
> utensil, so as not to conduct the performance of the commandment

in a contemptuous manner, thus treating God's commandments with scorn. For reverence [kavod] is due not to the commandments themselves, but to Him who has issued them. . . . [59]

It is the commandments that straighten out the crooked places and indicate the proper behavior for humanity. Indeed,

> Although the statutes in the Law [ḥukkei ha-Torah] are all of them divine edicts . . . yet it is proper to ponder over them and to give a reason for them, so far as we are able to give them a reason. . . . And both these laws (sc. Lev. 17:15; 27:10) serve to suppress man's natural tendency and correct his moral qualities.[60]

One aspect of the Law is thus reflected in its moral, ethical, and pedagogical lessons. There is no breach in the totality of Rambam's teachings, at least according to Twersky, who infers from this passage an attempt to integrate that aspect of the Law which commands with that which educates.[61] Yet Rambam states explicitly that it is proper to plumb for reasons "so far as we are able."

Maimonides hypothesizes that the generalities of commandments have causes and a certain utility; the details one might say, were given merely for the sake of commanding something. In turning from ritual slaughter to sacrifices, it may be alleged that the offering of sacrifice in general has great utility, yet what of the particulars; do they have any cause.[62]

Maimonides posits that certain particulars exist without specific causes and that it is unreasonable to imagine that this should be different with the Law. For particular sacrifices, particular species were chosen. If a lamb were chosen, one could ask why a lamb and not a ram; and if a ram had been chosen, one could ask why not a lamb? One species, either a lamb or a ram, or some other animal had to be chosen, and similarly, if seven lambs were prescribed for a particular act, one could ask why were not eight prescribed? And if eight had been prescribed, one could ask why had not ten, twenty, or any other number been mandated? Just as one species had to be chosen necessarily, one number had to be chosen necessarily; that is, one particular or one detail had to be selected; and this merely resembles the nature of the possible, for it is certain one of the possibilities will occur.[63] It does one no good to ask why one possibility instead of another came to pass since this leads to a philosophical cul-de-sac.

Maimonides asserts convincingly that, while all commandments have reasons, great utility, and purpose, certain commandments necessitated choices. If they did not and were deemed irrational and without a purpose, to attribute them to God is not only the height of folly, but blasphemous as well. Maimonides realized fully that there exist certain "innocents, intellectually naive and misguided people who presume to laud God while they actually demean him."[64] Maimonides contends:

> There is a group of human beings who consider it a grievous thing that causes should be given for any law; what would please them most is that the intellect would not find a meaning for the commandments and prohibitions. . . . For they think that if those laws were useful in this existence and had been given to us for this or that reason, it would be as if they derived from the reflection and the understanding of some intelligent being. If, however, there is a thing for which the intellect could not find any meaning at all and that does not lead to something useful, it indubitably derives from God; for the reflection of man would not lead to such a thing. It is as if, according to these people of weak intellects, man were more perfect than His maker; for man speaks and acts in a manner that leads to some intended end; whereas the deity does not act thus, but commands us to do things that are not useful to us, and forbids us to do things that are not harmful to us. But He is far exalted above this; the contrary is the case, the whole purpose consisting in what is useful for us.[65]

Those people who imagine that mysterious and secretive practices exalt God are wrong. For they would then have to assert that divine wisdom and intent would merely be reflective of human understanding. In fact, Maimonides suggests that just the opposite obtains: The divine Law as a whole, including all of its parts, has a purpose even if it is independent of, and lies beyond, human insight.

The Law, as a whole, aims at two things: welfare of the soul and welfare of the body.[66] The first for Maimonides is perfection of the soul; the second, perfection of the body. The Law is the means by which these perfections are facilitated. And since an individual cannot acquire all things necessary for bodily welfare, save as a member of society, the Law seeks to establish civilized society governed by principles of social utility and justice. The Law also seeks to teach true beliefs and instill moral virtues in man or to train men in the acquisition of moral and intellectual virtues.[67]

According to Maimonides, certain commandments—be they prescriptions or prohibitions—which lead to a good social relationship, or abolish reciprocal wrongdoing, or encourage the attainment of noble, moral qualities, or convey true opinions, have clear causes and are of demonstrable utility. For example, one need not inquire concerning the prohibitions on murder, theft, or vengeance, nor ought one to wonder why the Law commands us that God is one. These present no difficulty.[68] The uneasiness lies in those commandments that seem to do none of these things, but only appear to command something. The difference between judgments [*mishpatim*] and statutes [*ḥukkim*] lies at the heart of the problem.[69] Since the Law as a whole is perfect, its components must also be perfect. The *ḥukkim* expose the impasse; and it is precisely in the *ḥukkim*, which seem to make the least, if any, sense and which seem to defy reason, that sense and reason must be sought.

In an engaging discussion of Maimonides' explication of Deuteronomy 4:6; "Keep, therefore, and do them [statutes]; for this is your wisdom and your understanding in the sight of the nations, which shall hear all these statutes [*ḥukkim*] and say: 'Surely this great nation is a wise and understanding people,'" Twersky has proposed that Maimonides interpreted the *ḥukkim* in a new manner. *Ḥukkim* are a source and sign of wisdom; they must be "intelligible and rational, otherwise they could not prove that the Torah, as a whole, is grounded in reason and wisdom."[70] If the *ḥukkim* are of no utility, why should anyone attach merit to or praise someone who believes in or observes them? Maimonides' approach to the dilemma not only establishes their utility, but demonstrates overwhelmingly the significance of accommodation in his thought.

What Maimonides established are the guidelines that lead humanity to perfection. He defined the problem and demonstrated that all commandments abet the establishment of civilized societies and foster the development and improvement of moral qualities and intellectual perfection. This is schematic and straightforward. All that one had to do was show how the 613 commandments relate to these goals. This was Maimonides' proof from philosophy.[71]

Yet Maimonides set forth a second proof employing divine accommodation, which approximates an argument from historical contingency. He tackled the problem by reinterpreting antique pagan history, a method that afforded him entry to the subject, much as it had for Petrus Alphonsi.[72] For Maimonides, sacrifice marked one stage in the ineluctable march of human history, and it enabled him, in an anthropological fashion, to examine foreign cultures and beliefs without ever abandoning his own. One such example lies in a responsum concerning Islam. His response to a query, sent by Obadiah the Proselyte, established the intellectual ambience in which his theory developed.[73]

Obadiah was puzzled. One of his teachers told him that Moslems were idolatrous because they threw stones at statues called Mercolis and Terufah;[74] and Obadiah wished to know if, in fact, Moslems were idolatrous. Peter Alphonsi and William of Auvergne describe similar Moslem actions, though they were not concerned with the issue of Moslem idolatry.[75] Maimonides responded to Obadiah fully and directly:

> Those Ishmaelites are not idolators, for long [idolatry] has been eradicated from their mouth and heart and they unify the exalted properly. . . . And if one should claim that the house they worship [the Ka'aba] is a house of idolatry, what of it. Those who kneel against it today have no other intention save towards heaven. . . . Indeed, the Ishmaelites once held in their places three kinds of idolatry, "pe'or," "margolis" [mercurius?] and "khemos"; they admit it openly today and give them Arabic names.[76]

Having dispensed with the charges leveled against Islam, Maimonides proceeds to explain how historical causality may be used to unearth ancient practices:

> All these matters were clearly known to us long before Islam emerged, but the Ishmaelites of today say that the reason for untying the hair and refraining from sewn clothes is so as to submit oneself to God. . . . And some of their sages give a reason and claim there were idols there, and we throw stones on the place of the idols; that is, we do not believe in the idols which stood there, and in a manner of rebuke we throw stones on them. Others say it is a custom.[77]

Maimonides, in fact, described customs of the hajj still observed today, but reinterpreted pre-Islamic elements that survived the transition from paganism to Islam. The idols that may have once been historically significant have become over time significantly historic and, hence, no longer pose any threat nor create any problem. Not so different, perhaps, is the Vatican Museum, housing statues of pagan gods today—statues that represent a vanished, vanquished past.[78]

It is this historical understanding of ages past that permitted Maimonides to analyze Jewish history with more than merely antiquarian glee. The Law was perfect and had to be cherished and obeyed. It was more than merely a textbook of the past that afforded an opportunity to investigate both historical change and continuity; it held out the possibility of moral and ethical perfection.[79] The textbook lay before him; he had but to open it and understand.

Maimonides' explorations of the Jewish past led him to a novel reformulation of it. His history lesson commences in chapter 29 of the third part of the *Guide,* where he focuses upon the world at the time of Abraham. He relies upon a narrative that purported to tell of an ancient community of Sabians, a group that recognized only the stars as the deity. This Sabian textbook, *The Nabatean Agriculture,*[80] told him that Abraham had been imprisoned for objecting to certain Sabian beliefs and that he was banished to Syria lest he ruin the polity of the Sabian monarch. This pagan civilization held dominion over the entire world, and regarded Noah as a husbandman who did not approve of idol worship. Noah, because he never worshiped idols, had been held up to ridicule and scorn, and was mocked and incarcerated because he worshiped God. The Sabians spread marvelous tales about Adam and his ventures in Babylon. They used these stories to buttress their belief in the eternity of the world in order to demonstrate that the stars and the heavenly sphere were divine.

Abraham, as he matured, denounced their ravings, and proclaimed the unity of the Lord and his creation of the world in time. In conformity with their beliefs, the Sabians erected statues for the stars (planets) and assigned different minerals and climes to specific planets. Temples were constructed, statues were erected, and the populace believed that the forces of these planets overflowed to the statues, which, in turn, spoke, gained understanding, and gave prophetic revelation to the people.

Maimonides discloses that all this was possible because these opinions were generally accepted, ignorance was rampant, and the world was frequently given over to such ravings. With such folly unchecked, it became inevitable that some became soothsayers, necromancers, charmers, wizards, and so on. It fell to Abraham to refute these opinions by argument and gentle preaching, by conciliating people, and by drawing them toward divine obedience. In the course of time, Moses received prophetic inspiration and perfected the process. He commanded the Sabians to be slain, their beliefs eradicated, and their traces extirpated. In fact, the Law existed to guide these efforts:

> You know from texts of the Torah figuring in a number of passages that the first intention of the Law as a whole is to put an end to idolatry, to wipe out its traces and all that is bound up with it, even its memory as well as all that leads to any of its works . . . and to warn against doing anything similar to their works, and all the more against repeating the latter. It is explicitly stated in the text of the Torah that everything that was regarded by them as worship of their gods and as a way of coming near to them, is hateful and odious to God.[81]

The first intention of the Law is the eradication of idolatry, which the commandments facilitate. It is the statutes [*hukkim*], even though they may appear to defy reason, which are ultimately utilitarian.

Maimonides applies accommodation only to the statutes; their utility, as he argues, emerges clearly upon examination:

> How great then is the utility of every commandment that delivers us from this great error and brings us back to the correct belief, namely that there is a deity Who is the Creator of all this; that it is He Who ought to be worshiped and loved and feared and not the things that are deemed to be gods; and that to come near to this true deity and to obtain His good will, nothing is required that is fraught with any hardship whatever, the only things needed being love of Him and fear of Him and nothing else.[82]

Maimonides notes that the meaning of the laws became clear to him, and their reasons became known to him, through the study of the Sabian doctrines. On this knowledge of the Sabians, Maimonides' thought converges with that of a possible forerunner, al-Qirqisani.[83] However, where al-Qirqisani rejects the Sabian hypothesis as the misguided assertions of "modern Christian philosophers," Maimonides spins his entire theory of accommodation about it.
Indeed:

> The knowledge of these opinions and practices is a very important chapter in the exposition of the reasons for the commandments. For the foundation of the whole of our Law and the pivot around which it turns, consists in the effacements of these opinions from the minds and of these monuments from existence.[84]

One goal of the Law was obvious; Maimonides tried to explain how the Law strove to achieve that goal.
Maimonides, with the eyes of a physician, treats the divine method of effacing all vestiges of idolatry and commences with medical and biological metaphors. He cites Galen's *De usu partium humani corporis*[85] and posits an organological development of man in order to infer a biological accommodation. Maimonides states:

> If you consider the divine actions—I mean to say the natural actions—the deity's wily graciousness and wisdom, as shown in the creation of living beings, in the graduation of the motions of the limbs, and the proximity of some of the latter to others, will through them become clear to you. Similarly His wisdom and wily graciousness, as shown in the gradual succession of the various states of the whole individual, will become clear to you.[86]

The use of biological accommodation is hardly something original to Maimonides; from Galen onward instances abound.[87] And it is not surprising that, as has been seen, the Antiochene exegetes skillfully incorporated this theme in their writings.[88] The divine, wily graciousness, taking cognizance of human limitations, legislated accordingly:

> Many things in our Law are due to something similar to this very governance on the part of Him Who governs. . . . For a sudden transposition from one opposite to another is impossible. And therefore man, according to his nature, is not capable of abandoning suddenly all to which he was accustomed. . . . and as at that time the way of life generally accepted and customary in the whole world and the universal service upon which we were brought up consisted in offering various species of living beings in the temples in which images were set up, in worshiping the latter and in burning incense before them . . . His wisdom . . . and His gracious ruse . . . did not require that He give us a law prescribing the rejection, abandonment and abolition of all these kinds of worship. For one could no more then conceive the acceptance [of such a law], considering the nature of man, which always likes that to which it is accustomed.[89]

Man cannot change radically, nor switch from one opposite to another; he prefers that to which he is accustomed. Biological development serves as a paradigm for behavioral development. Man, like a fragile reed—to use Nazianzus' metaphor—might break if too drastic a switch were made suddenly.[90] To protect man's fragile nature, change was achieved almost imperceptibly. As Maimonides notes, for man to relinquish sacrifice at that time would have been tantamount to someone in his day urging people to forego prayer for meditation. Sacrifice could not be eliminated at once:

> Therefore, He, may He be exalted, suffered the abovementioned kinds of worship to remain, but transferred them from created or imaginary and unreal thinks to His Own Name . . . commanding us to practice them with regard to Him . . . Thus He commanded us to build a Temple for Him . . . to have an altar for His Name; to have the sacrifice offered up to Him . . . to bow down in worship before Him, and to burn incense before Him. And He forbade the performance of any of these actions with a view to someone else. . . . [91]

The form was kept, but the intentions were transformed. All the appurtenances of idolatry were retained, but the Lord, not idols, was venerated. As Maimonides wrote:

> Through this divine ruse it came about that the memory of idolatry was effaced and that the grandest and true foundation of our belief . . . was firmly established, while at the same time the souls had

no feeling of repugnance and were not repelled because of the abolition of modes of worship to which they were accustomed and than
which no other mode of worship was known at that time.[92]

And so God, by means of accommodation— a divine ruse—eliminated sacrifice. Maimonides goes even further in his interpretation of
sacrifice. Although sacrifice was permitted, the ritual was severely
curtailed. Sounding a theme similar to Christian exegetes—such as
Chrysostom[93] and Aphrahat[94]—Maimonides notes that sacrifices were
limited to a Temple and that temples could not be built in any "fortuitous place" nor by any " fortuitous man." Rather, a priestly hierarchy was established to offer the oblations, and Maimonides notes
trenchantly: "All this was intended to restrict this kind of worship,
so that only the portion of it should subsist whose abolition is not
required by His wisdom."[95]

Maimonides comprehended the difficulty with this explanation.
It is infuriating to contemplate a deity who resorts to ruses to accomplish his goals, and legislates commandments that only cloak his true
intentions. Simply put: Why could God not have dispensed with the
entire pedagogical technique and instilled in man a natural disposition that would not have necessitated the use of ruses or wily graciousness? The Torah and history provided another vantage point
from which to view this problem.

Maimonides recalls Israel's delivery from Egypt and the wandering of the people in the desert. Indeed, when Pharaoh finally let the
people go, God led them, not by way of the Philistines (though it was
near), but roundabout by way of the wilderness of the Red Sea (Exod.
13:17–18). God did this lest the people have a change of heart when,
and if, they experienced battle and would pine to return to Egypt.
Maimonides explicates the reason behind this divine action:

> For just as it is not in the nature of man that, after having been
> brought up in slavish service occupied with clay, bricks and similar
> things, he should all of a sudden wash from his hands the dirt
> deriving from them and proceed immediately to fight against the
> children of Anak [Num. 13:28], so it is not in his nature that, after
> having been brought up upon so very many modes of worship and
> customary practices, which the souls find so agreeable, that . . . he
> should abandon them all of a sudden. And just as the deity used
> a gracious ruse in causing them to wander perplexedly in the desert
> until their souls became courageous . . . so did this group of laws
> derive from a divine grace, so that they should be left with the kind
> of practices to which they were accustomed.[96]

So, in a sense, the historical process, if not history, repeated itself. The biblical example did not answer the question, but raised yet another one: Why did God not lead the Children of Israel through the land of the Philistines and make them capable of waging war?

Maimonides grasped the folly of this question. Certainly, had God desired, the Israelites could have fought the Philistines; however, for them to have done so would have required a radical change in human nature—that is, a miracle. Were God to have changed human nature, he could have implanted in man the natural disposition to incline always toward God's will. This would have obviated the exigency for all ruses. Why then did not God resort to miracles to change human nature? The answer is swift and sure: God does not change human nature by miracles.[97]

Maimonides held that miracles are rare and temporary adjustments of nature intended for a specific purpose. They are not an enduring trespass upon the natural process. For man to change radically, the necessary miracle would have removed man's free will, and the miracle, rather than being a temporary trespass, would have had to become a permanent, natural change.[98] The Lord acted through natural laws to change man; he acted with and not *contra naturam*. His plans were accommodated to existing, contingent circumstances and employed contingent elements within nature to bring about organic change.[99] To have resorted to the miraculous to eradicate idolatry would have been tantamount to a confession of not having established the proper natural parameters at creation. That the Lord could fight polytheism with its own weapons, on its own terms, with its own forms of worship; and transform these weapons, terms, and forms of worship to divine service and fruitful deceit, proves divine omnipotence conclusively: "Sacrifices were conceded with maximal restrictions and changed intents. They are turned into fruitful error."[100]

The explanation offered by Maimonides brings into sharp relief the excruciatingly delicate nature of accommodation. The very fact that no one recognized it for what it was shows the extraordinary triumph accommodation enjoyed. Maimonides postulates a theory that details the original *ratio praeceptorum,* while demonstrating its success by the fact that it was so totally forgotten. Not only was idolatry and its method effaced, but the very method by which this was achieved went undetected. Since the entire world in Maimonides' time was monotheistic, or so he believed, no greater proof could be adduced for his theorem. "The fact that the reasons for certain commandments were forgotten is in itself a testimony to the success of the divine 'cunning' or pedagogy."[101]

162   *The Footprints of God*

Yet, did this entire philosophical excursus serve any other function than merely to provide intellectual exercise to its author and readers or was it just another application of the exegetical principle of accommodation? The Christian attack on the Law as a burden was being echoed in the world of Islam in Maimonides' own day.[102] Maimonides' description of these ancient pagan practices showed conclusively what a burden they were. God mercifully sought "to efface this error from our minds and to take away fatigue from our bodies through the abolition of these tiring and useless practices and to give us laws through the instrumentality of Moses our Master."[103] Those things, which one might consider unpleasant or burdensome, appear so only because we "do not know the usages and teachings that existed in those days."[104] Maimonides, after showing the futility of past paganism, gives his opinion quite candidly: "For I for one do not doubt that all this was intended to efface those untrue opinions from the mind and to abolish those useless practices, which brought about a waste of lives."[105]

Pagan practices were a great burden imposed upon humanity. They tired the body and wasted men's lives. Thus, "most of the commandments serve . . . to lighten the great and oppressive burdens, the toil and the fatigue, that those people imposed upon themselves in their cult."[106] Paganism had no purpose. Judaism does:

> As for those who deem its burdens grievous, heavy, and difficult to bear—all of this is due to an error in considering them. I shall explain later on how easy they are in true reality, according to the opinion of the perfect. . . . everyone who is deficient in any respect considers that a hindrance in the way of the vice that he prefers because of his moral corruption is a great burden. Accordingly the facility or difficulty of the law should not be estimated with reference to the passions of all the wicked, vile, morally corrupt men, but should be considered with reference to the man who is perfect among the people. For it is the aim of the Law that everyone should be such a man.[107]

The Law is not a burden. And given the goal of the Law, its means for achieving perfection are far from onerous.[108] Perfection demands its price, and considering the reward, the price is quite reasonable. Further, as Twersky suggests, Maimonides' approach attempted to bridge the gap between the traditionalist and the philosopher. The call to action could be harmonized with the plea to contemplation.[109]

This is an attempt to harmonize Maimonides' philosophical tendencies with his traditional religious ones, an issue that began in Maimonides' own time and continues almost unabated in our time.[110]

For example, it is reflected in the reactions of Naḥmanides (R. Moses ben Naḥman, 1195–c. 1270), who attacked the Maimonidean position in his commentary on Leviticus 1:9,[111] where Naḥmanides repeated the arguments advanced by Maimonides concerning the origin and institution of sacrifice. Naḥmanides mentions that the biblical sacrifices consisted of the same species—the herd, flock, and goats—used by idolators and wonders how mimicry of this sort would eliminate sacrifice. Not to be outdone, Naḥmanides, in his effort to refute Maimonides, uses the Maimonidean method, that is, an appeal to history.

Naḥmanides urges his reader to consider Noah's actions upon emerging from the ark: Noah brought an offering that was pleasing before the Lord. Why, wonders Naḥmanides, did Noah sacrifice when there was neither one Sabian nor one Egyptian in the whole world? How could anyone attribute sacrifice to them? He expressed himself clearly and minced no words:

> The Rabbi [Maimonides] wrote in the *Guide* that the reason for the sacrifices is because the Egyptians and the Chaldeans ... always used to worship the herd and the flock. These are his words, and he expounded them lengthily. They are utter nonsense. ... God forbid that these rituals should have no other purpose and intention, save the elimination of idolatrous opinions from the minds of fools.[112]

This clash prompted the Ritba (R. Yom Tob ben Abraham Ishbili, d. c. 1360)[113] to pen his *Sefer HaZikaron*, which encapsulates the opinions exchanged between the proponents and opponents of the Maimonidean position. Maimonides' supporters never claimed infallibility for his words; his opponents claimed the theory definitive as posited. The Ritba was a proponent of the Maimonidean position and could say only that Naḥmanides did not fully comprehend the entire Maimonidean position.[114]

The dispute between these two towering figures of Jewish scholarship raises more fundamental problems than differences of personality and temperament. Certainly, Maimonides' own works raise critical problems, even though one is tempted to be drawn into the discussion over the unity or duality of Maimonides' thought, we shall resist that temptation.[115] However, a few words are necessary to explain some of the larger issues.

The problems with Maimonides arise from seeming contradictions in his writings.[116] For example, why did Maimonides incorporate repentance—*teshuvah*—as a chapter of his *Mishneh Torah*, while not listing it among the 613 commandments in his *Book of Com-*

mandments? Unlike repentance, sacrifice is a biblically mandated law— *d'oraita*—which no Halachist could ever imagine changing. And one might well ask why did he deal with sacrifice when many other Halachists ignored the issue? This ultimately goes back to Rambam's view of humanity, and the belief that the "mob" needs laws to restrain them, especially from relapsing into idolatry.

For the most part, other Halachists condensed issues debated in only four orders of the Mishnah and excluded discussion of those legal issues—*Kodashim* and *Tohorot*—that for practical reasons do not obtain in the post-Temple and premessianic era. Not that other Halachists voiced negative opinions about the resumption of sacrifice; they simply avoided the discussion since sacrifices were irrelevant until the messianic redemption. Maimonides' two chief works, the *Guide* and the *Mishneh Torah* do not agree on the matter of sacrifice either; the latter offers no hint or trace of the *Guide*'s historical explanation for sacrifice. This is usually interpreted as originating in the different purposes, different audiences, and purposes of each book.[117] The *Guide* was a philosophical work, the *Mishneh Torah,* a legal work. Yet it is perhaps curious that his law collection, which aimed to be comprehensive, including laws not part of the curriculum of his time, does not end with an eye toward the practical needs of his readers, be they judges or laymen.

One might ask an additional question: What was Maimonides' attitude toward sacrifice in messianic times? Again there seems to be no unambiguous answer. He seems to have left the issue open to future leaders, especially those who would have to face the messianic advent. Since Maimonides insisted that the nature of the world would not change in messianic times, but that it would simply become a better place in which to live because civilization would improve, one might assume that in this advanced world people might not need sacrifices. Yet, always suspicious of the masses, Maimonides believed that laws of the Torah, including those of sacrifice, were eternal because the chance of people becoming idolators was eternal.

The list of Jewish opponents and adherents of divine accommodation is a long and distinguished one, and to peruse that list would take us far afield. However, a few views ought to be considered. One of the earliest discussions of the Maimonidean position occurs in David Kimhi of Narbonne's (1160–1235) commentary to Jeremiah 7:22, where he notes that "perhaps" Maimonides offered the proper interpretation.[118] Another early appearance of the Maimonidean position occurs in Sa'ad Ibn Mansur Ibn Kammuna's (1215–85) *Examination of Three Faiths*.[119] What is of interest, besides Ibn Kammuna's polite objection to Maimonides, is his discussion of the Nabatean Agriculture and the fact that Maimonides' opinions were well known, within a brief span of time, to Ibn Kammuna in Baghdad.

Gersonides (Levi ben Gerson, 1288–1334), the Ralbag,[120] an important critic of Maimonides, rejects Maimonides historical anthropology and educational psychology as applied to sacrifices. Unlike Maimonides, who saw sacrifices as commandments of second intention, for Ralbag they are of primary intention. Sacrifices were commanded to help establish prophecy. Ralbag conveys his opinions of Maimonides' interpretation of sacrifices in his exegesis of the story of Noah:

> The *Rav Ha-Moreh* [Maimonides] explained the sacrifices commanded in the Torah as secondary intentions, not as intended in themselves. . . . But if this were so, why were the prophets stimulated to build altars and to offer sacrifices, as we have found in the case of Noah, Abraham, Isaac, Jacob and Moses? . . . Now we claim that sacrifices have not only a secondary purpose but a primary purpose as well. . . . Concerning the latter, I believe that some of the sacrifices were intended as instruments of the reception of prophecy. . . . Thus, Balaam said to Balak after the latter had built the altars and offered up the cow and ram, "Stand here by the sacrifices, but I will go on and perhaps God will meet me" (Num. 23:3). . . . Thus, it is clear from these cases [including Noah and the patriarchs] that sacrifices have something to do with prophecy.[121]

Echoing Nahmanides' claim that sacrifices predate Israel's sojourn in Egypt and that God found them pleasing on those occasions, Gersonides rejects out of hand Maimonides' anthropological interpretation. Sacrifices, in and of themselves provide a context for prophecy.

Gersonides supplies the link between sacrifices and prophecy, even though some prophetic utterances (Isa. 1:11–17 and Amos 5:21–25) seem to refute this claim:

> It has been explained in Book Two of *The Wars* that prophecy requires the isolation of the intellect from all other faculties of the soul. Hence, prophecy will not be attained unless the activities of these other faculties are suppressed. Thus, it is necessary for the prophet, when he wants to prophesy, to stimulate his intellect and to suppress his other powers. One finds, therefore, that prophets used to perform certain actions to bring about prophecy, as was the case with Elisha . . . [II Kings 3:15 ff., 4:33–34]. Now the practice of sacrifices stirs up the intellect and suppresses the sensitive powers. For when the animal is slaughtered, dissected and burned . . . the

sensitive powers . . . are humiliated and suppressed by the destruction of their sensible objects [i.e., the animal] . . . a person then says
to himself that destruction is the end of all sensible and lower
things [i.e., bodies], and thus the animalic soul is humiliated and
its power suppressed.[122]

As certain types of acts are necessary for mystical contemplation, so
are certain acts helpful for prophecy. Sacrifices help isolate the intellect and better facilitate the mantic art. The immolation of the animal is equated with the dominance of form over matter—the intellect
over the body. Sacrifices were not an accommodation to puerile Israel,
but a vehicle to accomplish prophecy.

Ralbag's contemporary Joseph ibn Kaspi (1279–1349), was disap-
pointed in the inability of Maimonides' students to penetrate the
Guide, but he did profit from Maimonides' observations of Mediterra-
nean culture which he applied to his own biblical studies.[123] Ibn Kaspi
approached Maimonides' explication of sacrifice in his discussion of
the attempted sacrifice of Isaac. Unlike Ralbag, ibn Kaspi argues that
the patriarchs were never *commanded* to offer sacrifices and that
neither the patriarchs nor Moses offered sacrifices. Sacrifices are described as smelling sweet simply for the benefit of the masses.[124]
Sacrifices in ibn Kaspi's opinion are an "abomination" (*davar nitav*)
on the way toward truth. The masses should not be told this, although sacrifices help maintain the community, especially since they
think that sacrifice is truly desired by God![125] He echoes Maimonides'
claim that prayer is superior to sacrifice, but that meditation would
be preferable to prayer.[126] He then posits that Judaism does allow
sacrifice when directed to the Lord, and Moses' narration demonstrates "truth to us individuals, and coarse knowledge to the masses,
teaching them how to act in relation to God."[127] Of course, those who
know better, will know better, and the masses will offer sacrifice
thinking God desires them. He concludes: "It is clear, for those who
can see, that from the way in which sacrifices are described in the
Torah, they were [permitted] only by way of necessity [*ones uletachlit*],
for the reason mentioned by Maimonides."[128] This is buttressed by
appeal to Jeremiah's description of child sacrifice to Moloch and Baal
(Jer. 7:31, 19:5), and the biblical narrative of the binding of Isaac.

Isaac Arama,[129] the fifteenth-century philosopher and exegete, objected to Maimonides' ideas in his exegetical opus, *Akedat Yitzhak*;
while his contemporary Don Isaac Abrabanel (1437–1508) warmly
supported the Maimonidean position. Abrabanel reiterates the
Maimonidean position[130] and concludes with the Midrashic parable

transmitted in the name of R. Pinhas ben Levi.[131] For Abrabanel, this Midrash proved conclusively that the position advanced in the *Guide* was perfectly consistent with the sages of blessed memory.

With the fourteenth and fifteenth centuries, the debate over Maimonides and his concepts continued apace. The shock waves generated by the calamitous upheaval spread far and wide from the epicenter before being spent. In the process, the course of Jewish intellectual development was altered unequivocally. The forces marshaled on both sides fought a bitter and divisive battle; a Pyrrhic victory was the most either could have attained.[132]

Maimonides' use of divine accommodation as an explanation for sacrifice had repercussions in Christian writings, and he may also have known of al-Qirqisani's work. We may speculate but not prove. Yet, in his hands, divine accommodation emerged from the shadows and was catapulted to the cutting edge of Jewish learning. Divine accommodation, as integrated into Maimonides' oeuvre, received a suppleness and pliancy that permitted it to serve as a tool in historical inquiry, to elucidate biblical abstruseness, and to wage polemical warfare.

If Maimonides' utilization of accommodation represented its apogee in Jewish philosophical circles, such a malleable and supple heuristic device was not overlooked in Jewish mystical circles.[133] In Jewish sources of the era of the *Zohar*, a discussion of the divine realm (that is, the world of the Sefirot) in Azriel of Gerona's *Commentary on Talmudic Aggadot* differentiates among *hokhmah, tebunah* and *da'at*, and states: *ve-ain shinnui ha-shemot ella lefi shinnui ha-hassagot.*[134] This may echo Sa'adia Gaon's description of God and his attributes of life, power, and wisdom as one derived "by means of our faculty of ratiocination."[135] Indeed, as Sa'adia writes of the divine attributes:

> Now these three aspects of God, which occur to our Reason in combination, cannot be expressed by one single word in our language. For we do not find a word in language which covers all these three aspects. We must needs express them by three different words, but it should be well understood that Reason conceived them as one single idea. Let nobody assume that the Eternal (blessed be He) contains a plurality of attributes. For all the attributes which we assign to Him are implied in the one attribute of Creator, and it is merely the deficiency of our language which makes it necessary for us to express our notion of God in three different words, since there exists no word in our vocabulary which covers all the three aspects.[136]

Sa'adia continues this line of argument by asserting that any newly minted term used to describe these three concepts in one word would serve no purpose at all, but merely lead to greater confusion. Such confusion would arise because humans might think that any term that implies a diversity of attributes within God might imply diversity within God. Creatures, not the creator, are subject to diversity and change.[137] Of course, Azriel's observation and Sa'adia's type of disclaimer permit manifold interpretations according to human perceptions while preserving the divine unity. This is accomplished quite handily by the accommodation of the Sefirot themselves to human nature.[138]

In several striking passages, the *Zohar* incorporates accommodation in its mystical exegesis. Indeed, in trying to explain the seeming differentiations and fluctuations within the divine realm, the *Zohar* explains: *kulei hai lo iskerai, eleh mi-sitra di-lan.*[139] There are changes only from our perspective *(mi-sitra di-lan);* the message does not change, but its reception and perception are responsible for any seeming change. Since these changes occur only from our perspective, accommodation may be invoked to explain other seeming differences and fluctuations.[140]

One such mystery is that of divine revelation within Torah, or in the form of the Torah, accommodating itself to our world so that we may comprehend it from our particular point of view *(mi-sitra di-lan).* Another arises from standard Gnostic reading of texts—including the New Testament—which maintains that Gnostics, due to superior insight, gain more from any texts than mere mortals, and thus we learn that the *mekubbalim,* since they are on a different spiritual and intellectual level than mere mortals, gain more from Torah than mere mortals. What is of interest in the examples that follow is that all have parallels in Christian writings, and the attention of both Jews and Christians to this aspect of divine revelation merits our scrutiny as a phenomenon within the study of religions.

In a parable of an old man and a beautiful maiden, the *Zohar* presents revelation as an accommodation to humanity. The Torah reveals herself, little by little, to no one but her lover:[141]

> At first when she begins to reveal herself to a human she first beckons him with a hint. If he knows, good; if not, she sends him a message, calling him a fool. Torah says to her messenger: "Tell that fool to come closer, so I can talk with him!" as it is written: "Who is the fool without a heart? Have him turn in here!" (Prov. 9:4) He approaches. She begins to speak with him from behind a curtain

she has drawn, words she can follow, until he reflects a little at a time. This is *derasha*. Then she converses with him through a veil, words riddled with allegory. This is *haggadah*. Once he has grown accustomed to her, she revelas herself face to face and tells him all her hidden secrets, all the hidden ways since primordial days secreted in her heart. Now he is a perfect human being, husband of Torah, master of the house. All her secrets she has revealed to him, withholding nothing, concealing nothing. She says to him, "Do you see that word, that hint with which I beckoned you at first? So many secrets there! This one and that one!" Now he sees that nothing should be added to those words and nothing taken away. Now the *peshat* of the verse. Just like it is! Not even a single letter should be added or deleted. Human beings must become aware! They must pursue Torah to become her lovers! . . .

The text presents the Torah's strategy for revelation. She reveals only her face to her lover, beckoning him with a hint. She speaks to him in comprehensible language, giving him time to think. Then she proceeds from the *derash* to the allegory *(millin de-hida)*, and finally teaches him mystical truths. Ironically, the *peshat* is seen as the highest revelation containing all truths, even though various layers may be turned back. The lover is, in this way, returned to the text by way of educational revelation.[142]

If the Torah accommodates her manner of teaching to the human level, she also does so with her very being; that is her hypostatization within the world. Indeed, as R. Shim'on exlaimed:

Woe to the human being who says that Torah presents mere stories and ordinary words *(millin de-hedyotei)*! If so, we could compose a Torah right now with ordinary words and better than all of them. To present matters of the world? Even rulers of the world possess words more sublime. If so, let us follow them and make a Torah out of them! Ah, but all the words of Torah are sublime words, sublime secrets! Come and see: The world above and the world below are perfectly balanced: Israel below, the angels above. Of the angels it is written: "He makes His angels spirits" (Ps. 104:4). But when they descend *(de-naḥtin letata)*, they put on the garment of this world *(bilvusha de-hai alma)*. If they did not put on the garment of this world they could not endure in this world and the world could not endure them. If this is so with the angels how much more so with Torah who created them and all the worlds and for whose sake they all exist! In descending to this world, if she did not put on the garments of this world the world could not endure. So this story of Torah is the garment of Torah.[143]

Were the Torah merely stories, humans could write a better Torah than the one they possess, but the true Torah is much more sublime. In applying the theory of accommodation to angels, the *Zohar* insists that those angels who visited Abraham did so in the flesh, in the garments of this world. They could not have endured this world were they not properly equipped, and the world could not have endured their luminescence. All the more so with the Torah, whose unbearable brilliance had to be accommodated to the physical limitations of this world. Without any condescension being made to the realities of physical existence, the Torah could not endure in this world, and perhaps more importantly, this world could not bear the Torah.

The *Zohar* continues this metaphor when discussing the high priest's garments:

> Observe that man's soul does not ascend to appear before the Holy King unless it is worthy first to be dressed in the supernal raiment. Likewise, the soul does not descend into this world [*naḥta letata*] until clad in the garments of this world. Similarly, the holy heavenly angels, [of whom it is written, "Who makest thy angels into winds and thy ministers into flaming fire" (Ps. 104:4)] when they have to execute a message in this world do not come down to it before they clothe themselves in the garments of this world. The attire thus has always to be in harmony with the place visited. . . .[144]

That is why Adam wore garments of celestial radiancy in Eden but changed garments of *or* (light) for garments of *'or* (skin).[145] Indeed, the attire must always be proper for the place visited, and mankind, at least in this world, wears earthly, rather than celestial, clothing.[146]

If angels and the Torah have been accommodated to the physical realities of this world, humans must therefore be able to comprehend and interpret the Torah, even if on different levels, for the accommodated Torah makes its own accommodations to its readers. The *Zohar* suggests that anyone who confuses the garment of the Torah with the real Torah will have no share in the world to come.[147] The reader receives the information of which he is capable, according to his ability and capacity, which is conditioned by knowledge and preparation:

> Come and see: There is a garment visible to all. When those fools see someone in a good-looking garment they look no further. But the essence of the garment is the body; the essence of the body is the soul. So it is with Torah. She has a body: the commandments of Torah called *gufei torah*.[148]

The commandments are the body of Torah, and one needs distinguish between the stories of the Torah and its inner essence. That ability depends upon individual capacities, and those capacities are accommodated by the Torah:

> This Body is clothed in garments: the stories of this world. Fools of the world look only at that garment, the story of Torah; they know nothing more. They do not look at what is under the garment. Those who do know more do not look at the garment but rather at the body under the garment. The wise ones, servants of the King on High, those who stood at Mt. Sinai look only at the soul, root of all, real Torah![149]

In an idiom common to other religious systems, Scripture is compared to human beings who consist of body, soul, and spirit.[150] It is of course the fools of the world who see only the garments of Torah; the more educated concentrate on the body—the *mitzvot*—while only the mystic perceives the *oraita mammash,* the real Torah. There is of course but one Torah, whose teachings operate on many levels, each level accommodated to different readers. The matter is presented with striking clarity; the Torah does not change, but each person receives only that which he is capable of receiving.

The different levels of meaning contained in the *Zohar* that are visible to the fool, the more educated, and the kabbalist find further expression in a parable offered in its commentary on Exodus 27:17:

> There was a man who lived in the mountains. He knew nothing about those who lived in the city. He sowed wheat and ate the kernels raw. One day he entered the city. They brought him good bread. He said, "What is this for?" They said, "Bread, to eat!" He ate, and it tasted very good. He said, "What is it made of?" They said, "Wheat." Later they brought him cakes kneaded in oil. He tasted them and said, "And what are these made of?" They said, "Wheat." Finally they brought him royal pastry made with honey and oil. He said, "And what are these made of?" They said, "Wheat." He said, "I am the master of all these, for I eat the essence of all these: wheat!" Because of that view, he knew nothing of the delights of the world; they were lost to him. So it is with one who grasps the principle and does not know all those delectable delights deriving, diverging from that principle.[151]

Fools of the world may look only at the outer garment or know only of wheat. The text of course criticizes one who claims omniscience by concentrating on only the wheat, while losing out on richer, more varied, and delicious products.

As we have seen thus far, the *Zohar* employs accommodation to explain the differences that obtain between the kabbalistic and nonkabbalistic reading of Scripture; between the Torah's accommodation to the physical world and its accommodated method of revelation as well as the accommodation of angels to this world. It does all of this without denying divine unity, while discoursing about differentiation within that unity.

The seemingly divine multiformity was an issue that, as we have seen, was discussed by Sa'adia in terms of the linguistic limitations of human speech. Such limitations did not obtain among kabbalists, who sought to explain the seeming multiformity of the divine in two basic ways: The first focused upon the manner of revelation through instruments or tools of God *(kelim)*, which, in fact, could be seen as the manner in which the divine could "stoop" to humanity. This emphasis upon divine tools enabled divinity to communicate with humanity and implied no change in the divinity. The second approach focused upon the nature of the essence of God *(atzmut)* and debated the Midrashic contention of accommodation. That is, the history of accommodation would bifurcate on the issue of essence *(atzmut)* and tools *(kelim)*.[152]

One more aspect of this theory needs to be discussed, what Gershom Scholem called the "relativization" of Torah.[153] The theory of relativization as set forth in the *Sefer ha-Temunah* maintains that in a series of successive creations, each governed by one of the seven lower *sefirot,* God's creative power is exerted and governed by that particular *sefirah.* Each creation is governed by one of God's attributes, and only in the totality of *shemmitoth* will the total creative power of God be revealed. Thus, in each successive *shemmitah,* the Torah is manifested in a manner determined by the individual *sefirah* and unique to that particular *shemmitah.* "In other words: in every *shemmitah* men will read something entirely different in the Torah, because in each one the divine wisdom of the primordial Torah appears under a different aspect."[154] In this series of cycles, the nature of creatures changes, and what in one age applies to angels may in another obtain among humans. Scholem wrote of the changes in concept in pre- and post-Sabbatian kabbalah, of shifts between the *torah de-beriah* and the *torah de-atzilut,* and the similarities to the ideas described by the Calabrian abbot Joachim of Fiore.[155]

The whole issue of the relativization of Torah, regardless of its striking similarity to Joachimite ideas, seems to fit very well with earliest Christian views of Judaism in general. That is, from the earliest writings stamped with the *auctoritas patrorum antiquorum,* it is quite evident that Christianity relativized the Torah of Moses. For Christian exegetes, the scriptural stories may have been true, the garments may have been fine, but they no longer told spiritual truths nor suited a new age. And just as the kabbalists could argue for different Torot for different *shemmitoth,* so could and did Christianity argue for a different Torah. It was, as we have seen, the twelfth-century scholar Anselm of Havelberg who, observing the plurality of religious orders within Christendom, noted:

> This variety [*varietas*] (of religious practice) is explained not on account of the mutability of an immutable God [*non propter invariabilis Dei . . . mutabilitatem*] who is "always the same and whose years shall have no end" (Ps.101:28), but on account of human infirmity, which is mutable [*propter humani generis variabilem mutabilitatem*], and on account of the temporal changes from age to age.[156]

It is perhaps no accident that as Christianity saw changes within its uniformity, especially with the struggle of Reformation, that new varieties of religious expression had to be explained in order to legitimize them. Just as Jewish mystics would argue over the idea of *shemmitoth* and the Torah that governed each *shemmitah,* it was Christian reformers who had to explain and defend new forms of Christianity. As we shall see, the task was handled best perhaps by Calvin, who, echoing Anselm of Havelberg, produced a strikingly familiar argument:

> . . . God ought not to be considered changeable merely because he accommodated diverse forms to different ages, as he knew would be expedient for each. If a farmer sets certain tasks for his household in the winter, other tasks for the summer, we shall not on this account, accuse him of inconstancy, or think that he departs from the proper rule of agriculture, which accords with the continuous order of nature. In like manner, if a householder instructs, rules and guides his children one way in infancy, another in youth, and still another in his young manhood, we shall not on this account call him fickle and say he abandons his purpose. Why, then, do we brand God with the mark of inconstancy because he has with apt and fitting marks distinguished a diversity of times? Paul likens the Jews to children, Christians to young men [Gal. 4:1ff]. What was irregular about the fact that God confined them to rudimentary teaching commensurate with their age, but has trained us through a firmer and, so to speak, more manly discipline? Thus, God's constancy shines forth in the fact that he taught the same doctrine to

all ages, and has continued to require the same worship of his name that he has enjoined from the beginning. In the fact that he has changed the outward form and manner, he does not show himself subject to change. Rather, he has accommodated himself to men's capacity, which is varied and changeable.[157]

What does emerge clearly from this examination of accommodation in various Jewish mystical sources is that the exegetical device of accommodation was among the traditional elements employed in various Jewish sources including the *Zohar.* It was perhaps R. Menahem Mendel of Kotzk who understood our subject very well when he noted that a man receives a heavenly gift the way he prepares himself to receive it[158] and that *Shavuot*—the Feast of Weeks/Pentecost—was termed *zeman mattan torah* and not *zeman mekabbel torah* because Torah is given equally to everyone, but each sees in it what he is.[159]

Thus, accommodation served as a powerful tool in diverse hands; Karaites and Rabbanites, philosophers and mystics. As a potent interpretive device, it gave Mamonides a tool to examine and explain divine legislation; it permitted mystics to speak with certainty about uncertainties, and admirably served mystical gnosticism. As an overwhelmingly successfully employed exegetical device, it had a brilliant philosophical career that ended in the Maimonidean controversy.

The educational aspects of accommodation, which were richly exploited by Calvin and others, enjoyed a fascinating career in Jewish mystical sources as well. The *Zohar,* after a lengthy discussion on the issue of the evil inclination, offers the following:

This is a parable to a king, who had an only son whom he loved exceedingly, and for that reason warned him not to be lured by bad women, saying that anyone defiled might not enter the king's palace. The son agreed to follow his father's will in matters of love. Outside the palace, however, there lived a beautiful harlot. After some time, the king said: "I will see how much my son is devoted to me." So he summoned the harlot and commanded her, saying: "Entice my son, for I wish to test his obedience to me." So she used all her wiles to lure him into her embraces. But the son, being obedient, obeyed his father's command. He refused her and rejected her. Then the father rejoiced greatly, and bringing his son into the innermost chambers of the palace, gave him the rarest of gifts and showered him with honors. And who was responsible for such joy? The harlot! Is she to be praised or blamed? Surely to be praised on all accounts, for on the one hand she obeyed the king's command and fulfilled his plans, and on the other hand she caused the son to receive gifts and deepened the mutual love between father and son.

Therefore it is written: "And the Lord saw all that He had made, and behold it was very good."[160]

Of course, this parable is based on Proverbs 7 and is a riveting example of the seductive element as an educational means in Jewish mystical thought. It would reappear in a different version in the eighteenth century in the *Ben Porat Yosef* of Jacob Joseph of Polonnoye, the faithful disciple of the Ba'al Shem Tov. As R. Jacob Joseph told the tale:

> I heard from my teacher . . . a story of a king who had a son and wanted him to be taught several types of sciences which are relevant for him, and he hired some scholars who would study with him, but the son could not succeed to fathom any science, so that they lost hope in teaching him. One scholar remained with him, and once the king's son saw a certain virgin, and coveted [*hamad*] her beauty. The scholar complained to the king about this matter, and the king answered that if his son has this lust [*hemdah*] through the physical or material he will achieve mastery [*yavo*] over all the sciences. The king ordered the virgin brought to his court, and ordered her, if the prince demands her,[161] she will not obey him until he masters [*yekabbel*] one science. She did so, and then said that he should study yet another science, so, that he learned all the sciences. When he thus became a scholar he despised the virgin and he will want to marry a king's daughter like himself.[162]

A gifted homilist, R. Jacob Joseph, added his own interpretation to the story of the virgin:

> By the evil eye which the king's son had, it made him see the beauty of virgins. He mastered all the sciences and virtues and destroyed nature. Then the evil eye which is from the side of the evil impulse became a chair for the holy and from the evil impulse was made the good impulse. In truth all of this was from the scholar who is the king and who knew the end of a thing from its beginning, which is characteristic of *hakham ha-roeh et ha-nolad.* . . .[163]

Of course, we should note how outrageous it is to employ sexual intercourse as an educational device, especially since the union of two unmarried people, if not for the sake of marriage, is prostitution. Indeed, one of the most common ancient ways of establishing marriage was by means of the sexual act.[164]

The original version of this story in Proverbs and its use in the *Zohar* emphasize the element of seduction, but abstain from introducing sexual intercourse into the narrative. It is the Hasidic tale that makes sexual intercourse part of the pedagogical curriculum, without, however, identifying the religion of either the king or the virgin, thus invalidating the rabbinic prescriptions mentioned above. The tale is an example of different means by which one could devote oneself to God, although the attitude toward and treatment of the virgin in the Hasidic version of the story are unacceptable and unforgivable. Yet it is the woman who is destined to cultivate and unearth the great wisdom of humanity, regardless of the price she must pay or the mistreatment she must suffer.

Accommodation as an educational device reappears in Dov Baer's—the Maggid of Mezhirech—*Likkutei Amarim (Maggid Devarav La-Ya'akov).*[165] Dov Baer invokes the same verse as did Bahya, Hosea 11:1, "When Israel was a child, then I loved him," together with Midrashic parallels to analogize divine and human actions. As the Lord loved the child Israel, so must a father act when playing with his own offspring. The father must lower his intellectual level *(tzimtzaym sikhlo)* and sophistication, as well as speak on the child's level for both to reap the maximum enjoyment.[166] Of course, Dov Baer employed the metaphor to apply to a model of a human father teaching his child, or a rebbe teaching his Hasidim. He applied a mystical concept to human psychology; for just as we have seen the Midrash anthropomorphized divinity reducing itself between the staves of the Ark for the sake of the children of Israel, so the rebbe—or father— reduces himself for his Hasidim—or children.

The powerful metaphor of the divine teacher stooping to aid his pupils is perhaps the lengthiest and most vibrant example of accommodation's many uses. Never, save perhaps for Maimonides' historical-anthropological reconstruction of nascent Israel's environment, was accommodation invoked without recourse to traditional sources. From the Midrash to Maimonides and the Maggid of Mezhirech is a long time and way. Only divine accommodation appears irrefutably in such diverse literary genres, and as such, it should be recognized as an enthralling literary, philosophical, mystical, historical, and pedagogical motif and principle in Jewish sources for almost two millennia.

CHAPTER SEVEN

THE SCHOOL OF THE HOLY SPIRIT

Wherefore I gave them also statutes that were not good, and
judgements whereby they should not live.

—Ezekiel 20:25

While Maimonides' historical interpretation of biblical ritual may
not have received unanimous and cordial acclaim within the Jewish
world, it would not go away, and it could not be ignored.[1] It was the
high-water mark of medieval Jewish philosophy, and its philosophical
waters overran the Jewish banks, only to water neighboring fields.
Alexander of Hales, William of Auvergne, and Thomas Aquinas received some of the overflow. Thomas was to put it to profitable use.[2]
In this chapter, we shall consider briefly William of Auvergne and
Thomas Aquinas, before crossing the divide between medieval and
Reformation thought. We shall tackle the use of accommodation in
late medieval and Reformation thinkers, especially Calvin, and see
how biblical exegesis became intertwined with the rise of "modern
science."[3]

The scholastics, heirs to the Latin patristic tradition, stressed, as
did their forebears, the links between the two testaments. Allegorical,
anagogical, and tropological interpretations could be adduced, or found,
for almost any situation; Scripture was a renewable resource. A late
twelfth-century anonymous writer, a priest or canon of Troyes, expressed the relationship in an accurate, if rather coarse, metaphor:
the "letter" of Scripture was "a harlot [*meretrix*], open to any sense
whatsoever."[4]

What the masters of the sacred page of Scripture accepted generally as true was that the precepts commanded in the Mosaic Code
conveyed a literal truth. Their point of departure was a text attributed to Augustine, but whose origin has defied more modern attempts
at attribution. The fact simply was: "The Law was given as a sign to
the perfect, as a burden and scourge to the forward, as tutor to the
simple and sucklings."[5]

177

This reading safeguarded allegorical interpretations, continued the penal interpretation favored by some church fathers, and maintained the ideas adumbrated in Galatians, that the law was a pedagogue in Christ. Additionally, discussion among theologians of the thirteenth century focused, as had earlier debate, on the role of legal enactments—the *legalia*—of the Law. These theologians, perhaps under the cloud of the Cathari, who echoed the Marcionite rejection of the Hebrew scriptures, stressed the divine origin of Scripture and all within it. This wholesale attack on the Mosaic Code in general must have forced Catholic thinkers to ponder the efficacy—conveyed to the Jews in the literal sense—of God's commands. It is of course not surprising that Maimonides' *Guide*, with its rationalistic explanation of biblical law, especially sacrifice, found an eager and receptive audience in its Latin translation.

If some Jewish exegetes attacked Maimomides because he never explained why the Law—or certain parts of it— should have retained value after fulfilling its historical mission, Christian exegetes were all too avid to supply an answer. The ceremonial precepts were simply historically necessary for a particular period in history that was now passé.

Just as Gnostics insisted they had a special gnosis that enabled them to penetrate and perceive more than the "common folk," so could the Maimonidean position foster the idea that scholars could understand more than the "common folk." If medieval scholars believed that Scripture contained all truth—all science and metaphysics—then certainly those areas were the province of the elite, not the masses. Even rabbinic tradition reserved to the few those areas—the matter of creation and the matter of the chariot (*ma'ase bereshit* and *ma'ase merkavah*). What the *Guide* seemed to advocate, at least to its Christian readers, was a hierarchy not only of knowledge, but of the divine sciences as well. Maimonides' well-known comment about meditation replacing prayers in his time being equivalent to prayer replacing sacrifices in earlier times, quite adequately suggests his position. The theory of accommodation posited by Maimonides in the *Guide* not only conformed to his entire intellectual outlook, but Christians could make it conform to their tradition:

> His belief in a hierarchy of wisdom corresponded to the Christian teaching that the elite of the Old Testament already belonged to the New, in that they perceived the prefiguration of the Gospel in *legalia*. Hence the *Guide* accorded with Christian tradition in presenting the Law as wholesome for all, sufficient for the people, and a mine of deeper wisdom for the elite.[6]

Perhaps it was William of Auvergne who most fully brought the *Guide* into Christian circles. William became bishop of Paris in 1228 after Gregory IX settled a disputed election, and he remained in that position until his death, in 1249. Disputations with Jews, the burning of the Talmud in Paris in 1240, in which William took a hand, Muslim advances in the Near East and Spain no doubt colored his view of religion. William displays an inquisitive attitude toward other faiths. His study of the *Guide* and its influence upon him is well known. Indeed, a recent student of the issue has written: "William made the *Guide* his own."[7] And William adopted as his own Maimonides' assertion that such *legalia* as sacrifices were prophylactic devices to wean Israel away from idolatry.[8] William follows, though not blindly, in Maimonides' steps.

William's interpretation of the Law concludes with what amounts to a manifesto of historically conditioned accommodation. William asserts that seemingly absurd precepts must have had reasonable and just causes that necessitate a literal interpretation. They were imposed upon a simple people (*populi ruditas*) who needed to be weaned from idolatry; the time required them (*quod tempus . . . requirebant*).[9] William's argument on behalf of accommodation did not end in the past, but it continued to his own day. He maintains that similar bans exist "even among us" (*etiam nos extant*) to ward off superstitious practices that smack of Judaism and "Saracenism." Little wonder then that Scripture contained the prohibitions it did, considering that primitive people existed in a world nurtured on ubiquitous idolatry.[10] For William, the Law was honest and did not violate natural law. It revealed partially the eternal truths of the Gospel and served as a preparation for the final complete dispensation of truth.[11] Indeed, the Mosaic Code was proper for its time and place; it did not contradict nature, and it had been put into writing. As William observed:

> The whole Law contains nothing which lacks a rational cause for commanding, forbidding or narrating. There is nothing absurd or irrational in it, and this appears clearly in many items which have obvious worth and usefulness.[12]

William seems to follow in Maimonides' wake when he suggests that the Lord gave so many precepts because the Children of Israel, like all children, could not understand generalizations and needed detailed specific instructions. Further, William believes that they required piecemeal instruction just as children need to have their bread cut into small pieces before they can eat it. This metaphor was a common one to express divine accommodation and was often used with apples, which had to be cut up because children have small mouths and tender teeth. In fact, the multiplicity of commands and prohibitions would certainly keep the Jews engrossed with their study.[13] The Law would truly keep the Jews occupied and away from "Greek wisdom," to use the rabbinic idiom.

Indeed, William suggests that when the Jews became attracted to philosophy they began to look upon some of the biblical commandments as absurd or irrational, and was that not the historical truth that prompted Maimonides to write the *Guide*? Maimonides had repeatedly stated that the first intention of the Law was to extirpate idolatry, and when William suggested that Maimonides had in fact said it was the Law's "one and only intention," he was playing fast and loose with the text.[14] William posits seven other reasons for sacrifices in addition to the "first intention," and even comments on the prayers and ceremonies surrounding the sacrifices.[15] William goes so far as to explain that those prayers would have allowed us to comprehend fully the reasons for the sacrifices. Apparently untroubled by the fact that Scripture contained no mention whatsoever of the liturgical practices surrounding sacrifices, William used Maimonides' methodology. Just as there existed no proof of the ancient Sabian culture, upon which Maimonides' views of sacrifice were erected, so were the ancient prayers and liturgy lost. William had truly learned well.

William saw accommodation at work in the Mosaic Code. Were not the leaders of ancient Israel faced with the task of educating a crude and irksome folk. The Law provided an education that sought to eradicate idolatry. He differed from other Christian exegetes in embracing the Law as a whole and in acknowledging that, in toto, it did possess a literal truth and meaning for the Jews in its original context; that was no doubt based upon Maimonides' great historical insight. Unlike other Christian scholars, who viewed Scripture as possessing a spiritual truth intended for Christians which was veiled by the Jewish letter, William saw each, without losing sight of either.

He suggests that contemporary Jews do not comprehend Scripture properly because they have simply neglected to study the Law due to avarice, to which they are prone, and because they prefer "Greek wisdom." William's spiritual reading of the Mosaic Code is "rather elusive: perhaps it was intended to be."[16] Scripture contains a profusion of potential readings and meanings depending on the capacity of the reader. Had not David desired to behold "the wondrous things of the Law" (Ps. 119:18)? God, just like a human schoolmaster faced with students of different capabilities, could not have provided sufficient instruction with one reading assignment, but gave different assignments all in one book.[17] Just as a human teacher teaches individual students according to their various capabilities, did not God accommodate his lessons to all kinds of students?

William employs diverse metaphors to describe the multiplicity of meanings in Scripture: it is like a mine, with veins of precious metals and jewels, like a garden of delights, like a wine cellar, and like a medicine chest.[18] Scripture is also similar to a table set with a multitude of different dishes, where each guest will find food suitable for his appetite.[19]

William, as Beryl Smalley has so insightfully shown, does not interpret Jewish biblical legal commands as types foreshadowing Christian teachings.[20] If they did not prefigure Christian sacraments, then William must, and does, explain why Christianity did not retain them. He posits a novel and rather questionable—at least from the Christian point of view—interpretation of biblical *legalia*.

Sacrifices did not cleanse sins; they were "pleasing unto the Lord" because they showed devotion and obedience, and helped, inter alia, provide for the priests. Christianity has simply found a better and more noble system (*melius et honestius*) of establishing divine service and taking care of priests.[21] Therefore, the legal enactments no longer serve the same purpose and may be set aside.

William employs Maimonides' view of an elite in ancient Israel possessing superior knowledge and wisdom when he ponders why these legal precepts were made incumbent upon all Jews, since the elite certainly did not need them to be restrained from idolatry as did the great mass of the Israelites. And William also wonders why God did not reveal the true means of expiation to his "chosen" people?

He answers the first question with the expected observation that the commandments were observed in order to prevent dissension and social problems, and the second question with the familiar charge that the people would not have comprehended the truth.[22] William then affirms his conviction that divine education took place in stages and that the prophets marked an advance over Scripture. Citing Jeremiah 4:4, 6:10, and 9:26, William declares that the prophets slowly (*paulatim*) encouraged people to spiritual worship and inner sanctity in place of externalities [*unde postmodum per prophetas paulatim ad spiritualem cultum et interiorem sanctificationem invitati sunt*].[23] The prophetic teachings, which more closely approached perfection, followed upon the Law; perfection was reached with the Gospels [*et doctrinae legis successit doctrina prophetarum tanquam perfectioni vicinior; tandem autem avenit evangelicae perfectionis excellentia, ultra qua non est*].[24]

William concludes with a discussion of the seven sacraments as the historical successors to biblical sacrifice, without, however, seeing the latter as prefiguring the former.[25] William's views are rather surprising in light of the tradition to which he was heir; the Mosaic Code was a textbook, but did it teach the elite of ancient Israel about the Incarnation, the Trinity, and human redemption through Christ as Christian tradition heretofore asserted? William never answers. His contribution to the history of accommodation and the role of the *Guide* in the hands of at least one provocative thinker is unique. In the words of one astute observer:

> We depend upon *De Legibus* for the surprising information that one period of reaction against allegory occurred at Paris in the second quarter of the thirteenth century. William wrote under its impact. He threw out suggestions which would have altered the technique of medieval exegesis, had they been followed. They were not followed: allegory survived. William's theory suffered from a fatal combination of flaws. It was both original and inchoate, too original to appeal and too inchoate to be adopted.[26]

Had William's theory been accepted by his contemporaries and successors, the thread of accommodation might have ended here. For better or worse, his theory was not accepted, and Thomas Aquinas would help restore an equilibrium, which, as we shall see, was to last until the intellectual convulsions of the modern era severed almost irreparably the traditional lines of Western thought.

Thomas undertakes his general review of the ceremonial and legal statutes of the Mosaic Code in question 98 of his *Summa*. He asks rather simply "whether it is good."[27] Thomas rebuts objections by affirming that the Law conformed to reason, restrained desires, and forbade all sins that were contrary to reason. While human law seeks to establish the temporal peace of the political unit, divine law endeavors to bring humanity toward eternal happiness. The Old Law is good, but inferior to the New, which brought grace.

Thomas's argument is built upon exegesis of Ezekiel 20:25, "Wherefore I gave them statutes that were not good . . . ." Thomas's reading of the text teaches that it was the ceremonial precepts of the Mosaic Code that were not good in that they demonstrated humanity's need for removing sin, but did not provide the means to do so. The New Law was superior, for it could fulfill what the Old could not. Consequently, the prophetic words taught that the Old Law was good on one level, but not perfect.[28] It is in question 101 that a full examination of the ceremonial precepts of the Old Law is undertaken.

Thomas poses the question: "Does the reason of the ceremonial precepts lie in the fact that they concern the worship of God?"[29] After giving several objections to his idea, including a citation from the *Guide*, Thomas remarks that the ceremonial precepts are applications of moral precepts establishing relations to God, just as judicial precepts are applications establishing relations between people. They are also rules for salvation.[30] Furthermore, anything that "is preparatory to a particular end comes under the science dealing with that end."[31] Thus, those precepts that concern the worship of God are called ceremonial.[32] The question and answer rotate about the axis of "ends," and therefore, Thomas inquires about the purpose of the precepts and the "ends" they sought to accomplish.

In trying to ascertain their ends, Thomas asks if the ceremonial precepts, which he has defined as those that regulate the worship of God, were figurative?[33] Thomas explains that worship is twofold: internal and external. "For since man is made up of soul and body, both must be used for the worship of God; the soul by interior worship, the body by exterior. . . ."[34] As the body is governed in its relationship with God by the soul, so interior worship governs the exterior. Interior worship consists in being joined to God by mind and affections, and since there are various means by which that end may be achieved, there are various ways of applying external acts to divine worship.[35]

In a state of future beatitude, the human mind will intuit divine truth in itself, and then external worship will not consist in anything figurative. However, at present that situation does not obtain, and various sensible figures, corresponding to the various states of human understanding, are necessary. The ceremonial precepts of the "Old Law"—in the form of external worship—prefigured the truth of the "New Law" and Christ, the way leading to it.[36]

Certainly the ceremonial precepts had a figurative cause, and Thomas offers a familiar reason for that principle:

> The things of God should be revealed to mankind only in proportion to their capacity; otherwise, they might despise what was beyond their grasp, with disastrous consequences. It was, therefore, better for the divine mysteries to be conveyed to an uncultured people as it were veiled by means of figures, so that at least they should have an implicit knowledge of them in using these figures for the honor of God.[37]

So much for the figurative cause, which is seen as accommodation, but what about the literal cause, since Thomas claims that the ceremonial precepts also had a literal cause.[38]

Thomas at first asserts that circumcision and the Paschal offering, for example, were only figurative, *a fortiori* all the other ceremonial precepts. He further claims that proportionality exists between the cause and the precept itself; all precepts that are figurative should have had only figurative causes. Additionally, he maintains that various precepts, such as the number of animals offered at a sacrifice, were simply a contingency, with no literal meaning. Yet, since we know that the ceremonial precepts had both figurative and literal causes, what was the literal cause of these ceremonies? His answer is not surprising: The literal causes for these ceremonies, which provided for divine worship, were ordained "at that time" (*pro tempore illo*). They fought idolatry, brought to mind divine goodness, and disposed the intellect toward divine worship.[39] In Thomas's scheme of things, one perhaps finds repercussions of Maimonides. The ceremonial precepts of the Mosaic Code had both figurative and literal causes; as the particulars of human laws may vary according to the desire of the legislators, such was the case with the Mosaic Code. Indeed, "many particulars in the ceremonies of the Old Law have no literal cause, but only a figurative, though taken in the abstract, they have also literal causes."[40] This middle road was more than a definitive maybe.

Thomas compares the ceremonial and judicial precepts; in different ways both were figurative.[41] And precepts may prefigure in two ways: they prefigure *in se* and in something additional. That is, the purpose of the ceremonial precepts prefigured, in some way, divine worship and the mystery of Christ. They were valid then as regulating Israelite worship and in prefiguring Christ. The judicial precepts, however, may be interpreted allegorically and tropologically just like the historical parts of Scripture; yet their literal value cannot be denied.

The Jewish precepts differ from those of Gentiles because the latter possessed literal value only and cannot be interpreted on other levels. Scripture reveals sacred history, and within it, Thomas must find the role of the ceremonial precepts. Both types of precepts have been rendered, in different ways, null and void by the New Law. As the angelic doctor explains: "The ceremonial precepts are not only dead, but deadly to those who observe them after the advent of Christ, while the judicial ones are dead because they have no authority, but they are not deadly."[42]

Observing the ceremonial precepts after the promulgation of the Gospels works against the faith, because the Christian faith has fulfilled the figures. Observing the judicial precepts would not be a mortal sin if they were not commanded to be observed because the "Old Law" was binding upon humanity, and further, they were not figures, but rather legislated to help order that society, and thus turn it toward Christ.[43] The ceremonial precepts differ from other precepts, primarily because they existed as figures of the mystery of Christ. Where William emphasized the literal importance of the ceremonial precepts at the expense of the figurative, Thomas sought to right the balance. For Thomas, the precepts of the "Old Law" were primarily prefigurations of those in the New,[44] and in the end, he sided with tradition and against William and innovation.

Thomas was convinced that the faith of the ancients was his own, save for the temporal difference. His truths were known to them directly or indirectly, and God poured forth knowledge—manifestly or furtively through signs—sufficient to the different times. Complete knowledge came only in Christ. The divine dispensation was accommodated to the prevailing conditions. The condition of human nature made it necessary that mankind not be led immediately to perfection, but rather from the imperfect to the perfect. Just as one observes in teaching children, who first learn the elementary things because they cannot grasp the more difficult, so a crowd cannot fathom at once unheard of things unless they have been accustomed to change in stages.[45]

William of Auvergne and Thomas Aquinas were both influenced by Maimonides' *Guide*. William went much further than a bishop of the thirteenth century should have been expected to go when he practically denied any figurative value to biblical precepts and stressed, perhaps too vigorously, their literal value. Thomas sought to right the scales that were tilted first by William in one direction, and then, as Smalley has so convincingly shown, by John of La Rochelle in the opposite direction.[46] Thomas steered the middle course, which may have been less exciting, but ultimately more long lasting. William asked the same questions as Maimonides: What did this all mean *then*, and how are we to interpret it in its original setting? Thomas sought reasons, not history. However, both, in their independent ways, helped ensure the vibrant continuation of divine accommodation in Western thought.

It was Aquinas' middle road between the extreme literalists and the extreme allegorists that ultimately bifurcated in the centuries between Thomas and John Calvin. Perhaps Nicholas of Lyra (c. 1270–1340), a Franciscan and Aristotelian who was strongly influenced by the exegesis of Rashi, became one of the foremost exponents of the literal approach toward Scripture. Indeed, scholars often point out that Lyra posited a "double literal sense" (*duplex sensus litteralis*), which could uncover some fascinating meanings. Lyra, in his interpretation of I Chronicles 17:13, where the Lord remarks to Solomon, "I will be a father to him and he will be like a son to me," notes that Paul had applied this verse to Jesus (Heb. 1:5) and suggests that the verse spoke of both Solomon and Jesus literally; Solomon being God's son by grace and Jesus by nature.[47] If Lyra's literal, nonfigurative reading of Scripture pointed in one of the two divergent directions, then the work of Jacques Lefevre d'Etaples (c. 1455–1536) betokened the other.

Lefevre, a humanist, reformer, and Christian Neo-Platonist, criticized Lyra as a "judaizer" who concurred more with the rabbis than with Christ. Just like Lyra, Lefevre saw only one sense in Scripture; the one intended by the Holy Spirit, and that meant the spiritual sense. For him, Scripture reverberated with the teaching of the Holy Spirit and its praise of the Son.[48]

Those were the two poles around which late medieval and Reformation exegesis gathered. History proved Lyra's approach to be the more long-lasting, though allegory was never really to disappear. Late medieval monastic schools, especially those of Luther's own order, the Augustinians, and English friars of the fourteenth century helped tilt the scales in favor of the literal-historical approach.[49] Both scholars and their approaches played a part in the development of Reformation theology, which, more than ever, stressed the attempt to understand and explain the sacred page.

In that undertaking, Luther's exegesis was built around the literal and the spiritual exegetical poles. In his first lectures on the Psalms (1531–15), which show his debt to Lefevre, Luther dismissed the literal-historical reading of Scripture as "carnal and Jewish," and incessantly searched for Christian meaning anywhere and everywhere.[50] For Luther, Christ seemed to be the literal sense of Scripture in toto; and some argue that this christological exegesis of Psalms provided the framework upon which Reformation theology rested. "Christ as the literal sense and faith in Christ as the moral sense, so faith became Jesus Christ tropologically understood, or what Jesus means *for me*."[51]

Against this position, some argue that Luther came, more and more, to side with Lyra's approach to Scripture, and he attempted to relate the theological content of the Psalms to their historical reality.[52] Luther came to see the divine promise to humanity within history. He spoke more frequently about the setbacks and successes in believing the word of God, and less frequently about achieving a spiritual union with Christ by means of faith. Luther began to recognize the Psalms as the historical record of the historical David, rather than the reverberations of the Holy Spirit's praise of Christ. Luther intuited that he and all Christians, like David in the Psalms, had to endure, despite difficulties, by faith—faith in God, his word, and his promise. "In this interpretation it was the correlations of existential faith with God's biblical promise rather than with Jesus Christ as a hidden speaker in the Psalms that gave birth to Reformation theology."[53] Luther's exegesis may have devalued the medieval four senses of Scripture to two, the literal and moral, but in so doing the value of faith—"or what Jesus means *for me*"—was inflated.

It was precisely faith, defined as knowledge, not ignorance, that was the bedrock upon which John Calvin would erect a grand exegetical structure.[54] Calvin, who held that God was inaccessible to humanity—either because of God's "infinite fulness"[55] or because of our "hereditary pravity and corruption of our nature"[56]—made Christ the object of faith. As the divine intermediary, it is through Christ— and only through Christ—that humanity could comprehend and come to God.[57] What then precisely constitutes knowledge of Christ?

> This, then, is the true knowledge of Christ, if we receive him as he is offered by the Father, namely, clothed with his gospel. For just as he has been appointed as the goal [*destinatus*] of our faith, so we cannot take the right road to him unless the gospel goes before us. And there, surely, the treasures of grace are opened to us; for if they had been closed, Christ would have benefited us little.[58]

In order to obtain knowledge of Christ, one must look to the Gospels, and there one will find grace. Scripture consequently assumes major importance in Calvin's scheme of things.

Calvin establishes the vital link between Scripture and faith, before defining the knowledge of Christ that is the goal of faith:

> First, we must be reminded that there is a permanent relationship between faith and the Word. He could not separate one from the other any more than we could separate the rays of the sun from which they come.... The same Word is the basis whereby faith is supported and sustained; if it turns away from the Word, it falls. Therefore, take away the Word and no faith will then remain.[59]

There is then an external connection between faith and Scripture, and once having established the inseparability of the Word and faith, the relationship among Christ, the Gospels, and grace is announced:

In understanding faith it is not merely a question of knowing that God exists, but also—and this especially—of knowing what is his will toward us. For it is not so much our concern to know who he is in himself, as what he wills to be toward us. Now, therefore, we hold faith to be a knowledge of God's will toward us, perceived from his Word.[60]

For Calvin, God's "Word" contains the promises of grace and mercy; faith was completely defined as

a firm and certain knowledge of God's benevolence toward us, founded upon the truth of the freely given promise in Christ, both revealed to our minds and sealed upon our hearts through the Holy Spirit.[61]

Calvin paradoxically emphasizes knowledge, while admitting that men, in matters divine, are dependent upon the Holy Spirit. What knowledge mankind has must be given, and was *contained in* Scripture. If man had any hope of obtaining full and complete knowledge, and the gifts it bestowed, he had to return to the text:[62]

In short, let us remember that that invisible God, whose wisdom, power and righteousness are incomprehensible, sets before us Moses' history as a mirror in which his living likeness glows. For just as eyes, when dimmed with age or weakness or by some other defect, unless aided by spectacles, discern nothing distinctly; so, such is our feebleness, unless Scripture guides us in seeking God, we are immediately confused.[63]

Indeed, even the patriarchs themselves were taught by God, not only broad generalities, but specifics including a history of creation. Seeming almost to echo his twelfth-century forebears, Calvin observes: "Therein time was first marked so that by a continuing succession of years believers might arrive at the primal source of the human race and of all things."[64] And if one wished to examine things fully, Calvin did not give the answers, but the place to look for them: "For it is better, as I have already warned my readers, to seek a fuller understanding of this passage from Moses and from those others who have faithfully and diligently recorded the narrative of Creation" [*mundi historiam*].[65] Moses could know all those things that had occurred so long before his time because he did not present his own fabrications, but was "the instrument of the Holy Spirit for the publication of those things which it was of importance for all men to know."[66]

Since for Calvin all knowledge and truth were contained in Scripture, and since knowledge and truth could not be obtained by humans but had to be given them, then Scripture, in some way or other, had to be tempered to the human capacity. For Calvin, this meant that Scripture was accommodated to the human level, and as one scholar has observed, accommodation "is perhaps his most widely used exegetical tool."[67] In explicating the mystery of the Trinity, Calvin joins, and contributes to, the history of accommodation:

> For who even of slight intelligence does not understand that, as nurses commonly do with infants, God is wont in a measure to "lisp" (*balbutire*) in speaking to us? Thus such forms of speaking (that God has mouth, ears, eyes, hands and feet) do not so much express clearly what God is like as accommodate (*accommodant*) the knowledge of him to our slight capacity. To do this he must descend [*descendere necesse est*] far beneath his loftiness.[68]

God has chosen to "lisp" and his "lisping" has been preserved in the sacred page. Men's changeable minds are not the safest repository for truth, and thus, to prevent difficulties, God's words have been recorded in perpetuity:

> Suppose we ponder how slippery is the fall of the human mind into forgetfulness of God, how great the tendency to every kind of error, how great the lust to fashion constantly new and artificial religions. Then we may perceive how necessary was such written proof of the heavenly doctrine, that it should neither perish through forgetfulness nor vanish through error nor be corrupted by the audacity of men. It is therefore clear that God has provided the assistance of the Word for the sake of all those to whom he has been pleased to give useful instruction because he foresaw that his likeness imprinted upon the most beautiful form of the universe would be insufficiently effective.[69]

Natural signs and wonders would have proven inadequate to the task of instructing mankind in divine lessons. Therefore, the Lord has given mankind his Word; and there can be no doubt as to its divine source. Indeed, "faith can rest on no other foundation than his eternal veracity," and the Word "has proceeded from his sacred mouth."[70] Scripture itself therefore is an accommodation to human capacity.

If for Calvin the divine authorship of Scripture is its guarantee of truth, how does one explain seeming divergencies in the two testaments. Can the Holy Spirit be inconsistent? Any differences are only apparent, not actual, for the Holy Spirit could not contradict or disagree with itself. Calvin, in an expanded discussion of differences between the testaments, repeats themes heard centuries earlier:

> I reply that God ought not to be considered changeable merely because he accommodated [*accommodaverit*] diverse forms to different ages, as he knew would be expedient for each. If a farmer sets certain tasks for his household in the winter, other tasks for the summer, we shall not on this account accuse him of inconstancy, or think that he departs from the proper rule of agriculture, which accords with the continuous order of nature. In like manner, if a householder instructs, rules and guides his children one way in infancy, another way in youth, and still another in his young manhood, we shall not on this account call him fickle and say that he abandons his purpose. Why, then, do we brand God with the mark of inconstancy because he has with apt and fitting marks [*aptis et congruentibus notis*] distinguished a diversity of times? Paul likens the Jews to children, Christians to young men [Gal. 4:1 ff.]. What was irregular about the fact that God confined them to rudimentary teaching commensurate with their age, but has trained us through a firmer and, so to speak, more manly discipline? Thus, God's constancy shines forth in the fact that he taught the same doctrine to all ages, and has continued to require the same worship of his name that he enjoined from the beginning. In the fact that he has changed the outward form and manner, he does not show himself subject to change. Rather, he has accommodated [*attemperavit*] himself to men's capacity, which is varied and changeable.[71]

The teaching of Augustine reverberates in Calvin's account of the same truth being taught to all ages, and this selection gives prominence to several of Calvin's exegetical propensities. He gainfully employs the hermeneutical technique of accommodation, which along with synecdoche were his two favorite exegetical devices.[72] The metaphor of the teacher was among his favorite to describe the Holy Spirit.[73] Indeed, Calvin's three favorite biblical themes are God as father, as teacher, and as physician.[74] And the issue of God's constancy or mutability reflected his concern with anthropopatheia. Calvin defined this term: "It occurs when we attribute to God human passions, attachments and modes of life."[75] Calvin could not tolerate descriptions of God that seemed contaminated by anthropopatheia.

Calvin's description of the making of coverings for Adam and Eve (Gen. 3:21) starkly presents the problem:

> Moses here, in a homely style, declares that the Lord had undertaken the labor of making [*fecitque*] garments for Adam and his

wife. It is not indeed proper so to understand his words, as if God had been a furrier, or a servant to sew clothes. Now, it is not credible that skins should have been presented to them by chance; but, since animals had before been destined for their use, being now impelled by a new necessity, they put some to death, in order to cover themselves with their skins, having been divinely directed to adopt this counsel; therefore Moses calls God the Author of it.[76]

Calvin could not conceive of God as a furrier or tailor, which is how the biblical text reads; Calvin's exalted view of the Lord could not allow him to function in human fashion, be subject to human passions, or be involved in the material world. This theological position was made tenable by appeal to accommodation, and "he treats all references to God's remembering, resting, repenting, returning, sleeping, yearning, smelling, seeing, wondering, laughing, speaking, and using spears and bucklers" as accommodation.[77] No less accommodated were the words of the Lord's Prayer, the sacraments, and the Lord's Supper; perhaps the sublime example of accommodation was for Calvin, as for other exegetes, the Incarnation.[78]

This exposition implies that Scripture itself is an accommodation. An extreme example of scriptural accommodation appears in Calvin's commentary on Psalm 78:65, where God is depicted as a drunk. In an astonishingly frank comment, Calvin explains: "The figure of a drunken man, although somewhat harsh, has not without reason been put forward, for it is accommodated to the stupidity of the people" (*accommodatur ad populi stuporem*).[79] Indeed, humanity can be so thickheaded that it needs such a jolt to make the message intelligible. The same "shock therapy" was used in the case of "Thou shalt not kill" and "Thou shalt not commit adultery": "Of all the instances of one class of sins, the lawgiver has chosen the most heinous instance to be the shocking vehicle of all the rest."[80]

In discussing the question of whether an accommodated Scripture contains precepts that are capable of being observed by humanity, Calvin clashes with certain Roman Catholic thinkers. John Eck, according to Calvin, argues that, if the law were impossible to observe, it would have been given in vain. And surely, the commandments were accommodated (*attemperata esse*) to our faculties so that we might fulfill them. Calvin disagrees with the conclusion, but not with the method. Certainly, the Law was accommodated to human potential; but heaven forbid that one believe God did so, only to conclude that he acted in vain. The true accommodation of the Law consisted in establishing its requirements so far above us that it would point out our weakness, and point us, through love, to his grace.[81] This process too is the work of the Holy Spirit, and man cannot fathom its wonders.

Calvin, as we have seen, understood all of Scripture through the lens of accommodation because it so perfectly served his purposes: It strengthened his theological system in asserting the sublimity of the divine and frailty of the human; it placed Scripture front and center as authoritative in religion, and it permitted him to try to establish an unbreakable bond between Scripture and faith by positing one theory for establishing true faith based on correct exegesis.

While Calvin may have traveled comfortably down the avenue of accommodation, his exegesis contains ideas blown in by a fresh wind. Possibly two disparate events indicate best the direction and force of that wind, which has yet to be spent. The first event was John Colet's interpretation of the creation story in Genesis. According to Colet, a notable disciple of Lyra,[82] Moses did not attempt to give a scientific explanation in Scripture; rather he accommodated himself to his rude audience

> after the manner of a popular poet, in order that he may the more adapt himself to the simpler rusticity, picturing a succession of things, works and times, of such a character as is certainly not possible of so great a Workman.[83]

For Colet, in a way unthinkable for Calvin, Moses seemed to take the initiative and act on his own:

> Moses, after the manner of a good and pious poet, was willing to invent some figure not altogether worthy of God, if only it might be profitable and useful to men. . . . Thus accommodating himself to their comprehension, Moses endeavored by this most honest and pious poetic figure, at once to allure them and to draw them on to the worship of God.[84]

Moses described six days of Creation

> chiefly that he might lead the people on to the imitation of God, whom, after the manner of a poet, he had pictured as having worked six days and rested the seventh, so that they should devote the seventh to rest and contemplation of God and worship. . . . Moses never would have put forward a number of days, except that, by this most useful and wise poetic figment, the people might be provoked to imitation by an example set before them.[85]

This unfolding of creation is perhaps as far from the traditionally religious approach to Scripture as we might imagine. The literal truth no longer obtains, being usurped by a new allegory in which the poetic truth seems more profound than the incomprehensible truth it seeks to portray. It is, to use the Elizabethan idiom, an "Imitation of the Idea" in a "pleasant and pretie parable," which leads mankind to "vertuous action."[86]

Colet's boldness may have presaged, but it did not single-handedly inaugurate, change. He symbolized a nascent and soon to be powerful movement. Yet that seemingly head-long rush into new territory was checked—or at least it appeared to be slowed—by the attitudes of the conservative fathers of the Fifth Lateran Council (1512–17). This was a council that thought about many issues: of worldwide missions, especially to the shores of the newly discovered America; of confronting the Turkish threat in southeastern Europe; of reforming the *Corpus iuris canonici*; of reducing the number of mendicant houses; of reaffirming church doctrine on the immortality of the soul against the encroachments of humanist thought as well as liturgical standardization.[87] The mood of this last attempt for internal reform may be gauged most accurately by the equanimity displayed in the keynote address.

The keynote was delivered by Giles of Viterbo, the superior general of the Hermits of St. Augustine, Martin Luther's own order. Five years after the opening of the council, Giles would receive his cardinal's hat, and Luther his baptism as a reformer. Giles sounded a conservative note: "It is right that people be changed by religion, not religion by people [*homines per sacra immutari fas est, non sacra per homines*]; we should imitate divine things, not make them imitate us" [*imitemur enim divina nos oportet, non a divinis imitandi nos sumus*].[88] For Giles and those who shared his opinions, reform meant one thing, and one thing only, paradoxical adherence to tradition. "True reform consisted in resounding reaffirmation . . . of the ancient customs, the ancient laws, the ancient practices, the ancient beliefs, and the ancient traditions."[89] Within a brief period after such a resounding profession of faith in tradition, the view of the world was permanently altered; some ancient traditions were discarded, others altered, and others endured, albeit in different forms. Accommodation, as we shall see, would survive, and in a rather surprisingly, recognizable manner.

Accommodation perceived as order in the divine dispensation— which so tantalized Augustine and others—as biological order in nature—described by Maimonides and others—attracted Calvin's attention as well.[90] That same order, accommodated to creation by the providence of the creator, could, in the newly emerging post-Reformation world, win the praise of one of Calvin's contemporaries, one of the fathers of comparative anatomy, Volcker Coiter (1534–76).[91] If

Calvin urged his followers to return to the sources—the book of Scripture—nascent scientists also returned to the sources—the book of nature. With that return to sources, the biblical picture of the universe found its mirrored image strangely distorted by "scientific" facts. Perplexities and discrepancies of all kinds abounded, and people in search of solutions turned to Calvin's exegesis for help.

Calvin was too observant and perhaps too shrewd to hold that the Fall had led to a depravity in all areas of human endeavor. The mind of man, though fallen and perverted from its optimal wholeness, nevertheless was clothed and decorated with God's gifts, and the shining light of truth is perceptible in the works of secular writers:[92]

> If we regard the Spirit of God as the sole fountain of truth, we shall neither reject the truth itself, nor despise it wherever it shall appear, unless we wish to dishonor the Spirit of God. For by holding the gifts of the Spirit in slight esteem, we condemn and reproach the Spirit himself.[93]

As Calvin observes, ancient civilizations established civic order, philosophers described nature, learned men developed and wrote about oratory, medicine, and mathematics. These were not the ravings of madmen. They were all divine gifts and warrant our admiration.

Truth could not be denied regardless of its source. Calvin's understanding of Scripture being accommodated to humanity was exploited in the harmonizing of Scripture and science. In explaining the differences between the Mosaic cosmogony and Greek astronomy, which he recognized absolutely, Calvin, in a rather remarkable passage, presents a marriage of choice and not simply convenience between Holy Writ and scientific "fact." He notes that Moses

> First . . . assigns a place in the expanse of heaven to the planets and stars; but astronomers make a distinction of spheres, and, at the same time, teach that the fixed stars have their proper place in the firmament. Moses makes two great luminaries; but astronomers prove, *by conclusive reasons*, that the star of Saturn, which, on account of its great distance, appears least of all, is greater than the moon. Here lies the difference; Moses wrote in a popular style things which, without instruction, all ordinary persons, endued with common sense, are able to understand; but astronomers investigate with great labor whatever the sagacity of the human mind can comprehend.[94]

Differences between Scripture and science are due to the accommodative nature of Scripture; indeed, astronomers prove their assertions "by conclusive reasons." Ordinary people with common sense can read and understand Scripture, while astronomers explore more recondite areas. Calvin was a propagandist for the school of the Holy Spirit:

> Nor did Moses truly wish to withdraw us from this pursuit [sc astronomy] in omitting such things as are peculiar to the art; but because he was ordained a teacher as well of the unlearned and rude as of the learned, he could not otherwise fulfill his office than by descending to this grosser method of instruction. Had he spoken of things generally unknown, the uneducated might have pleaded in excuse that such subjects were beyond their capacity. Lastly, since the Spirit of God here opens a common school for all, it is not surprising that he should chiefly choose those subjects which would be intelligible to all. . . . Moses, therefore, rather adapts his discourse to common usage.[95]

Moses adapted his material to the "common usage"; and if Genesis 1 mentions "waters above the heavens," and "it appears opposed to common sense and quite incredible, that there should be waters above the heaven," the waters mentioned here "are such as the rude and unlearned may perceive."[96] Scripture was a "common school for all"; "he who would learn astronomy, and other recondite arts, let him go elsewhere."[97]

Calvin pushed his approach so far as to assert that the Holy Spirit, on occasion, accommodated itself to vulgar error in order to enhance the meaning of its message. In commenting on Psalm 58:4–5, "They are like the deaf adder that stoppeth her ear; which will not hearken to the voice of the charmers, charming never so wisely," Calvin wondered if it were possible for charmers to charm snakes and for adders to stop their ears. "He therefore suggests an alternative to the realistic interpretation: 'David borrowed the similitude out of the common error, as if he had said, there is no wiliness to be found in serpents which reigns not in these men; yea, though it be so that adders be fenced by their own slyness against enchantments, yet are these men as crafty as they.' "[98]

Calvin's approach and influence were so pervasive that even Copernican astronomers in Protestant countries echoed his sentiments. For example, Edward Wright, in his preface to William Gilbert's *De magnete* (1600), argued that neither Moses nor the prophets were trying to teach physics or mathematics when they spoke and wrote. Rather, Moses "accommodated himself to the understanding and the way of speech of the common people, like nurses to little children."[99] Philips van Lansbergen (1561–1632) a Reformed minister, Calvinist, famous astronomer, and ardent Copernican suggested that Scripture

could teach doctrine and righteousness, but not geometry and astronomy. Scripture, in his view, did not speak astronomically about
things as they really were, but according to appearances. And when
his son Jacob, a physician, wrote, in 1633, a defense of his father's
positions and view of Scripture, he quoted as support the comment of
"Calvinus noster" that "the Spirit, as it were, stammers with us," and
Jacob capped his argument with reference to Calvin's commentary on
Psalm 58.[100] Even a convinced Copernican like Johannes Kepler, who
could not quote Calvin, nevertheless sounded very much like a Calvinist in astronomical matters.[101]

The last and perhaps most interesting example of accommodation's
scientific career is that of Galileo. As a Catholic, Galileo had to read
Scripture as tradition and as the authority of popes and councils
dictated; yet as a scientist, he betrayed another side. Namely, Scripture was binding in matters of faith and morals, though in other
cases it is accommodated to the human level.[102] Galileo believed that
astronomical truth—the Copernican system—was in fact contained
in the Bible if one knew how to read properly. The same argument
was made centuries before by Gnostics in their battle with the early
church and reverberates in the Maimonidean view of scriptural levels
of truth, which reappears in the thought of William of Auvergne and
Thomas Aquinas. Joshua's command to the sun to stand still meant
that the sun did stand still in the middle of the heavens, instead of
revolving about its axis. This of course retarded the earth's rotation,
resulting in a lengthened day.[103] This could all be found, if one knew
how to search, in the biblical text itself.

Galileo's interpretation of Psalm 19:5–7 ("The sun like a bridegroom comes out of his chamber") did not suggest that this was poetic
language accommodated to humanity, but that the sun's rays spread
throughout the universe and are called "bridegroom" because of their
generative qualities. "Out of his chamber" refers to the light, not the
orb; the phrase in verse 7, "the law of the Lord is perfect, converting
the soul," signifies that God's law is more perfect than the sun, which
may be marred with sunspots, and the divine power to direct souls is
greater than the sun's power to guide the spheres. Galileo assumed,
of course, that the psalmist knew the seventeenth-century discoveries
of a heliocentric universe and sunspots and made use of the theories
he and Kepler posited that held that the sun's rotation powered the
movement of the planets.[104] As R. Hooykaas explains: "In Galileo's
view, then, Scripture, which at first sight was accommodating itself to
the vulgar opinion on the world system, was using this opinion as a
veil through which the learned could perceive scientific truth. At the

same time he entrusted the final exegesis of such biblical texts to the hands of enlightened scientists. The supposed conformity of the two Books, Scripture and Nature, which led the literalists to the condemnation of the Copernican system, served Galileo for its verification, and in this respect he used the same system as his opponents."[105]

Galileo remained a faithful son of the Church having declared that the pope had absolute authority to admit or condemn any thesis, even outside matters of faith; he ran afoul of tradition when he asserted that no creature can render theses true or false when they are not so according to their own nature and in fact.[106] The shape that the future would assume is discernible in Pascal's protest to the Jesuits over Galileo's condemnation:

> It was also in vain that you did obtain that decree of Rome against Galileo which condemned his opinion touching the motion of the earth, for that will not prove that the earth is standing still, and if one had solid observations demonstrating that she does turn round, the whole of mankind together would neither be able to prevent the earth from turning round nor themselves turning round also, with her.[107]

Even though Pascal earned a place on the Index, and Galileo's bishop refused to look through a telescope, the modern world could not be denied or suppressed. The view of the world as an accommodation to humanity maintained a high profile in the exegesis of William of Auvergne and Thomas Aquinas because it served their purposes so well; William's to elevate literalism and Thomas' to restore the delicate balance between the literal and the allegorical in medieval exegesis. Calvin, who, except perhaps for Chrysostom, is almost unequaled in his exploitation of accommodation, employed it to explain: the relationship between a sublime deity and his mundane creation and creatures; the authority of Scripture; the importance of the Word and not institutions in religious life. Finally, it provided a method by which the book of Scripture could be read along with the book of nature. Together the Bible and the world constituted the "school of the Holy Spirit," which came under attack in the New World of the seventeenth century. It is to the changed role of accommodation in, and its influence upon, that New World that we must now turn in order to complete our tale.

CHAPTER EIGHT

CONFRONTING TRUE AND FALSE GODS

> The thing that hath been, it is that which shall be; and that which
> is done is that which shall be done: and there is no new
> thing under the sun.
>
> —Ecclesiastes 1:9

This study of the career of divine accommodation ends with a brief survey of accommodation's survival after leaving the friendly confines of late antiquity and the medieval and Reformation worlds. Accommodation was to confront a new, bizarre, and hardly recognizable landscape. Religious ideas and institutions, its former haven, seemed besieged and embattled by the forces of so-called reason and enlightenment. On the seventeenth- and eighteenth-century battlegrounds, amidst a flurry of intellectual activities of diverse sorts, accommodation would find new lodgings and endure.

It is accommodation's rather remarkable survival in the modern period that shall concern us in this concluding chapter. That survival has been documented by others, and there is no need to be repetitive; therefore, by way of concluding the history of accommodation, we shall simply offer several prominent examples of its new uses.[1]

The eighteenth century, which belongs to our modern time, and the age of Voltaire, Montesquieu, Holbach, Diderot, Hume, Locke, and others, raised "Reason" as its battle cry in its struggle to overthrow the seeming forces of darkness, superstition, and ignorance. With reason, they were prepared to "let the facts prevail," and with those facts storm the benighted battlements of their time, especially those vestiges of darkness embodied in the still potent ecclesiastical residue of centuries past. The *philosophes* harassing attitude toward religion and its doctrines leaps out from the pages of such a representative work as Voltaire's *Philosophical Dictionary* (1764). His battle cry *Ecrasez l'infame* ("Crush the vile thing") epitomizes the situation, with certain reservations.

Religion might be a vital hodgepodge of ancient nonsense, but it had shown its utility in restraining the ignorant masses, who, without fear of eternal chastisement, would have fallen totally victim to crime, vice, and lunacy of every description. Of course, priests taught falsehoods and helped forge shackles for mankind, but religion, one might grudgingly concede, did curb humanity's worst tendencies. Of course, reason would now hold universal—at least European—dominion and would replace its inferior predecessor. This apologia came not to praise but to bury, and was fraught with danger.

It was perhaps Holbach and his successors who pushed these views to their extreme limits. Having dubbed religion "the sacred malady," they denied the possibility of any apology for what religion had done. A disease—especially a noxious holdover from humanity's remote past—could only be cured or eradicated, and they set out not only to destroy the god of fear but to replace him with devotion to humanity and society. As Holbach observed: "In the matter of religion men are only big babies."[2]

The *philosophes* could laugh at these babies because they were the adults who could dispense with all the childish biblical teachings that prevented them from experiencing freedom; freedom in thought first, and then in any way possible. Humans could act properly and morally by listening to, and voluntarily obeying, the fundamental laws of their own human nature. Nature was the sole source of those laws, and men's consciences were in tune with nature as well as with the rational order of things. Morals could teach as much about the world as science, and God could be detected through his laws of creation. Moral searching and questioning might lead humanity to discover the divine rules imbedded in mankind's created nature, and that search would eventually yield statutes to replace those granted by revelation. God could now be worshiped through obedience to the dictates of human nature guided by reason, rather than through outmoded and childlike ceremonies. Natural religion and natural law could replace manufactured law and religion. This was heady stuff, indeed, and in the evolution of these ideas, the *philosophes* moved, as we shall see, from a reinterpretation of religion, especially Christianity, to its rejection.

Enlightenment thinkers scoured man's history and tried to piece together the shattered remnants of religious experience and teachings accumulated from creation to their own time; in creating this mosaic, they felt one could use the litmus test of reason and common sense to distinguish between the true and false, the noble and ignoble pieces of ages past. Reason and common sense could separate the real from the imaginary, the facts from fables, and those facts, once assembled, would enable truth to emerge. An intoxication with reason prevented the *philosophes* from comprehending a fatal flaw in their system: They lacked the historical imagination and empathy that had been present in Western thought since Maimonides. That is, Maimonides, William of Auvergne, and even Thomas Aquinas sought to grasp how the biblical narrative corresponded to the historical reality of the time in which it was given; in fact, that was one of Maimonides' startling achievements. For the *philosophes*, the literary remains—containing myths, legends, and other monuments of ancient people's self-description—bore witness, not to their actual historical record, but to their irrationality; that is, the *philosophes* could not understand that people in other times might not have seen or described themselves as the *philosophes* would have liked them to see and describe themselves. Very simply put, the *philosophes* could not explain—let alone comprehend—how the rationality of their time had been planted, grew, and flowered out of the irrational past they knew man to have. Only a still, small voice offered some sort of solution, and that voice, which went long ignored, belonged to Giambattista Vico.

Vico's *Nouva Scienza* posited *corsi e ricorsi* as the norm for nations, with one notable exception: the Jews. Yet Vico's three-stage cycle, which recurs throughout history, involves three different types of human nature corresponding to three distinct levels of historical and psychological changes.[3] The divine, heroic, and human ages succeed each other seriatim; the figures of the first age are strong and violent; those of the heroic age are cruel and punctilious; the last are slothful and oversophisticated. In the course of the cycle, progress is arrested, and Vico's "barbarism of reflection" turns men into worse brutes than the primordial "barbarism of sense."[4] At the point where people have reached premeditated malice, divine providence remedies the situation by returning them to a more primitive and simple state, when the cycle is renewed.[5] For Vico, the affairs of each period are proper to it, and he will speak of "harmony," "correspondence," and "accommodation."[6]

Vico's answer, unfortunately, went largely ignored. His reconstruction of history did away with the focus on individuals and on little battles between petty figures fighting for political prizes. For Vico, the real actors in history were larger units, the nations, and classes within those nations. Each age was unique and had its own reality. Where the *philosophes* spurned ancient myth and fable, Vico embraced them as primary sources of knowledge; all these remnants told of man's quest for the divine. "Primitive religion was not non-sense, idiotic babbling, but man's first striving toward the divine truth. Pagan laws and customs were no empty accidents or shadows of truth; they were necessary stages in the attainment of rational justice. God's order, the principles of the laws of nations, were embod-ied in the most remote corners of human experience."[7]

Vico appreciated the difficulties those primitives overcame as they set about the task of creating language, religion, indeed civiliza-tion. The alien quality and character that so attracted Vico to the process of those primitives repulsed the *philosophes*, who denied it any value and meaning. This Neapolitan professor outraged and scan-dalized his contemporaries and coreligionists. What resemblance was there between those primitives struggling to create something and good Catholics in eighteenth-century Venice? If, indeed, the *corsi e ricorsi* were inevitable, where did Christ's redemptive sacrifice fit into the scheme? And if the *corsi e ricorsi* were inevitable, what good, if any, had Christianity itself achieved? Vico proposed a view of history that contained similarities to the theory of accommodation, but for the lasting incorporation of accommodation in modern thought one must look at other thinkers, including Gotthold Lessing (1729–1781), Johann Hamann, and especially Johann Herder.

Lessing's famous play *Nathan the Wise* (1779) came as a defini-tion of universal toleration, and according to this reinterpretation of Christianity, it emerges as one of several roads man could choose to follow to moral improvement. In 1780, with the publication of his *Education of the Human Race*, Lessing describes a progressive plan for humanity that unfolds gradually through time, demonstrating divine providence and goodness. Humanity now had the unique op-portunity to improve itself with divine guidance watching at a dis-tance. The change was not external through religious institutions and forms, but rather internal.

In a scheme similar to that employed by Christian exegetes, man's inner nature would be transformed in three stages: The first brings revelation only to the Jews, the second to Christians, and the last would embrace all humanity. Judaism held out material rewards and punishments in this world; Christianity spiritualized and post-poned those to the next world; and the third stage would usher in a period when internalized moral reason, totally free from restraints in this or the next world, would reign supreme.[8]

Lessing, in his one hundred paragraphs, invokes accommoda-tion, knowingly or unknowingly. The ideas, language, and historical outlook blend beautifully with the entire tradition, and even the En-lightenment belief that "education gives to Man nothing which he might not educe out of himself; it gives him that which he might educe out of himself, only quicker and more easily"[9] had been used centuries earlier to explain revelation by Sa'adia Gaon.[10] Just as education effects human powers of development differently, and a teacher cannot impart knowledge all at once, so God had to temper his dispensation and his revelation.[11] Human reason, left to its own devices in those primordial times, broke the "Immeasurable" into many "Measurables," which led to the rise of idolatry and polytheism. It was divine goodness that acted to correct the situation, and a people, not an individual, was chosen for special education.[12]

As Lessing explains:

> To this rude people God caused Himself to be announced first, simply as "the God of their fathers" in order to make them acquainted and familiar with the idea of a God belonging to them also, and to begin with confidence in him.[13]

> But of what kind of moral education was a people so raw, so incapable of abstract thoughts, and so entirely in their childhood capable? Of none other but such as is adapted to the age of children, an education by rewards and punishments addressed to the senses.[14]

The same view is voiced concerning the giving of the Mosaic Law, though Lessing believes the "sanction of his [sc. Moses'] law only extended to his life. For why should it extend further?"[15] The answer is not surprising. Moses was

> surely sent only to the Israelitish people of that time, and his commission was perfectly adapted to the knowledge, capacities, yearnings of the then existing Israelitish people, as well as to the destination of that which belonged to the future.[16]

The law was a primer for children: "But," as Lessing observes, "every primer is only for a certain age."[17] At the proper moment, "a better Instructor must come and tear the exhausted Primer from the child's hands. Christ came!"[18] This is accommodation in its new setting, and only in his last few paragraphs did Lessing face the crucial issue of how individual education could enlighten humanity as a whole. He seems to resort to some sort of theory of metempsychosis, which leaves one wondering and a bit perplexed. However, accommodation had crossed the medieval-early modern divide and had emerged into the modern period. It was to take up permanent residence.

Lessing was the first editor and defender of Hermann Samuel Reimarus, whose *Fragments* became part and parcel of the debate over the meaning and worth of Christianity.[19] In trying to interpret the value of religion and the history of mankind, the Bible emerged as the foremost literary monument of ancient Israel. Could the view of the records of the past advanced by the *philosophes* apply also to Holy Writ? That is, was Scripture simply a relic of the past, and as such no longer relevant, valuable, or meaningful? And if not, how did one go about interpreting this ancient code in the modern world? If Reimarus could deny Christ's resurrection, and if only natural religion, independent of revelation, were true religion, how could one protect the theological necessity of revelation against such charges? The problem is the same Vico faced.

Two poles can be quickly established: complete acceptance of revelation or complete rejection. One way out was an historical understanding of Scripture that held that the biblical narrative ought be examined, not only to discover simply what had taken place, but to understand how those ancient authors "experienced and thought, in their own distinctive culturally or historically conditioned consciousness."[20] Some affirmed the correspondence between the real and intended meanings of biblical narratives; that is, the literal text was historically reliable. Others dissented; the historical reliability must be judged anew in each case, and its reliability existed independent of the literal text. The texts concerning human salvation became the center of attention, and since the quest began with creation the Mosaic cosmogony was debated first. The great debate over Christ's mission awaited 1835 and the appearance of Strauss's *Life of Jesus*.[21]

Johann Gottfried Herder (1768–1834) was one of the leading figures in the fight against the encroachments of the Enlightenment. Herder's prolific production includes a special empathy (*Einfühling*) for language, which he inherited from his brooding mentor, "the magus of the North," Johann Georg Hamann.[22] Poetry was "the mother tongue of the human race,"[23] and as Goethe phrased Herder's views, "Poetry is a gift to the world and its peoples, not the private inheritance of a few elegant, educated men."[24] The truest and best expression of poetry was found in the Hebrew Bible, and poetry that divine in a human form of expression could, and should, be read in human fashion.

> In human fashion must one read the Bible; for it is a book written by men for men: Human is the language, human the external means with which it was written and preserved; finally human is the sense with which it may be grasped, every aid that illumines it, as well as the aim and use to which it is applied.[25]

Not accidentally, Herder wrote a study of biblical poetry entitled, *Concerning the Spirit of Hebrew Poetry* (1782–83), and his entire corpus is marked with striving to touch the "spirit" of a time, a people, a work. *Einfühling*—empathy—was what one needed to strive for, the very quality the *philosophes* shunned. Herder graphically expresses the process in words that Vico would have incontestably approved:

> Become with shepherds a shepherd, with a people of the sod a man of the land, with the ancients of the Orient an easterner, if you wish to relish these writings in the atmosphere of their origin; and be on guard especially against the abstractions of dull, new academic prisons, and even more against all so-called artistry which our social circles force and press on those sacred archetypes of the most ancient days.[26]

Herder maintained, as fully and cogently as he could, that to read the Bible in the most human way was to read it as a divine gift. He repeatedly stresses the veracity of Christianity on the basis of historical truth, though he was not adverse to analyzing the literary origins of the Gospels.[27] He may have detested the spirit of the Enlightenment and Rationalism, but he could not, and would not, have turned the intellectual clock back. For him, "history develops slowly and without missing stages between earlier and later times."[28] For Herder, a certain imperceptible providence seems to emerge from the biblical narrative that connected events and their descriptions. Historical unity seemed to mark Scripture, and as Herder noted:

> You are right, my friend, that if the sum of what the Bible teaches us is theology, and in its application practical theology, the chief perspective of pupil and teacher must be directed upon this. As a consequence it does not matter alone what every splint and nail signified individually in its own place, but what it means to us now, beyond times and cultures, in the totality of the building in which providence has placed it. The purpose of the first is simply its own isolated knowledge; the second is necessary for its use in our time. The first makes the biblical antiquarian, the second the biblical theologian.[29]

We, and not the biblical figures, must see the whole edifice. One ought not ask

> whether this or that person in the Old Testament recognized himself clearly as a type, or whether his time recognized him as such, but whether in the sequence of times he was pointed to as an archetype. . . . Only later illumination, the clear succession of the developing sense in the sequence of time, together with the analogy of the whole, shows us the building in its light and shadow.[30]

Unity was the hallmark of Scripture. Christ, the sum of revelation, heralded the kingdom promised by the prophets. Biblical unity was verifiable through its history—a history that combines divine providence and human aspirations. The largest part of Scripture is given over to history, and all poetry, doctrine, and prophecy are based on that history. "... God wanted to speak to us in scripture as he speaks to us in nature, in his intimate word as in his open works—naturally and actively."[31] History thus becomes the channel for divine revelation, a revelation that aims primarily at the education of the human race. And while Hamann may have seen the "cyphers, hidden signs," and "hieroglyphs" of God in history, Herder would offer another vision.[32]

Lessing saw the religious development of humanity, not merely as the mechanism of divine revelation, but as revelation itself. A revelation adapted to different peoples, times, and places. Herder, in a similar way, focused upon the development of humanity's "spirit" in the educational process. The figurative reading of Scripture is the glue that holds the whole together. No specific prophecy of Scripture may be torn from its place and applied haphazardly to Christ, but that does not negate the possibility that such passages, broadly speaking, may anticipate future events. The utterances of biblical figures arose in their time; what those words would come to mean was beyond their ken. The future, not they, decided meaning. Thus, those statements of yore could be understood and represented by a changing phenomenon over time, and not necessarily by one, unique reading.

That view of Scripture enabled Herder to interpret the Bible as a continually unfolding story, in which, one may consider the Hebrew Bible to be fulfilled in the New Testament. The New did not merely complete the Hebrew Bible, but prevented its amputation from the whole. As Hans Frei has stated:

> Though the process is gradual, general, and anticipatory, it is more than mere natural anticipation: God's providence is at work through the historical direction. The historical facts, including miracle but especially fulfillment of prophecy, are the foundation of Christianity. Though the fulfillment can be seen only retrospectively, as the synergistic effect of providential revelation and immanent, natural historical education, its substance is a *genuine* fulfillment of earlier vistas by later events and the fuller perspectives that go with them.[33]

Herder delicately balances divine providence, revelation, and immanent historical development. The unity of the Bible, displayed in the narrow thread of the prophetic sayings and happenings that fascinated Augustine and his fellows in the early Church, demonstrated to Herder the ever-increasing elucidation of divine providence in the spirit of his chosen people, which could only be uncovered through the historical events themselves. It was precisely the empathy for the text that permitted that type of interpretation. Where Enlightenment figures sought to bring ancient man to their world, Herder tried to step back into the past.[34] Herder could understand Scripture because the biblical narrative merged with the spirit of its time to give the text meaning for the present; empathy for the spirit of the past gave him a chance to bring it into his own time because he positioned himself within that spirit, or at least tried to do so. A spiritual and historical empathy unifies the text and links us to it, in the same way that allegory did for readers in earlier times.

Herder's view of Scripture spilled over into his philosophy of history. History implied constant movement; yet within this change there are islands at rest: nations. Nations are organisms that have a spirit and lifespan, and historians must try to understand them. And Herder fought, as we have seen, against judging other ages and civilizations by the standards of his time. Just as the Bible needed empathy for proper understanding so did history.[35]

History—the channel through which divine providence poured forth—thus became a benevolent process. As he believed: "Providence guides the path of development onward."[36] Nature, the creation, and history reflect the majesty and splendor of God. Herder compared history to a stream rushing to the ocean, or to a growing tree. History is meaningful, the "scene of a guiding intention on earth, although we do not perceive this ultimate purpose at once."[37]

Herder, according to a critic,

> had laid the foundations for a historicism which spread far beyond the German boundaries. Herder's theory directly contributed to the reawakening of historical interest. His writings were translated into the Slavic languages, as well as French and English. His ideas merged with the broad stream of Romantic philosophy to challenge Enlightenment doctrines throughout Europe; yet the historicist doctrine by no means had been fully developed. Herder had presented the most coherent theory of historicism, but several important concepts that later played a significant role in the German historical tradition of the nineteenth century were still missing in his writings or had not been fully developed by him.[38]

Herder's historicism witnessed the ways of God in history and not merely in the cosmic order. His ideas on Scripture, religion, and history had roots nourished in the fertile soil of accommodation.

CONCLUSION

Let the wise consider these things and let him who considers take
note; for the Lord's ways are straight and the righteous walk in
them, while sinners stumble.

—Hosea 14:9

There is, of course, a certain danger in attempting to describe the
history of an idea and capture its myriad applications in seemingly
countless different literatures and times. Indeed, in tracing the development—the uses and abuses—of accommodation, it becomes obvious
that it originated in the realm of religious polemics and apologetics
and was confined to that sphere throughout the patristic, medieval,
and Reformation periods. For Christian patristic authors from
Tertullian and Irenaeus onward, accommodation was but one arrow
in the polemical quiver that could be shot unerringly at Jews and
Judaism in an attempt to undermine the legitimacy of Judaism and
bolster nascent Christianity. With the loss of its Temple and home-
land, the divine promise could be seen by Christians to have indeed
departed from Israel and have been passed on to a new, and needless
to say, true, Israel. The actual political changes could be seen to
reflect the theological shifts; accommodation helped explain the movement from an outmoded religion to a fresh and vibrant faith.
Athanasius perhaps voiced the idea most trenchantly. The Jews could
not understand the historical—not to mention religious—significance
of the Incarnation and new revelation; they continued to walk in
darkness. They did not stumble when they saw, for they were blind
and incapable of seeing truth.

For Irenaeus, Origen, Eusebius, and other early fathers, Jewish
history marked one stage in human development, a stage that had
been appropriate for its time, had become obsolete, and ultimately
had been superseded. Of course, accommodation could be and was

wielded effectively not only in the polemic against Judaism, but on diverse fronts including battling with Christian heretics, elucidating the mystery of the faith, and buttressing a developing Christianity.

For the Cappadocian fathers, accommodation became a utilitarian exegetical tool. In advocating church and civil harmony, rather than the fraternal strife that rent the fabric of early Christianity, Basil the Great frequently invoked accommodation as the salve and medicine to soothe Christian conflict. Gregory of Nazianzus not only employed accommodation in his historical interpretation of biblical laws, but sustained his theological speculations on the role of the Holy Spirit in the trinitarian scheme by an appeal to the role of accommodation in theological speculation. Gregory of Nyssa applied the theory of accommodation to his mystical and philosophical teachings on human nature, as well as to metaphysical speculation on the creation, role, and functioning of time in the divine plan.

The writings of the "father of accommodation," John Chrysostom, are suffused with the lexical and intellectual vocabulary of accommodation. For Chrysostom, accommodation helped illuminate countless thorny theological and mundane issues ranging from virginity to the Incarnation and the incomprehensible nature of God. Accommodation not only superbly fit John's rhetorical fancy, but meshed well with his pastoral pressures. With his imprimatur, accommodation became an exegetical fixture in Christian thought.

Accommodation's influence was prevalent among the Syriac fathers as well from the mild polemics of Aphrahat to the vicious attacks of Ephrem. Ephrem's "tasters of blood" and "crucifiers" could be vilified because history had passed them by; they observed outdated laws, and time and theology had left them behind. For Isaac of Antioch and Jacob of Sarug, history was a series of historically conditioned, accommodated covenants. The Jews were abandoned by the tides of history when their carnal knowledge failed to become spiritual.

It was Augustine, Hugh of Saint Victor, and Anselm of Havelberg, representatives of the Latin tradition from late antiquity through the Middle Ages, who demonstrated convincingly the pervasive potency of accommodation in the Latin Christian tradition. From theology to historical interpretation, accommodation conformed to similar and dissimilar situations and needs, just as it had in the eastern Christian world.

In the exegetical works of rabbinic Judaism, accommodation not only aided in the explication of Scripture, but helped the rabbinic establishment strengthen its own raison d'être; for, if the Lord had bestowed laws upon Israel that needed to be expounded and made relevant for changed times and circumstances, was that not the entire rabbinic enterprise? That is, if the Lord could accommodate his laws to humanity, what better model for the rabbis, the arbiters of legal wisdom and religious regulation, to follow? If the Lord spoke Egyptian to manumitted Israelites, and could change his mode of revelation depending on the circumstances in order for Israel to comprehend him, had not the pattern been established for subsequent interpretation?

It was of course Maimonides who elevated accommodation to the pinnacle of religious philosophy. In his hands, it became an all-encompassing hermeneutical implement of history, explaining the very reason not only for the commandments, but more importantly why they existed as they did in this contingent world. Accommodation, for him, was a gradualistic, quasi-evolutionary tool to help explain historical and religious change; a device anchored securely in his entire view and understanding of history and the role of divine providence in the world. His work approached the very limits of religious speculation. While his supporters could not advance those limits, his enemies could not retract them; they could only argue over them.

From the thirteenth century to Calvin, accommodation underwent some important shifts and changes. It enabled the scholastics to fathom and interpret religious history in novel and not so novel ways. Accommodation was not employed in the course of the ongoing Christian conversionary activities of the thirteenth century, yet it entered scholastic thought via the Maimonidean corpus, and that route opened up the need for new and "modern" philosophical polemics against Jewish speculative thinking. The continual battle over scriptural interpretation seems all but unthinkable without recourse to some form of accommodationist sentiments.

It was Calvin who brought accommodation into the Protestant camp and exploited it in a manner not seen since Chrysostom. With the concomitant collapse of an all-embracing Christian *oikouménē*, the rise of new scientific thinking, and the triumph of "new and false" gods, accommodation underwent its greatest changes as it entered the modern world.

Indeed, if nothing else, the history of accommodation demonstrates not only the longevity of an idea in various guises, but something much more meaningful. This study of accommodation reveals how an idea, once confined to the realm of religion, developed and evolved in the course of its existence into a nineteenth-century philosophy of history and nationalistic theory. Such a study demonstrates, on the one hand, that the seeming novelty of this system of ideas is partly due to the novelty of its application and the arrangement of old and new elements that enter into it. On the other hand, and perhaps even more compelling, is the recognition that ideas are not baton sticks handed from one century to the next, unchanged and unchanging.

Accommodation in the modern world came to be what it had been all along: a bridge between the secular and the sacred, the palpable and the intangible. It nurtured rationalistic exegesis and a rationalistic interpretation of history. In our view of history and the world, accommodation certainly fears heaven no less, but perhaps serves Clio a bit more.

LIST OF ABBREVIATIONS

ACW	*Ancient Christian Writers,* ed. by J. Quasten and J. C. Plumpe. Westminster (Md.) and London, 1946–.
ANF	*Ante-Nicene Fathers.* Buffalo and New York.
ANL	*Ante-Nicene Christian Library.* Edinburgh, 1864–.
AThR	*Anglican Theological Review.* New York, 1918–.
BJR	*Bulletin of John Rylands Library.* Manchester, 1903–.
CBQ	*The Catholic Biblical Quarterly.* Washington (D.C.), 1939–.
CCL	*Corpus Christianorum.* Series Latina. Turnhout and Paris, 1953–.
CH	*Church History.* Chicago, 1931–.
ChQ	*Church Quarterly Review.* London, 1875–.
CHR	*The Catholic Historical Review.* Washington (D.C.), 1915–.
CR	*Corpus Reformatorum.* Halle, 1834–.
CSCO	*Corpus Scriptorum Christianorum Orientalum.* Louvain, 1903–.
CSEL	*Corpus Scriptorum Ecclesiasticorum Latinorum.* Vienna, 1866–.
DOP	*Dumbarton Oaks Papers.* Cambridge (Mass.), 1941–.
ECQ	*Eastern Churches Quarterly.* Ramsgate, 1936–.
EHR	*English Historical Review.* London, 1866–.
FC	*The Fathers of the Church,* ed. R. J. Deferrari. New York, 1947–.
GCS	*Die griechischen christlichen Schrifsteller.* Leipzig, 1897–.
HThR	*Harvard Theological Review.* Cambridge (Mass.), 1908–.
HUCA	*Hebrew Union College Annual.* Cincinnati, 1924–.
JBL	*Journal of Biblical Literature.* New Haven and Boston, 1881–.
JEH	*The Journal of Ecclesiastical History.* London, 1950–.

JHI	*Journal of the History of Ideas.* Philadelphia, 1940–.
JJS	*Journal of Jewish Studies.* Cambridge, 1948–.
JQR	*Jewish Quarterly Review.* Philadelphia, 1888–.
JThSt	*Journal of Theological Studies.* London, 1900–1905; Oxford, 1906–1949; N.S.: Oxford, 1950–.
LCC	*Library of Christian Classics,* ed. J. Baillie, J. T. McNeill, H. P. van Dusen. Philadelphia and London, 1953–.
LCL	*Loeb Classical Library.* London and Cambridge (Mass.), 1912–.
LNPF	*A Select Library of Nicene and Post-Nicene Fathers of the Christian Church,* ed. by Ph. Schaff and H. Wace, Buffalo and New York, 1886–1900; reprinted: Grand Rapids, 1952–.
LThK	Lexikon für Theologie und Kirche. Freiburg i.B., 1930–1938.
LThK²	Lexikon für Theologie und Kirche. 2nd ed. Freiburg i.B., 1957–.
MGWJ	*Monatsschrift für Geschichte und Wissenschaft des Judentums.* Breslau, 1851–.
MS	*Mediaeval Studies.* Toronto, 1939–.
NRTh	*Nouvelle revue théologíque,* Tournai, 1869–.
NS	New Series.
OCh	*Oriens Christianus.* Leipzig, 1901–41. Weisbaden, 1953–.
OS	Old Series.
PAAJR	*Proceedings of the American Academy for Jewish Research.* NY 1928/30–.
PG	Migne, Jacques Paul (ed.). *Patrologiae Cursus Completus Series Graeca.* 161 Vols. Paris, 1857–1912. References are by volume and columns.
PL	Migne, Jacques Paul (ed.). *Patrologiae Cursus Completus Series Latina.* 221 Vols. Paris, 1844–1890. References are by volume and columns.
PO	*Patrologia Orientalis,* ed. by R. Graffin and F. Nau. Paris, 1903–.
PS	*Patrologia Syriaca,* ed. by R. Graffin. Paris, 1894–1926. 3 vols.
PSt	*Patristic Studies,* ed. by R. J. Deferrari. Washington, 1922–.
RB	*Revue Bénédictine.* Maredsous, 1884–.
RBibl	*Revue Biblique.* Paris, 1891–. N.S.: 1904–.

RE   Realencyklopädie für protestantische Theologie und Kirche, founded by J. J. Herzog, 3rd ed. by A. Hauck. Leipzig, 1896–1913.

REAug   *Revue des Études Augustiniennes.* Paris, 1955–.

REG   *Revue des Études grecques.* Paris, 1888–.

REJ   *Revue des Études Juives.* Paris, 1880–.

RHE   *Revue d'Histoire Ecclésiastique.* Louvain, 1900–.

RSR   *Recherches de Science Religieuse.* Paris, 1910–.

RSRUS   *Revue des Sciences Religieuses.* Strasbourg and Paris, 1921–.

SCh   *Sources Chrétiennes,* ed. by H. de Lubac and J. Daniélou. Paris, 1941–.

SPCK   Society for Promoting Christian Knowledge. London

SRHJ   Salo Baron, *A Social and Religious History of the Jews,* 2nd rev. ed., New York, 1952–.

ST   *Studi e Testi.* (Biblioteca apostolica vaticana:) Rome, 1900–.

TRHS   *Transactions of the Royal Historical Society.* London, 1871–.

TS   *Theological Studies.* Woodstock (MD.), 1940–.

VC   *Vigiliae Christianae.* Amsterdam, 1947–.

NOTES

INTRODUCTION

1. See *The Fathers According to Rabbi Nathan*, trans. Judah Goldin, (New York, 1974), Chap. 34, 140–141. For additional uses of the number ten, see *Pirkei Avot* V,1–8 in *Shishah Sidre Mishnah*, ed. Ch. Albeck (Jerusalem, 1952–59) 374–76, and Herbert Danby, trans., *The Mishnah: Translated from the Hebrew with Introduction and Brief Explanatory Notes* (Oxford, 1933), pp. 445–56. The scriptural events are mentioned in the following order: Gen.:3:8; 11:5; 18:21; Exod. 3:8; II Sam. 22:10; Exod. 19:20; Num. 11:25; Ezek. 44:2. One additional descent will take place in the future, Zech. 14:4. These ten descents—actually only *nine* are listed—are contrasted with ten ascents: II Sam. 22:11; Ezek. 10:4; 10:18; Prov. 21:9; Amos 7:7; 9:1; Micah 6:9; Ezek. 11:23; Prov. 21:19; Hos. 5:15.

2. Marcia Colish, *The Mirror of Language: A Study in the Medieval Theory of Knowledge* (New Haven and London, 1968), 2.

3. Ibid., 2.

4. Ibid., 3.

5. Ibid., 3.

6. *Pirkei Avot*, 5, 25. The attribution is to Ben Bag Bag, a possible convert to Judaism and disciple of Hillel.

7. Claude Henri, Comte de Saint-Simon, *Introduction aux travaux scientifiques du dix-neuvième siècle* (Paris, 1808), in *Oeuvres choisie,* (Bruxelles, 1959), I, 68.

8. See Richard Walzer, *Galen on Jews and Christians,* (Oxford, 1949), and Glen W. Bowersock, *Greek Sophists in the Roman Empire* (Oxford, 1969).

9. See below Chapter VI, pp. XXX for the use and history of the motif in medieval sources, and Gershon D. Hundert, "Jewish Children and Childhood in Early Modern East Central Europe," in *The Jewish Family: Metaphor and Memory,* ed. David Kraemer (Oxford, 1989), 81–94.

10. It was published in Cambridge, 1685. I have used the 1732 edition that contains Spencer's *dissertatio de Urim et Thummim*. For much of this see Stephen D. Benin, "The 'Cunning of God' and Divine Accommodation," *JHI* 45, (1984), 179–191, esp. 179–80.

11. *De Legibus,* 196.

12. Benin, "The 'Cunning of God' ", 179.

13. *De Legibus,* 196.

14. Originally published in 4 volumes in London, 1738–65. I have used the reprint in *British Philosophers and Theologians of the Seventeenth and Eighteenth Centuries,* ed. René Wellek (New York and London, 1978), 2, 280–475. (Book 4, section 6 of *The Divine Legation*).

15. Warburton, 2, 298 (Book 4, sect. 6).

16. Warburton, 2, 298 (Book 4, sect. 6).

17. See for example, Warburton, 2, 298–306 (Book 4, sect. 6).

18. See Julius Wellhausen *Geschichte Israels* (Berlin, 1878), and C. P. Tiele *Histoire compareé des anciennes religions de l'Egypte et de peuples sémetiques* (Paris, 1882).

19. Henry Pinard, Les Infiltrations paiennes dans l'ancienne loi d'après les Peres de l'"église," *RSR* 9 (1919), 197–221.

20. Fabio Fabbi, "La "Condiscendenza" Divina Nell'Ispirazione Biblica secondo S. Giovanni Crisostomo," *Biblica* 14 (1933), 330–347.

21. Karlfried Grunder, *Figur und Geschichte. Johann Georg Hamanns "Biblische Betrachtungen" als Ansatz einer Geschichtsphilosophie* (Freiburg-Munich, 1958).

22. Johanna Kopp, *Brudlerliebe im Licht der Inkanartion (Studia Salesiana)* Eichstatt and Veinna, 1963.

23. K. Duchatelez, "La notion d'économie et ses richesses théologiques," *NRTh* 92 (1970)267–292; "La 'condescendance' divine et l'histoire du salut," *NRTh* 95 (1973), 594–621.

24. John H. Erickson, *"Oikonomia* in Byzantine Canon Law," *Law, Church and Society: Essays in Honor of Stephan Kuttner,* eds. Kenneth Pennington and Robert Sommerville (Philadelphia, 1977), 225–236.

25. See most recently Amos Funkenstein, *Theology and the Scientific Imagination from the Middle Ages to the Seventeenth Century* (Princeton, 1986), esp. 202–267. Funkenstein however does not explore the Syriac sources, nor does he delve as deeply as I have into the individual thinkers I examine in this book. For others of his studies, see the bibliography.

26. F. Freyfus, "Divine Condescendence (*synkatabasis*) as a Hermeneutic Principle of the Old Testament in Jewish and Christian Tradition," *Immanuel*

19 (1984/85), 74–86 originally published in French in *Congress Volume, Salamanca 1983 (Vetus Testamentum Supplement 36)*, ed. J. A. Emerton (Brill, 1985), 96–107. On p. 83 Dreyfus argues that accommodation is not so much an evolutionary, as a synchronic, process: "at all times there are both learned and simple people, but God places himself within reach of the simple." See the following: Hans W. Frei, *The Eclipse of Biblical Narrative: A Study in Eighteenth and Nineteenth Century Hermeneutics* (New Haven, 1974); John Reumann, "Oikonomia as 'Ethical Accommodation' in the Fathers, and Its Pagan Backgrounds." *Studia Patristica* 3, I (1961), 370–79; James S. Preus, *From Shadow to Promise Old Testament Interpretation from Augustine to the Young Luther* (Cambridge, MA., 1969); and Ford Lewis Battles, "God Was Accommodating Himself to Human Capacity," *Interpretation* 31 (1977), 19–38.

CHAPTER ONE

1. See Stephen D. Benin, "The 'Cunning of God' and Divine Accommodation" *JHI*, 45(1983), 179–191, for a statement of the issues.

2. For a brief summary, see Theodore G. Stylianopoulos, *Justin Martyr and the Mosaic Law (SBL Dissertation Series, 20)* (Missoula, MT, 1975), hereafter I refer to *JMML*; Leslie W. Barnard, *Justin Martyr: His Life and Thought* (Cambridge, 1967), and A. Harnack, "Judentum und Judenchristentum in Justins Dialog mit Tryphon," in *Texte und Untersuchungen zur Geschichte der Altchristlichen Literatur* 39, (1913), 47–98.

3. For theories of the Mosaic Law see Carl Andresen, *Logos und Nomos: Die Polemik des Kelsos Wider Das Christentum* (Berlin, 1955), 189–224, 312–344; Hans Dieter Betz, *Galatians (Hermeneia Commentary)* (Philadelphia, 1979), passim; E. P. Sanders, *Paul, the Law and the Jewish People* (Philadelphia, 1983), (hereafter, Sanders, *PLJP*).

4. See Betz, *Galatians,* 161–80, and contra Betz, see Lloyd Gaston, "Angels and Gentiles in Early Judaism and Paul," in *Sciences Religieuses / Studies in Religion* 11 (1982), 65–75.

5. For a fuller discussion of this difficult topic, see Betz, *Galatians,* 161–72, and Sanders, *PLJP,* 70–105.

6. We need not comment on the authenticity of the event here, and for a brief outline, see *JMML*, 8–44. See also Lloyd Gaston, "Legicide and the Problem of the Christian Old Testament: A Plea for a New Hermeneutic of the Apostolic Writings" (unpublished draft), who suggests that the apology of the *Dialogue* is directed to potentially interested pagans in the light of the Marcionite challenge. For an overview of later developments see: Bernhard Blumenkranz, *Juifs et Chrétiens: Patristique et Moyen Âge* (London, 1977), and *Juifs et Chrétiens dan le Monde Occidental, 430–1096* (Paris, 1960).

7. *Dialogue,* 44.2 Text in *PG* 6, 461–800.

8. Though Justin's list (*Dial.* 93:1–2) is not identical with the rabbinic list (prohibition of idolatry; blasphemy; murder, incest and adultery, eating flesh with the blood still in it, *Sanhedrin,* 56a), in that he mentions only three examples, yet the idea of universally valid ethical rules seems to be similar. What is also of importance for the rabbis is the idea of the righteous among the nations of the world. There is no evidence that the early church had knowledge of the noachic commandments.

9. *Dialogue,* 42.4, where Justin talks of *typoî, sýmbola,* and *kataggelías.*

10. See *Dialogue,* 41:4; 18:2; 29:1; 43:2; 16:2ff.; 19:2; 92:2–3; 113:6–7; and 114:4.

11. See for example *Dialogue,* 18:2; 23:2; 30:1; 46:4–5; 67:8, 10; 92:4.

12. See Betz, *Galatians,* 169; Sanders *PLJP,* 65–81.

13. *Dialogue,* 35:6.

14. *Dialogue,* 67:5–6.

15. *Dialogue,* 67:6. For the idea of *oïkonomía,* see below note 139, and Chapter II, note 6.

16. *Dialogue,* 18.

17. *Dialogue,* 19.

18. *Dialogue,* 22.

19. Justin's repeated use of the prophets is encountered on almost every page of the *Dialogue.* For a reasonable summary of Justin's usage, see *JMML,* 76–108.

20. References are to W. W. Harvey, *Sancti Irenaei Episcopi Lugdunensis, Libros quinque adversus Haereses,* 2 vols. (Cambridge, 1857). References are to book, chapter, and section of the Harvey edition, abbreviated as *AH.* See also: Andre Benoît, *Saint Irenée: Introduction a l'étude de sa théologie,* (Paris, 1960).

21. *AH,* 4, 25, 2.

22. *AH,* 4, 25, 2.

23. *AH,* 4, 25, 3.

24. *AH,* 4, 25, 3.

25. *AH,* 4, 26, 1.

26. *AH,* 4, 26, 1.

27. *AH,* 4, 26, 1 and 4, 26, 2.

28. *AH,* 4, 26, 2. I cite the text in the *SCh* edition, which differs from the Harvey text as follows. Harvey reads: . . . *ut per eas* (sc. *praedictas observationes*), *munera dent ei, et detenti ab eo.* . . . The *SCh* text reads: . . . *ut*

per eas (sc. *praedictas observationes*) *salutarem Decalogi absorbentes hamum et detenti ab eo....* For the use of a similar metaphor, see Gregory of Nyssa, *Oratio catechetica magna (The Great Catechism),* 24; "Thus it was that God, in order to make himself easily accessible to (the devil)... veiled himself in our nature, so that, as with ravenous fish, he might swallow the Deity like a fishhook along with the bait of the flesh"; cf. John of Damascus, *De Fide Orthodoxa,* 3, 27. "Therefore Death will advance, and gulping down the bait of the body, be transformed with the hook of the divinity...."

29. According to this commandment, a sheaf forgotten in the field during harvest belongs to the poor; the owner of the field was forbidden to go to the field and harvest it. The Hebrew term is *mitzvat shik^ehah.* This was a commandment that was impossible to fulfill as long as one thought of it.

30. *Tosefta Peah,* 22, and parallel in *Midrash Zuta,* 51b in Buber's edition. I follow the translation in Solomon Schechter, *Aspects of Rabbinic Theology Major Aspects of the Talmud* (New York, 1961), 149. Hereafter, I refer to Schechter, *Aspects.* Yet compare the translation and commentary in Efraim E. Urbach, *The Sages, Their Concepts and Beliefs,* 2 vols. trans. by I. Abrahams (Jerusalem, 1979), I, 473. Hereafter, I refer to Urbach, *Sages.*

31. See the remarks in Schechter, *Aspects,* 148–69.

32. See Schechter, *Aspects,* 242–92, for sources and references cited below. Cf. George Foot Moore, *Judaism in the First Centuries of the Christian Era: The Age of the Tannaim,* 2 vols. (New York, 1971), I, 474–96.

33. See the story in *Yoma,* 87a, cited in Urbach, *Sages,* I, 21–22, 479, and II, 898, about R. Ḥanina and R. Yoḥanan, who, when they had a choice of two roads, one leading to an idolatrous shrine and the other to a brothel, chose the latter since "the craving for idolatry had already been destroyed." On this, see also, E. E. Urbach, "The Rabbinic Laws of Idolatry in the Second and Third Centuries in the Light of Archaeological and Historical Facts," I–II, *Israel Exploration Journal,* 9 (1959–60), 149–65; 229–45, and Saul Lieberman, "Rabbinic Polemics against Idolatry," in *Hellenism in Jewish Palestine: Studies in the Literary Transmission, Beliefs and Manners of Palestine in the I Century B.C.E. IV Century C. E.* (New York, 1962), 115–27.

34. *Song of Songs Rabbah,* I, 2, and see Schechter, *Aspects,* 290–92.

35. See Urbach, *Sages,* I, 472–73.

36. *TB, Kiddushin,* 30b. Occupying oneself with Torah meant study and observance since Judaism emphasizes the deed.

37. *Sifre,* sec. 45 cited in Moore, *Judaism,* I, 481.

38. *AH,* 3, 5.

39. Cited in Elaine Pagels, *The Gnostic Gospels* (New York, 1981), 123. For the Gnostic attack on orthodoxy, see Klaus Koschorke, *Die Polemik der*

Gnostiker gegen das kirchliche Christentum (Nag Hammadi Studies 12) (Leiden, 1978).

40. Cited in Pagels, *Gnostic Gospels,* 128.

41. See Koschorke, *Die Polemik,* 175–85, esp. 180–83, where Koschorke entitles a subsection "Akkomodation."

42. AH 3, 5. Irenaeus uses Luke 5:31–32 as a proof text. "They that are whole need not a physician, but they that are sick. I came not to call the righteous, but sinners to repentence."

43. AH, 4, 26, 1.

44. Cf. Clement's comment in *Strom.* 2.16.72. For Philo and Origen's use of Philonic thought and language, see R. P. C. Hanson, *Allegory and Event: A Study of the Sources and Significance of Origen's Interpretation of Scripture* (Richmond, Va., 1959). For Origen, the word *symperiphorá* will be used for accommodation together with the key words *sygkatábāsis* and *asthéneia.* For language as an accommodation cf. the rabbinic maxim, *dibbᵉrah torah kilᵉshon bᵉnei adam,* for example *TB, Berakhot,* 31b; *TB, Ketubot,* 67b; *TB, Yebamot,* 71a; *Sifre* on Numbers 15:31 and its use as an exegetical tool.

45. Origen, *On First Principles,* trans. G. W. Butterworth (New York, 1966), 275–76; referred to as *FP. FP,* 4, 2, 4.

46. *FP,* 4, 2, 6.

47. See the valuable remarks of Henry Chadwick, *Early Christian Thought and the Classical Tradition: Studies in Justin, Clement, and Origen.* (New York, 1966), 74–93, and 150–53 for references, and *Origen: Contra Celsum,* trans. H. Chadwick (Cambridge, 1952). 3:78–79; 4:10, 19; 6:26, 72.

48. See Chadwick, *Early Christian Thought,* 76.

49. *FP,* 4, 1, 7; 4, 3, 7; 4, 3, 13.

50. Chadwick, *Early Christian Thought,* 92–93. For sources, see 153 nn. 71–72. For the analogy of the Bible and the Incarnation, see *in Matt. Sermon,* 27; *Hom. in Exod.* 12:4; *Hom. in Lev.* 1:1. For the idea of a future gospel, see *Comm. in Rom.* 1:4; *FP,* 2, 8, 7; 3, 6, 8; 4, 2, 4. Irenaeus takes the same position in *AH* 4, 9, 2, in opposition to Jerome, *Ep.* 124:12.

51. *FP,* 4, 2, 9.

52. For example, see below p. 186–192, for Luther and Calvin on Scripture.

53. *FP,* 4, 3, 15. This is in the Latin, not in the Greek, text.

54. *Frag. on Deut.* 1:21, *PG,* 17, 24.

55. Chadwick, *Early Christian Thought,* 75.

56. *Contra Celsum,* 5, 16; 4, 71. Cf. the use of *harmózo* as in Justin, p. 4 of this version.

57. *Homilies sur Jérémie, SCh,* 238 (Paris, 1977), ed. Pierre Nautin, and trans. P. Husson. Homily 18, 6; 198–200. The last sentence reads: *kaì ho theòs dè laleî paidíois.* (Note the emphatic *dè.*) Cf. pp. 202–4 for a further discussion of God's anger and repentance, and cf. *Contra Celsum,* 4, 72. For the use of *oikonomía,* see below n. 139. See also: Marguerite Harl, *Origene et la Fonction Révélatrice de Verbe Incarne (Patristica Sorbonensia* 2) Paris, 1958.

58. Origen comments on sacrifice very briefly; in his *Selecta in Leviticum, PG* 12, 397, and *Selecta in Numeros, PG,* 12, 580. There are comments scattered through the *Contra Celsum,* but his major use of accommodation lies in his exegetical works and reflects attempts to explain certain philosophical issues prevalent in the second and third centuries among Christian and pagan thinkers alike.

59. For Eusebius, see Timothy D. Barnes, *Constantine and Eusebius* (Cambridge, Ma., 1981) (hereafter, *C and E*); D. S. Wallace-Hadrill, *Eusebius of Caesarea* (London, 1960).

60. *C and E,* 104–5.

61. *C and E,* 72–73.

62. *C and E,* 164–69. For the text, see *PG,* 22, 1021–62.

63. *C and E,* 169.

64. *Prophetic Extracts,* 1.2. I use the translation in *C and E,* 166.

65. *Prophetic Extracts,* I.3–12; 1.15; 3.26.

66. The *Second Theophany* is the last book of the *General Introduction* and follows the four books of the *Prophetic Extracts.*

67. *Prophetic Extracts,* 1.8; 3.6. I use the translation in *C and E,* 171–72.

68. All quotations are from *The Proof of the Gospel,* 2 vols. trans. W. J. Ferrar (London, New York, 1920), hereafter cited as *Proof* with reference to book and chapter number of Eusebius' text, and page in this translation. Thus, *Proof,* I, 6; pp. 28–29.

69. *Proof,* I, 6; p. 33.

70. *Proof,* I, 6; p. 33. For the term *pareiselthón* and its use, see Benin, "The 'Cunning of God,'" 181–82. The editor of *Proof* notes on p. 33, n. 3 that the "Egyptian customs" *(homoitropías)* were understood by Gaisford as idolatry *(hoc est idolatria).*

224					*Notes*

71. *Proof,* I, 6; pp. 33–34.

72. *Proof,* I, 6; p. 34.

73. See James H. Oliver, *The Civilizing Power: A Study of the Panathenaic Discourse of Aelius Aristides Against the Background of Literature and Cultural Conflict, with Text, Translation and Commentary [Transactions of the American Philosophical Society, N.S.]* Vol. 58, part 1 (Philadelphia, 1968). Hereafter referred to as *Civ. Power.*

74. In general, see the entire introduction to *Civ. Power,* 5–44, and for the date of composition, see 33–34.

75. Diodoros Siculus, *Diodorus of Sicily,* ed. and trans. C.H. Oldfather *(LCL)* 1933–67, XIII, 26.

76. *Civ. Power,* pp. 18–19. Cf. the language in n. 72.

77. *Civ. Power,* sec. 225–30; pp. 82–83; 140–43.

78. *Civ. Power,* sec. 271–75; pp. 89–90; 148–51.

79 *Civ. Power,* sec. 2, 3, 4, 5, 83, 84; pp. 45, 46, 58; 91–94; 117.

80. See Andresen, *Logos und Nomos,* 292–372.

81. See Louis Ginzberg, *Legends of the Jews,* 7 vols. (Philadelphia, 1909–28). I, 62; V, 113–14; IV, 94; V, 402–03. Ginzberg cites Moses Isserles as a source for Socrates studying with Ahitophel *(Torat ha-Olah,* 1.11, "quoting an old source"). Azariah de Rossi would bring up Plato's study with Moses as a "fact" accepted by Jews and Christians during the Renaissance. See Salo W. Baron, "The Historical Outlook of Maimonides," *PAAJR* 6 (1935), 9–113 reprinted in *History and Jewish Historians: Essays and Addresses* (Philadelphia, 1964), 184–87; 415, n. 69, where we read that Azariah rejected the opinion that Socrates converted to Judaism in his old age. See also Danton B. Sailor, "Moses and Atomism," in *JHI,* 25, 3–16; and John J. Collins, *Between Athens and Jerusalem: Jewish Identity in The Hellenistic Diaspora* (New York, 1983), for the Jewish-Hellenistic background.

82. *Numenius Fragments,* ed. E. Des Places (Paris, 1973), 51. *Ti gár ésti Plátōn è Mosès attikítzōn.*

83. Eusebius, *Preparatio Evangelica,* 9:27. It is worth mentioning that Artapanus' writings are preserved mainly in Eusebius and also in the *Stromata* of Clement.

84. *Proof,* I, 6; 34–35.

85. *Proof,* I, 6:35.

86. *Proof,* I, 6:35. For the use of *stoicheiōsis* cf. *Proof,* and it is used for the "alphabet" in Epiphanius.

87. *Proof,* I, 6; 38.

88. *Proof,* I, 6; 40.

89. *Proof,* I, 6; 42.

90. *Proof,* I, 6; 42.

91. See the different opinions in Karl Baus, *From The Apostolic Community to Constantine* [*Handbook of Church History* I,] (Freiburg/Montreal, 1965), 364–65; H. J. Schoeps, *Theologie und Geschichte des Judenchristentums* (Tubingen, 1949); ibidem, *Jewish Christianity,* trans. Douglas R. A. Hare (Philadelphia, 1969); Jean Daniélou, *The Theology of Jewish Christianity,* ed. and trans. J. A. Baker (London, 1964); and for a recent review of the scholarship on recensions, dating, etc., see F. Stanley Jones, "The Pseudo-Clementines: A History of Research," Part I and Part II, *The Second Century* II (1982), 1–33; *The Second Century* II (1982), 63–96. The edition to be cited is Bernhard Rehm, ed. *Die Pseudoklementinen II: Rekognitionen in Rufins Übersetzung,* prepared for the press by F. Paschke, *GCS,* 51 (Leipzig, 1965–69). Geord Strecker. *Das Judenchristentum in den Pseudoklementinen* (*Texte und Untersuchungen zur Geschichte der Altchristlichen Literatur,* Bd. 70) Berlin, 1958.

92. *Recognitions,* Book I, chap. 32.

93. *Recognitions,* Book I, chap. 33.

94. *Recognitions,* Book I, chap. 34.

95. *Recognitions,* Book I, chap. 35 and cf. Midrash.

96. *Recognitions,* Book I, chap. 36.

97. *Recognitions,* Book I, chap. 37.

98. *Recognitions,* Book I, chap. 38–41. I, 38 reads: igitur Moyses his administrandis, Ausen quendam nomine praeponeus populo, qui eos revocaret ad patriam terram ... defunctus est. Note that a variant for Ausen is Iesunaven. (See the critical apparatus on p. 30 of the *GCS* text.)

99. Schoeps, *Jewish Christianity,* 82.

100. Schoeps, *Jewish Christianity,* 82; cf. his *Theologie,* 155–59. Whether or not this reflects Ebionite theology as Schoeps argues is not our point.

101. Schoeps, 118–20. See also Walter Bauer, *Orthodoxy and Heresy in Earliest Christianity,* 2nd German ed. eds. with appendices by Georg Strecker, Robert A. Kraft and Gerhard Krodel (Philadelphia, 1971); esp. Appendix 1, "On the Problem of Jewish Christianity," 241–85.

102. See *Didascalia Apostolorum,* ed. and trans. R. Hugh Connolly (Oxford, 1929) (hereafter, *DA*) and *Didasclia Apostolorum et Constitutiones Apostolorum,* 2 vols. ed. F. X. Funk (Paderborn, 1905) (hereafter, *DCA*). The former dates from the first half of the third century according to Strecker n. 101 above, and cf. Paul Galtier, "La date de la Didascalie des apôtres," in *Aux origines du Sacrement de pénitence* (Rome, 1951), 189–221; the latter

226   *Notes*

from the late fourth century according to Baus, *Handbook of Church History*, 342–49. The *Apostolic Constitutions* contain eight books: the first six based on an abbreviated form of the *Didascalia;* the seventh derived from the *Didache*, and the eighth from the *Apostolic Constitutions* of Hippolytus. See *DA*, xx–xci.

103. *DA*, chap. 2, 3, and 26. One might compare the idea of syzygies in Gnostic and Jewish-Christian literature and examine the idea of pairs in light of the two inclinations in rabbinic thought; see Daniélou, *Theology*, 61.

104. *DA*, chap. 26. For Origen, of course, *Deuteronomy* was especially esteemed since it was the last book of the Old Law and thus nearest the New Testament in order of the books as presented in written texts.

105. *DA*, chap. 26.

106. *DA*, chap. 26.

107. *DCA*, chap. 20.

108. *DCA*, chap. 20.

109. *DCA*, chap. 20. See Daniélou, *Theology*, 61, for other instances and references to parts of Scripture suppressed by certain Jewish-Christian groups.

110. On Athanasius' career, see Eduard Schwartz, "Zur Geschichte des Athanasius," in *Nachrichten der K. Gesselschaft der Wissenschaften zu (Göttingen)*. Philologische-Historische Klasse (1904), 333–56; Gustave Bardy, *Saint Athanase (Les Saints)* (Paris, 1914); and H. F. von Campenhausen, *Greichische Kirchenväter* (Stuttgart, 1955); Hermann Joseph Sieben, "Hermeneutique d' l'exégése dogmatique d'Athanase," in *Politique et théologie chez Athanase d'Alexandrie, Actes des Colloque de Chantilly 23–25 Septembre 1973*, ed. Charles Kannengiesser (Paris, 1974), 195–214, and much of my discussion of Athanasius and Arianism comes from Robert C. Gregg and Dennis E. Groh, *Early Arianism—A View of Salvation* (Philadelphia, 1981). This is a learned and valuable book. (Hereafter, *Early*). See also George L. Prestige, *God in Patristic Thought* (London, 1964).

111. *Early*, 1–42, and *Four Discourses Against the Arians*, in *LNPF,* series 2, vol. 4, trans. A. Robertson (New York, Oxford, London, 1892), 303–447 (hereafter cited as *Or. contra Ar.* by oration and section number), and G. Christopher Stead, "Rhetorical Method in Athanasius," in *VC*, 30 (1976), 121–37.

112. *Early*, 18–21.

113. Cited in *Early*, 20; *Or. contra Ar.*, 1:40.

114. *Early*, 25–31. Note the citation from *Or. contra Ar.*, 3:10 on p. 26, and the use of the terms *sumphonia, symphonos*.

115. *Early,* 28–29. As Gregg and Groh observe: "The life of the redeemer is a *charis* in the sense of a gift, in that, it is seen entirely as a divine 'condescension' with none of the elements of that transaction which we observed in Arianism" (p. 29).

116. I have used the English translation of H. Burgess of the letters in the text cited in n. 111 (pp. 506–553) above (the Latin edition is in *PG,* 26, 1351–1432), and the Syriac text in *The Festal Letters of Athanasius,* ed. William Cureton (London, 1848), and for the *Contra Gentes* (hereafter *Contra G.*) and *De Incarnatione* (hereafter *De I.*), all references will be to *Athanasius, Contra Gentes and De Incarnatione,* ed. and trans. Robert W. Thomson (Oxford, 1971).

117. *Epistle,* 12, and cf. the *Epistola Encyclica,* 4, 5.

118. *Epistle,* I, 7, 8; *De I.* 39, 40.

119. *Epistle,* I, 7; 5, 4. cf. above p. 000.

120. *Epistle,* 6, 2; 6, 6; 14, 3; 19, 1–8.

121. *Epistle,* 5, 4; 6, 1–2; 14, 3.

122. *Epistle,* 19, 2.

123. *Epistle,* 19, 2; *PG,* 26, 1424.

124. *Epistle,* 19, 2.

125. *Epistle,* 19, 3; *PG,* 26, 1425.

126. *Epistle,* 19, 3; *PG,* 26, 1426. *Credo itaque per vestras orationes concessarum, ut quae ego dicam, a veritate tramite, neque devient. Mandatum ac lex sacrificiis, antiqua non fuerunt, neque holocausta erant ex mente Dei qui legem statuit; sed ejus potius rei gratia exstiterunt quae in figuris antecedebat: lex autem bona illa adumbrat, quae depositi loco usque ad tempora reparationis.*

127. *Epistle,* 19, 4.

128. *Epistle,* 19, 4; cf. 6, 12.

129. *Epistle,* 19, 4.

130. *Contra G.,* 8.

131. *Contra G.,* 19; As Athanasius continues: *taûta mèn hoútōs ekeînoi mythologoûsin. où gàr theologoûsi.* See *Contra G.,* 55, n. 19: The image of *grámmata toîs ánthrōpois* is in Athenagoras, *Supplicatio,* 18.1; and cf. Eusebius *Proof,* 3, 7 (quoting Porphyry), where he discusses the idea of the statues of the gods as images *(eikónes)* and books *(biblía)* from which one can learn *tá perí theôn grammáta.* This is an old metaphor usually associated in the Christian tradition with Gregory the Great.

132. *Contra G.,* 45, 46.

133. *Contra G.,* 47.

134. *De I.,* 4, 5, 6.

135. *De I.,* 8.

136. *De I.,* 8.

137. *De I.,* 12.

138. *De I.,* 12.

139. See, for example, John H. Erickson, *"Oikonomia* in Byzantine Canon Law," in *Law, Church, and Society: Essays in Honor of Stephan Kuttner,* eds. Kenneth Pennington and Robert Somerville (Philadelphia, 1977), 225–36; K. Duchatelez, "La notion d'économie et ses richesses théologiques," in *NRTh* 92 (1970), 267–92; J. Reumann, *"Oikonomia* as 'Ethical Accommodation' in the Fathers, and Its Pagan Backgrounds," in *Studia Patristica* 3 (1961), 370–79; R. A. Markus, Trinitarian Theology and the Economy," *JThSt* n.s. 9(1958), 89–102; and R. A. Markus, "Pleroma and Fulfillment," *VC* 8, (1954), 193–224, and Don S. Lauerer, "Die kondesczendenz gottes" *Das Erbe Martin Luthers und die gegenwartige theologische forschung* ed. Robert Telke (Leipzig, 1928), 258–272. For further references, consult these articles. See above n. 13, and the text from Origen, pp. 16–17.

140. Erickson, *"Oikonomia,"* 230.

141. Erickson, *"Oikonomia,"* 230–34.

CHAPTER TWO

1. See Henry Pinard, "Les Infiltrations Painnes dans l'Ancienne Loi D'après les Pères de l'Église," in *RSR,* 9 (1919); 197–221. This is a fine study and at 209, Pinard calls Chrysostom "le docteur de la condescendance."

2. Johannes Quasten, *Patrology* (Utrecht/Antwerp 1966).

3. Quasten, *Patrology,* III, 204. For Basil, see also *Basil of Caesarea, Christian, Humanist, Ascetic; A Sixteen Hundredth Anniversary Symposium,* 2 vols., ed. Paul J. Fedwick (Toronto, 1981) (hereafter, *BoC*). See also: E. Lamirande, "Etude bibliographique sur les Péres de l'Église et l'aggada," *VC* 21 (1967), 1–11, and G. Quispel, "The Discussion of Judaic Christianity," *VC* 22 (1968), 81–93.

4. *Epistle,* 58. *Saint Grégoire de Nazianze Lettres* 2 vols. ed. and trans. Paul Gallay Paris, 1967.

5. Athanasius, *Epistle,* 62 and 63. in *LNPF* sec. 2, vol. 4.

6. *Epistle,* 58, and for what follows, see George L. Kustas, "Saint Basil and the Rhetorical Tradition," in *BoC,* I, 221–79. See also, K. Duchatelez,

"La notion d'économie et ses richesses theologiques," in *NRTh*, 92 (1970), 267–92, esp. 288–89; James D. Hester, "The 'Heir' and Heilsgeschichte: A Study of Galatians 4:1 ff.," in *Oikonomia*, ed. Felix Christ (Hamburg-Bergstedt, 1967), 118–25; John Reumann, "'Stewards of God'—Pre Christian Religious Application of Oikonomos in Greek," in *JBL* 77 (1958): 339–49; "Oikonomia = 'Covenant'; Terms for Heilsgeschichte in Early Christian Usage," in *Novum Testamentum* 3 (1959); 282–92; "Oikonomia as 'Ethical Accommodation' in the Fathers, and Its Pagan Backgrounds," in *Studia Patristica* 3, I (1961), 370–79; Sidney Sowers, "On the Reinterpretation of Biblical History in Hellenistic Judaism," in *Oikonomía*, ed. Felix Christ (Hamburg-Bergstedt, 1967), 18–25; Wilfred Tooley, "Stewards of God," in *Scottish Journal of Theology*, 19 (1966), 74–86; H. Pierre, "Économie ecclésiastique et réitération des sacrements," in *Irenikon* 14 (1937), 228–47; Adhémar D'Alés, "Le Mot Oikonomia dans la langue théologique de Saint Irénée, " in *Revue des Etudes Grecques*, 32 (1919), 1–9; W. Gass, "Das patristiche Wort *oikonome*," in *Zeitschrift für Wissenschaftliche Theologie*, 17 (1874), 465–504; John A. Douglas, "The Orthodox Principle of Economy and Its Exercise," in *Theology*, 24 (1932), 39–47; C. Dyovouniotes, "The Principle of Economy," in *ChQ*, 116 (1933), 93–101.

7. Gregory of Nazianzus, *Oration* 43, 68–69. I use the translation in Quasten, *Patrology* III, 231–32, and *Epistle* 58.

8. See above, p. 29–30, and Kustas, "Saint Basil" passim.

9. See Duchatelez, "La Notion," 289–91, and see Gregory of Nazianzus, *Oration* 21, 35 on Anthanasius.

10. Kustas, "Saint Basil," 223, n. 6 and 224–25, nn. 7 and 8 for references.

11. Kustas, "Saint Basil," 224–30. See also his full and valuable footnotes with a myriad of references.

12. Kustas, "Saint Basil," 224–25.

13. See *LNPF*, ser. 2, vol. 5, 490, n. 8

14. See K. Duchatelez, "La 'condescendance' divine et l'histoire du salut," in NRTh, 95 (1973), 593–621, esp. 607 and 614. See also *Realëncyklopaedie für protestantische Theologie und Kirche*, ed. A. Hauck (Leipsig, 1896), I, 127–30.

15. See *Homiliae in Psalmos*, Psalm 44:6; 44:9; 48:4; 114:2; *PG* 29, 400, 408, 441, 485. Also *Homily on the Faith*, 2, *PG* 31, 468. I follow Duchatelez, "La 'condescendance,'" 607 and n. 64. Indeed, Suidas' *Lexicon* defines *sygkatábāsis* using the words of Chrysostom cited on p. 68 and p. 239, n. 186.

16. Rosemary R. Ruether, *Gregory of Nazianzus. Rhetor and Philosopher* (Oxford, 1969), 156 (hereafter, Ruether, *Gregory*). See also, Thomas E.

230 *Notes*

Ameringer, *The Stylistic Influence of the Second Sophistic on the Panegyrical Sermons of St. John Chrysostom, A Study in Greek Rhetoric* (Washington, D.C., 1921); James M. Campbell, *The Influence of the Second Sophistic on the Style of the Sermons of St. Basil the Great* (Washington, D.C., 1922); L. Méridier, *L'influence de la seconde sophistique sur l'oeuvre de Grégoire de Nysse* (Rennes, 1906), was unavailable to me.

17. Kustas, "Saint Basil," 232, and see Jaroslav Pelikan, "The 'Spiritual Sense' of Scripture," *BoC* I, 337–60, esp. 355–56.

18. Kustas, "Saint Basil," 233 with credit to B. Pruche, *Basile de Césarée, Traité du Saint-Esprit,* 2nd ed. (Paris, 1968).

19. *De Spiritu Sancto,* 14, 31 (hereafter, *DSS* by chapter and paragraph number). Text is in *PG* 32, 67–217.

20. *DSS,* 14, 31.

21. *DSS,* 14, 31. For skiāgrăphía cf. Plato, *Critias,* 107c, where it is "indistinct and deceptive," and Aristotle, *Nichomachean Ethics,* i, 3, 4, where it is "paxylós kaí en túpō," coarsely, roughly in the type. cf. Chrysostom, p. 65 below.

22. *Address to Young Men on Reading Greek Literature: St. Basil, in Letters v. 4* trans. R. J. Defferrari and Martin R. P. McGuier (London, 1934), 378–435 at 426–31, and 428, n. 1. Also see the usages in Clement, *Stromata* 1, 1; *Protrepticus ad Graecos* 1; Gregory of Nazianzus, *Oration* 4, 47; 18, 4; 28, 19; Gregory of Nyssa, *In Psalmorum Inscriptiones, PG,* 44, 585.

23. *DSS,* 14, 31; and see Pelikan, n. 17 above.

24. Kustas, "Saint Basil," 244 and n. 74.

25. Gregory of Nazianzus, *Oration* 43, 23.

26. Gregory of Nazianzus, *Oration* 7, 7; cf. 7, 8, and *Epistle* 7.

27. *Oration* 7, 10.

28. *Oration* 7, 8.

29. See the remarks of Glenn W. Bowersock, *Greek Sophists in the Roman Empire* (Oxford, 1969), 59–75.

30. See Quasten, *Patrology,* 206–7. It should be noted that Basil's *Epistle* 70 was sent to Pope Damasus asking him to visit the East in the interests of Church unity.

31. *Epistle* 2, 27.

32. Cited in Kustas, "Saint Basil," 256.

33. See examples throughout Duchatelez, "La Notion."

34. See Kustas, "Saint Basil," 262–63, esp. nn. 157–64. For the same distinction between *theología* and *oikonomía* in Gregory of Nazianzus, see *Oration* 38, 8.

35. See Campbell, *The Influence*, 96–145.

36. *Epistle* 2, 3.

37. *De Baptismo* 1.1, *PG* 31, 1516.

38. *Epistle* 46, 6: *ho mégas tôn psychôn iatrós.*

39. *DSS,* 14, 32.

40. *DSS,* 14, 33.

41. *DSS,* 14, 33.

42. See n. 4 above.

43. See Quasten, *Patrology* III, 239–54; Ruether, *Gregory;* M. E. Kennan, "St. Gregory of Nazianzus and Early Byzantine Medicine," in *Bulletin of the History of Medicine* 9 (1941), 8–30; John F. Callahan, "Greek Philosophy and the Cappadocian Cosmology," in *DOP,* 12 (1958), 29–57; Brooks Otis, "Cappadocian Thought as a Coherent System," *DOP,* 12 (1958), 95–124. For the letters, see *Saint Grégoire de Nazianze Lettres,* 2 vols. ed. and trans. Paul Gallay (Paris, 1967).

44. *Oration* 38, 12. Numerous passages are repeated in *Or.* 2.

45. See references in note 43.

46. *Oration* 38, 12.

47. See briefly, Gerhart B. Ladner, *The Idea of Reform; its impact on Christian thought and action in the age of the Fathers* (New York, 1967), 153–212, esp. 157, n. 14; 174–78 (hereafter, Ladner, *Reform*) and idem. "The Philosophical Anthropology of Saint Gregory of Nyssa," *DOP* 12 (1958), 59–94 (hereafter, Ladner, "Anthropology"); and Ruether, *Gregory,* 135–36. See the *Pirke de Rabbi Eliezer,* chap. 14.

48. *Oration* 38, 13 and cf. *Oration* 2, 10–25.

49. *Oration* 45, 11.

50. *Oration* 45, 11.

51. *Oration* 45, 12.

52. Plutarch uses *boétheia* to mean both medical aid and a cure.

53. *Oration* 45, 12.

54. For the date, see Ruether, *Gregory,* 179, and Quasten, *Patrology* III, 242, for a summary of the contents.

55. *Oration* 31, 25. (*Fifth Theological Oration, 25.*)

56. *Oration* 31, 25.

57. *Oration* 31, 25.

58. See Quasten, *Patrology* III, 248–54, for a brief and lucid discussion.

59. *Oration* 30, 19.

60. *Oration* 30, 26. cf. Chap. VI below for similar Jewish exegesis.

61. See, for example, Quasten, Patrology III, 254–96.

62. Quasten, Patrology III, 255; L. Méridier, n. 16, was unavailable to me. See also Jean Daniélou, *Platonisme et théologie mystique: Essai sur la doctrine spirituelle de Saint Grégorie de Nysse,* 2nd ed. (Paris, 1954), and his *Introduction* (3–78) in *From Glory to Glory: Texts from Gregory of Nyssa's Mystical Writings,* ed. and trans. H. Musurillo (New York, 1961) (hereafter, *Glory*), Hans Urs von Balthasar, *Présence et Pensée: Essai sur la philosophie religieuse de Grégoire de Nysse* (Paris, 1942), Harold F. Cherniss, *The Platonism of Gregory of Nyssa (California Publications in Classical Philology* 11) (Berkeley, 1930), and Evangelos G. Konstantinou, *Die Tugendlehre Gregors von Nyssa in Verhältnis zu der Antik-Philosophischen und Judisch-Christlichen Tradition (Das Ostliche Christentum,* Neue Folge, Heft 17) Wurzburg, 1966.

63. J. Daniélou, *"Akolouthia* chez Grégoire de Nysse," in *RSR* 43 (1953), 219–249. Cited in *Glory,* 72, n. 8.

64. See Ladner, *Reform* and "Anthropology"; Ernest V. McClear, "The Fall of Man and Original Sin in the Theology of Gregory of Nyssa," in *TS* 9 (1948), 175–212; Eugenio Corsini, "Plerome Humain et Plerome Cosmique chez Grégoire de Nysse," *Écriture et Culture Philosophique dans la Pensée de Grégoire de Nysse, Actes du Colloque de Cheretogne (22–26 Septembre, 1969)* ed. Marguerite Harl (Leiden, 1971), 111–125.

65. See Cherniss, *Platonism,* and Ladner, "Anthropology," 61–63.

66. Ladner, "Anthropology," 63–66, see 64, n. 12.

67. *De opificio hominis* 8 (hereafter, *De hom.*). References to chapters and translations, unless otherwise indicated, are by H. A. Wilson in *LNPF,* ser. 2, vol. 5, 387–427. See Daniélou, *Platonisme,* 17–123.

68. *De hom.,* 8, 14, 27, 28, and cf. Ladner, "Anthropology," 67–77.

69. *De hom.,* 12–13; Gregory of Nazianzus, *Oration* II, 17, cited in Ladner, "Anthropology," 77.

70. *De hom.,* 16–18; Ladner, "Anthropology," 80–94 and Corsini, "Plerome Humain."

71. *De hom.*, 17.

72. *De hom.*, 17–22, Ladner, "Anthropology," 83–93.

73. *De Anima et resurrectione*, PG, 46, 148. For a history of this idea, see Daniélou, *Platonisme*, 27ff and 55ff; and Ladner, "Anthropology," 88, n. 136.

74. *De Anima et resurrectione*, *PG*, 46, 148–49, and for what follows, see *Glory*, 10–23 and McClear, "Fall."

75. *De hom.*, 16.

76. *Glory*, 12–13. See also, *On the Dead, PG*, 46, 522–24.

77. *Oratio catechetica magna*, 8. I use the translation in *LNPF* 5 and their chapter numbers (hereafter, *Cat. Or.*).

78. *Cat Or.*, 8.

79. See Daniélou, in *Glory*, 14; ibidem., *Platonisme*, 53–56; Ladner, "Anthropology," 88–89, esp. nn. 136 and 137.

80. See Ladner, "Anthropology," 88–89, esp. n. 137.

81. *Glory*, 14.

82. Daniélou, *Platonisme*, 27ff. and 55ff; and Ladner, "Anthropology," 90–91, esp. nn. 141–149.

83. See the edition of Jean Daniélou, *Grégoire de Nysse, La Vie de Moïse ou Traité de la Perfection en Matière de Vertu*, (*SCh* 1) 2nd edition, (Paris, 1955). See Daniélou's introduction ii–xxxv. [Hereafter, *Life*].

84. See *Life* I, 5; II, 225; and xviii–xxiv. Cf. *Homily* 8 of Gregory's *Accurate Exposition of the Canticle of Canticles*, PG, 44, 940–941.

85. *De hom.*, 25, 7.

86. *De hom.*, 25, 7.

87. *De hom.*, 25, 12; cf. *De hom.*, 25: 8–12.

88. *Adversus Eunomium*, 12, 3 (hereafter, *Ad Eu.*). *PG*, 45, 900.

89. *Ad. Eu.*, 12, 1; *PG*, 45, 889, 892. See also, McClear, "Fall," 194–96.

90. For the various references, see McClear "Fall," 196, nn. 113–117. Christ is described as a sheperd in *Ad. Eu.* 2, 4, 12; *PG*, 45, 541, 636, 888; a physician in *Ad. Eu.*, 3; PG, 45, 612.

91. *Cat. Or.*, 17.

92. *Cat Or.*, 17.

93. *Cat. Or.*, 20. Section 18 takes up the rejection of the Jews and the destruction of the Temple repeated and exploited by Chrysostom. I do not

focus on it since it does not contribute effectively to Gregory's main line of thought.

94. *Cat Or.*, 24. For an outline of the longevity of this idea, see Robert Longsworth, *The Cornish Ordinalia: Religion and Dramaturgy* (Cambridge, Mass., 1967), 72–102. I am indebted to Professor David Fowler for this reference.

95. *Cat. Or.*, 24, where several times Gregory employs language similar to: *tò tēn pantodŭnámon phúsin pròs tò tăpeinȏn tês anthrōpótētos katabénai ïsxusai.* Cf. *Cat. Or.*, 14.

96. *Cat. Or.*, 24.

97. See *Glory*, 23–32, for darkness as an image in Gregory's works.

98. For Rufinus, see *A Commentary on the Apostle's Creed*, trans. J. N. D. Kelly (Westminster, Md. and London, 1955), 51. For Augustine, see *Sermo*, 130, 2; *PL*, 38, 726. Both cited in Longsworth, *Ordinalia*, 74–75.

99. *Cat. Or.*, 23.

100. *Cat Or.*, 26.

101. *Cat Or.*, 26.

102. See, for example, *Ad. Eu.*, 2, 9; 8, 4: *PG*, 45, 505–508; 780–81, and *Ad. Eu.*, *Logos IB, PG*, 45, 932–33; 984–85; 988–96; 1049–52; LNPF, 113–17, 204–5, 257, 272–75, 292–93.

103. *Ad. Eu.*, *Logos IB, PG* 45, 992–93 (*LNPF*, 274–75).

104. *Ad. Eu.*, *PG*, 45, 992.

105. *Ad. Eu.*, *PG*, 45, 996–97.

106. *Ad. Eu.*, *PG*, 45, 1048–49, quotation on 1049.

107. See, for example, Benin, "The 'Cunning of God' "; J. Heinemann, *Aggadah and its Development* (Jerusalem, 1974), (Hebrew) 12, 96–102, 183; Abraham Joshua Heschel, *Theology of Ancient Judaism* (London and New York, 1962), (Hebrew) 2 vols., I, 3–23; Harry A. Wolfson, "Extradeical and Intradeical Interpretations of Platonic Ideas," in *Religious Philosophy: A Group of Essays* (New York, 1965), 27–68, also in *JHI*, 22, (1961), 3–32.

108. I rely heavily on Brooks Otis, "Gregory of Nyssa and the Cappadocian Conception of Time," in *Studia Patristica* 14, (1979), 327–57 (hereafter, "Gregory and Time"); ibidem, "Cappadocian Thought," *DOP*, 12, (1958), 95–124; John F. Callahan, "Basil of Caesarea: A New Source for St. Augustine's Theory of Time," in *Harvard Studies in Classical Philology*, 63 (1958), 437–54; ibidem, "Greek Philosophy," *DOP*, 12, (1958), 29–57; Ladner, *Reform*, 203–12; ibidem, "Philosophical Anthropology"; Daniélou, *Platonisme*, passim; Balthasar, *Présence*, passim.

109. Otis, "Gregory and Time," 337–41, esp. 340, nn. 1 and 2. *Ad. Eu.*, I, 26; *Logos* IB; *PG,* 45, 364, 1064.

110. Otis, "Gregory and Time," 341, and Danielou, "Platonisme," 186–333, which Otis notes deals inter alia with the progress of the soul that operates both with human desire for the divine and with divine love for humanity. Cf. chap. 6 below for the Maimonidean position concerning divine actions.

111. *Ad. Eu., Logos IB, PG,* 45, 932–33; *LNPF,* 257; I use the translation in Otis, "Gregory and Time," 243.

112. Balthasar, *Présence,* 8–11, cited in Otis, "Gregory and Time," 345, n. 1.

113. *Hom. VII on Ecclesiastes, PG,* 44, 729, cited in Otis, "Gregory and Time," 346: *tò dé diástēma oùdén 'állo ē' ktísis ëstín.*

114. *De hom.,* 16, 17, and 22.

115. Otis, "Gregory and Time," 351.

116. Otis, "Gregory and Time," 353; ibidem, "Cappadocian Thought"; Jerome Gaith, *La conception de Liberté chez Grégoire de Nysse (Études de Philosophie Médiévale,* 43) Paris, 1953; S. De Boer, *De Anthropologie van Gregorius van Nyssa* (Assen, 1968), was unavailable to me, and see Balthasar, *Presénce.*

117. *De hom.,* 2.

118. Otis, "Gregory and Time," 354, and n. 1. For comparison with other writers, especially Augustine, see Callahan, "Basil of Caesarea," and Ladner, *Reform,* 185–223.

119. See Sozomen, *Historica Ecclesiastìca,* 8, 2, where bibliographical information on Chrysostom, is provided. Also of interest is Palladius, *Dialogue of the Life of Saint John Chrysostom, PG,* 47, 5–82. For Chrysostom, one must consult the excellent study by Robert L. Wilken, *John Chrysostom and the Jews (The Transformation of the Classical Heritage 4)* (Berkeley, Los Angeles, London, 1983) (hereafter, Wilken, *Chrysostom*), which appeared while I was working on this manuscript. While I profited greatly from Wilken's analysis, I have decided to retain Chrysostom in this work because Wilken never deals directly with the use of *sugkatábāsis,* and Chrysostom's use of accommodation and condescension merits examination. Also of use, but now of secondary value to Wilken, is Chrysostomus Baur, *John Chrysostom and His Time* (trans. M. Gonzaga) (Westminster, Md., 1959), 2 vols. For bibliography, see Wilken, Chrysostom, 165–83.

120. Cited in J. Quasten, *Patrology,* III, 396.

121. See Quasten, III, 397; and on Theodore, see J. M. Voste, "L`Oeuvre exégétique de Théodore de Mopsuestia au IIe concile de Constantinople," in *R. Bibl.*, 38 (1929), 382–95, 542–54.

122. Diodoros of Tarsus, *Fragmenta in Genesim, PG,* 33, 1580.

123. *Fragmenta in Genesim, PG,* 33, 1571 on Genesis 8:20.

124. See Stephen D. Benin, "Sacrifice as Education in Augustine and Chrysostom," in *CH,* 52(1983), 7–20.

125. Wilken, *Chrysostom,* passim.

126. See above p. 68–74 for Basil.

127. *De Sacerdotio,* 5, 5. I use the translation in Wilken, *Chrysostom,* 106.

128. *Oration,* 42, 24. See also Harry M. Hubbell, "Chrysostom and Rhetoric," in *Classical Philology,* 19 (1943), 261–76.

129. *Sur la vaine gloire et l' education des enfants,* ed. A-M. Malingrey, *SC,* 188 (Paris, 1972) (hereafter, *Vaine gloire*), and in M. L. W. Laistner, *Christianity and Pagan Culture in the Later Roman Empire together with an English translation of John Chrysostom's Address on Vainglory and the Right Way for Parents to bring up their Children* (Ithaca, NY 1951), 85–122 (hereafter, Laistner, *Culture*).

130. *Jean Chrysostome, La Virginité,* ed. and trans. H. Musurillo and B. Grillet, *SCh,* 125 (Paris, 1966) (hereafter, *Virginity*).

131. The text, *Peri Akataleptou,* may be found in *Jean Chrysostome, Sur L'Incompréhensibilité de Dieu,* (*SCh,* 28 bis) ed. A.-M. Malingrey (Paris, 1970) (homilies I-IV); there is also the text in *PG,* 48, 701–812, and *St. John Chrysostom on the Incomprehensible Nature of God,* trans. Paul W. Harkins, *FC,* 72 (Washington, D.C., 1984) (hereafter, Harkins, *On the Incompreh.*).

132. Trans. Paul W. Harkins, *FC,* 68 (Washington, D.C., 1979).

133. For the dating, see Laistner, *Culture,* 78–79; *Vaine gloire,* 41–47, where the relevant scholarship is reviewed, with the end of 393 to early 394 being favored.

134. *Vaine gloire,* sect. 15.

135. *Vaine gloire,* sect. 19.

136. *Homiliae XVIII in Epistolam I ad Timotheum* 9, 2 in *PG* 62, 545–46.

137. *Vaine gloire,* sect. 20–25.

138. *Vaine gloire,* sect. 37.

139. See, for example, *Virginity*, 30, 1; 50, 1–2; *Homilia in Epistolam ad Colossenses hom.*, 4, 1: *PG*, 62, 328–31; *Homilia in Epistolam ad Colossenses*, 4; *PG* 62, 328–31; and Benin, "Sacrifice as Education," 17–20.

140. *Vaine gloire*, sect. 37–53.

141. See above pp. 28–35.

142. *Vaine gloire*, sect. 52 and cf. *De Lazaro conciones*, 3, 1, *PG*, 48, 991, for the image of a mother who feeds her children with tiny morsels.

143. *Vaine gloire*, sect. 54. Note the use of *oĭkouménē* as above in Origen, Eusebius, and Athanasius. See above pp. 34–35, 37–42, 61–62 for the use of *oĭkouménē.*

144. *Vaine gloire*, sect. 56–59.

145. *Vaine gloire*, sect. 61; cf. *Ad Stagirium a daemone vexatum libri*, II, 12; *PG*, 47, 470; *Homiliae in Genesim*, 62, 4; *PG*, 54, 537; *Homilia in epistola ad Coloss. hom.*, 10, 5; *PG*, 62, 372 and for other references, see Laistner, *Culture*, 139, n. 34, and *Vaine gloire*, 159, n. 5.

146. *Vaine gloire*, sect. 90.

147. For a brief summary, see Laistner, *Culture*, 49–73, and H. I. Marrou, *A History of Education in Antiquity*, trans. G. Lamb (New York, 1956). P. Koukoules, *Basil, Gregory of Nazianzus and John Chrysostom as Educators* (Athens, 1951) (in Greek), was unavailable to me.

148. *PG*, 31, 563–90, and *Saint Basil, The Letters*, IV, 365–435, trans. Roy J. Defarrari and Martin R. P. McGuire (*LCL*), sect. 4, p. 390.

149. Bernard Grillet favors the earlier date in "Introduction générale," *Virginity*. Herbert Musurillo, who did the Greek text for the above edition, favors the later date in "Some Textual Problems in the Editing of the Greek Fathers," in *Studia Patristica* III = *Texte und Untersuchungen*, 78 (Berlin, 1961), 92. The date of *On the Incompreh.* is agreed to by Wilken, *Chrysostom*, 14–16, and Harkins, *On the Incompreh.*, 22–23.

150. Bernard Grillet, "Introduction générale," *Virginity*, p. 8.

151. *Virginity*, 14, 3–6.

152. *Virginity*, pp. 57–64.

153. *Virginity*, pp. 142–43, n. 3, for references.

154. *Virginity*, 15, 1.

155. *Virginity*, 15, 3.

156. *Virginity*, 16 is entitled *hóti sugkatábaseōs ho gámos.*

157. *Virginity*, 16, 1. See below for the same expression in the Syriac authors, and compare Augustine in Benin, "Sacrifice as Education."

158. *Virginity,* 16, 1.

159. *Virginity,* 16, 2.

160. *Virginity,* 17, 1.

161. *Virginity,* 17, 2.

162. *Virginity,* 17, 3. Cf. 47, 4.

163. *Virginity,* 17, 4.

164. *Virginity,* 17, 5.

165. *Virginity,* 19, 1–2.

166. *Virginity,* 44, 1.

167. *Virginity,* 78, 1.

168. *Virginity,* 13, 1.

169. *Virginity,* 78, 2.

170. *Virginity,* 78, 3.

171. *Virginity,* 82, 1–3.

172. *Virginity,* 83, 1.

173. *Virginity,* 83, 2.

174. See *Homiliae 9 in Genesin,* 27, *PG,* 53, 242; *Homiliae in Psalmum,* 49; *PG,* 55, 247; *Homiliae in Psalmum,* 121; *PG,* 55, 349; *In Isaiam,* I; *PG,* 56, 18–19; *Adversus Judaeos,* 4; *PG,* 48, 880–81, as a few examples, and for fuller discussion, see Pinard, "Les Infiltrations," and Benin, "Sacrifice as Education."

175. *Adversus Judaeos,* 4; *PG,* 48, 880.

176. *Hom. in. Epist. ad Coloss.* 4; *PG,* 62, 329–29. Cf. Basil's use of *skiagraphia* on pg. 69.

177. *Hom. in. Epist. ad Coloss.* 4; *PG,* 62, 329–330.

178. *Hom. in. Epist. ad Coloss.* 4; *PG,* 62, 330–331. *"Kaì baskánoi dè málista pántōn ēsan, kaì mikrópsychoî, kaì pánta áteleîs."* See also, M. Simon, "La polémique anti-juive de S. Jean Chrysostome et le mouvement judaïsant d'Antioche," in *Annuaire de l'Institut de philologie et d'histoire orientales et slaves,* IV, 1936 (*Mélanges Franz Cumont*), 403–21, and R. A. Kraft, "In Search of 'Jewish-Christianity' and Its 'Theology' Problems of Definition and Methodology," *Judeo-Christianisme Daniélou Festschrift* (Paris, 1972), 81–92.

179. References will be to homily number and section according to the divisions in *PG* 48; page numbers in *PG* and in the *SCh* edition will be given. I, 6, 707/130. I use the translation in Harkins, *On the Incomprehen.* unless otherwise indicated; text of homilies I–V is in *Sur L'incompréhensibilité de Dieu, SCh* 28 bis, ed. A.-M. Malingrey (Paris, 1970).

180. Harkins, *On the incompreh.*, II, 1, 709–10/144.

181. *Sygkatabaínō* appears III, 5, 723/208; IV, 3, 730/244; 731/246; V, 3, 739/288; *sygkatábāsis* appears I, 6, 707/128; III, 3, 722/200–1 (five times); III, 5, 724/212–14 (twice); IV, 1, 729/234; IV, 3, 730/242; IV, 3, 731/246. *Ástheneía* appears I, 3, 704/110; III, 1, 720/192; III, 3, 722/200; III, 4, 722/204; IV, 3, 731/244; V, 3, 739/288; V, 3, 740/290 (twice); V, 6, 745/314.

182. *On the incompreh.*, III, 2, 720–21/195–6.

183. *On the incompreh.*, III, 2, 721/196.

184. *On the incompreh.*, III, 2, 721/196–98.

185. *On the incompreh.*, III, 3, 722/198.

186. *On the incompreh.*, III, 3, 722/200. My translation.

187. *On the incompreh.*, III, 3, 722/200–2. As Malingrey points out, 202–3, n. 2, *sygkatábāsis* is modified by *dmudrós*, meaning indistinct or faint, which indicates that God chooses one manifestation for this revelation to a prophet. This individual, temporary manifestation is a result of condescension.

188. *On the incompreh.*, III, 4, 722–24/202–04. As Maligrey notes, 204, n. 1. Chrysostom refers to Daniel as *hágios*, which he uses often with people of the Hebrew Bible as a sign of their faith and piety.

189. *On the incompreh.*, III, 5, 723/208–9; *sygkatabaínōn* is used.

190. *On the incompreh.*, III, 5, 724/212.

191. *On the incompreh.*, VI, 3, 753.

192. *On the incompreh.*, VII, 3, 759.

193. *On the incompreh.*, VII, 3, 759.

194. *On the incompreh.*, VII, 3, 759.

195. *On the incompreh.*, VII, 3, 759–60.

196. *On the incompreh.*, X, 2, 785. *Sygkatábāsis* is used.

197. *On the incompreh.*, IX, 2, 782. Note also the medical imagery in the section. Cf. X, 3, 787–88.

198. *On the incompreh.*, X, 2, 786. I amend Harker's translation. See also X, 4–6, 788–94 for even more references.

199. See Quasten, *Patrology*, III, 536–554, and Theodoret's *Letters, PG* 83, 1173–1409; *Letters*, 81, 113.

200. Letter, 113, I use the translation *LNPF*, III, 294.

201. See below, pp. 2–5 and pp. 76–80.

202. See *Bibliotheca*, sect. 46, where the style is called "clear and clean," and his thoughts "well ordered."

203. *In Isaiam*, I, 81, 225. Cf. Arthur Bedford, *The Temple Musick* (London, 1712), 231–32: "Musick was corrupted by the Egyptians when they were wont to set forth thereby the praises of their false gods; and yet Moses made no scruple to use it for the Honour of the True God: Neither do we even find that he was blamed for it. Nay, when God was more particularly cautious in the time of Moses, and forbade the Israelites to retain the customs of other nations, because they were abused, these customs were in themselves lawful before the prohibition, when He forbade everything which might have the tendency to idolatry. . . ."

204. The text is in *PG*, 83, 783–1152, and in P. Canivet, ed. and trans. *Théodoret de Cyr, Thérapeutique des maladies helléniques*, 2 vols., *SCh* 57, (Paris, 1958). Sacrifices are the subject of Sermon 7.

205. *Curatio*, 7, *PG*, 83, 995. See also Amos Funkenstein, "Gesetz und Geschichte, zur historisierenden Hermeneutik bei Moses Maimonides und Thomas von Aquin," *Viator* I (1970), 147–78; *ibidem:* 'Maimonides: Political Theory and Realistic Messianism," in *Miscellanea Medievalia*, XI (1977), 81–103. (Hereafter, Funkenstein, "Messianiam".)

206. *Curatio*, 7, *PG*, 83, 996–97.

207. *Curatio*, 7, *PG*, 83, 997.

208. *Curatio*, 7, *PG*, 83, 997.

209. See Funkenstein, "Messianism," 94, n. 44, for the references to Manetho, who, according to Josephus, inverted biblical history and claimed that the leader of the Jews instructed them to kill and consume all animals revered in Egypt. Of course, Tacitus, when speaking of Jewish practice, remarked succinctly: *"Profana illic omnia quae apud nos sacra, rursum concessa apud illos quae nobis incesta."* (History V, 4)

210. *De Providentia, Oratio X, PG*, 83, 764. Diá toûto mónon lambánei tòn perì toû phutoû mónon, nēpiódē tinà, kaì bréphesin artitókois harmóttonta.

211. *De Providentia, Oratio X, PG*, 83, 764–74.

212. See *Commentarii in Exodum, PG*, 87:1, 601–2; 663–66; *Commentarii in Leviticum, PG*, 87:1, 749; *Catenae Graecae in Genesim et in Exodum I*, ed. F. Petit in *Corpus Christianorum Series Graeca*, introduction, xiii–xxi. For Procopius, see K. Krumbacher, *Geschichte der Byzantinischen Literatur von Justinian bis zum ende des ostromischen Reiches* (Munich, 1897), 125–27.

213. *Quaestiones, Quaestio, 46, PG*, 89, 597, where he says that sacrifices were a condescension to human weakness: állà [thusiai] sygkatabaínōn têekeínōn astheneía. *Dialogus Parvus ad Judaeos, PG*, 89, 1271–73; *Disputatio adversus Judaeos, PG*, 89, 1277. See also Krumbacher, *Geschichte*, 64–65, where Anastasius is dubbed "der Wanderapostel der Orthodoxie." The latter two works are of spurious origin.

214. See the *Trophies of Damascus,* "Les Trophées de Damas, Controverse Judeo-Chretienne du VIIe siècle," ed. and trans. G. Bardy. *PO,* XV (Paris, 1920). See p. 198, where sacrifices are described as a condescension to human weakness: *ástheneían toutô eípēn sygkatabaínōn aútoîs.* On p. 248, the issue of dietary laws is also introduced but the text merely parrots Theodoret and Anastasius.

215. *De Dei circa hominem oeconomia* I, PG, 120, 1293–96.

216. *Exposito in Pauli Epistolas: Ad Hebraeos, PG,* 125, 324.

CHAPTER THREE

1. For much of what follows I am indebted to the seminal study of Robert Murray, *Symbols of Church and Kingdom, A Study in Early Syriac Tradition* (London, 1975), 1–38. (hereafter, Murray, *Symbols*) Cf. the very valuable study of Judah B. Segal, *Edessa "The Blessed City"* (Oxford, 1970), 9–62. (hereafter, Segal, *(Edessa).* See also Stephen D. Benin, "Commandments, Covenants and the Jews in Aphrahat, Ephrem and Jacob of Sarug" in *Approaches to Judaism in Medieval Times (Brown Judaic Studies* 54) ed. David R. Blumenthal (Chico, CA., 1984), 135–56 (hereafter, Benin, "Commandments") and in general see Marcel Simon, *Verus Israel: étude sur les relations entre chrétiens et juifs dans l'empire roman (135–425)* (Paris, 1948). G. Richter, "Uber die älteste Auseinandersetzung der syrischen Christen mit den Juden," *Zeitschrift für die Neutestamentliche Wissenschaft* 35 (1936), 101–114.

2. Murray, *Symbols,* 19. See also Frank S. B. Gavin, "Aphraates and the Jews," *Journal of the Society of Oriental Research* 7 ((1923), 95–166, (hereafter, Gavin, *Aphraates).* See also H. J. W. Drijvers, "Edessa und das judische Christentum," *VC* 24 (1970), 4–33; Frank, S. B. Gavin, *Aphraates and the Jews: A Study of the Controversial Homilies of the Persian Sage in their relations to Jewish Thought (Contributions to Oriental History and Philology),* vol. IX, New York, 1966 (reprint of 1923 edition), Jacob Neusner, *Aphrahat and Judaism. The Christian-Jewish Argument in Fourth-Century Iran* (Leiden, 1971), 1–15, 123–49 (hereafter, Neusner, *Aphrahat),* Paul Schwen, *Afrahat: seine Person und sein verstandnis des Christentums* (Berlin, 1907), and Arthur Vööbus, "Methodologisches zum Studien der Anweisung Aphrahats," *OCh* 46 (1962), 25–32..

3. Segal, *Edessa,* 101.

4. Segal, *Edessa,* 102.

5. Murray, *Symbols,* 29.

6. Murray, *Symbols,* 29; Neusner, *Aphrahat,* 4, suggests 1–10 were written in 337, the next thirteen in 344.

7. Neusner, *Aphrahat,* 4–5, 144–9, 150–195, where Neusner reviews the literature; demonstrates similarities, parallels, and affinities; and suggests that these commonalities may only indicate that Semitic Christianity preserved some elements of the Pharisaic heritage.

8. Neusner, *Aphrahat,* 144–49.

9. Segal, *Edessa,* 100, and Arthur Vööbus, *Peschitta und Targumim des Pentateuchs: neues Licht zur Frage der Herkunft der Peschitta aus dem altpalastenischen Targum,* (Stockholm, 1962).

10. The text is in *PS,* I, II, 1–489, ed. J. Parisot (Paris, 1894, 1907). References are to homily (Demonstration) and section according to the *PS* text. See Gavin, *Aphraates* 1–18; Neusner, *Aphrahat,* 196–244; Murray, *Symbols,* 279–340. See also Stanley Kazan, "Isaac of Antioch's Homily Against the Jews," in *OC,* 45 (1961), 30–53; 46 (1962), 87–95; 47 (1963), 89–97; 49 (1965), 57–78 (hereafter, Kazan, *OC*).

11. The work is attributed to the school of Bardaisan. Segal, *Edessa,* 36, suggests that his pupil Phillip was the probable author. The text is *Bardasanes Liber Legum Regionum,* ed. F. Nau, *PS,* 2 (Paris, 1907), 604 (sec. 43). See in general, Anton Baumstark, *Geschichte der syrischen Literatur* (Bonn, 1922), 12–17.

12. *Dem.* I, 19.

13. Segal, *Edessa,* 100.

14. *Dem.* 15, 1–3.

15. *Dem.* 15, 4.

16. *Dem.* 15, 4.

17. *Dem.* 15, 4.

18. Little has been done on Aphrahat's style save for M. Maude, "Rhythmic Patterns in the Homilies of Aphraates," in *AThR,* 17 (1935), 225–33, and Murray, *Symbols,* 30 and passim.

19. *Dem.* 15, 4.

20. *Dem.* 15, 4.

21. See *Gen. R.,* 34:10; *TB Berachot,* 17a; *PT Berachot,* 7d. See Schechter, *Aspects,* 262–67; Moore, *Judaism,* I, 480, notes, 146–47. Gavin points out the use of this metaphor in Aphrahat; and Neusner, *Aphrahat,* 152, agrees "that for Aprahat and the rabbis the evil impulse meant pretty much the same thing."

22. *Dem.* 15, 4.

23. Murray, *Symbols,* 54 and n. 5.

24. *Dem.* 15, 6. For the idea of "peoples," see Murray, *Symbols,* 41–68.

25. See Schechter, *Aspects,* 250–52.

26. *Dem.* 11, 4.

27. *Dem.* 11, 2.

28. *Dem.* 11, 11.

29. *Dem.* 11, 11. Cf. Benin, "Commandments," 138–42, and the discussion in Murray, *Symbols,* 14–17.

30. See Murray, *Symbols,* 41, n. 3.

31. Murray, *Symbols,* 56–68, for what follows, and Murray's comment is on 68. See also Arthur Vööbus, *History of the School of Nisibis, CSCO* 266, (Louvain, 1965), and *ibidem,* Ed. and trans. *The Statutes of the School of Nisibis,* (Stockholm, 1961).

32. I use the translation in Kazan, *OC,* 47, 96–97.

33. *Hymn,* 21, 18. I use the translation in *LNPF,* 13, 11, trans. J. T. Sarsfield Stopford, p. 192; the Syriac text was unavailable to me. See T. Jansma, "Narsai and Ephrem. Some Observations on Narsai's Homilies on Creation and Ephraem's Hymns on Faith," *Parole de l'Orient* I (1970) 49–68; and compare J. Gribomont, "Les Hymnes de Saint Ephrem sur la Paques," in *Melito,* 1–2 (1967), 147–82.

34. Murray, *Symbols,* 63.

35. *Sermo de Domino Nostro,* sec. 6, ed. E. Beck, *CSCO,* 270–71, (Louvain, 1966), Syriac 116–17.

36. *Sermo de Domino Nostro,* sec. 6.

37. *Sermo de Domino Nostro,* sec. 17 and cf. 18–21; which is an expanded exegesis comparing *Exodus* 32 with *Luke* 7:44–47.

38. See the fruitful discussion in Murray, *Symbols,* 41–68.

39. I use the translation in Kazan, *OC,* 46, 97.

40. Kazan, *OC,* 46, 97.

41. Kazan, *OC,* 46, 98.

42. Kazan, *OC,* 46, 98.

43. Cited in Murray, *Symbols,* 63; see 62, n. 6. See also Ephrem's *Commentaire de l'Évangile Concordant, Version armenienne,* ed. and trans. L. Leloir, *CSCO,* 137, (Louvain, 1953/54), 144–47.

44. Cited in Kazan, *OC,* 46, 97.

45. *Hymns on the Crucifixion* 3.3 and 12. I use the translation in Murray, *Symbols,* 63.

46. For Aphrahat's comment, see *Dem.,* 21, 1, where he writes that one day a *gbr' dmtqr' ḥkym' dyhwdy'.* For Ephrem, see Murray, *Symbols,* 41. See also N. Sed, "Les hymnes sur le paradis de Saint Ephrem et les traditions juives," in *Le Muséon,* 81 (1968), 455–501; Robert Murray, "A Hymn of St. Ephrem to Christ on the Incarnation, the Holy Spirit and the Sacraments," in *Eastern Churches Review,* 3 (1970), 142–50; and *ibidem,* "St. Ephrem the Syrian on Church Unity," in *Eastern Churches Quarterly,* 15 (1963), 164–70.

47. See Baumstark, *Geschichte,* 142–152, and 152, n. 2.

48. I use the text and translation in Kazan, *OC,* 45, 31–53.

49. In Kazan, *OC,* 45, 35, lines 81–84; the word *kbl'* may be a slave's neckchain. It is in any case some sort of restraining device.

50. In Kazan, *OC,* 45, 35, lines 87–96.

51. In Kazan, *OC,* 45, 43–48, lines 285–372.

52. In Kazan, *OC,* 45, 34, lines, 54–58.

53. In Kazan, *OC,* 45, 42–43, lines 235–284.

54. In Kazan, *OC,* 45, 40, lines 201–208.

55. *TB Shabbat,* 105b attributed to Yohanan ben Nuri; the same teaching is attributed to his contemporary, R. Akiba, in *The Fathers According to Rabbi Nathan,* chap. 3.

56. Immortality and propogation, *Gen. R.,* 8, 11; no evil inclination, *Gen. R.,* 68, 11.

57. *Lev. R.,* 27, 3, and see Urbach, *Sages,* I, 554–64.

58. *TB, Sanh.* 102a; cf. *Exod. R.* 43, 2. On the whole issue, see Levy Smolar and Moshe Aberbach, "The Golden Calf in Postbiblical Literature," *HUCA,* 39 (1968), 91–116.

59. The title was given to Jacob in an anonymous biography published by Assemani, *Bibliotheca Orientalia* 1, 286, cited in Kazan, *OC,* 49, 60, n. 1. I use the text in Micheline Albert, *Jacques de Saroug, Homélies Contre Les Juifs PO* 38, (1976). References are to homily number, page, and lines. For parallels with earlier Syriac writers, see Albert's *Introduction,* 9–23. I am indebted to Fr. F. Graffin of Paris for advising me, while I was a graduate student, to search these homilies. (This in a private letter of 11 November 1978.)

60. For a brief outline, see Kazan, *OC,* 49, 61–64, and Albert, *Homélies,* 11–14; see on Jacob, Segal, *Edessa,* 170–73.

61. *Hom.,* I, 52, lines 125–30.

62. *Hom.,* I, 62, lines 287–88. *ẓrh wḥtmh lnbywt' brh d'lh'; 'p 'sh'y' ẓwr shdwt' mtnb' hw'.* The on of God bound (*ẓrh*) and sealed (*ḥtm*) calls to mind Mohammed as the seal of prophecy. The Arabic cognate root is *khtm.*

63. *Hom.,* 2, 69, line 19.

64. *Hom.,* 2, 75, lines 103–8.

65. *Hom.,* 2, 69–84, lines 25–252.

66. *Hom.,* 3, 87–88, lines 15–46.

67. As E. E. Urbach has written: "The rabbinic viewpoint in regard to the creation of the world found succinct expression in the epithet 'He who spoke and the world came into being.' See Urbach, *Sages,* 213; see on the entire issue, *Sages* I, 184–213.

68. *Hom.,* 3, 90, lines 70–74.

69. *TB Taanit,* 7a. Cf. Moore, *Judaism,* 2, 96–97.

70. *Hom.,* 7, 190, lines 145–55.

71. *Hom.,* 7, 190–92, lines 145–200, esp. 165–186.

72. *Hom.,* 7, 192, line 177: *h' wryt' by't 'mm' hshyb' h'm'.*

73. *Hom.,* 7, 195, lines 197–200.

74. *Hom.,* 7, 210, lines 445–457.

75. Cf. *Hom.,* 3, 90, line 79.

76. *Hom.,* 7, 212, lines 480–84. The source for he image may be Basil of Caesarea, *Comment. in Isaiam Prophetam,* 2, *PG,* 30, 245. (Though as Quasten points out, *Patrology* 3, 219, it may be a spurious work.) The translation by Dom Wilstan Hibberd, in J. Daniélou, *From Shadows to Reality: Studies in Biblical Typology of the Fathers* (London, 1960), 190, reads: "If we think a man is ridiculous to have a lighted lamp in full daylight, how much more ridiculous when the Gospel has been proclaimed to linger in the shadows of the Law"— does not seem to capture the full strength of the Greek: *Ei' dè géloios hēliou lámpontos, ho lýxnon heatọ paraphaínōn, pollọ geloióteros ho Eyangeliou kēryssoménou, tẹ skiậ tẹ nomikẹ paraménōn.* The language is close to Jacob's where he uses the verb *t̑n,* for carrying the lamp (as a burden one might carry the Law?) is the Syriac for *paraphérō* (see Payne-Smith, 179, s.v. *t̑n.*)

77. *Hom.,* 7, 198, lines 259–60 and cf. 345–346.

78. *Hom.,* 7, 182, lines 7–8.

79. *Hom.,* 4, 112–14, lines 25–30, and cf. *San.* 98a: "Rabbi Yohanan said: 'The Son of David will come only in a generation which is wholly innocent or wholly guilty.' "

80. *Hom.,* 4, 122, lines 153–76.

81. *Hom.,* 4, 120–22, lines 145–52.

82. *Hom.,* 4, 120, line 1. The root is *gmr,* and it implies perfection and full growth. Jacob writes about bodily perfection in opposition to being virtuous *(spyr),* or even perhaps orthodox. See Payne-Smith, p. 590, s.v. *spyr.*

83. *Hom.,* 4, 120, lines 125–30. The root is *nhr* and the text would be read *nuhr* (light) or *nuhar* (instruction or enlightenment), cf. Payne-Smith, s.v. *nwhr.* Jacob may either be comparing the fact that the Jews neither *see* nor accept Christ with their acceptance of the Law in Exodus 19:8 and 24:3, where they promise to do all that God *spoke,* that is, they heard, but could not see then either! He may also be punning on light as sight as in the case of the great kabbalist Isaac the Blind, known as R. Yitzḥak Sagi Nahor—a use attested in Jacob's time, see Jastrow, *Dictionary,* 881, s.v. *n'hwr.*

84. Kazan, *OC,* 49, 76. The text *Against the Jews,* ed. J. de Zwaan (Leiden, 1906), was unavailable to me, I relied on summaries in A. Lukyn Williams, *Adversus Judaeos; A Bird's Eye View of Christian Apologiae Until The Renaissance* (Cambridge, 1935), 107–112, and Kazan, *OC,* 49, 66–78.

85. *Dem.,* 11, 11.

86. Cited in Kazan, *OC,* 49, 73.

87. See Kazan, *OC,* 49, 72–78, at 73; *l' mshtḥl'p pwqdn'.* Cf. Aphrahat, *Dem.,* 11, 11, *qy'm' dl' mshtḥlp.*

88. Cf. the comments in Kazan, *OC,* 49, 74, for the idea of a lost Aramaic anti-Jewish polemical tradition.

CHAPTER FOUR

1. I wish to thank Rev. Lawrence Frankovich of Kansas Newman College for his suggestions, comments and criticisms on Augustine in an earlier draft of this chapter. For Tertullian see for example: *Adversus Marcionem* 2, 18; in *CCL* I, ed. A. Kroymann (Turnhout, 1954) *de Virginibus Velandis* 2, 1; *De Monogamia* 3, 8; both in *CCL* II ed. E. Dekkers (Turnhout, 1954) *Adversus Judaeos* 2, 9. *CCL* II, ed. A. Kroymann (Turnhout, 1954). For Thomas Moore, see *Utopia* I, in *The Complete Works of Thomas More* vol. 4, ed. Edward Surtz and J. H. Hexter (New Haven and London, 1965), 100: *Nisi quod concionatores homini calide, tuum illud consilium secuti puto, quando mores suos homines ad CHRISTI normam grauatim paterentur aptari, doctrinam eius uelut regulam plumbeam accommodauerunt ad mores, ut aliquo saltem pacto coniungerentur scilicet.* See also 376 for uses of the *regulam plumbeam.* And for Dante see, Dante Alighieri, *The Divine Comedy, Paradiso,* 2 vols. trans. and ed. Charles S., Singleton (Princeton, 1970–75), I, 38; Canto 4, lines 28–48; II, 79–82. "Così parlar conviensi al vostro

ingegno, pero che solo da sensato apprende ciò che fa poscia d'intelleto degno. Per questo la Scrittura condescende a vostra facultate, e piedi e mano attribuisce a Dio e altro intende; e Santa Chiesa con aspetto umano Gabriel e Michel vi rappresenta, e l'altro che Tobia rifece sano."

2. For a survey of other medieval Latin authors see the unpublished dissertation of Stephen D. Benin, " 'Thou Shalt Have No Other Gods Before Me': Sacrifice in Medieval Jewish and Christian Thought" (Univ. of California, Berkeley, 1980), 120–64.

3. For Augustine and editions of his works and translations, see Peter R. L. Brown, *Augustine of Hippo* (Berkeley, Los Angeles, 1969); for much of what follows, see R. A. Markus, "St. Augustine on Signs," in *Phronesis* II (1957), 60–83; R. A. Markus, " 'Imago' and 'similitudo' in Augustine," in *REAug*, 10 (1964), 125–43; Ulrich Duchrow, " 'Signum' und 'superbia' beim jungen Augustin (386–390)," *REAug*, 7 (1961), 369–72; Paul Archambault, "The Ages of Man and the Ages of the World. A Study of Two Traditions," *REAug*, 12 (1966), 193–228; Stephen D. Benin, "Sacrifice as Education in Augustine and Chrysostom," in *CH*, 52 (1983), 7–20; William M. Green, "Augustine on the Teaching of History," *Univ. of California Publications in Classical Philology*, 12 (1944), 315–32; Herbert Musurillo, "History and Symbol: A Study of Form in Early Christian Literature," in *TS*, 18 (1957), 357–87.

4. *De Magistro*, I, 1. CSEL, 77, ed. Guenther Weigel, Vienna, 1961 (hereafter, *De Mag.*)

5. *De Mag.*, I, 2; Markus, "Augustine on Signs," 66–67.

6. *De Mag.*, XI, 36; Markus, "Augustine on Signs," 69–70.

7. *Retractions* I, 12. (*CSEL* 36, ed. P. Knoll, Vienna, 1902).

8. See Markus, "Augustine on Signs," 71, and n. 1 for the details. See also R. A. Markus, *Saeculum: History and Society in the Theology of St. Augustine,* Cambridge 1970. The *De Doctrina Christiana* was written in 397 as far as III, 25, 35, revised in 427, when the remainder of book III and book IV were added. See B. Darrell Jackson, "The Theory of Signs in St. Augustine's *De doctrina christiana,*" in *REAug*, 15 (1969), 9–49. I use *De Doctrina Christiana* in *CSEL,* 80 ed. William M. Green, (Vienna, 1963).

9. *De Doc. Christ.*, II, 1, 1. Cf. Markus "Augustine on Signs," 71–72.

10. *De Doc. Christ.*, I, 2, 2. For a detailed discussion, see Jackson, "Theory of Signs."

11. *De Doc. Christ.*, I, 2, 14–23.

12. See Brown, *Augustine,* 259–69.

13. See Duchrow, " 'Signum' und 'superbia.' " Cf. Brown, *Augustine,* 265–69.

14. *City of God,* 16, 3.

15. See David S. Katz, *Philo-Semitism and the Readmission of the Jews to England 1603–1655* (Oxford, 1982), 60–61.

16. *De Doc. Christ.,* II, 14, 21; II, 4, 5; II, 13, 19, and cf. Brown, *Augustine,* 265.

17. *De Doc. Christ.,* III, 5, 9–III, 9, 13.

18. Brown, *Augustine,* 266.

19. *De Doc. Christ.,* II, 40, 60.

20. *Retractions,* I, 13, 1. I use the translation in *LCC,* vol.6, 218.

21. *Retractions,* I, 13, 3.

22. *De Doc. Christ.,* II, 40, 60. This is discussed in Benin, "Sacrifice as Education."

23. *De Doc. Christ.,* II, 40, 60; cf. Benin, "Sacrifice as Education," 8–9.

24. Benin, "Sacrifice as Education," 9. *De. Doc. Christ.,* II, 40, 60; *Sed etiam liberales disciplinas usui veritatis aptiores et quaedam morum praecepta utilissima continent, deque ipso uno deo colendo nonnulla vera invenientur apud eos.* Note the use of *aptum* and its comparison with *pulcher,* in notes 30, 34, 37, 38, 85, and 86 below, cf. p. 111.

25. *De Vera Religione,* VII, 13. I use *De Vera Religione, CSEL* 77 ed. G. Weigel (Vienna 1961). For renewal and restoration see Gerhart B. Ladner, *The Idea of Reform; its impact on Christian thought and action in the age of the Fathers* (Cambridge, MA, 1959), and more recently, Karl F. Morrison, *The Mimetic Tradition of Reform in the West* (Princeton, 1982), esp. 54–97.

26. *De Vera Relig.,* VIII, 14, 15; IX, 16–17; X, 18–20.

27. *De Vera Relig.,* XI, 19. Cf. XXVI, 48. See the similarity to Eusebius' use of *pareisēlthón,* above, chap. 1., n. 70.

28. *De Vera Relig.,* XXVII, 50; XXVIII, 51.

29. *De Vera Relig.,* XVI, 30.

30. *De Vera Relig.,* XL, 76; *LCC,* 264. Note the use of *pulcher* n. 34, 37, 38, 85, and 86 below cf. p. 111.

31. *De Vera Relig.,* XVII, 34.

32. *De Vera Relig.,* XVII, 34; *LCC,* 241.

33. *De Vera Relig.,* XXX, 56; *LCC,* 253: "This standard of all the arts is absolutely unchangeable, but the human mind, which is given the power to see the standard, can suffer the mutability of error"; cf. XXVIII, 51; XXIX,

52, 53; XXX, 54–56; XXXI, 57–58; XXXII, 59–60; XXXIX, 72; XL, 74–76; XLII, 79; XLIII, 80–81 for examples of proportionality.

34. *De Vera Relig.*, XLIII, 80; LCC, 267.

35. *De Vera Relig.*, L, 98.

36. *Confessions*, 4, 13 (hereafter, *Conf.*). I use the Latin text in *CCL*, 27, ed. L. Verheijen (Turnhout, 1981).

37. *Conf.*, 4, 13.

38. *Conf.*, 4, 15.

39. See, for example, Takeshi Kato, " Melodia interior. Sur le traite *De Pulchro et Apto*," in *REAug*, 12 (1966), 229–40, which argues for the Manichaean background as well as the influence of Cicero and other authors; see 229–31, notes 2–11 for the relevant scholarship.

40. *Conf.*, 4, 15.

41. *Conf.*, 3, 7.

42. *Conf.*, 3, 7.

43. *Conf.*, 3, 7.

44. *Conf.*, 3, 8.

45. *Conf.*, 3, 8.

46. *Conf.*, 3, 10.

47. *Conf.*, 5, 3.

48. *Contra Faustum Manichaeum* 19.2 (*CSEL*, 25.1; 497–98) (hereafter, *C. Faust.*) References to book and section and pages in CSEL 25:1, ed. J. Zycha, (Vienna, 1896). See also Benin, Sacrifice as Education" for much of what follows.

49. *C. Faust.*, 6, 1, 284–5.

50. *C. Faust.*, 6, 5, 290–91.

51. *C. Faust.*, 12, 9, 337–38.

52. *C. Faust.*, 12, 13, 342–43.

53. *C. Faust.*, 12, 9–13, 337–343.

54. *C. Faust.*, 18, 6, 494; cf. 22, 17, 604–6.

55. See M. F. Berrouard, " 'Similitudo' et la définition du réalisme sacramental d'après l'Épître XCVIII, 9–10, de saint Augustin," in *REAug*, 7 (1961), 321–37 (hereafter, Berrouard, " 'Similitudo' "); Ladner, *The Idea of Reform*, 185–190. See in Augustine, *In Iohannis Evangelium*, 26.11; 15. 18; 50.2;

116.4; 120.3; 123.2 (*CCL* 36. ed. R. Willems (Turnhout 1916), 264–65; 268; 433–34; 648; 661–62; 676) and *De Civitate Dei*, 10.17, 32; 16.43; 19.23 (*CSEL*, 40: 1, 476–77; 503–10; 40:2, 200–3; 411–18).

56. *City of God*, 10:19. I use the translation by Henry Bettenson in *Augustine, City of God*, ed. David Knowles (London, 1972).

57. *City of God*, 10:17.

58. *City of God*, 10:20.

59. See Brown, *Augustine*, 212–32.

60. Brown, *Augustine*, 222.

61. *Conf.*, 3, 4; Brown, *Augustine*, 222.

62. *C. Faust.*, 19, 11; 510.

63. *C. Faust.*, 20, 21, 22; 564–65.

64. *C. Faust.*, 20, 21; 563.

65. *C. Faust.*, 20, 21; 563–4.

66. *C. Faust.*, 20, 21; 564.

67. For much of what follows, see Benin, "Sacrifice as Education"; see Augustine, *Epistle* 98.7 (*CSEL* 44.2; 528–29). (Hereafter references to Epistle number, section, and page in *CSEL* edition.) See the article by Markus in n. 3, "Imago and similitudo," and Berrouard, " 'Similitudo.' "

68. *Ep.*, 98.9; 530.

69. *Ep.*, 98.9; 531. *Si enim sacramenta quandam similitudinem rerum earum, quarum sacramenta sunt, non haberent, omnino sacramenta non essent; ex hac autem similitudine plerumque iam ipsarum rerum nomina accipiunt.*

70. *Ep.*, 98.9; 531.

71. *Ep.*, 98.10; 531–33.

72. *C. Faust.*, 19.13, 19, 7; 510, 503–5. *Proinde prima sacramenta, quae observabantur et celebrabantur ex lege, praenuntiativa erant Christ venturi: quae cum suo adventu Christus inplevisset, ablata sunt, et ideo ablata, quia inpleta; non enim venit legem solvere, sed adinplere.* Note the skillful chiasmatic construction: *inplevisset / ablata: ablata / inpleta.*

73. *C. Faust.*, 19.16; 512-13.

74. *C. Faust.*, 19.17; 514.

75. *C. Faust.*, 19. 17; 514–15.

76. See Bede's *Ecclesiastical History of the English People, (Oxford Medieval Texts)* eds. B. Colgrave and R. A. B. Mynors (Oxford, 1969). The introduction and notes are most valuable. The letter is contained in book 1, chap. 30. On the authenticity of the Gregorian letters preserved in Bede, see Paul Meyvaert, *Benedict, Gregory, Bede and Others* (London, 1977), a reprint of articles, especially, "Bede and Gregory the Great," 8–13. See also E. A. Lowe, "The Script of the Farewell and Date Formulae in Early Papal Documents as Reflected in the Oldest Manuscripts of Bede's *Historia Ecclesiastica*," in *RB*, 69 (1959), 22–31. See the story of Raedwald's conversion in book 2, chap. 15, 188–91.

77. See *History*, I, 30, 31; II, 10, 13–15; III, 8, 22, 30. For the problem in a larger context, see the texts and discussion in J. N. Hillgarth, *The Conversion of Western Europe, 350–750* (Englewood Cliffs, N. J., 1969).

78. *History*, I, 30.

79. *History*, I, 30.

80. *Ep.*, 102.2.12 *(CSEL* 34, 555); cf. *Ep.* 138, 1.9, 5 and 7 *(CSEL* 44, 130–33).

81. *Ep.*, 136.1 *(CSEL* 44, 93).

82. *Ep.*, 138.1.1, 2 *(CSEL* 44, 126–27).

83. *Ep.*, 138.1.2 *(CSEL* 44, 127).

84. *Ep.*, 138.1.3 *(CSEL* 44, 128).

85. *Ep.*, 138.1.5 *(CSEL* 44,130).

86. *Ep.*, 138.1.5 *(CSEL* 44, 130). I have used the translation in Brown, *Augustine*, 317–18.

87. Cf. Brown, *Augustine*, 318–19.

88. *City of God* 10, 14–15. On the giving of the Law through angels, see Lloyd Gaston, "Angels and Gentiles in Early Judaism and Paul," in *Sciences Religieuses / Studies in Religion*, 11 (1982) 65–75.

89. *De Doc. Christ.*, 3, 10. For much of what follows, see the masterful study of Marie Dominique Chenu, *Nature, Man and Society in the Twelfth Century: Essays on New Theological Perspectives in the Latin West* trans. and ed. Jerome Taylor and Lester K. Little (Chicago and London, 1968) (hereafter, *Man and Society*). One might also consult R. W. Southern, "Aspects of the European Tradition of Historical Writing: Hugh of Saint Victor and the Idea of Historical Development," in *TRHS*, Series V, 21 (1971), 159–79; Beryl Smalley, *The Study of the Bible in the Middle Ages* (Notre Dame, 1978) (hereafter, Smalley, *Bible*); Amos Funkenstein, *Heilsplan und natürliche Entwicklung Formen der Gegenwartsbestimmung im Geschichtsdenken des hohen Mittelalters* (Munich, 1965) (hereafter, Funkenstein, *Heilsplan*); and *The Cambridge History of the Bible*, II, ed., G. W. H. Lampe (Cambridge,

1969), 155–280. For additional studies of biblical exegesis in Judaism and in Islam see: J. Heinemann "Scientific Allegorization During the Jewish Middle Ages," *Studies in Jewish Thought,* ed. A. Jospe (Detroit, 1981) 247–69; the elegant study by Frank E. Talmage, "Apples of Gold: The Inner Meaning of Sacred Texts in Medieval Judaism," *Jewish Spirituality,* ed. Arthur Green (New York, 1986–87), 312–355, and for Islam see Paul Nwiya, *Exégèse Coranique et Langage Mystique: nouvel essai sur le lexique technique des mystiques musulmans. (Recherches publiees sous le direction de l'institut de lettres orientales de Beyrouth t. 49 Serie 1: Pensée arabe et musulmanes* (Beyrouth, 1970).

90. *De tribus diebus,* iii, *PL,* 176, 814, cited in Chenu, *Man and Society,* 117, n. 44, which identifies Augustine, *Enarrationes in psalmum* 45, 7, *PL,* 36, 518 as the source. See Chenu, *Man and Society,* 99–145. (*PL* wrongly prints *de Tribus diebus* as book 7 of the *Didascalion.*)

91. Smalley, *Bible,* 87.

92. See William M. Green, "Augustine on the Teaching of History," 331.

93. Smalley, *Bible,* 88–89.

94. Green, "Augustine on the Teaching of History," 331–32.

95. *De Sacramentis,* Pro. ii, *PL,* 176, 183. I use the translation in Smalley, *Bible,* 89, and I rely on Hugh of Saint Victor, *On the Sacraments of the Christian Faith (De Sacramentis Christianae Fidei),* trans. Roy J. DeFerrari (Cambridge, Ma., 1951) (hereafter, DeFerrari, and page number). See also *The Didascalion of Hugh of St. Victor,* trans. Jerome Taylor (New York and London, 1961) (hereafter, *Didascalion*).

96. *De Arca Noe Mystica,* 3. Also cited in Smalley, *Bible,* 90, whose translation I use.

97. Smalley, *Bible,* 90.

98. *De Sacramentis,* prol. 6. DeFerrari, 5. *Historia est rerum gestarum narratio, quae in prima signifcatione litterae continentur.* Cf. Funkenstein, *Heilsplan,* 51–60.

99. *De Sacramentis,* I, 1, 29; DeFerrari, 27. Cf. *De Sacramentis,* I, 10, 6; DeFerrari; 173.

100. *In Eccles. praef. PL,* 175, 115 "... *in serie rerum gestarum ordo temporis inveniuntur.*"

101. *De arca Noe morali,* 4, 9 *PL,* 176, 667.

102. *De Sacramentis,* I, 8, 12.

103. *De Vera Relig.,* 7, 13. See also Morrison, *The Mimetic Tradition,* 54–97. Morrison explains Augustine's views solely on the basis of a mimetic tradition and uses as his terms, "inversion" and "subversion" with no indication of the role of accommodation. While *mimesis* was no doubt a very

powerful exegetical device, I think that the whole doctrine of accommodation and condescension is of no less importance and seems a simpler and more direct explanation than "inversion" and "subversion." I feel that my observations strengthen Morrison's position, and vice versa. Cf. Ladner, *Idea of Reform*, 222–83.

104. *De Vanitate Mundi*, 3, *PL*, 176, 721: *Haec autem dispensatio Creatoris magnae fuit machinationis principum. . . .*

105. *De arca Noe morali*, 4, 9 *PL*, 176, 667.

106. *De Sacramentis*, I, 1, 3; DeFerrari, 8–9.

107. *Tract. in Joan.*, 45, 9, *PL*, 35, 1722.

108. *De Sacramentis*, 1, 10, 6; DeFerrari, 173–78.

109. Chenu, *Man and Society*, 170–77; M. D. Chenu, "Contribution a l'histoire du Traite de la Foi," in *Melanges Thomistes* (Paris, 1923), 123–40.

110. *De Sacramentis*, I, 10, 6; DeFerrari, 178.

111. *De Sacramentis*, I, 10, 8; DeFerrari, 180.

112. *De Sacramentis*, I, 11, 1; DeFerrari, 182.

113. *De Sacramentis*, I, 11, 2–3; DeFerrari, 183.

114. *De Sacramentis*, I, 11, 4; DeFerrari, 183–84.

115. *De Sacramentis*, I, 11, 4; DeFerrari, 184.

116. *De Sacramentis*, I, 11, 5–7; DeFerrari, 184.

117. *De Sacramentis*, I, 11, 8; DeFerrari, 184.

118. *De Sacramentis*, I, 11, 8; DeFerrari, 184–85.

119. *De Sacramentis*, I, 11, 8; DeFerrari, 184.

120. See below pp. 122–23.

121. *De Sacramentis*, I, 11, 8; DeFerrari, 185–86.

122. *De Sacramentis*, I, 12, 1; DeFerrari, 187.

123. *De Sacramentis*, I, 12, 3; DeFerrari, 190–91.

124. *De Sacramentis*, I, 12, 4; DeFerrari, 191.

125. *De Sacramentis*, I, 12, 4; DeFerrari, 191.

126. *De vanitate mundi*, 4 *PL*, 176, 733. Cf. Chenu, *Man and Society*, 170, n. 18.

127. *De Sacramentis*, I, 12, 23; DeFerrari, 201–3.

128. *De Sacramentis*, I, 12, 4; DeFerrari, 191.

129. *De Sacramentis*, I, 12, 4; DeFerrari, 191.

130. *De Sacramentis*, I, 12, 5; DeFerrari, 191.

131. *De Sacramentis,* I, 12, 23, my translation.

132. *De Sacramentis,* I, 12, 23; DeFerrari, 203.

133. See, for example, *De vanitate mundi,* 4, *PL,* 176, 732–33; cf. Chenu, *Man and Society,* 173–201.

134. See Anselm de Havelberg, *Dialogues, Livre I,* ed. Gaston Salet, *SC* 118 (Paris, 1966), 7–13 (hereafter, *Dialogues*). The text is also in *PL* 188. For much of what follows, see A. Funkenstein, *Heilsplan,* 60–67; W. Berges, "Anselm von Havelberg in der Geistesgeschichte des 12. Jahrhunderts," in *Jahrbuch für die Geschichte Mittel—und Ostdeutschlands,* 5 (1956), 38–57. The study by M. Van Lee, "Les idées d'Anselme de Havelberg sur le développement des dogmes," in *Analecta Praemonstratensia,* 14 (1938), 3–35, was unavailable to me.

135. *Dialogues,* 7.

136. Anselm's monastic views may be gleaned from his *Epistola apologetica pro ordine canonicorum regularium PL,* 188, 1118–1140. See *Dialogues,* 13–21; Chenu, *Man and Society,* 202–38; John H. Van Engen, *Rupert of Deutz* (Berkeley, Los Angeles, London, 1983), 300–42.

137. *Dialogues,* 34; *PL,* 188, 1141. *Dialogues,* I, 1, pp. 34–39; *PL,* 188, 1141–43.

138. *Dialogues,* 3, 6; *PL,* 188, 1217; and cf. 3, 2; *PL,* 188, 1211.

139. Cited in Chenu, *Man and Society,* 215; see Rupert of Deutz, *Super quaedam capitula regulae divi Benedicti abbatis* 4, 13; *PL,* 170, 535–36.

140. *Dialogues,* I, 1, 34; *PL,* 188, 1141. Cf. Chenu, *Man and Society,* 217-18.

141. *Dialogues,* I, 13, 117; *PL,* 188, 1160.

142. *Dialogues,* I, 13, 117; *PL,* 188, 1160.

143. *Dialogues,* I, 4, 54–56; *PL,* 188, 1146–47. Cf. Hugh of Saint Victor, *De Sacramentis,* II, 6, 3; *PL, 176, 345: Sciendum est quod divinae dispensationis ordo et ratio poposcit, ut sicut ab initio, procurrente tempore, magis et magis adventus salvatoris appropinquavit, sic semper magis ac magis effectus salutis cresceret et cognitio veritatis. . . .* cited in Funkenstein, *Heilsplan,* 184, n. 73.

144. Salet in *Dialogues,* 58, n. 1, observes that in book II of the *Dialogues* Anselm cites Gregory twenty-six times—eighteen *ad sensum* and eight literally. And while Anselm cites other fathers explicitly, he never names Gregory.

145. *Dialogues,* I, 5, 58; *PL,* 188, 1147.

146. *Dialogues,* I, 5, 58–60; *PL,* 188, 1147.

147. *Dialogues,* I, 6, 62; *PL,* 188, 1147–48.

148. *Dialogues,* I, 6, 62; *PL,* 188, 1148. I follow in the main the transla-tion in Chenu, *Man and Society,* 174, n. 25.

149. Chenu, *Man and Society,* 174–75.

150. *Dialogues,* I, 6, 66; *PL,* 188, 1149, translated in Chenu, *Man and Society,* 184.

151. Mansi, 22, 1035, cited and translated in Chenu, *Man and Society,* 327, n. 44–45 for the decretal reference.

CHAPTER FIVE

1. *Leviticus R.,* 22, 8. I use the edition of M. Margulies (Jerusalem, 1951) 3 vols. I thank Professor Moshe Greenberg of the Hebrew University for communicating to me that *gas libo* is an inferior reading and *nazaz libo* is the preferred reading. See the Margulies edition and his discussion of the issue at 22, 8. Cf. *Leviticus* 10, 3 for another use of *nazaz libo.*

2. On Aphrahat, see Chapter III above.

3. See his *Talele Orot* (Jerusalem, 1972/3) .

4. *Mechilta d'Rabbi Ismael,* eds. S. Horovitz and I. A. Rabin, 2nd ed. (Jerusalem, 1970) (hereafter *MRI*); and the English translation, *Mekilta de-Rabbi Ishmael* (trans. Jacob Z. Lauterbach), 3 vols. (Philadelphia, 1976) (hereafter Laut.). References are given to tractate, chapter, and page of the Horovitz-Rabin and Lauterbach editions. *Pisha* (Bo) 5, 15, Laut., I: 33–38. On the *Mekilta,* see Max Kadushin, *A Conceptual Approach to the Mekilta* (New York, 1969) (hereafter, Kadushin *Approach*), and Judah Goldin, *The Song at the Sea being a commentary on a commentary in two parts.* (New Haven and London, 1971) (hereafter Goldin, *Song*). See also *Mekhilta D'Rabbi Simeon b. Yoḥai,* eds. J. N. Epstein and E. Z. Melamed (Jerusalem, 1955) [hereafter, *MRJ*].

5. *MRI,* Yitro, 5, 219; Laut., II, 231. Cf. Golden, *Song,* 126–28.

6. *MRI,* Yitro, 4, 216; Laut., II, 223. I follow the text in *MRI,* which reads ". . . *kedei leshachech et ha-ozen mah she-hi yicholah lishmoah,"* and cf. *MRI,* 3, 214; Laut., II, 218. Compare MRJ, Yitro, 19, p. 144. See also Max Kadushin, *The Rabbinic Mind,* 3rd. ed. (New York, 1972) (hereafter, Kadushin, *Mind*), 263–335, for a discussion of many of these themes. For the idea of the ear hearing, see the discussion in Kadushin, 312, n. 27. Kadushin refers to Solomon Schechter, *Aspects of Rabbinic Theology* (New York, 1975), (hereafter, *Aspects*), 35, which translates the phrase, "to sooth the ear (so as to make it listen to) what it can hear." Also of interest is Rashi's comment on Exodus 19:18, on the talmudic expression *"leshaber et ha-ozen*—to rupture the ear," that mankind is given a sign that is recogniz-able to them.

7. Kadushin, 303–24, esp. 312.

8. *Midrash Tehillim,* ed. S. Buber, 3a.

9. *MRI,* Va-yisa 4, 168; Laut., II, 118. I follow the reading in Lauterbach, cf. *MRI,* 118, alternate readings for 1, 13.

10. *Pesikta de Rav Kahana according to an Oxford Manuscript with variants from Known Manuscripts and Genizah Fragments and Parallel Passages with Commentary and Introduction* ed. Bernard Mandelbaum, 2 vols. (New York, 1962) (hereafter *Pesikta RK;* references to chapter and section); and the English translation by W. G. Braude and I. J. Kapstein (Philadelphia, 1975) (hereafter, *BK, Pestikta*).

11. See above pp. 57–58.

12. See above p. 58.

13. See Hermann L. Strack, *Introduction to the Talmud and Midrash* (New York, 1969), 115.

14. *Pesikta RK,* Piska 12:24, I: 223, *BK, Pesikta,* 248. I use the translation in *BK, Pesikta.* See the notes in *Pesikta RK* comparing *anokhi* to Coptic *Anok,* and cf. Piska 11:6, which states that Israel was redeemed since Israel did *not* change languages; cf. *Mekhilta Pisha* 5, *MRI,* 14; Laut., I; 34. Cf. *Midrash Tehillim,* Psalm 114:4; *Pesikta RK.* 21:12; *Esther R.* 4:12, and cf. *Acts* 2:5–12.

15. *Pesikta RK,* Piska 12:24, 223; *BK, Pesikta,* 248–49. Cf. *B. T. Erubin* 54b and *MRI* 3:1. Judah Goldin (in *Song,* 128) has suggested that the *Mekhilta* as an early tannaitic Midrash emphasizes the mercy of the Lord rather than his military prowess, as well as his compassion rather than his pedagogy, while later Midrashim such as the *Pesikta* stress divine pedagogy more than divine compassion. However, considering the matter from the point of view of accommodation, both seem to be of equal value—compassion controls the type of teaching. See also J. Heinemann, *Aggadah and Its Development* (Jerusalem, 1974) [Hebrew].

16. *Pesikta RK,* 12:25, I, 223–24; *BK, Pesikta,* 249. Cf. *Pesikta Rabbati,* 21:6 and *T. B. Sahabbat* 30b.

17. This is the opinion advanced by Leon Nemoy in *Pesikta Rabbati,* 424, n. 33.

18. The word is the Greek *eikōn* and appears, inter alia, *in Pesikta RK,* 7, 6; 127: *BK, Pesikta,* 146. Cf. *Pesikta Rabbati,* 21:6.

19. *Pesikta RK,* 12:25; 224; *BK, Pesikta,* 249. Cf. *Pesikta Rabbati,* 21:6. Cf. *Exodus R.* 3:6

20. Cf. *Pesikta R.* 21:6, where the teaching is again presented in the name of R. Levi. using Deuteronomy 5:4, "The Lord spoke with you face to face in the Mount" as the text to interpret.

Notes

21. *Pesikta RK,* 12:25, 224: *BK, Pesikta,* 249. Cf. *Exodus R.* 5:9; 29:1; *Tanhuma, Shemot,* 25; *Tanhuma Buber, Yitro* 17.

22. *Pesikta RK,* 12:25, 224; *BK, Pesikta,* 249.

23. *Pesikta RK,* 12:25, 224; *BK, Pesikta,* 249.

24. *Pesikta RK,* 12:25, 224; *BK, Pesikta,* 249–50. Also, the literal translation is "The voice of the Lord is in strength." For similar Hebrew syntax, cf. Genesis 29:1: "Jacob lifted his feet."

25. The influence of rabbinic thought on Origen is well known. One may see for example, N. R. M. DeLange, *Origen and the Jews: Studies in Jewish-Christian Relations in Third-Century Palestine (University of Cambridge Oriental Publications* 25) (Cambridge, 1976); S. Liebermann, *Siphre Zutta The Talmud of Caesarea,* 2 vols. (New York, 1968). The frequency of teachings (or when they are mentioned as tradents) attributed to the five rabbis mentioned in the homily in Pesikta RK, gives some indication of the frequency of their teachings.

	Gen. R.	*Pesikta R.*	*Midrash Tehillim*
Ḥanina b. Papa	15	8	10
Ḥiyya b. Abba	31	14	14
Yosi b. Ḥanina	34	13	11
R. Neḥemiah	105	15	31
R. Levi	246	82	74

26. The Jewish Publication Society translates *amon* as "confidant," The Jerusalem Bible renders it, "master craftsman." This section was completed before I came across David Stern, "Midrash and Indeterminancy," *Critical Inquiry* 15:1 (1988), 132–161, [hereafter, Stern, *Midrash*] whose approach to the issue while more literary than mine, nevertheless touches upon issues I discuss in Chapter 6.

27. These are all puns based on phonetic similarities and supported by the following verses: *Num.* 11:12; *Lamentations* 4:5; *Esther* 2:7; *Nahum* 3:8.

28. The text suggests that the first word of the Torah *bereshit* should be read *be-reshit* That is, *be* is a preposition usually translated "in", and the text of the midrash states "there is no *reshit,* but the Torah".

29. See Stern, *Midrash,* 150, n. 35. And on the background to the use of "wisdom" see, Hans Conzelmann, "The Mother of Wisdom," *Essays in Honour of Rudolph Bultmann The Future of Our Religious Past,* ed. James M. Robinson, trans. Charles E. Carston and Robert P. Scharlemann (New York, 1971), 230–243.

30. See pp. 8–9.

31. On God's "Otherness" see Kadushin, 288–303.

32. See briefly, *The Targum Ongelos to Genesis* (*The Aramaic Bible,* v. 6), trans. Bernard Grossfeld (Wilmington, Delaware, 1988), 1–35, (hereafter, Grossfeld, *Targum*), *Divine Name and Presence: The Memra* (Totowa, N.J., 1981). See also Joshua Abelson, *The Immanence of God in Rabbinic Literature: The Memra* (London, 1912), and Grossfeld for additional bibliography.

33. Psuedo-Jonathon also uses "before". On this issue see M. L. Klein, "The Preposition KDM ("Before") A Psuedo-Anti-Anthropomorphism in the Targums," *TS* n.s. 20 (1979), 502–507. See Grossfeld, p. 22.

34. Grossfeld, *Targum,* p. 20.

35. See Grossfeld, *Targum,* p. 30 for further discussion and bibliography.

36. *Guide,* I, 26, 28.

37. Commentary on *Gen.* 46:1.

38. See G. Scholem, *On the Kabbalah and Its Symbolism* (New York, 1969), 166–67. For the power of Hebrew see *Bereshit R.* 12;10 and *M. Avot* 5;1.

39. *Tanhuma, Va-Yikahel* 7. For the idea of a plan of Creation see *Bereshit R.* I, 1.

40. *Tanhuma, Va-Yikahel* 7. Cf. *Pesikta* Rabbati, 5:7

41. For Luria see briefly, G. Scholem, *Major Trends in Jewish Mysticism* (New York, 1974) The use of the term zimzen in Jewish thought would be a valuable contribution to scholarship to scholarship. I touch upon this below in Chapter 7 in reference to Dov Baer, the Maggid of Mezhirech, *Maggid devarov le-Ya'akov* ed. R. Schatz-Uffenheimer (Jerusalem, 1976), 295–99.

42. *Gen. R.* 5:7 Cf. *Tanhuma B.* Hukat, 29.

43. *Gen. R.* 5:7.

44. *Gen. R.* 5:7. See the parellels and comments in *Gen. R.* I:36–37.

45. *Avot* 5:8; *Gen. R.* 5:7; *Lev. R.* 10:9; *Songs of Songs R.* 7:5 *Bt. Yoma* 21a; *Pesikta R.* 21:8. *Tanḥuma B.* Yitro 14 records that Sinai was large enough to hold the Lord, and legions upon legions of engels before mentioning the expansive nature of Jerusalem.

46. Gen. R. 5:7.

47. *Mishna Pesaḥim* 10:4. For our purposes I do not wish to enter the arguments over the number and order of the questions since it is not important for our purposes.

48. *BT Pesaḥim* 116a.

49. *Mishneh Torah, Laws of Ḥametz and Matzah,* 7:2–3.

50. *Kitzur Shulkhan Arukh,* trans. Hyman E. Goldin (New York, 1963), section 119:4 Cf. 119:1 for giving children nuts. etc. See also *Shulkhan Arukh, Laws of Passover,* sect. 482, para. 16, and sect. 483, para. 6, and on this the *Misnah Berurah* notes that "Rabbi Y. Mi-Londros" used to recite the Haggadah in the vernacular.

CHAPTER SIX

1. On Sa'adia, see briefly Simon Rawidowicz, "Saadya's Purification of the Idea of God," in Simon Rawidowicz, *Studies in Jewish Thought,* ed. Nahum Glatzer (Philadelphia, 1974), 246–68 (hereafter, Rawidowicz, "Saadya."). and Sa'adia Gaon, *The Book of Beliefs and Opinions, Yale Judaica Series* I, trans. Samuel Rosenblatt (New Haven, 1948) (hereafter, Sa'adia, *BBO*), xxiii–xxxii. Also of value are Julius Guttmann, *Philosophies of Judaism; the history of Jewish Philosophy from Biblical Times to Franz Rosenzweig* (New York, 1964), 69–94; (hereafter, Guttmann, *Philosophies of Judaism*) A. Altmann, "Saadya's Conception of the Law," in *Bulletin of the John Rylands Library,* 28 (1944), 320–39; and Y. Elstein, "Torat Ha-Mitzvot be-Mishnat R. Saadyah," in *Tarbiz,* 38 (1968), 120–35. For Jewish exegesis see: Wilhelm Bacher, *Die Bibelexegese der jüdischen Religions-philosophen des Mittelalters von Maimoni,* (Strassburg, 1892), and Marvin Fox, "On the Rational Commandments in Saadia's Philosophy, a Re-Examination," *Modern Jewish Ethics: Theory and Practice* ed. M. Fox (Columbus, 1975) 174–87.

2. See *Encyclopedia Judaica,* vol. X, 1047–48; and L. Nemoy, *Karaite Anthology, Excerpts from the Early Literature* (New Haven, 1952), 44 ff. (hereafter *Anthology*); and "Al-Qirqisāni's Account of the Jewish Sects and Christianity," *HUCA,* VII (1930), 317–398.

3. On Jesus Sexa, see Nemoy, *Anthology,* 42 ff. for a fuller discussion.

4. The text is *Kitab al-'Anwar wal-Maraqib* and *Kitab al-Riyad wal-Hada'iq,* 5 vol. ed. L. Nemoy (New York, 1939–43). I am indebted to Professor W. Brinner for providing translations of parts of the Arabic text.

5. I follow Nemoy's translation in *HUCA,* 7 (1930), 319–97. On Karaites in general, see Z. Ankori, *Karaites in Byzantium the Formative Years, 920–1100.* (New York, 1959).

6. Nemoy, *HUCA,* VII (1930), 366. The text does not, however, state explicitly that al-Muqammis rejected Christianity:

> Da'ud al-Muqammis ... learned thoroughly the origins of Christianity and its mysteries and mastered philosophy. But [afterward] he composed two books against the Christians in which he attacked them; these two books are well known.

7. Nemoy, *Anthology,* 59.

8. Nemoy, *Anthology,* 63.

9. Nemoy, *Anthology,* 63.

10. Nemoy, *HUCA* 7, 356–66.

11. On the Sabians, see *Kitab al-'Anwar,* vol. I, 44 and vol. II, 214; and Funkenstein *"Messianism,"* 94 and n. 43. See also D. Chwolson, *Die Ssabier and der Ssabismus* (St. Petersburg, 1856), 2 vols. reprint (Amsterdam, 1965).

12. For example, see Rawidowicz, "Saadya," 248 and 424, n. 2, and for some medieval Christian comments on this principle, cf. Aquinas, *Summa Theologica* 1–2 q. 98 ad 3: *"secundum opinionem populi loquitur scriptura."* Cf. Oresme, *Livre du ciel,* 2.25, 530. *"L'em diroit que elle se conforme en c'est partie a la manier de commun parler."* Both cited in Amos Funkenstein, *Theology and the Scientific Imagination from the Middle Ages to the Seventeenth Century* (Princeton, 1986), 213, n. 1; 213–70. See Funkenstein's discussion of what he calls the *minimalist* and the *maximalist* approaches of this principle (hereafter, Funkenstein, *Theology.*) See also Amos Funkenstein, "Gesetz und Geschichte, zur historisïerenden Hermeneutik bei Moses Maimonides und Thomas von Aquin," *Viator* 1 (1970), 147–78 (hereafter, Funkenstein, "Gesetz").

13. Rawidowicz, "Saadya," 248 and 424, n. 2.

14. Sa'adia, *BBO,* II, 8–13; pp. 109–136; esp. II, 10 for anthropomorphic terms used in Scripture. See Rawidowicz, "Saadya," 250–52.

15. See below in this chapter, pp. 142–160.

16. *Duties of the Heart,* trans. Moses Hyamson (Jerusalem/New York, 1970), 52. (Hereafter, *Hyamson*).

17. *Kuzari,* ed. and trans. H. Hirschfeld (New York, 1964), 5; 7; p. 295.

18. See Rawidowicz, "Saadya," 253–66, for a thorough discussion.

19. Rawidowicz, "Saadya," 267.

20. Sa'adia, *BBO* 3:7, 157–63 at 160. I thank Professor Seymour Feldman of Rutgers for the reference. Neither Funkenstein, *Theology* nor Twersky, *Introduction to the Code of Maimonides* (New Haven/London, 1980) (hereafter, Twersky, *Introduction*) (see 373, n. 47 for additional bibliography) addresses this issue. For what follows, cf. Rawidowicz, "Saadya," 267–68; Sa'adia, *BBO,* 3; 7, 157–63 at 160.

21. See below pp. 167–168.

22. I have consulted two editions of this text: *Duties of the Heart,* 2 vols. trans. M. Hyamson (Jerusalem/New York, 1962), and the text of A. Zifroni

(Tel Aviv, 1928) (hereafter, Zifroni). The Hebrew text is the Ibn Tibbon translation from the Arabic in both editions. Also of value is Georg Golinski, *Das
Wesen des Religionsgesetzes in der Philosophie des Bachja ibn Pakuda* (Berlin, 1935); cf. Salo W. Baron *A Social and Religious History of the Jews* 2nd
rev. ed. v. 6 (New York, 1958) (hereafter, Baron, *SRHG*) vol. 6, p. 398, n. 172;
and Funkenstein, "Gesetz," 150. *Hovot Ha-Levavot* became a classic in Jewish ethical treatises. And when S. Y. Agnon wished to portray nineteenth-
century orthodoxy, he placed quotations from *Hovot Ha-Levavot* in the "hero's"
mouth. See Joseph Dan, *Jewish Mysticism and Jewish Ethics* (Seattle, 1986),
22–25.

23. *Duties of the Heart;* Zifroni, chap. 3, 2, p. 220; and Hyamson, vol. I,
pp. 196–97.

24. Zifroni, chap. 3, 3, p. 227; and Hyamson, vol. I, pp. 198–99.

25. Zifroni, chap. 3, 3, p. 227; and Hyamson, Vol. I, pp. 206–7.

26. Zifroni, chap. 3, 3, p. 227; and Hyamson, vol. I, pp. 206–7/208–9.

27. Zifroni, chap. 4, 4, p. 329; and Hyamson, vol. I, pp. 350–51.

28. Zifroni, chap. 4, 4, p. 329; and Hyamson, vol. I, pp. 350–51. For
further use of the verse from Hosea, see S. Pines, " 'Israel My Firstborn' and
the Sonship of Jesus: A Theme of Moslem Anti-Christian Polemics," in *Studies in Mysticism and Religion Presented to Gershom G. Scholem on His
Seventieth Birthday by Pupils, Colleagues and Friends,* eds. E. E. Urbach, R.
J. Zwi Werblowsky, and Ch. Wirszubski (Jerusalem, 1967), 177–89. (hereafter, *Studies in Mysticism*).

29. Zifroni, chap. 4, 4, pp. 329–30; and Hyamson, vol. I, pp. 350–53.

30. Zifroni, chap. 4, 4, pp. 330–31; and Hyamson, vol. I, pp. 350–54.

31. See Gershon David Hundert, "Jewish Children and Childhood in
Early Modern East Central Europe," in *The Jewish Family: Metaphor and
Memory,* ed. David Kraemer (Oxford, 1989), 81–94.

32. I have consulted the English translation by H. Hirschfeld in *The
Kuzari* (New York, 1946); and the Hebrew text edited by A. Zifroni (Tel Aviv,
1948), which contains the Ibn Tibbon Hebrew translation. References are to
the English text.

33. See *BT Hagiga* 14b; *Tosefta Hagiga* 2:3–4; *PT Hagiga* 2:1, 77a; and
G. Scholem, *Jewish Gnosticism, Merkabah Mysticism, and Talmudic Tradition* (New York, 1960), 14–19. For one teaching, see *M. Avot* 4, 25.

34. *Kuzari,* Pt. 3, 65, p. 190.

35. *Kuzari,* Pt. 1, 97, p. 67.

36. *Kuzari,* Pt. 1, 97, pp. 68–69.

37. See chap. II, pp. 64–65.

38. *Kuzari,* Pt. 1, 97, pp. 69–70.

39. *Kuzari,* Pt. 2, 99; p. 72.

40. There is a wealth of biographical material, but I do not intend to present an exhaustive list of such works. The following are helpful: D. Yellin and I. Abrahams, *Maimonides* (Philadelphia, 1903), with a biographical supplement by J. Dienstag. The study by Meier Orian *Ha-Moreh le-Dorot* (Jerusalem, 1956) is valuable also. The pages in Y. Baer, *A History of the Jews in Christian Spain* (Philadelphia, 1961), vol. I, 96–110; and Baron, *SRHS,* vol. 6, 97 ff., are useful. J. Guttmann, *Philosophies of Judaism* 83–150, is good on Maimonides' philosophy; and now one should consult I. Twersky, *Introduction,* 1–96, on the man and his works; and the bibliography, 561–610, lists a wealth of bibliographical material. See also Funkenstein, *Theology,* 213–39. I approach the same problems, but place Maimonides' work within the exegetical/philosophical tradition, rather than the scientific tradition that Funkenstein seeks to elucidate. The works of Leo Strauss are critical for one approach to Maimonides; see, for example, his *Persecution and the Art of Writing* (Glencoe, 1952) (hereafter, Strauss, *Persecution*). Leo Strauss, *Philosophy and Law: Essays toward the Understanding of Maimonides and his Predecessors* trans. Fred Baumann, (Philadelphia, 1987); "Notes on Maimonides' 'Book of Knowledge,'" in *Studies in Mysticism,* 269–283, and for a totally different analysis of Maimonides and his work, see David Hartman, *Maimonides: Torah and Philosophic Quest* (Philadelphia, 1986) (hereafter, Hartman, *Quest*). For a mediating position between Strauss and Hartman, see Georges Vajda, "La pensée religieuse de Moïse Maïmonide: unité ou dualité?" in *Cahiers de Civilisation Médiévale,* 9 (1966), 29–49.

41. The works are: responsa; works on astrology and resurrection; a compostion on logic; one on ethics; a commentary on the Mishnah; the *Mishneh Torah;* and *Moreh Nebukim [Guide of the Perplexed].* The editions are: The responsa are found in *Responsa of Maimonides,* 3 vols., ed. J. Blau (Jerusalem, 1958) (hereafter *Responsa M.*). The *Letter on Astrology* was published by A. Marx in *HUCA,* (1926), 349–58; and translated into English in *Medieval Political Philosophy,* eds. R. Lerner and M. Mahdi (Glencoe, 1963), 227–37. *The Treatise on Resurrection* is edited by J. Frankel in *PAAJR* IX (1939). *Treatise on Logic,* ed. I. Efros (New York, 1938), published by the American Academy for Jewish Research. *Eight Chapters,* ed. J. Gorfinkle (New York, 1912). *Mishnah Commentary,* published in numerous editions, including one with the Arabic original by J. Kafih (Jerusalem, 1963), in seven volumes. *The Mishneh Torah* in standard editions and available in English in the *Yale Judaica Series. Guide of the Perplexed* exists in the Tibbonide Hebrew translation. In addition to the Hebrew text, I have consulted both the translation by S. Pines (Chicago, 1963) and the French translation in S. Munk, *Le Guide des Égares,* 3 vols. (Paris, 1856–66). All references are to Parts 1, 2, and 3 and to chapter; and I employ the English of the Pines's translation of the *Guide* (hereafter referred to as *Guide*).

42. See Twersky, *Introduction,* 356–507. This book appeared after most of this chapter was written, but I was pleased to note that many of my observations were to be found in Twersky's opus.

43. Twersky, *Introduction,* 373–74.

44. On the structure of the *Guide,* see Strauss, "How to Begin the Study of the *Guide of the Perplexed,* in Pines, *Moreh* xi–lvi; L. V. Berman, "The Structure of Maimonides' *Guide of the Perplexed,"* in *Proceedings of the Sixth World Congress of Jewish Studies,* v. 3 ed. Avigdor Shinan (Jerusalem, 1977), 7–13; L. V. Berman, "The Structure of the Commandments of the Torah in the Thought of Maimonides," in *Studies in Jewish Religious and Intellectual History,* eds. Siegfried Stein and Raphael Lowe (University, Al., 1979), 51–66; S. Rawidowicz, "She'elat mivnehu shel Moreh Nevukhim," in *Tarbiz,* 6 (1935), 285–333 [reprinted in his *Iyyunim ba-Mahshevet Yisra'el,* ed. B. C. I. Ravid (Jerusalem, 1969), I, 237–96]; Kalman P. Bland, "Moses and the Law According to Maimonides," in *Mystics, Philosophers, and Politicians, Essays in Jewish Intellectual History in Honor of Alexander Altmann,* eds. J. Reinharz and D. Swetchinski (Durham, N.C., 1982), 49–66. H. A. Davidson, "The Study of Philosophy as a Religious Obligation," *Religion in a Religious Age,* ed. S. D. Goitein (Cambridge, 1974) 53–68; Jacob I Dienstag, "The Relationship of Maimonides to his Predecessors," *The Jewish Law Annual I* (1978), 42–60; J. Faur, "Mekor Hiyyuban shel ha-mitzvot le-daat ha-Rambam," *Tarbiz* XXXVIII (1969), 43–53; J. Faur, "The Origin of the Classification of Rational and Divine Commandments in Medieval Jewish Philosophy," *Augustinianum* IX (1969), 299–304; Alfred Ivry, "Islamic and Greek Influences on Maimonides' Philosophy," *Maimonides and Philosophy,* eds. Shlomo Pines and Yirmiyahu Yovel (Dordrecht, 1986), 139–56; Hanna Kasher, "Commandments Between Man and God in the Guide of the Perplexed," *Daat* 12 (1984), 23–28; Hanna Kasher, "Maimonides' Philosophical Division of the Laws," *HUCA* LVI (1985), 1–7 (both articles in Hebrew); Abraham Nuriel, "Providence and Governance in *More ha-Nebukhim,"* *Tarbiz* IL (1980) 346–55; A. Nuriel, "The Question of a Created or Primordial World in the Philosophy of Maimonides." *Tarbiz* XXXIII (1964), 372–87 (both articles in Hebrew); Alvin J. Reines, "Maimonides' Concept of Mosaic Prophecy," *HUCA* XL–XLI (1969–70), 325–61, *ibid.* "Maimonides' Concepts of Providence and Theodicy," *HUCA* XLIII (1977), 169–206, and C. Touati "Les Deux Théories de Maimonide sur La Providence," *Studies in Jewish Religions and Intellectual History Presented to Alexander Altmann on the occasion of his seventieth birthday.* eds. S. Stein, R. Loewe (University, Alabama, 1977), 331–343.

45. Introduction to *Commentary on the Mishnah,* 35–37. Cf. *Introduction* to the first part of the *Guide,* 10–14; *Guide,* 1, 34 and Hartman, *Quest,* 219, n. 23.

46. *Introduction* to the first part of the *Guide,* 10–14.

47. *Introduction to Ḥelek* (Kapah ed. 134–35); I use the translation in Twersky, *Maimonides Reader,* 404–5.

48. Twersky, *Maimonides Reader,* 404–5 (Kapah ed. 134–35).

49. See the discussion in Hartman, *Quest,* 66–101, for his analysis of fear and love and God's authority (*ahavah, yireh, din*).

50. Twersky, *Maimonides Reader,* 406–7 (Kapah ed. 135–36). See also Hartman, *Quest,* 72–76 and 228, n. 18, 19. Hartman, *Quest,* 74, comments: "The rabbis, though committed to the need to transcend lower forms of religious experience, were careful not to develop a system catering solely to the elite."

51. If Maimonides was indebted to Alfarabi, who scorned the masses, then Hartman's assertion needs greater proof. See Lawrence V. Berman, "Maimonides, the Disciple of Alfarabi," in *Israel Oriental Studies,* 4 (1974), 154–78, at 159 and 166–67, and 167, n. 43. See the translation of the *Book of Letters,* 171–78, for the relationship of philosophy and religion; cf. *Guide,* 1, 71.

52. *Book of Commandments,* trans. C. Chavel (London, 1967), 2 vols. and see Twersky, *Introduction,* 377, n. 58.

53. *Guide,* 3, 26.

54. For a discussion of the above, see Twersky, *Introduction,* 377 ff. and I. Twersky, "Some Non-Halakic Aspects of the *Mishneh Torah,*" in *Jewish Medieval and Renaissance Studies,* ed. Alexander Altmann (Cambridge, 1967), 95–118 (hereafter, Twersky, *Aspects*), and the suggestive comments of Josef Stern, "The Idea of a *Hoq* in Maimonides' Explanation of the Law," in *Maimonides and Philosophy* eds. S. Pines and Y. Yovel (Dordrecht/Boston/Lancaster, 1986), 92–130 (hereafter, Stern, *Hoq*); Arthur Hyman, "A Note on Maimonides' Classification of Law," *PAAJR,* 46/47:323–43 (hereafter, Hyman, *"Note"*) L. Epstein, "Le-shitat La-Rambam ba-ta'amei ha-korbanot," *Yad Shaul, Memorial Volume for Rabbi Dr. Saul Weinfurt,* eds. J. J. Weinberg and P. Biberfeld (Tel Aviv, 1719), 145–52. Alexander Altmann, "Maimonides' 'four perfections.'" *Israel Oriental Studies* I (1972), 15–24; Y. Ben-Sasson, "Le-Heker Mishnat Ta'amei ha-Mitzvot be *Moreh Nevukhim,*" *Tarbiz* 29 (1960), 268–82; L. V. Berman, "The Political Interpretation of the Maxim: The Purpose of Philosophy is the Imitation of God." *Studia Islamica* V (1961), 53–61; L. V. Berman, "The Ideal State of the Philosophers and Prophetic Laws," *The Straight Path,* ed. Ruth Link-Salinger, (Washington, D.C. 1988), 10–22, and Leo Strauss, "Maimonides' Statement on Political Science," *PAAJR* 22 (1953), 115–130.

55. *Guide,* 3, 26.

56. *Guide,* 3, 26, where Maimonides writes: "The Sages always say with regard to the verse, 'For it is no vain thing' [Deut. 32:47]. And if it is vain, it is because of you—meaning that this legislation is not a vain matter without useful end; and that if it seems to you that this is the case with regard to some of the Commandments, the deficiency resides in your own apprehension. You already know the tradition that is widespread among us, according

to which the causes for all the Commandments, with the exception of that concerning the Red Heifer, were known to Solomon; and also, their dictum that God hid the causes for the Commandments in order that they should not be held in little esteem, as happened to Solomon with regard to the three commandments whose causes are made clear." See Louis Finkelstein, "Maimonides and the Tannaitic Midrashim," *JQR* 25 (1935), 469–517.

57. *Guide*, 3, 26.

58. *MT, Book 5; Holiness, Slaughtering*, I, 4.

59. *MT, Book 5; Holiness, Slaughtering*, XIV, 16.

60. *MT, Book 9; Substitute Offerings*, IV, 13.

61. This is of course an attempt to unify the seemingly divergent views of Maimonides the Halachist and Maimonides the philosopher. Twersky, *Introduction*, 78–79; Hartman, *Quest*, 15–27. For a different point of view, see Strauss, *Persecution*, 78–94; and "Notes on Maimonides' 'Book of Knowledge,'" *Studies in Mysticism*, 269–83. See also S. Pines, "The Philosophical Purport of Maimonides' Halachic Works and the Purport of *The Guide of the Perplexed*," in *Maimonides and Philosophy*, eds. S. Pines and Y. Yovel (Dordrecht/Boston/Lancaster, 1986), 1–15.

62. Of course, one might reply with the Midrashic comment cited above that the orders of a king must be obeyed. But such an answer does not of course *explain* the reasons for the details.

63. See Stern, *Hoq*, 104–6; Funkenstein, *Theology*, 227–35; A. Funkenstein, "Maimonides: Political Theory and Realistic Messianism," in *Miscellanea Medievalia* 11 (1971) (hereafter, Funkenstein, "Maimonides"), 81–103; Julius Guttman, "Das Problem der Kontingenz in der Philosophie Maimonides," in *MGWJ* 83 (1939), 406–30.

64. Twersky, *Introduction*, 379.

65. *Guide*, 3, 31.

66. *Guide*, 3, 31; and see Twersky, *Introduction*, 380, n. 64.

67. In *Guide*, 3, 27. Maimonides writes: "The true Law then . . . has come to bring us both perfections. . . . The letter of the Torah speaks of both perfections and informs us that the end of this Law in its entirety is the achievement of these two," *Guide* 3, 27; and see the observations of A. Funkenstein, "Maimonides," 86–96, esp. 93. Also see the two introductory essays to the Pines edition of the *Guide:* "How to Begin to Study The Guide of the Perplexed," pp. lvi–cxxxiv. See also Hartman, *Quest*, 139–86 and passim for his attention to the importance of the notion of community in understanding Rambam.

68. *Guide*, 3, 26.

69. *Guide,* 3, 26; cf. Twersky, *Introduction,* 374–97, esp. 391–97. Note that Maimonides applies accommodation only to statutes, not to judgments. See Stern, *Hoq,* passim; Lenn Evan Goodman, "Maimonides' Philosophy of Law," in *Jewish Law Annual,* I (1977), 72–107 (hereafter, Goodman, *Law*); Hyman, *Note,* 331–39; Michael Nehorai, "Maimonides' System of the Commandments" *Da'at* 13 (1984) [Hebrew], 29–42, esp. 35–42, where the sacrifices are discussed. For the ends of the Law, see Miriam Galston, "The Purpose of the Law According to Maimonides," *JQR,* n.s. 69 (1978), 27–51. A. Hyman. "Maimonides on Causality," *Maimonides and Philosophy* eds. Shlomo Pines and Yirmiyahu Yovel (Dordrecht, 1986), 157–71; and "Maimonides' Thirteen Principles," *Jewish Medieval and Renaissance Studies,* ed. Alexander Altmann (Cambridge, Ma., 1967) 119–144.

70. Twersky, *Introduction,* 385. See also Stern, *Hoq,* 126, n. 11, for discussion of the rabbinic background and references to the concept in Maimonides' works.

71. This was one approach advanced by Maimonides. Cf. Twersky, *Introduction,* 387–88, and observe his comments on 388 in n. 80. H. A. Wolfson in "Spinoza and the Religion of the Past," in *Religious Philosophy: A Group of Essays* (Cambridge, 1961), 260–61 expressed the idea with masterful clarity:

> Religion, to religious philosophers, was not only a truth, a way of knowing, but also a good, a way of living. To them, God, in His governance of the world, by His individual providence, in His infinite wisdom, not only endowed men with freedom, but has also revealed to them laws of conduct by which, through the exercise of their freedom, they are guided to their destined good. These divinely revealed laws, it was insisted upon by the religious philosophers, were not the prescripts of an arbitrary ruler; they were based upon reason. In fact, there were the virtues which philosophers, in their fumbling way, were trying to discover by their own faulty reason as rules of conduct whereby men were to attain their highest good.

Twersky cites Maimonides' *Commentary on the Mishnah,* chap. 10, of Sanhedrin in Twersky, *Intro.,* p. 358, n. 80.

> The truth has no other purpose than knowing that it is truth. Since the Torah is truth, the purpose of knowing it is to do it. A good man must not wonder: "If I perform these commandments, which are virtues, and if I refrain from these transgressions, which are vices that God commanded us not to do, what will I get out of it?"

See also Eliezer Goldman, "The Worship Peculiar to Those Who Have Apprehended True Reality," *Bar Ilan Annual Studies* in *Judaica and the Humanities* VI (1968), 287–313. On Maimonides' approach, one should also consult Isaak Heineman, *Ta'amei ha-Mitzvot be Sifrut Yisra'el* (Jerusalem, 1966),

79–97. See also Goodman, *Law,* 93–104; Warren Zev Harvey, "Political Philosophy and Halakhah in Maimonides" in *Iyyun,* 29 (1980), 198–212 [Hebrew].

72. See B. Septimus, "Petrus Alfonsi on the Cult at Mecca," *Speculum* 56 (1981), 517–33 (hereafter, Septimus, "Petrus Alfonsi.")

73. *Responsa of Maimonides,* 3 vols., ed. J. Blau (Jerusalem, 1958), vol. II, 726–28, esp. 726–27 (hereafter *Responsa M.*) and A. Funkenstein, "Changes in the Patterns of Christian Anti-Jewish Polemics in the 12th Century," in *Zion,* 33 (1968), 125–44 (Hebrew) esp. 136 ff. See also B. Septimus, "Petrus Alfonsi" 517–33.

74. Saul Lieberman, "Palestine in the Third and Fourth Centuries," in *JQR,* 36, (1949), 329–79, and 37 (1946), 31–54 (reprinted in *Texts and Studies* [New York, 1974], 112–77). See esp. vol. 36, 366, n. 266 (reprinted in *Texts and Studies,* 165–77), for an exhaustive study of Mercurius in rabbinic literature. On the prevalence of idolatry in the rabbinic period, one need but look at the *Mechilta d'Rabbi Ishmael, Bahodesh* VI: "If the name of every idol were to be specifically mentioned, all the skins [parchments] in the world would not suffice."

75. On Peter Alphonsi see Septimus, "Petrus Alfonsi" and on William see Stephen D. Benin, "Maimonides and Scholasticism: Sacrifice as Historical Hermeneutic," IV, *Proceedings of the Eighth World Congress of Jewish Studies Division C* (Jerusalem 1982) 41–46. Cf. Peter Alfonsi, *Dialogi, PL,* 527–672.

76. *Responsa M.,* vol. II, 726–27; and cf. Funkenstein, "Maimonides," 91–92, n. 35.

77. *Responsa M.,* vol. II, 727.

78. See Joseph Levenson, *Confucian China and Its Modern Fate: A Trilogy* (Berkeley/Los Angeles, 1968), vol. III, 114–15.

79. See Goodman, *Law,* 93–97; and Hartman, *Quest,* passim.

80. *Guide,* 3, 29. As Pines notes (518, n. 25), Abu Bakr Ahmad Ibn Ali Ibn Wahshiyya seems to have been the author, and he attempted to pass it off as a translation from the Chaldean. It appeared in 904. See also Pines, *Introduction,* cxxii–cxxiv.

81. *Guide,* 3, 29. See also *Guide,* 3, 30: "For the foundation of the Law consists in putting an end to this opinion [Sabian notions] and effacing its traces . . . " and see *Guide,* 3, 49: "In the case of most of the statutes whose reason is hidden from us, everything serves to keep people away from idolatry."

82. *Guide,* 3, 29.

83. See chap. V on al-Qirqisani, 232–236 and see also Funkenstein, "Maimonides," 94, n. 43. Twersky, *Introduction,* does not mention or indicate al-Qirqisani as a possible antecedent of Maimonides' theory.

84. *Guide,* 3, 29.

85. *Guide,* 3, 32; cf. Pines, *Introduction,* i–xxvii to i–xxviii. For Galen, see the English translation by Margaret Tallmadge May: *Galen, On the Usefulness of the Parts of the Body* (Ithaca, 1968), 2 vols.; and the Greek text, *De Usus Partium,* ed. D. C. G. Kuhn (Leipzig, 1822). I am indebted to Peter Brown for calling my attention to more references than those provided by Pines in his *Introduction;* i.e., book XI, chaps. 14 and 15. See also the comments of Robert L. Wilken, *The Christians as the Romans Saw Them* (New Haven and London, 1984), 68–93.

86. *Guide,* 3, 32.

87. See chap. II and III for some instances.

88. See chap. II for Antiochene exegesis.

89. *Guide,* 3, 32.

90. See chap. II, 40.

91. *Guide,* 3, 32.

92. *Guide,* 3, 32.

93. See chap. II, 65–66.

94. See chap. III, 79.

95. *Guide,* 3, 32.

96. *Guide,* 3, 32.

97. *Guide,* 3, 32. See also Twersky, *Introduction,* 389–90; and Funkenstein, "Maimonides," 84–90. See also S. Pines, "Ibn Khaldun and Maimonides," in *Studia Islamica,* 32 (1970), 265–70; and cf. Maimonides' *Treatise on Resurrection* concerning miracles of the "category of the possible." See also Funkenstein, *Theology,* 227–39, on the indeterminacy of nature, and Alvin J. Reines, "Maimonides' Concept of Miracles," *HUCA* XLV (1979), 243–85.

98. *Guide,* 3, 32; and cf. Funkenstein, "Maimonides," 91 ff.

99. Funkenstein, "Maimonides," 91.

100. Funkenstein, "Maimonides," 91–92.

101. Funkenstein, "Maimonides," 94.

102. Twersky, *Introduction,* 404.

103. *Guide*, 3, 30.

104. *Guide*, 3, 47.

105. *Guide*, 3, 49.

106. *Guide*, 3, 49.

107. *Guide*, 2, 39.

108. *Guide*, 2, 39; and cf. Twersky, *Introduction*, 405, especially n. 128, for the parallels in ha-Levi, R. David Kimhi, and others, and his reconciliation of tradition and philosophy. Cf. Hartman, *Quest*, passim and contrast with Strauss, *Persecution*, 78–94.

109. Twersky, *Introduction*, 402–6.

110. For a recent overview of some of the issues, see the helpful comments of Warren Zev Harvey, "The Return of Maimonideanism," in *Jewish Social Studies*, 42 (1980), 249–68, and for nineteenth-century views, see Jay Harris, "The Image of Maimonides in Nineteenth-Century Jewish Historiography," in *PAAJR*, 54 (1987) 117–39. Of course, this is an issue of dispute between Strauss's general approach, that the *Guide* was written for the elite, the *Mishneh Torah* for the masses; that the *Guide* was more important than the *Mishneh Torah*. This position is attacked by Hartman, who seeks to explain that one cannot expect that Maimonides kept himself neatly divided into two distinct halves: the philosopher and the rabbi and never the twain met. Twersky seeks a middle path to mediate these difficulties.

111. Commentary printed in standard editions of the Bible and an edition by C. Chavel (Jerusalem, 1966–67). There is also an English translation by C. Chavel (New York, 1971–74).

112. Naḥmanides' commentary on Leviticus 1:9.

113. On the Ritba, see *Encyclopaedia Judaica* 16, 846–48.

114. The edition used is in *Kitvei Haritva*, ed. M. Y. Blau (New York, 1956). The relevant discussion is found on 35–40, esp. 36 and 37. The edition by K. Kahana (Jerusalem, 1955) was unavailable to me.

115. Twersky *Introduction*, 430–59, reviews some of the issues with pertinent bibliography. See also Vajda, "La pensée religieuse de Moïse Maimonide: unité ou dualité?" in *Cahiers de Civilization Médiévale*, 9 (1966), 29–49.

116. See Twersky, *Introduction*, 447–59 for an overview.

117. See Twersky, *Introduction*, 430–33.

118. On Kimhi, see the excellent monograph by Frank E. Talmage, *David Kimhi, The Man and His Commentaries* (Cambridge, Ma., 1975), as well as "A Hebrew Polemical Treatise," in *HThR*, 60 (1967), 3232–348; "R.

David Kimhi as Polemicist," *HUCA,* 38 (1967), 213–35; and "Introduction" to *The Book of the Covenant of Joseph Kimhi* (Toronto, 1972), 9–26. See also I. Twersky, "Aspects of the Social and Cultural History of Provencal Jewry," in *Journal of World History,* XI (1968), 185–208. Kimhi on discussing the reasons for the building of the Temple in his comment on Jeremiah 7:22 writes: *binyan habayit la-avodah efshar she-hu kemo she katav moreh tzadik Rabenu Moshe, z"l, le-heatik ha-deot hazarot....* Frank E. Talmage, "David Kimhi and the Rationalist Tradition," *HUCA* XXXIX (1968), 177–218, and "David Kimhi and the Rationalist Tradition II: Literary Sources," *Studies in Jewish bibliography, history and literature in Honor of I. Kiev.* Ed. Charles Berlin. New York, 1972, 435–478.

119. I have used the translation by Moshe Perlmann (Berkeley/Los Angeles/London, 1971). See the translator's brief but informative introduction, 1–9.

120. On Ralbag, see most recently, *Gersonides, The Wars of the Lord,* 2 vols., trans. Seymour Feldman (Philadelphia, New York, Jerusalem, 1987), I:11–17 and II:213–47, esp. 238–47 for Halachic exegesis, and for a helpful overview of Levi's works and approach (hereafter, *Gersonides, Wars*).

121. *Gersonides, Wars,* 246.

122. *Gersonides, Wars,* 246.

123. See Basil Herring, *Joseph Ibn Kaspi's Gevia' Kesef: A Study in Medieval Jewish Philosophic Bible Commentary* (New York, 1982), for the Hebrew text, translation and commentary (hereafter, Herring, *ibn Kaspi*).

124. Herring, *ibn Kaspi,* chap. 6, p. 14 of Hebrew text; 160 English.

125. Herring, *ibn Kaspi,* chap. 6, p. 13 of Hebrew text; 159 English.

126. Herring, *ibn Kaspi,* chap. 6, p. 13 of Hebrew text; 159 English.

127. Herring, *ibn Kaspi,* chap. 6, p. 13 of Hebrew text; 159–60 English.

128. Herring, *ibn Kaspi,* chap. 6, p. 14 of Hebrew text; 161 English.

129. On Arama, see Sarah Heller Wilensky, *The Philosophy of Isaac Arama in the Framework of Philonic Philosophy* (Jerusalem and Tel Aviv, 1956), (Hebrew) esp. 191–221. I have used the Pressburg (1849) edition of *Akedath Jitzchak,* III, 1–11.

130. On Abrabanel, see B. Netanyahu, *Don Isaac Abravanel, Statesman and Philosopher* (Philadelphia, 1972).

131. Abrabanel, *Commentary* (Tel Aviv, 1963) See above Chap. 5, 127–28. See his preface to Leviticus 11–12, where Abrabanel tells of the great conflict that arose over the words of Maimonides. He argues that Maimonides' words were not words of emptiness, but words of sanctity. One should note the sixteenth-century example of accommodation in Samuel de Uceda's *Midrash Shmuel,* where accommodation is employed in his explanation of *Ethics of the Fathers,* I:1.

132. The view of others should not be forgotten. See *Sefer Or Adonai* by Hasdai Crescas (I consulted a reprint of the 1555 Ferrara edition). On Crescas and Joseph Albo's *Sefer Ha-Ikkarim (Book of Principles)*, see I. Heinemann, *Ta'amei* 102–16. See also Isaac Cardoso, *Las Excelencias de los Hebreus* (Amsterdam, 1679) p. 44 quoted in Yosef Hayim Yerushalmi, *From Spanish Court to Italian Ghetto Isaac Cardoso: A Study in Seventeenth-Century Marranism and Jewish Apologetics* (Seattle and London, 1981) p. 407 for further use of the medical imagery.

133. See the following works for helpful background: Gershom G. Scholem, *Major Trends in Jewish Mysticism,* 3rd. rev. ed. (New York, 1961), 224 (hereafter, *Trends*); Gershom Scholem, *On the Kabbalah and Its Symbolism,* trans. Ralph Mannheim (New York, 1977), 32–86 (hereafter, *Kabbalah*). Gershom Scholem, "The Name of God and the Linguistic Theory of the Kabbala," trans. Simon Pleasance, in *Diogenes* 79 (1972), 59–81 and in 80 (1972), 164–94. (Hereafter, *Name of God.*) Moshe Idel, "Infinites of Torah in Kabbalah," in *Midrash and Literature,* eds. G. H. Hartman and S. Budick (New Haven and London, 1986), 141–57 (hereafter, "Infinities"); Harry A. Wolfson, "Extradeical and Intradeical Interpretations of Platonic Ideas, in *"Religious Philosophy: A Group of Essays* (New York, 1965), 27; also in *JHI,* 22 (1961); Stephen D. Benin, "The 'Cunning of God' and Divine Accommodation," in *JHI,* 45 (1984), 179–91; for much of what follows see: Stephen D. Benin, "The Mutability of an Immutable God: Exegesis ad Individual Capacity in the Zohar and Several Christian Sources," in *Proceedings of the Theird(sic) International Conference on the History of Jewish Mysticism The Age of the Zohar, Jerusalem Studies in Jewish Thought* 8, ed. J. Dan (Jerusalem, 1989), 67–86.

134. *Ma'arekhet ha-Elohut,* ed. I. Tishby (Jerusalem, 1982), 85, 147.

135. See Sa'adia, *BBO,* 2:4, 101–2, and I quote from Sa'adia Gaon, *Book of Doctrines and Beliefs,* book II, ed. and trans. Alexander Altmann, in *Three Jewish Philosophers* (New York, 1969) 82–84. Cf. the Hebrew edition of J. Kappah (Jerusalem, 1970), 89. As Altmann notes, 82, n. 3. the Tibbon translation of Sa'adia reads *"be-koah sikhlenu."*

136. Sa'adia, *BBO,* 2:4, 101–2 and *Book of Doctrines,* book II, 82–83.

137. Sa'adia, *BBO,* 2:4–8; 101–12; *Book of Doctrines,* book II, 83.

138. *Ma'arekhet ha-Elohut,* Mantua edition of 1588, 6b, 7b and cf. Scholem, *Trends,* 402, n. 66.

139. *Zohar* 2:176a; 3:14a/b. I use the edition of R. Margaliot, Jerusalem, 1964.

140. The phrase the *Zohar* uses is *mi-sitra di-lan. Zohar* 2:176a/b and 3:141b.

141. I use the translation in Daniel C. Matt, *Zohar (The Classics of Western Spirituality)* (New York, Toronto, 1983), 123–55 (hereafter, Matt,

Zohar). Cf. Gershom G. Scholem, *Zohar, The Book of Splendor: Basic Readings from the Kabbaleh* (New York, 1974), 89–91 (hereafter, Scholem, *Zohar*).

142. On the issue of hidden and revealed meanings in texts and on the erotic nature of reading, see R. Barthes. *The Pleasure of the Text,* trans. Richard Miller (New York, 1975), 9–14.

143. *Zohar,* 3:152a, cf. Matt, *Zohar,* 43 and commentary on 204–7; Cf. Scholem, *Zohar,* 121. This is of course the issue of *sod hamalbush.*

144. *Zohar* 2:229b.

145. Cf. *Pirke de Rabbi Eliezer,* 3, and Gregory of Nazianzus *Oration,* 38, 12.

146. Concerning human "clothing" compare the concept of *haluqa derabbanan,* the mystical garment, woven of the commandments fulfilled in this world, in which the soul is outfitted in the world to come.

147. *Zohar* 3:152a; cf. 3:3:149b.

148. *Zohar* 3:152a. I use the translation in Matt, *Zohar,* 44 and see notes 205. Cf. *Zohar* 2:85b and Scholem, *Zohar,* 122.

149. *Zohar* 3:152a; Matt, *Zohar,* 44 and notes 205; cf. Scholem, *Zohar,* 122. See also *The Wisdom the Zohar* 2 vols., ed. I. Tishby (Jerusalem, 1971), 2, 402–3 (Hebrew), (hereafter, Tishby, *Wisdom*).

150. See Matt, *Zohar,* 205 for parallels in Philo, Origen, and Rumi.

151. *Zohar,* 2:176a; Matt, *Zohar,* 38–39.

152. For a discussion of this issue, see Efraim Gottlieb, *Studies in the Kabbalah Literature,* ed. Joseph Hacker (Tel Aviv, 1976), (Hebrew) esp. 288–317 (hereafter, Gottlieb, *Studies*), and Efraim Gottlieb, *The Kabbalah at the End of the Thirteenth Century* (Jerusalem, 1969) (Hebrew) (hereafter, Gottlieb, *Kabbalah*).

153. Scholem, *Trends,* 178–80, and *Kabbalah,* 77–86.

154. Scholem, *Kabbalah,* 78.

155. Scholem, *Trends* 178–80, and *Kabbalah,* 77–86.

156. *Dialogues,* I, 13, 117 (*PL,* 188, 1160). See also W. Berges, "Anslem von Havelberg in der Geistesgeschichte des 12. Jahrhunderts," in *Jahrbuch für der Geschichte Mittel-und Östdeutschlands,* 5, (1956), 38–57, and cf. above chap. IV, p. 124.

157. *Institutes of the Christian Religion,* II, 11, 13. Cf. II, 7, 2; I, 11, 3; II, 11, 2: *Commentary on Genesis, Argument* 1:16; 2:8. See below, chap. VII, for Calvin.

158. See Yaacov Levinger, "Torato shel HaRebi Mi-Kotzk," in *Tarbiz*, 55 (1986), part II, 427. The post-Zoharic uses of accommodation, be they in the doctrine of *shemmitoth* and the relativization of Torah and *mitzvot* to differ- ent times and observances, or in mystical speculation on the infinities of Torah, need further study.

159. Yaacov Levinger, "Torato shel HaRebi Mi-Kotzk," 419. For a re- working of this tale, see Martin Buber, *Tales of the Hasidim, The Later Masters,* trans. Olga Marx (New York, 1974), 278.

160. *Zohar,* 2, 163a–163b; Tishby, *Wisdom,* 1, 121–23. I am indebted to Dr. Ze'ev Gries for pointing out these sources to me and sharing his interpre- tation of them. The story is also found in Mendel Paikarz', *Biyemei Tzemikat Ha-Ḥasidut* (Jerusalem, 1978), 229–31, but without reference to the *Zohar,* its source in Proverbs, or the idea of the seductive nature of education.

161. Hebrew *im yitbaneha* meaning demand sexual intercourse cf. *Hagigah* 15a.

162. Jacob Joseph of Polonnoye, *Ben Porat Yosef* (Pietrokov, 1884) 85a.

163. Ibid.

164. See *Temurah* 29b–30a, which states that such a union "makes a whore out of her."

165. See the critical edition by Rivka Schatz-Uffenheimer (Jerusalem, 1976) (hereafter, *Maggid*).

166. *Maggid,* 296–97. The parable is on 297. A study of the use of *tzimtzaym* as it occurs in the Midrash, where God reduces his presence through Luria's use of the *tzimtzum* as a divine internal procedure before creation, would be welcome.

CHAPTER SEVEN

1. On reactions in general see Daniel J. Silver, *Maimonidean Criticism and the Maimonidean Controversy* (Leiden, 1965), and for a sampling of original sources see Abraham S. Halkin, *After Maimonides An Anthology of Writings by His Critics, Defenders and Commentators* (Jerusalem, 1979) (Hebrew). See also Joseph Saracheck, *Faith and Reason: The Conflict over the Rationalism of Maimonides* (Williamsport, 1935).

2. See J. Guttmann, "Guillaume d'Auvergne et la litterature Juive," *REJ* 18 (1889), 243–55; J. Guttmann, "Alexandre de Hales et le Judaisme," *REJ,* 19 (1889), 224–34; J. Guttmann, "Der Einfluss der Maimonidischen Philosophie auf das christliche Abenland," *Moses ben Maimon; sein Leben, seine Werke und sein Einfluss,* eds. W. Bacher, M. Brann, D. Simonsen (Leipzig, 1907). 175–204. For much of what follows see Stephen D. Benin, "Maimonides and Scholasticism: Sacrifice as Historical Hermeneutic," *Proceedings of the Eighth World Congress of Jewish Studies, Division C* (Jerusalem, 1982), 41–

46; and the longer, masterful study of Beryl Smalley, "William of Auvergne, John of La Rochelle and St. Thomas Aquinas on the Old Law," *St. Thomas Aquinas Commemorative Studies*, (Toronto, 1974) II, 11–71. (Hereafter, Smalley, "Old Law"). For William see *Tractatus de Fide et Legibus* in *Guilelmi Alverni Episcopi Parisiensis, Opera Omnia* Vol. 1 (Paris/Orleans, 1674) (hereafter, *de Legibus*) I have used a photocopy of the text, and references are to sections of the work and page numbers of Vol. I. For other twelfth century commentators see Beryl Smalley, "Ralph of Flaix on Leviticus" *Recherches de théologie ancienne et médiévale*, 35 (1968), 35–82, and "An Early Twelfth-Century Commentator on the Literal Sense of Leviticus", *Recherches de théologie ancienne et médiévale*, 35 (1969), 78–99. See also Seymour Feldman, "A Scholastic Misinterpretation of Maimonides' Doctrine of Divine Attributes," *JJS* 19 (1968) 23–40, and Wolfgang Kluxen, "Maimonides and Latin Scholasticism," *Maimonides and Philosophy*, eds. Schlomo Pines and Yirmiyahu Yovel (Dordrecht, 1986), 224–31.

3. This manuscript was completed before the publication of Amos Funkenstein, *Theology and the Scientific Imagination from the Middle Ages to the Seventeenth Century* (Princeton, 1986) which deals with similar ideas but focuses on the development of modern scientific thought rather than on biblical exegesis. For example, he has no Syriac material, he does not consider the works of Calvin at all, and has but one brief reference to Luther. For an examination of the relationship between the ideas of accommodation, economy and the rise of modern science, one should now consult Funkenstein.

4. Smalley, "Old Law," 17; "sicut enim meretrix, immo quam plurimis, sese exponit, ita in littera multiplex est sensus: set enim sensus historialis, allegoricus, tropologicus."

5. Smalley, "Old Law," 19, see n. 25 for sources and attempts to identify the quotation.

6. Smalley, "Old Law," 25. See the *Guide* 3, 32. And on the strictures of the rabbis on certain studies see David J. Halperin, *The Merkabah in Rabbinic Literature* (New Haven, 1980). Cf. Maimonides position in *Sefer ha-Mitzvot*, negative commandment 365, where he asserts all the precepts had a reason and rationale even if undecipherable by the masses.

7. Smalley, "Old Law," 31.

8. *de Legibus*, 8; 38–40.

9. *de Legibus*, 15; 46.

10. *de Legibus*, 15; 46.

11. *de Legibus*, 1; 18, 2; 29 and cf. 16, 47.

12. *de Legibus*, 2, 29; cf. 16; 47.

13. *de Legibus*, 1, 24. For a particularly nice illustration of the same metaphor that depicts God's accommodative and condescending nature, see

Notes 275

Memorials of St. Anselm, eds. Richard W. Southern and F. S. Schmitt (London, 1969), 274: *Puerorum more cibandos existimo, qui si quando grossum aliquod pomum edendum percipiunt, illud ob dentium teneritudinem et oris angustiam absumere nequeunt, si pro illorum capacitate primo non fuerit particulatim divisum.*

14. Smalley, "Old Law," 35, and 35, n. 41.

15. *de Legibus*, 2, 29 and 24, 72. The seven reasons are: (1) to honor God and teach the Jews to observe the commandments given especially to them; (2) to signify divine justice and mercy; (3) to impress upon the Jews what they had studied in Scripture; (4) to sanctify those who offered them; (5) to bring people closer to God; (6) to unify God's people; and (7) to unify humanity through worship. He also suggests (*de Legibus*, 2, 30) that sacrifices provided for the priests and permitted them to officiate in the Temple and to teach the Israelites. Perhaps the biblical idea of pilgrimage mentioned by Maimonides, (*Guide*, 3, 39 and 3, 46) as a unifying feature of religious life together with knowledge of the hajj, which Maimonides certainly knew about and William probably did, influenced William's last reason.

16. Smalley, "Old Law," 39.

17. *de Legibus*, 16, 47.

18. *de Legibus*, 16, 47–48.

19. *de Legibus*, 16, 47.

20. Smalley, "Old Law," 39–44.

21. *de Legibus*, 28; 97.

22. *de Legibus*, 28; 97.

23. *de Legibus*, 28; 99.

24. *de Legibus*, 28; 99.

25. *de Legibus*, 28; 99–101.

26. Smalley, "Old Law," 46.

27. I refer to Thomas Aquinas, *Summa Theologiae*, Leonine text, ed. P. Caramello (Turin, 1952–56). References are to part/question/article/response. All citations from the *responsio* are given as *in corp*. Unless indicated otherwise, I give the translation in the Blackfriars edition (New York, 1964).

28. I, IIae, 98, 1 *ad* 1. Smalley, "Old Law," 60, states: "St. Thomas refers it (Ezek. 20:25) to the ceremonial precepts, as had normally been done. Ralph of Flaix, representing the older tradition, had used it to discredit the educative value of *caeremonalia*, whereas William of Auvergne, following Maimonides, had taken *not good* as referring to the disposition of those who performed ceremonies unworthily." Smalley also explains Ezek. 20:25 with reference to *Guide* 3, 32 and its use of I Sam. 15:22; Isa. 1:11, and Jer. 7:22–

23. While Maimonides may indeed have understood Ezek. 20:25 in that way, the text is not used either in the *Guide* or in the *Mishneh Torah.* The Vulgate read *"praecepta non bona, et iudicia"* for the Hebrew *"ḥukkim lo tovim u-mishpatim,"* but see above pp. 151–155 for Maimonides' interpretation of *ḥukkim.*

29. I, IIAE, 101, 1. My translation.

30. I, IIAE, 101, *in corp.* He quotes the *Guide,* 3, 28.

31. I, IIAE, 101, 1, *ad* 1.

32. I, IIAE, 101, 1, *ad* 3.

33. I, IIAE, 101, 2.

34. I, IIAE, 101, 2, *in corp.*

35. I, IIAE, 101, 2, *in corp.*

36. I, IIAE, 101, 2, *in corp.*

37. I, IIAE, 101, 2, *ad* 1.

38. I, IIAE, 102, 2, *in corp.*

39. I, IIAE, 102, 2, *in corp.*

40. I, IIAE, 102, 2 *ad* 3.

41. I, IIAE, 104, 2 *in corp.*

42. I, IIAE, 104, 3, *in corp.*

43. I, IIAE, 104, 3, *in corp.*

44. See, for example, IIIa, 48, 3, where Christ's passion was the true sacrifice prefigured by the blood offerings of Scripture.

45. *Summa contra gentiles,* 4, 55, (London, 1923). Smalley, "Old Law," 65, n. 21, incorrectly cites *Summa contra gentiles,* 4, 23. See also H. Liebeschutz, "Judaism and Jewry in the Social Doctrine of Thomas Aquinas," *JJS,* 13 (1962), 57–81.

46. Smalley, "Old Law," 47–51.

47. James S. Preus, *From Shadow to Promise Old Testament Interpretation from Augustine to the Young Luther,* (Cambridge, Ma., 1969), 68–68 (hereafter, Preus, *Shadow*); also cited in Steven Ozment, *The Age of Reform, 1250–1550: an intellectual and religious history of late Medieval and Reformation Europe* (New Haven, 1980), 69 (hereafter, Ozment, *Reform*). For the transition from Aquinas to Calvin, I rely on Ozment, *Reform,* 22–134, for a very helpful and informative overview. Also of value is Owen Chadwick, *The Reformation (Pelican History of the Church,* 3) (London, 1964). For Lyra and Rashi, Herman Hailperin, *Rashi and the Christian Scholars* (Pittsburgh, 1963), ought to be used with some attention to the sources.

48. See Ozment, *Reform*, 22–134, for a helpful, sober, and insightful account of different approaches to the period; cf. Preus, *Shadow*, 72–149, and see also Heiko Oberman, *Forerunners of the Reformation: The Shape of Late Medieval Thought* (Philadelphia, 1981), 279–315, for translated excerpts from late medieval exegesis including (297–301) Lefevre's *Introduction* to his *Commentary on the Psalms* (1508).

49. Ozment, *Reform*, 18–21, 70–71; and see Beryl Smalley, *English Friars and Antiquity in the Early Fourteenth Century* (New York, 1960).

50. Cited in Preus, *Shadow*, 145. Ozment, *Reform*, 71, n. 118, cites one of Luther's tabletalks of 1531, where he remarks: *"Lyram contemnebam, quanquam post viderem eum valere ad historiam."*

51. Ozment, *Reform*, 71.

52. Preus, *Shadow*, 176–91.

53. Ozment, *Reform*, 71. This is Preus' position in *Shadow*; and Ozment, *Homo Spiritualis. A Comparative Study of the Anthropology of Johannes Tauler, Jean Gerson and Martin Luther (1509–16) in the context of their theological thought.* (Leiden, 1969), supports this view.

54. For Calvin, I rely upon H. Jackson Forstman, *Word and Spirit, Calvin's Doctrine of Biblical Authority* (Stanford, 1962) (hereafter, Forstman, *Word*). References are to *Ioannis Calvini Opera quae supersunt omnia* eds. J. W. Baum, E. Cunitz and E. Reuss. (*Corpus Reformatorum* v. 29–87). I use the translation of the *Institutes of the Christian Religion* (*LCC*, 20, 21) ed. John T. McNeill and trans. Ford Lewis Battles (Philadelphia, 1960) (hereafter, *ICR*, references to book, and chapter). See also Ford Lewis Battles, "God Was Accommodating Himself to Human Capacity," in *Interpretation*, 31 (1977), 19–38 (hereafter, Battles, *Accommodating*). Battles, 19 n. 1, states that he knows "of only one contemporary study explicitly devoted to accommodation: Clinton Ashley, "John Calvin's Utilization of the Principle of Accommodation and Its Continuing Significance for an Understanding of Biblical Language," unpub. Ph.D. Dissertation, Southwest Baptist Theological Seminary, 1972." I have read that work, and it is of no help to this study.

55. *ICR*, I, 1, 1.

56. *ICR*, II, 1, 8.

57. *ICR*, III, 2, 1.

58. *ICR*, III, 2, 6.

59. *ICR*, III, 2, 6.

60. *ICR*, III, 2, 6; cf. *ICR*, I, 2, 1; I, 10, 2.

61. *ICR*, III, 2, 7.

62. *ICR*, I, 6, 2. Cf. *Commentary on Philipians* 1:9 (*CR* 52, 12).

63. *ICR*, I, 14, 1; cf. I, 5, 12, 15; I, 6, 1.

64. *ICR*, I, 14, 1.

65. *ICR*, I, 14, 20.

66. *Commentary on Genesis, Argument.* I use the translation in Jean Calvin, *Commentaries on the First Book of Moses called Genesis*, trans. John King (Grand Rapids, 1948), I, 58 (hereafter, *Com. Gen*).

67. Forstman, *Word*, 13.

68. *ICR*, I, 13, 1.

69. *ICR*, I, 6, 3.

70. *Com. Gen. 17:4;* 446–47.

71. *ICR*, II, 11, 13, Cf. *ICR*, II, 7, 2; I, 11, 3; II, 11, 2; *Com. Gen. 1:16; 2:8,* 86–87; 113.

72. Forstman, *Word*, 107–9.

73. Forstman, *Word*, 75–85.

74. Battles, "Accommodating," 20.

75. *Commentary on Psalm 10:1*; cf. *Commentary on Matthew 23:37.* The definition is cited in Forstman, *Word*, 114.

76. *Com. Gen. 3:21*, 181.

77. Forstman, *Word*, 115, and 164, nn. 50–61, for references.

78. Battles, "Accommodating," 35–38. For the Lord's Prayer see *ICR*, III, 20, 40; Sacraments, *ICR*, 4, 14, 3; Lord's Supper, *ICR*, 4, 17, 11; 36; 4, 18, 12–18; Incarnation, *ICR*, I, 13, 5; II, 6, 1.

79. Cited in Battles, "Accommodating," 35.

80. *ICR*, II, 8, 39, 41, cited in Battles, "Accommodating," 35.

81. *ICR*, II, 5, 6–7. Battles, "Accommodating," 35, n. 10, identifies the source of Eck's remarks as *Enchiridion*, Chap. 31, *Concerning Free Will.*

82. See Ozment, *Reform*, 72.

83. Cited in Israel Baroway, "The Bible as Poetry in the English Renaissance: An Introduction," in *Journal of English and German Philology*, 32 (1933), 447–80, at 462 (hereafter, Baroway, "Bible").

84. Cited in Baroway, "Bible," 462.

85. Cited in Baroway, "Bible," 462.

86. Cited in Baroway, "Bible," 463.

87. See Ozment, *Reform*, 400–2. I have not discussed the accommodation of Christianity in regard to the Jesuit missions to China. See on this: Arnold H. Rowbotham, *Missionary and Mandarin The Jesuits at the Court*

of China (Berkeley, 1992) and Amos Funkenstein, *Perceptions of Jewish History*, p. 98 (Forthcoming).

88. Cited in John O'Malley, *Giles of Viterbo on Church and Reform. A Study in Renaissance Thought* (Leiden, 1968), 140, and in Ozment, *Reform*, 401.

89. O'Malley, *Giles*, 161, 191, cited in Ozment, *Reform*, 402, n. 16.

90. *ICR*, I, 2, 1; I, 5, 5; I, 14, 2, 20; I, 16, 3, 5, 7; II, 1, 5; III, 3, 12; IV, 17, 25.

91. See Reijer Hooykaas, *Religion and the Rise of Modern Science* (Grand Rapids, 1972) (hereafter, Hooykaas, *Religion*). I thank Professor Thomas Hankins for suggesting this and other worthwhile readings.

92. *ICR*, II, 2, 15.

93. *ICR*, II, 2, 15.

94. *Com. Gen.*, I, 16 (86). Emphasis added.

95. *Com. Gen.*, I, 16 (87). Cf. *Com. Gen* I, 5 (78): The Latin reads: *Quanquam Moses legem hic preafigure noluit quam violare sit nefas: sed receptae consuetudini (ut iam dictum est) accommodavit sermonem suum.* Cf. Thomas Aquinas, *Summa Theologiae* I, IAE 68, 3 *in corp.* concerning the biblical description of the creation, the second day. "*Sed considerandum est quod Moyses rudi populo loquebatur, quorum imbecillitati condescendens, illa solum eis proposuit, quae manifeste sensui apparent.*" See Giorgio de Santillana, *The Crime of Galileo* (Chicago, 1955), xi where he observes that at Galileo's first trial (1616) history might have been different if a 'youthful Aquinas' had been present instead of an 'aged Bellarmine'. Also of note is the prosecutor's conclusion against Lavoisier: "La République n'a pas besoin de savants."

96. *Com. Gen.*, I, 6 (79–80).

97. *Com. Gen.*, I, 6 (79).

98. Cited in Hooykaas, *Religion*, 118–19.

99. Cited in Hooykaas, *Religion*, 122–23, 155, n. 33b.

100. Cited in Hooykaas, *Religion*, 123, 155, n. 37.

101. See J. Kepler, *Atronomia Nova* (1609), Introduction: cited in Hooykaas, *Religion* 155, n. 38: "Holy Scriptures speak about common things (for the instruction in which they have not been instituted) with human beings in a human way, so that they may be understood by mankind; they use what is generally acknowledged by men, in order to bring home to them other things, more lofty and divine."

102. Hooykaas, *Religion*, 124–25.

103. Hooykaas, *Religion*, 125, 155, nn. 41, 42.

104. Hooykaas, *Religion*, 126, 155, n. 43.

105. Hooykaas, *Religion*, 126.

106. Hooykaas, *Religion*, 134.

107. Cited in Hooykaas, *Religion*, 135, 156, n. 69.

CHAPTER EIGHT

1. See first and foremost, Hans W. Frei, *The Eclipse of Biblical Narrative: A Study in Eighteenth and Nineteenth Century Hermeneutics* (New Haven, 1974) (hereafter, Frei, *Eclipse*). This is an excellent survey of biblical study from Luther to Strauss, and in many ways, my study provides the history behind the figures and movements Frei discusses. See also Hayden V. White, "Romanticism, Historicism, Realism: Toward a Period Concept For Early 19th Century Intellectual History," in *The Uses of History*, ed. Hayden V. White (Detroit, 1968), 45–58; Hayden V. White, *Metahistory: The Historical Imagination in Nineteenth Century Europe* (Baltimore, 1973) (hereafter, White, *Metahistory*) (hereafter, White *Meta*); Frank E. Manuel, *The Eighteenth Century Confronts the Gods* (Cambridge, Ma., 1959) (hereafter, Manuel, *Gods*); idem., *Shapes of Philosophical History* (Stanford, 1965) (hereafter, Manuel, *Shapes*); idem., *The Changing of the Gods* (Hanover, London, 1983) (hereafter, Manuel, *Changing*); and for a general historical survey, I have relied upon Leonard Krieger, *Kings and Philosophers*, 1689–1789, (New York, 1970) (hereafter, Krieger, *Kings*); also of provocative use is Carl L. Becker, *The Heavenly City of the Eighteenth Century Philosophers* (New Haven, 1932) (hereafter, Becker, *City*); and of interest is J. G. A. Pocock, "The Origins of the Study of the Past: A Comparative Approach," in *Comparative Studies in Society and History*, 4 (1961–62), 209–46. Of use also are: Basil Willey, *The Seventeenth Century Background: Studies in the Thought of the Age in Relation to Poetry and Religion* (London, 1949), and *The Eighteenth Century Background: Studies on the Idea of Nature in the Thought of the Period* (London, 1949).

2. Cited in Manuel, *Gods*, 235, and 321, n. 93. Cf. Krieger, *Kings*, 152–86, and for ideas on the historiography of the period, see White, *Metahistory*, 45–59.

3. See Manuel, *Changing*, 161–65; Manuel, *Shapes*, 46–69; White, *Metahistory*, 51–53; and for Vico, I use *The New Science of Giambattista Vico*, trans. Thomas G. Bergin and Max H. Fisch (Ithaca, London, 1979) (hereafter, *New Science*). See also, Amos Funkenstein, "Natural Science and Social Theory: Hobbes, Spinoza and Vico," in *Giambattista Vico: An International Symposium*, ed. Giorgio Tagliacozzo (Baltimore, 1969), 187–212, cf. June T. Fox, "The Pedagogical Theory of Giambattista Vico: In Appreciation of an International Symposium," in *Educational Theory*, 20 (1970), 292–303. See also, J. Faur, "The Splitting of the Logos: Some Remarks on Vico ad Rabbinic Tradition," *New Vico Studies*, 3 (1985), 85–103; and G. Costa, "Vico

Notes 281

and Ancient Rhetoric," *Classical Influences on Western Thought AD 1650–1870*, ed. R. R. Bolger (Cambridge, 1979), 247–262.

4. *New Science, Conclusion*, 381.

5. *New Science, Conclusion*, 381.

6. See Amos Funkenstein, "Periodization and Self-Understanding in the Middle Ages and Early Modern Times," *Medievalia et Humanistica*, n.s.5 (1974), 3–23. Cf. Manuel, *Shapes*, 58–59.

7. Manuel, *Gods*, 154.

8. See Gotthold Ephraim Lessing, *The Education of the Human Race*, trans. F. W. Robertson (London, 1927). (Hereafter, Lessing, *Education*, reference to paragraph number and page). Cf., Manuel, *Shapes*, 70–82.

9. Lessing, *Education*, 4, 195.

10. See *Book of Opinions and Beliefs*, Prologue.

11. Lessing, *Education*, 5, 195–6.

12. Lessing, *Education*, 6–9, 196.

13. Lessing, *Education*, 11, 197.

14. Lessing, *Education*, 16, 197–98.

15. Lessing, *Education*, 23, 200.

16. Lessing, *Education*, 23, 200.

17. Lessing, *Education*, 51, 207.

18. Lessing, *Education*, 53, 207.

19. See Frei, *Eclipse*, 105–23, and *Reimarus, Fragments*, ed. Charles H. Talbert (Philadelphia, 1970).

20. Frei, *Eclipse*, 63.

21. Cf. Frei, *Eclipse*, 63–65.

22. See Frei, *Eclipse*, 183, and F. J. Schmitz, *The Problem of Individualism and the Crises in the Lives of Lessing and Hamann (Univ. of California Publications in Modern Philology)* 27 (1944), 125–48. See also: Karlfield Grunder, *Figur und Geschichte. Johann Georg Hamann's "Biblische Betrachtungen" als Ansatz einer geschichtsphilosophie* (Freiburg-Munich, 1958). For Herder, see Robert T. Clark, *Herder, His Life and Thought* (Berkeley, Los Angeles, 1955) and F. M. Barnard, *Herder's Social and Political Thought; from Enlightenment to Nationalism* (Oxford, 1965).

23. Cited in Frei, *Eclipse*, 183, 334, n. 3.

24. Cited in Frei, *Eclipse*, 184, 334, n. 4.

25. Herder, *Letters*, cited in Frei, *Eclipse*, 184, 334, n. 5.

26. Herder, *Letters*, cited in Frei, *Eclipse*, 185, 334, n. 9.

27. See the examples in Frei, *Eclipse*, 187.

28. Frei, *Eclipse*, 193.

29. Cited in Frei, *Eclipse*, 193–94.

30. Cited in Frei, *Eclipse*, 194.

31. Cited in Frei, *Eclipse*, 195.

32. See Georg G. Iggers, *The German Conception of History*, rev. ed. (Middletown, 1983), 34 (hereafter, Iggers, *History*), and Georg G. Iggers, "The Dissolution of German Historicism," *Ideas in History Essays Presented to Luces Gottschalk by his former students,* eds. Louis Richard Herr and Harold T. Parker, (Durham, N.C., 1965) 288–329.

33. Frei, *Eclipse*, 197.

34. That is the view of Thomas Willi, presented in Frei, *Eclipse*, 198, 334, n. 17.

35. Iggers, *History*, 35, 302, n. 22.

36. Cited in Iggers, *History*, 36, 302, n. 28.

37. Cited in Iggers, *History*, 36–37, 302, n. 29.

38. Iggers, *History*, 37; cf. Manuel, *Shapes*, 115–35; cf. White, *Meta*, 69–80; cf. Manuel, *Changing*, 135–68.

BIBLIOGRAPHY

GREEK AND LATIN SOURCES

Alexander of Hales. *Summa Theologica.* [Quarrachi edition]. Florence, 1924.

Alighieri, Dante. *The Divine Comedy, Paradiso.* Trans. and Ed. Charles S. Singelton. 2 vols. Princeton, 1970–75.

Anastasius Sinaites. *Disputatio Adversus Judaeos. PG* 89, 1203–1272.

————. *Dialoga Parvus ad Judaeos. PG* 89, 1271–73.

————. *Quaestiones et Responsiones. PG* 89, 327–824.

Anselm of Havelberg. *Dialogi. PL* 188, 1139–1248.

————. *Dialogues. SCh 118.* Ed. and trans. Gaston Salet, Paris, 1966.

————. *Epistola apologetica pro ordine canonicorum regularium. PL* 188, 1118–1140.

Anselm of Laon. (Saint Anselm) *Memorials of St. Anselm.* Eds. Richard W. Southern and F. S. Schmitt, London, 1969.

Aristotle. *Aristotle: The Nicomachean Ethics.* Ed. and trans. Loby H. Rackham, *(LCL),* Cambridge, MA, 1934.

Athanasius. *De Incarnatione. PG* 25, 95–198.

————. *Contra Gentes. PG* 25, 3–96.

————. *Athanasius Contra Gentes and De Incarnatione.* Ed. and trans. R. W. Thompson, Oxford, 1971.

————. *Four Discourses Against the Arians. PG* 25, 12–468. Translated by A. Robertson in *LNPF,* series 2, vol. 4, 303–447.

————. *The Festal Letters of Athanasius.* Ed. William Cureton, London, 1848. Trans. by H. Burgess, *LNPF,* ser. 2, vol. 4, 506–553.

Athenagoras, *Apologia. PG* 6, 887–972.

Augustine. *Adversus Judaeos. PL* 42, 51–63.

——. *Contra Faustum Manichaeum. CSEL* 25:1. Ed. Joseph Zycha, Vienna, 1896.

——. *De Civitate Dei. CSEL* 40:1 and 40:2. Ed. E. Hoffman, Vienna, 1899–1900.

——. *Augustine. City of God.* Ed. David Knowles, trans. Henry Bettenson, London, 1972.

——. *Confessions. CCL* 27. Ed. L. Verheijin, Turnhout, 1981.

——. *De vera Religione. CSEL* 77. Ed. Günther Weigel, Vienna, 1961.

——. *De Diversis Quaestionibus. CCL* 44A, pp. 1–249. Ed. A. Mutzenberger. Turnhout, 1955.

——. *Enarrationes in Psalmos. CCL* 38, 39, 40. Eds. D. E. Dekkers and I. Fraipont. Turnhout, 1956.

——. *Epistolae. CSEL.* 44. Ed. A. Goldbacher, Vienna 1895.

——. *In Iohannis Evangelium. CCL* 36. Ed. R. Willems, Turnhout, 1954.

——. *De Magistro. CSEL* 77. Ed. Günther Weigel, Vienna, 1961.

——. *De Doctrina Christiana. CSEL* 80. Ed. William M. Green, Vienna, 1963.

——. *Retractionum libri duo. CSEL* 36. Ed. P. Knöll, Vienna, 1902.

——. *Sermones. PL* 38, 23–1484; *PL* 39, 1496–1718.

Basil of Caesarea. *Address to Young Men on Reading Greek Literature.* St. Basil, *Letters,* vol. 4 (*LCL*), trans. R. J. Defarrari and Martin R. P. McGuire, London, 1934, 249–348.

——. *Homiliae 1–9 in Hexameron. PG* 29, 3–208.

——. *Homiliae in Psalmos. PG* 29, 209–494.

——. *De Fide. PG* 31, 675–692.

——. *De Bapismo. PG* 31, 1513–1628

——. *Comment in Isaiam Prophetam. PG* 30, 118–668.

——. *Homilia de Spiritu Sancto. PG* 31, 1429–1438.

——. *Liber de Spiritu Sancto. PG* 32, 67–217.

——. *The Letters.* (*LCL*) 4 vols. Trans. R. J. De farrari, London 1926–39.

Bede. *De Ratione Temporum. PL* 96, 203–578.

——. *Ecclesiastical History of the English People.* Eds. B. Colgrave and R. A.B. Mynors. [Oxford Medieval Texts]. Oxford, 1969.

Clement of Alexandria. *Protrepticus ad Graecos. GCS* 12. Ed. Otto Stählin, Leipzig, 1905.

———. *Stromata. GCS* 15. Ed. Otto Stählin, Leipzig, 1906.

Cyril of Alexandria. *De Adoratione et cultu in Spiritu et Veritate. PG* 68, 133–1126.

———. *Glaphyra in Pentateuchum. PG* 69, 9–678.

———. *Contra Julianum. PG* 76, 509–1064.

Didascalia Apostolorum. Ed. and trans. R. Hugh Connolly, Oxford, 1929.

Didascalia et Constitutiones Apostolorum. 2 Vols. Ed. F. X. Funk, Paderborn, 1905.

Diodore of Tarsus. *Exegetica ex Catena. PG* 33, 1561–1628.

Diodorus of Sicily. *Diodorus of Sicily.* Ed. and trans. C. H. Oldfather, (*LCL*) 1933–67.

Eusebius of Caesarea. *The Ecclesiastical History.* With an English Translation. (*LCL*) 2 vols. Trans. K. Lake and J. E. L. Oulton. London, 1926, 1932.

———. *Praeparatio Evangelica. GCS* 43:1, *GCS* 43:2. Ed. K. Mras, Leipzig, 1954, 1956.

———. *Demonstratio Evangelica. GCS* 23. Ed. I. A. Heikel, Leipzig, 1973.

———. *Proof of the Gospel.* 2 vols. Trans. W. J. Ferrar, London, New York, 1920.

Galen. *De Usu Partium.* Ed. D. C. G. Kuhn. Leipzig, 1822.

———. *Galen on the Usefulness of the Parts of the Body.* 2 vols. Trans. Margaret Tallmadge May, Ithaca, 1968.

Glossa Ordinaria, Biblia Sacra cum Glossis et Ordinaria. Lyons, 1650.

Gregory of Nazianzus. *Saint Grégoire de Nazianze Lettres.* 2 vols. Ed. and trans. Paul Gallay, Paris 1967.

———. *Orationes. PG* 35–36.

———. *Die funf theologischen Reden. (Testimonia, Schriften der altchristlichen Zeit).* Vol. 3. Ed. T. Barbel, Dusseldorf, 1963.

Gregory of Nyssa. *Oratio catechetica magna. PG* 45, 9–106.

———. *In Psalmorum Inscriptiones. PG* 44, 431–608.

———. *De Opificio Hominis. PG* 44, 125–256; trans. H. A. Wilson, *LNPF*, Ser. 2, vol. 5, 387–427.

———. *De Anima et resurrectione. PG* 46, 11–160.

———. *Grégoire de Nysse La Vie de Moïse ou Traité de la Perfection en Matière de Vertu. SCh* 1, 2nd edition. Ed. and trans. J. Daniélou, Paris, 1955.

————. *Adversus Eunomium. PG* 45 237–1122.

————. *Accurate Exposition of the Canticle of Canticles. PG* 44, 755–1120.

————. *On the Dead. PG* 46, 522–24.

Gregory the Great. *Magna Moralia. PL* 75, 76; *CCL* Vols. 143, 143A. Ed. M. Adriaen, Turnhout, 1979.

Hesychius Presbyter. *In Leviticum. PG* 93, 787–1180.

————. *In Isaiam. PG* 93, 1369–1386.

Hugh of St. Victor. *De Sacramentis Naturalis et Scriptae Legis. PL* 176, 17–40.

————. *De Sacramentis Christianae Fidei. PL* 176, 173–616.

————. *On The Sacraments of the Christian Faith (De Sacramentis Christianae Fidei)*. Trans. Roy J. DeFerrari, Cambridge, MA, 1951.

————. *In Ecclesiasten homiliae. PL* 175, 113–256.

————. *De arca Noe Morali. PL* 176, 618–680.

————. *De arca Noe Mystica. PL* 176, 681–703.

————. *De Vanitate mundi. PL* 176, 703–740.

————. *De tribus diebus. PL* 176, 811–838.

————. *The Didascalion; a Medieval Guide to the Arts*. Trans. Jerome Taylor, New York, 1961.

Irenaeus of Lyon. *Sancti Irenaei Episcopi Lugdunensis, Libros quinque Adversus Haereses*. Ed. W. Wigan Harvey. 2 Vols. Cambridge, 1857.

Jean Calvin. *Ioannis Calvin Opera quoe suspersunt omnia. (Corpus Reformatorum*, 29–87). Eds. J. W. Baum, E. Cunitz, E. Reuss, Brunsvigae, 1863–1900.

————. *Commentaries on the First Book of Moses called Genesis*. Trans. John King, Grand Rapids, 1968.

————. *Institutes of the Christian Religion. LCC* 20, 21. Ed. John T. McNeill, trans. Ford Lewis Battles, Philadelphia, 1960.

John Chrysostom. *Adversus Judaeos*. 1–8; *PG* 48, 843–892.

————. *Discourses Against Judaizing Christians. FC 68*, trans. Paul W. Harkins, Washington, D.C., 1979.

————. *Contra Judaeos et Gentiles quod Christus sit Deus. PG* 48, 813–838.

————. *De Sacerdotio. PG* 47, 623–692.

————. *Sur la Sacerdoce Dialogue et Homélies. SCh 272*. Ed. A-M. Malingrey, Paris, 1980.

———. *De Lazaro conciones. PG* 48.

———. *In diem natalem Christi. PG* 49, 351–362.

———. *Homilae IX in Genesim.* 1–67; *PG* 53, 23–386; *PG* 54, 385–580.

———. *Homiliae in Psalmos. PG* 55, 35–498.

———. *In Isaiae. PG* 56, 11–94.

———. *Homélies sur Jérémie. SCh 238.* Ed. Pierre Nautin, trans. Pierre Husson, Paris, 1977.

———. *Homiliae in Acta Apostolorum. PG* 60, 13–384.

———. *Homiliae XII in Epistolam I ad Timotheum. PG 62,* 501–98.

———. *Homilia in Epistola ad Colossenses. PG* 62, 299–392.

———. *Sur L'incompréhensibilité de Dieu. SCh* 28 bis. Ed. Anne-Marie Malingrey, Paris, 1970.

———. *On the Incomprehensible Nature of God. FC,* 78, trans. Paul W. Harkins, Washington, D.C., 1979.

———. *Sur la vaine gloire de l'education des enfants. SC* 188. Ed. Anne-Marie Malingrey, Paris, 1972.

———. M. L. W. Laistner. *Christianity and Pagan Culture in the Later Roman Empire together with an English translation of John Chrysostom's Address on Vainglory and the Right Way for Parents to bring up their children.* Ithaca, NY, 1951.

———. *Jean Chrysostome La Virginité. SCh 125.* Ed. and trans. H. Musurillo and B. Grillet, Paris, 1966.

John of Damascus. *De Fide Orthodoxa. PG* 94, 789–1228.

John of Haghia Sophia. *De Dei Circa Hominem Oeconomia. PG* 120, 1293–1296.

Justin Martyr. *Dialogus cum Tryphone Judaeo. PG* 6, 461–800.

Lactantius. *Divinae Institutiones. CSEL.* 19. Ed. S. Brandt, Vienna, 1890.

Moore, Thomas. *Utopia I* in *The Complete Works of Thomas Moore.* Vol. 4, eds. Edward Surtz and J. H. Hexter, New Haven and London, 1965.

Numenius. *Fragments.* Ed. E. Des Places. Paris, 1973.

Origen. *Selecta in Leviticum. PG* 12, 397–404.

———. *Homiliae in Exodum. PG* 12, 297–396.

———. *Die acht Bucher gegen Celsos. GCS,* 1 and 2; Ed. P. Koetschar. Leipzig, 1897–1899.

———. *Origen: Contra Celsum.* Trans. H. Chadwick, with Introduction and Notes. Cambridge, 1952.

———. *In Genesim Homiliae. GCS* 29, 1–144. Ed. W. A. Baehrens, Leipzig, 1920.

———. "Origenis in Exodum Homiliae" in *Homilien zum Hexateuch in Rufins Ubersetzung. GCS* 29, 145–280. Ed. W. A. Baehrens, Leipzig, 1920.

———. "Origenis Homiliae in Isaiam" in *Homilien zu Samuel I, zum Hohenlied und zu den Propheten. Konmentar zum Hohenlied in Rufins und Hieronymus Ubersetzungen. GCS* 33, 200–507. Ed. W. A. Baehrens, Leipzig, 1920.

———. "In Numeros Homiliae" in *Die Homilien zum Hexateuch in Rufins Ubersetzung. GCS* 30. Ed. W. A. Baehrens, Leipzig, 1921.

———. *On First Principles.* Trans. G. W. Butterworth, New York, 1966.

———. *Selecta in Deuteronomium. PG* 12, 805–813.

———. *In Matthaeum. PG* 13, 829–1600.

———. *Selecta in Numerous. PG* 12, 573–584.

———. *In Epistolam ad Romanos. PG* 14, 831–1294.

Palladius. *Dialogue on the Life of St. John Chrysostom. PG* 47, 5–82.

Peter Alphonsi. *Dialogi. PL* 157, 527–672.

Peter Damiani. *Dialogus inter Judaeum Requirentem et Christianus e Contrario Respondentem. PL* 145, 57–68.

Photius. *Bibliothèque.* Ed. R. Henry. Paris, 1959.

Procopius of Gaza. *In Genesim. PG* 87:1, 21–512.

———. *In Exodum. PG* 87:1, 511–690.

———. *In Leviticum. PG* 87:1, 689–794.

———. *In Numeros. PG* 87:1, 793–894.

———. *In Deuteronomium. PG* 87:1, 893–992.

———. *In Isaiam. PG* 87:2, 1817–2718.

Pseudo-Augustine. *De Mirabilius Sacrae Scripturae. PL* 35, 2149–2199.

Pseudo-Clement. *Recognitions of Clement, Bibliotheca Patrum Ecclesiasticorum Latinorum I.* Ed. E. G. Gersdorf. Leipzig, 1838.

———. *Die Pseudokelmentinen II: Rekognitionen in Rufins Ubersetzung.* prepared for the press by F. Paschke, *GCS* 51. Ed. Bernhard Rehm, Leipzig, 1965–69.

Rabanus Maurus. *Commentariorum in Genesim Libri Quattuor*. *PL* 107, 439–670.

———. *Expositiones in Leviticum*. *PL* 108, 45–586.

Rupert of Deutz. *De Victoria Verbi Dei*. *PL* 168, 743–836.

———. "In Isaiam"and "In Leviticum" in *De Sancta Trinitate*. *PL* 168, 1271–1362; and *CCL* 21–24. Ed. H. Haacke, Turnhout, 1971–72.

———. *Hermanni ex Judeo Christiani*. *PL* 170, 805–835.

———. *Annulus, sive Dialogus inter Christianum et Iudaeum*. *PL* 170, 545–559.

———. *Super quaedam capitula regulae Benedicti abbatis*. *PL* 170, 477–538.

Socrates. *Historia Ecclesiastica*, 1–7. *PG* 67, 29–842.

Sozomen. *Historia Ecclesiastica*, 1–9. *PG* 67, 843–1630.

Tacitus, *The Histories*. *LCL*. Ed. and trans. Clifford H. Moore, London, 1931.

Tertullian. *Adversus Marcionem*. *CCL* I. Ed. A. Kroymann, 437–726, Turnhout, 1954.

———. *Adversus Judaeos*. *CCL* II, 1337–1415. Ed. A. Kroymann, Turnhout, 1954.

———. *De Carne Christi*. *CCL* II, 871–917. Ed. A. Kroymann, Turnhout.

———. *De Monogamia*. *CCL* II, 1253–1277. Ed. E. Dekkers, Turnhout.

———. *De Resurrectione Mortuorum*. *CCL* II, 919–1012. Ed. J. G. Borleffs, Turnhout.

———. *De Pallio*. *CCL* II, 733–778. Ed. A. Gerlo, Turnhout.

———. *De Virginibus Velandis*. *CCL* II, 1207–1226. Ed. K. Dekkers.

Theodore of Mopsuestia. *Fragmenta in Vetus Testamentum*. *PG* 66, 633–700.

———. *Expositiones in Psalmos*. *CCL* 88A. Ed. L. DeConink, Turnhout, 1977.

Theodoret of Cyrus. *Quaestiones in Octateuchum*. *PG* 80, 75–528.

———. *de Providentia*. *PG*, 83, 555–774.

———. *Epistolae*. *PG* 83, 1173–1409.

———. *In Isaiam*. *PG* 81, 215–494.

———. *In Jeremiam*. *PG* 81, 495–760.

———. *Graecorum Affectionum Curatio*. *PG* 83, 783–1152.

———. *Théodoret de Cyr Thérapeutique des maladies helléniques*. 2 vols. *SCh* 57. Ed. and trans. P. Canivet, Paris, 1958.

————. *Catena graecae in genesim et in exodum.* Ed. F. Petit, Turnhout, 1977–

Theophylact of Ochrida. *Expositio in Acta Apostolorum.* PG 125, 483–848.

————. *Expositio in Pauli Epistolas: Ad Hebraeos.* PG 125, 185–404.

Thomas Aquinas. *Summa Theologiae.* Ed. P. Caramello. 3 Vols. Turin, 1952–1956.

————. *Summa Contra Gentiles.* Trans. English Dominican Fathers, London, 1923–.

Trophies of Damascus. *Les Trophées de Damas, Controverse Judeo-Chretienne du VII siècle. PO* XV. Ed. and trans. G. Bardy, Paris, 1920.

Walafrid Strabo. *De Exordiis et Incrementis Quarundam in Observationibus Ecclesiasticus rerum.* Ed. A. Knoepfler. Munich, 1899.

William of Auvergne. *Tractatus de Fide et Legibus in Guilielmi Alverni Epicsopi Parisiensis. Opera Omnia.* Vol. I. Paris, 1674.

SYRIAC SOURCES

Aphraatis Sapientis Persae Demonstrationes. Ed. J. Parisot; *PS.* Vols. I and II, 1–489. Paris, 1894, 1907.

Bardasanes, Liber Legum Regionum. Ed. F. Nau, PS vol. 2, Paris, 1907.

Des hl. Ephraem des Syrers, *Paschahymnen.* Ed. E. Beck; *CSCO,* vols. 248–249, Louvain, 1964.

Des hl. Ephraem des Syrers, *Hymnen de Fide.* Ed. E. Beck; *CSCO,* vols. 154–155, Louvain, 1955.

Des hl. Ephraem des Syrers, *Sermones.* Ed. E. Beck. Vols. I–IV; *CSCO* I, 305–306, 1970; *CSCO* II, 311–312, 1970; *CSCO* III, 320–321, 1972; *CSCO* IV, 334–335, Louvain, 1973.

Des hl. Ephraem des Syrers, *Sermo de Domino Nostro.* Ed. E. Beck; *CSCO,* vol. 270–271, Louvain, 1966.

Des hl. Ephraem des Syrers, *Sermones de Fide.* Ed. E. Beck; *CSCO,* vols. 212–213, Louvain, 1961.

Assemani, Joseph-Simon. *Sancti Patris Nostri Ephraem Syri Opera Omnia, Syriace et Latine.* Vols. I–III. Rome, 1740.

Isaac of Antioch. *Opera.* Ed. G. Bickell. Giessen, 1873–1877.

————. *Homiliae.* Ed. P. Bedjan. Vol. I. Paris, 1903.

————. "Isaac of Antioch's Homily Against the Jews." Ed. and trans. Stanley Kazan, *OC* 45. (1961), 30–53; 46 (1962), 87–95; 47 (1963), 89–97; 49 (1965), 57–78.

Jacob of Sarug. *Homélies Contre les Juifs.* Ed. M. Albert; PO 38, No. 174, Turnhout, 1976.

———. "Mimro de Jacques de Saroug sur lex deux oiseaux" [trans. F. Graffin]; *L'Orient Syrien* 6. (1961), 51–66.

HEBREW SOURCES

A. Rabbinic Sources and Translations (arranged alphabetically by texts).

Abot de-Rabbi Natan:

Schechter, Solomon. *Aboth de Rabbi Nathan.* 3rd ed. New York, 1967.

Judah Goldin. *The Fathers According to Rabbi Nathan.* (*Yale Judaica Series 10*), New Haven and London, 1955.

Babylonian Talmud: Standard Vilna edition.

Deuteronomy Rabbah:

Liebermann Saul, ed. *Midrash Debarim Rabbah.* Edited for the first time from the Oxford, MS No. 147 with an Introduction and Notes. Jerusalem, 1974.

Genesis Rabbah:

Theodor Julius and Albeck, Chanoch, eds. *Midrash Bershit Rabbah: Critical Edition with Notes and Commentary.* Three volumes. Wahrmann Books, Jerusalem, second edition. 1965. (Originally published Berlin. 1903–1936).

Leviticus Rabbah:

Margulies, Mordecai. *Midrash Leviticus Rabbah.* 3 Vols. Jerusalem, 1972. Originally published Jerusalem, 1953–60.

Mekhilta of R. Ishmael:

H. S. Horovitz and I. A. Rabin, eds. *Mechilta d'Rabbi Ismael.* Jerusalem, 1970. Originally published Frankfurt A. M., 1931.

Lauterbach, Jacob Z., editor and translator. *Mekhilta de-Rabbi Ishmael: A Critical Edition on the basis of the Manuscripts and Early Editions. The Schiff Library of Jewish Classics*, Philadelphia, 1933–1935, 1949.

The Song at the Sea being a commentary on a commentary in two parts. Trans. Judah Goldin, New Haven and London, 1971.

Mekhilta of R. Simeon b. Yochai:

Epstein, Jacob N. and Ezra F. Melamed, eds. *Mekhilta d'Rabbi Simeon b. Yochai.* Jerusalem, 1955.

Midrash on Proverbs:

Buber, Salomon, ed. *Midrasch Mishle.* Originally published by Romm. Vilna, 1893. Reprinted in Jerusalem, 1965 (bound with *Midrash Shemu'el*).

Midrash on Psalms:

Buber, Salomon, ed. *Midrasch Tehillim. (Schocher Tob).* Vilna, 1891.

Midrash Rabbah:

Sefer Midrash Rabbah. Two volumes. Jerusalem, n.p., 1961. Originally published by Romm. Vilna, 1878.

Midrash Zuta:

Buber, Salomon, ed. *Midrash zuta al Shir hashirim, Rut, Ekhah, ve-Kohelet al pi ketav yad.* Berlin, 1895.

Mishnah:

Albeck, Chanock, ed. *Shishah Sidre Mishnah (The Six Orders of the Mishnah, with Commentary).* Six volumes. Jerusalem, 1952–1959.

Danby, Herbert, trans. *The Mishnah: Translated from the Hebrew With Introduciton and Brief Explanatory Notes.* Oxford, 1933.

Pesiqta de-Rab Kahana:

Buber, Salomon, ed. *Pesikta, die älteste Hagada, redigirt in Palästina von Rab Kahana.* Lyck, 1868.

Madelbaum, Bernard, ed. *Pesikta de Rav Kahana, according to an Oxford Manuscript with Variants from Known Manuscripts and Genizoth Fragments and Parallel Passages with Commentary and Introduction.* 2 volumes. New York, 1962.

Pesiqta Rabbati:

Friedmann, Meir, ed. *Pesikta Rabbati. Midrasch für den Fest-Cycle und die ausgezeichneten Sabbathe.* Vienna, 1880.

Pesikta Rabbati. Trans., William G. Braude, 2 Vols. New Haven/London, 1968.

Pirqe de-Rabbi Eliezer:

Friedman, Meir. *Seder Eliahu Rabba und Seder Eliahu Zuta.* Vienna, 1902.

Sifra:

Finkelstein, Louis, ed. *Sifra or Torat Kohamin According to Codex Assemani LXVI.* Facsimile edition, with introduction by the editor. New York, 1956.

Sifre, Deuteronomy:

Finkelstein, Louis, ed. *Sifre on Deuteronomy.* New York 1969. Originally published Berlin, 1939.

Sifre, Numbers:

H. S. Horovitz, ed. *Siphre d'Be Rab. Siphre ad Numeros Adjecto Siphre Zutta.* Wahrmann Books, Jerusalem, 1966. Originally published by G. Fock, Leipzig, 1917.

Siphre Zutta

Siphre Zutta (Midrash of Lydda) The Talmud of Caesarea. 2 vols. Ed. Saul Lieberman, New York, 1968.

Tanhuma:

Buber, Salomon, ed. *Midrasch Tanchuma: Ein agadischer Commentar zum Pentateuch von Rabbi Tanchuma ben Rabbi Abba.* n.d. Israel. Originally published Vilna, 1885.

Midrash Tanhuma al Hamishshah Humshe Torah. Jerusalem, 1973. The standard "printed text" with the *'Etz Yosef* and *'Anaf Yoseh.*

Targum:

Miqra'ot Gedolot. Five volumes, Jerusalem, 1974. Originally published in Vienna, 1859, and Warsaw, 1862–1866.

The Targum Onkelos to Genesis (The Aramaic Bible vol. 6). Trans. Bernard Grossfeld, Wilmington, DE, 1988.

Tosefta:

Lieberman, Saul. *The Tosefta: According to Codex Vienna. With Variants From Codex Erfut, Genizah Mss. and Editio Princeps (Venice 1521). Together with references to Parallel Passages in Talmudic Literature and a Brief Commentary.* Four volumes, covering the orders *Zera'im Mo' ed.* and *Nashim.* New York, 1955–73.

Zuckermandel, M. S. *Tosephta Based on the Erfurt and Vienna Codices.* Wahrmann Books. Jerusalem, 1970. Reprint of the second edition, Jerusalem, 1937. (This edition contains Zuckermandel's edition of 1880 with supplements by Zuckermandel (1882, 1899), and a "Supplement to the Tosephta" by Saul Liebermann so the name is spelled on the title page.

B. MEDIEVAL AND MODERN SOURCES (arranged alphabetically by authors or editor)

Abarbanel, Isaac. *Commentary on the Pentateuch.* 3 Vols. Jerusalem, 1963.

Abraham Isaac Kook, *Talele Orot.* Jerusalem, 1972/3.

After Maimonides: An Anthology of Writings by His Critics, Defenders and Commentators. Ed. Abraham Halkin, Jerusalem, 1979. [Hebrew]

Albo, Joseph. *Sefer Ha-Ikkarim.* Ed. and trans. I. Husik, Philadelphia, 1930.

Arama, Isaac. *Akedath Jitzchak.* Ed. H. J. Pollack. Pressburg, 1849.

Bahya Ibn Pakuda. *Duties of the Heart.* Ed. A. Zifroni. Jerusalem, 1928; [ed./ trans. M. Hyamson] 2 Vols. Jerusalem/New York, 1962.

Code of Jewish Law (Kitzur Shulkhan Arukh). Ed. Solomon Ganzfried, trans. Hyman E. Goldin, New York, 1961.

David Kimhi. [Radak]. *Commentary.* [Printed in standard editions of the Hebrew *Bible*].

Dov Baer of Mezhirech. *Maggid Devarav Le-Ya'akov of the The Maggid Dov Baer of Mezhirech, Critical Edition with Commentary, Introduction and Indices.* Ed. Rivka Schatz-Uffenheimer, Jerusalem, 1976.

Hasdai, Crescas, *Or ha-Shem.* Jerusalem, 1989/90.

Israel Meir ha-Cohen (Hofez Hayyim). *Sefer Mishnah Berurah.* Standard editions.

Jacob al-Qirqisani. *Kitab al-Anwar wal-Maraqib* and *Kitab al-Rivad wal-Hada'iq.* Ed. L. Nemoy. 5 vols.

Joseph ibn Kaspi, *Joseph ibn kaspi's Gevia kesef: A Study in Medieval Jewish Philosophic Bible Commentary.* Ed. and trans. Basil Herring, (New York, 1982).

Levi ben Gerson [Ralbag: Gersonides]. *Commentary.* [Printed in standard editions of the Hebrew *Bible*].

———. *Gersonides, The Wars of the Lord.* 2 vols. trans. Seymour Feldman. Philadelphia, 184–87.

Ma'arekhet ha'Elohut. Jerusalem, 1963. Originally published, Mantua, 1558.

Mishnat ha-Zohar. 2 vols. Eds. Isaiah Tishby and Fishel Lachover, Jerusalem 1961, 1971.

Moses ben Maimon [Rambam:Maimonides]. *Letters of Maimonides.* Ed. D. H. Baneth. Jerusalem, 1946.

———. *Crisis and Leadership: Epistles of Maimonides.* Philadelphia, 1985.

———. *Epistle to Yemen.* [Arabic original and 3 Hebrew versions]. Ed. A. S. Halkin [English trans. B. Cohen]. New York, 1952.

———. *Collection of Maimonides' Responsa and Letters.* Ed. A. Lichtenberg. Leipzig, 1859.

———. *Letter on Astrology* in *Medieval Political Philosophy.* Eds. R. Lerner and M. Mahdi. Glencoe, 1963, pp. 227–237.

———. *The Guide of the Perplexed.* [Trans. S. Pines]. Chicago, 1963.

———. *Le guide des égarés.* 3 vols. trans. S. Munk, Paris, 1856–66.

———. *Mishneh Torah.* Standard editions and in *Yale Judaica Series.*

———. *Treatise on Resurrection.* Ed. J. Finkel, in *PAAJR.* Vol. IX. 1939.

———. *Mishnah Commentary.* Ed. J. Kafih. 7 Vols. Jerusalem, 1963.

———. *Book of Commandments.* [English trans. by C. Chavel], *The Commandments.* 2 Vols. London, 1967.

———. *Eight Chapters.* Ed. J. Gorfinkle. New York, 1912.

———. *Responsa of Maimonides.* Ed. J. Blau. 3 Vols. Jerusalem, 1958.

Moses ben Nahman [Ramban: Nahmanides]. *Commentary on the Pentateuch.* Ed. C. Chavel. Jerusalem, 1966–1967.

Saadya ben Joseph Gaon. *The Book of Beliefs and Opinions.* Trans. Samuel Rosenblatt (Yale Judaica Series 1) New Haven, 1948.

Sa'id ibn Mansur Ibn Kammuna. *Sa'id Ibn Mansur Ibn Kammuna. Examination of the Three Faiths.* Ed. and trans. M. Perlmann. Berkeley and London, 1971.

Samuel de Uceda, *Midrash Shemuel: ve-hu beur al Pirke Avot.* Jerusalem, 1966 (reprint of Warsaw edition. of 1869).

Sefer Ha-Zohar. 3 vols. 4th edition. Ed. Reuven Margaliot, Jerusalem, 1964.

Shulkhan Arukh. Jerusalem, 1975 (reprint of Vilna edition).

Yom Tob ben Abraham Ishbili [Ritba]. *Kitvei Haritva.* Ed. M. Y. Blau. New York, 1956.

Zohar The Book of Enlightenment. Trans. Daniel C. Matt, New York, Ramsey, Toronto, 1983.

Zohar, The Book of Splendor: Basic Readings from the Kabbalah. Trans. Gershom Scholem, New York, 1949.

LEXICA CONCORDANCES

Alder, A. ed., *Suidae Lexicon.* Leipzig, 1935.

Hauck, A. ed., *Realencyklopaedie für protestantiische Theologie und Kirche,* Leipzig, 1896.

Jastrow, Marcus. A *Dictionary of the Targumin, the Talmud Babli and Yerushalmi, and the Midrashic Literature.* 2 Vols. New York, 1950.

Smith, R. P. *A Compendious Syriac Dictionary.* Ed. J. Payne Smith (Mrs. Marfoliouth). Oxford, 1957.

SECONDARY SOURCES

Abelson, Joshua. *The Immanence of God in Rabbinic Literature: The Memra.* London, 1912.

Altmann, Alexander, "Maimonides' 'four perfections.' " *Israel Oriental Studies,* I (1972), 15–24.

———. "Saadya's Conception of the Law." *BJR* 28 (1944), 320–339.

Ameringer, Thomas E. *The Stylistic Influence of the Second Sophistic on the Panegyrical Sermons of St. John Chrysostom, A Study in Greek Rhetoric.* Washington D.C., 1921.

Andresen, Carl. *Logos und Nomos: Die Polemik des Kelsos Wider Das Christentum.* Berlin, 1955.

Ankori, Zvi. *Karaites in Byzantium; the Formative Years, 920–1100.* New York, 1959.

Archambault, Paul. "The Ages of Man and the Ages of the World: A Study of Two Traditions." *REAug,* 12 (1966), 193–228.

Ashley, Clinton. "John Calvin's Utilization of the Principle of Accommodation and Its Continuing Significance for an Understanding of Biblical Language." [Dissertation (Ph.D.), Southwest Baptist Theological Seminary], 1972.

Bacher, Wilhelm. *Die Bibelexegese der jüdischen Religionsphilosophen des Mittelalters von Maimuni.* Strassburg, 1892.

Baer, Yitzhak F. *Israel Among the Nations.* Jerusalem, 1955. [Hebrew].

———. *History of the Jews in Christian Spain.* 2 vols. Philadelphia, 1961.

Balthasar, Hans Urs Von. *Présence et Pensée: Essai sur la philosophie religieuse de Grégoire de Nysse.* Paris, 1942.

Bamberger, Bernard J. "Revelations of Torah After Sinai." *HUCA,* 16 (1941), 97–113.

Bardy, Gustave. *Saint Athanase. (Les Saints)* Paris, 1914.

Barnard, Frederick M. *Herder's Social and Political Thought from Enlightenment to Nationalism.* Oxford, 1965.

Barnard, Leslie W. *Studies in the Apostolic Fathers and their Background.* New York, 1966.

———. *Justin Martyr: His Life and Thought.* Cambridge, 1967.

Barnes, Timothy David. *Constantine and Eusebius.* Cambridge, Mass., 1981.

Baron, Salo Wittmayer. "The Historical Outlook of Maimonides." *PAAJR* 6 (1935), 5–113. Reprinted in *History and Jewish Historians: Essays and Addresses.* Philadelphia, 1964, 109–167.

———. *A Social and Religious History of the Jews*. Vols. 6, 7, 8. Philadelphia, 1958.

Baroway, Israel. "The Bible as Poetry in the English Renaissance: An Introduction." *Journal of English and German Philology*, 32 (1933) 447–480.

Barthes, R. *The Pleasure of the Text*. Trans. Richard Miller, New York, 1975.

Battles, Ford Lewis. "God Was Accomodating Himself to Human Capacity." *Interpretation* 31 (1977), 19–38.

Bauer, Walter. *Orthodoxy and Heresy in Earliest Christianity*. Eds. Robert A. Kraft and Gerhard Krodel. Philadelphia, 1971.

Baumstark, A. *Geschichte der syrischen Literatur*. Bonn, 1922.

Bauer, Chrysostomus. *John Chrysostom and His Time*. Trans. by M. Gonzaga. 2 vols. Westminster, Md., 1959.

Baus, Karl. *From the Apostolic Community to Constantine*. (*Handbook of Church History I*) Freiburg/Montreal, 1965.

Becker, Carl Lotus. *The Heavenly City of the Eighteenth Century Philosophers*. New Haven, 1932.

Bedford, Arthur. *The Temple Musick*. London, 1712.

Benin, Stephen D. "The 'Cunning of God' and Divine Accommodation." *JHI*, 45 (1983) 179–191.

———. "Thou Shalt Have No Other Gods Before Me: Sacrifice in Medieval Jewish and Christian Thought" (Diss. (Ph.D.) University of California, Berkeley, 1980).

———. "Maimonides and Scholasticism: Sacrifice as Historical Hermeneutic," *Proceedings of the Eight World Congress of Jewish Studies, Division C*, Jerusalem, 1982, 41–46.

———. "Sacrifice as Education in Augustine and Chrysostom." *CH*, 52 (1983); 7–20.

———. "Commandments, Covenants and the Jews in Aphrahat, Ephrem and Jacob of Sarug." *Approaches to Judaism in Medieval Times*. (*Brown Judaic Studies 54*). Ed. David Blumenthal (Chico, Ca., 1984), 135–56.

———. "The Mutability of an Immutable God: Exegesis and Individual Capacity in the Zohar and Several Christian Sources." *Proceedings of the Theird (sic) International Conference on the History of Jewish Mysticism: The Age of the Zohar, Jerusalem Studies in Jewish Thought 8*. Ed. Joseph Dan, Jerusalem, 1989, 67–86 (English Section).

Benoît, Andre. *Saint Irénée: Introduction a l'étude de sa théologie*. Paris, 1960.

Ben-Sasson, Y. "Le-Heker Mishnat Ta'amei ha-Mitzvot *be-Moreh Nevuk-him.*" *Tarbiz,* 29 (1960), 268–82. [Hebrew]

Berges, W. "Anselm von Havelberg in der Geistesheschichte des 12. Jahrhunderts." *Jahrbuch für die Geschichte Mittel-und Ostdeutschlands.* Tubingen, 1956, 39–57.

Berman, L. V. "The Political Interpretation of the Maxim: The Purpose of Philosophy is the Imitation of God." *Studia Islamic,* 5 (1961), 53–61.

———. "The Ideal State of the Philosophers and Prophetic Laws." *The Straight Path.* Ed. Ruth Link-Salinger. Washington, D.C. 1988, 10–22.

———. "Maimonides, the disciple of Alfarabi." *Israel Oriental Studies,* 4 (1974), 154–178.

———. "The Structure of Maimonides' Guide of the Perplexed." *in Proceedings of the Sixth World Congress of Jewish Studies,* Vol. 3. Ed. Avigdor Shinan. Jerusalem, 1977, 7–13.

———. "The Structure of the Commandments of the Torah in the Thought of Maimonides." *Studies in Jewish Religious and Intellectual History.* Eds. Siegfried Stein and Raphael Loewe. University, Alabama, 1979, 51–66.

Berrouard, M. F. " 'Similtudo' et la définition du réalisme sacramental d'après l'Épître XCVIII, 9–10, de saint Augustin." *REAug* 7 (1961), 321–337.

Betz, Hans Dieter. *Galations (Hermeneia Commentary)* Philadelphia, 1979.

Bland, Kalman P. "Moses and the Law According to Maimonides." *Mystics, Philosophers, and Politicians, Essays in Jewish Intellectual History in Honor of Alexander Altmann.* Eds. Jehuda Reinharz and Daniel Swetschinski. Durham 1982, 49–66.

Blidstein, Gerald. "Maimonides on 'Oral Law.' " *The Jewish Law Annual,* I (1978), 108–122.

Blumenkranz, Bernhard. *Juifs et Chrétiens: Patristique et Moyen Age.* London, 1977.

———. *Juifs et chrétiens dans le monde occidental, 430–1096.* Paris, 1960.

Bowersock, Glen Warren, *Greek Sophists in the Roman Empire.* Oxford, 1969.

Brown, Peter Robert Lamont. *Augustine of Hippo.* Berkeley, Los Angeles 1969.

Buber, Martin. *Tales of the Hasidim, The Later Masters.* Trans. Olga Marx, New York, 1974.

Callahan, John F. "Greek Philosophy and the Cappadocian Cosmology." *DOP*, 12, 1958; 29–57.

—. "Basil of Caesarea: A New Source for St. Augustine's Theory of Time." *Harvard Studies in Classical Philology*, 63 (1958), 437–54.

Campbell, James Marshall. *The Influence of the Second Sophistic on the Style of the Sermons of St. Basil the Great*. Washington, D.C., 1922.

Chadwick, Henry. *Early Christian Thought and the Classical Tradition: Studies in Justin, Clement and Origen*. New York, 1966.

Chadwick, Owen. *The Reformation (Pelican History of the Church 3)*. London, 1964.

Chenu, Marie Dominique, *Nature, Man and Society in the Twelfth Century: Essays on New Theological Perspectives in the Latin West*. Trans. and eds. J. Taylor and L. K. Little. Chicago, 1968.

—. "Contribution a l'histoire du Traite de la Foi." *Mélanges Thomistes*. Paris, 1923, 123–40.

Cherniss, Harold F. *The Platonism of Gregory of Nyssa*. (*California Publications in Classical Philology V. 11*), Berkeley, 1930.

Chwolson, D. *Die Ssabier und der Ssabismus*. 2 Vols. St. Petersburg, 1856. (Reprint, Amsterdam, 1965.)

Clark, Robert Thomas. *Herder, His Life and Thought*. Berkeley, Los Angeles 1955.

Colish, Marcia L. *The Mirror of Language: A Study in the Medieval Theory of Knowledge*. New Haven and London, 1968.

Collins, John Joseph. *Between Athens and Jerusalem: Jewish Identity in the Hellenistic Diaspora*. New York, 1983.

Colombas, Garcia M. *Paradis et Vie angélique*. Paris, 1961.

Conzelman, Hans. "The Mother of Wisdom." *Essays in Honour of Rudolph Bultmann The Future of Our Religious Past*. Ed. James M. Robinson, trans. Charles E. Carston and Robert P. Scharlemann, New York, 1971, 230–243.

Corsini, Eugenio, "Plerome Humain et Plerome Cosmique chez Grégoire de Nysse." *Écriture et Culture philosophique dans la Pensée de Grégoire de Nysee. Actes du colloque de Chevetogne (22–26 Septembre 1969)*. Ed. Marguerite Harl, Leiden, 1971, 111–125.

Costa, G. "Vico and Ancient Rhetoric." *Classical Influences on Western Thought, AD 1650–1870*. Ed. by R. R. Bolgar. Cambridge, 1979, 247–262.

Dagens, Claude. *Saint Grégoire le Grand: Culture et Expérience Chrétiennes*. Paris, 1977.

D'Ales, Adhémar. "Le mot Oikonomia dans la langue théologique de Saint Irénée." *REG*, 32 (1919), 1–9.

Dan, Joseph. *Jewish Mysticism and Jewish Ethics.* Seattle, 1986.

Daniélou, Jean. *From Shadows to Reality: Studies in Biblical Typology of the Fathers.* London, 1960.

————. *Platonisme et théologie mystique: essai sur la doctrine spirituelle de Saint Grégoire de Nysse.* 2nd edition, Paris, 1954.

————. *"Akolouthia"* chez Grégoire de Nysse." *RSR* 43 (1953) 219–249.

————. *Primitive Christian Symbols.* London, 1964.

————. "Terre et Paradis chez les Péres de l'Église," *Eranos-Jahrbuch,* 22 (1913), 433–72.

————. *The Theology of Jewish Christianity.* Ed. and trans. J. A. Baker, London, 1964.

Davidson, H. A. "The Study of Philosophy as a Religious Obligation." *Religion in a Religious Age.* Ed. S. D. Goitein, Cambridge, 1974, 53–68.

De Boer, door Sobbele, *De Anthropologie van Gregorius van Nyssa.* Assen, 1968.

De Lange, Nicholas Robert Michael. *Origen and the Jews: Studies in Jewish-Christian Relations in Third-Century Palestine. University of Cambridge Oriental Publications* V. 25. Cambridge, 1975.

Dienstag, Jacob I. "The Relationship of Maimonides to his Predecessors." *The Jewish Law Annual,* 1 (1978), 42–60.

Douglas, John A. "The Orthodox Principle of Economy, and Its Exercise." *Theology,* 24 (1932), 39–47.

Dreyfus, F. "Divine Condescendence (sygkatabasis) as a Hermeneutic Principle of the Old Testament in Jewish and Christian Tradition," Immanuel 19 (1984/5), 74–86. French original in: *Congress Volume, Salamanca 1983 Vetus Testamentum Supplement 36.* Ed. J. A. Emerton. Brill, 1985, 96–107.

Drijvers, H. J. W. "Edessa und das jüdische Christentum." *VC,* 24, 1970, 4–33.

Duchatelez, K. "La notion d'économie et ses richesses théologiques." *NRTh,* 92 (1970); 267–292.

————. "La 'condescendance' divine et l'histoire du salut." *NRTh,* 95 (1973); 593–62.

Duchrow, Ulrich. " 'Signum' and 'superbia' beim jungen Augustin (386–390)." *REAug,* 7 (1961), 369–72.

Dyovouniotes, C. "The Principle of Economy." *ChQ* 116 (1933), 93–101.

Elstein, Y. "Torat Ha-Mitzvot be-Mishnat R. Saadyah." *Tarbiz* 38 (1968) 120–35.

Epstein, L. "Le-shitat ha-RaMBaM be-ta'amei ha-mitzvot." *Yad Shau'l, Memorial Volume for Rabbi Dr. Saul Weingurt.* Eds. Jechiel J. Weinberg and P. Biberfeld Tel Aviv, 5719, 145–52.

Erickson, John, H. "*Oikonomia* in Byzantine Canon Law." *Law, Church, and Society: Essays in honor of Stephan Kutter.* Eds. Kenneth Pennington and Robert Somerville. Philadelphia, 1977, 225–36.

Fabbi, Fabio. "La 'condiscendenza' Divina Nell'Ispirazione Biblica Secondo S. Giovanni Crisostomo." *Biblica* 14 (1933), 330–347.

Faur, J. "Mekor Hiyyuban shel ha-mitzvot le'daat ha-RaMBaM." *Tarbiz,* XXXVIII (1969), 43–53.

———. "The Splitting of the Logos: Some Remarks on Vico and Rabbinic Tradition." *New Vico Studies,* 3 (1985); 85–103.

———. "The Origin of the Classification of Rational and Divine Commandments in Mediaeval Jewish Philosophy." *Augustinianium,* IX, (1969) 299–304.

Fedwick, Paul Jonathan, ed. *Basil of Caesarea Christian, Humanist, Ascetic: A Sixteen Hundreth Anniversary Symposium.* 2 vols. Toronto, 1981.

Feldman, Seymour. "A Scholastic Misinterpretation of Maimonides' Doctrine of Divine Attributes." *JJS,* 19 (1968); 23–40.

Finkelstein, Louis. "Maimonides and the Tannaitic Midrashim." *JQR,* 25 (1935), 469–517.

Forstman, H. Jackson. *Word and Spirit, Calvin's Doctrine of Biblical Authority.* Stanford, 1962.

Fox, June T."The Pedagogical Theory of Giambattista Vico: In Appreciation of an International Symposium." *Educational Theory,* 20 (1970); 292–303.

Fox, Marvin. "On the Rational Commandments in Saadia's Philosophy, a Re-Examination." *Modern Jewish Ethics: Theory and Practice.* Ed. by M. Fox, Columbus, 1975, 174–87.

Frei, Hans W. *The Eclipse of Biblical Narrative: A Study in Eighteenth and Nineteenth Century Hermeneutics,* New Haven, 1974.

Funkenstein, Amos. "Gesetz und Geschichte, zur historisierenden Hermeneutik bei Moses Maimonides und Thomas von Aquin." *Viator,* I (1970), 147–178.

————. "Maimonides: Political Theory and Realistic Messianism." *Miscellanea Medievalia,* XI, (1977), 81–103.

————. "Periodization and Self-Understanding in the Middle Ages and Early Modern Times." *Medievalia et Humanistica,* N.S. 5 (1974), 3–23.

————. "Changes in the Patterns of Christian Anti-Jewish Polemics in the 12th Century." *Zion,* XXXIII (1968) 125–144. [Hebrew].

————. *Heilspan und natürliche Entwicklung. Formen der Gegenwarts–bestimmung in Geschichtsdenken des hohen Mittelalters.* Munich, 1965.

————. "Natural Science and Social Theory: Hobbes, Spinoza and Vico." *Giambattista Vico: An International Symposium.* Ed. Giorgio Tagliacozzo, Baltimore, 1969.

————. *Theology and the Scientific Imagination from the Middle Ages to the Seventeenth Century.* Princeton, 1986.

Gaith, Jerome. *La conception de Liberté chez Grégoire de Nysee. (Études de Philosophie Médiévale* 43) Paris, 1953.

Galtier, Paul. "La date de la Didascalia des apôtres." in *Aux origines du Sacrement de Pénitence.* Rome, 1951, 189–221.

Galston, Miriam, "The Purpose of the Law According to Maimonides." *JQR,* 69 (1978) 27–51.

Gass, W. "Das patristiche wort oikonomie." *Zeitschrift für wissenschaftliche Theologie,* 17 (1874), 465–504.

Gaston, Lloyd, "Angels and Gentiles in Early Judaism and Paul." *Sciences Religeuses / Studies in Religion* 11 (1982), 65–75.

————. "Legicide and the Problem of the Christian Old Testament: A Plea for a New Hermeneutic of the Apostolic Writings" [Unpublished].

Gavin, Frank Stanton Buins. *Aphraates and the Jews; A Study of the Controversial Homilies of the Persian Sage in their relations to Jewish Thought [Contributions to Oriental History and Philology.* Vol. IX.] New York, 1966. (Reprint of 1923 edition.)

————. "Aphraates and the Jews." *Journal of the Society of Oriental Research,* 7 (1923), 95–166.

Ginzberg, Louis. *Legends of the Jews.* 7 vols. Philadelphia, 1909–1928.

Goldman, Eliezer. "The Worship Peculiar to Those who Have Apprehended True Reality." *Bar Ilan Annual Studies in Judaica and the Humanities,* VI (1968); 287–313.

Golinski, Georg. *Das Wesen des Religionsgesetzes in der Philosophie des Bachja ibn Pakuda.* Berlin, 1935.

Goodman, Lenn Evan. "Maimonides' Philosophy of Law." *The Jewish Law Annual,* 1 (1978), 72–107.

Gottlieb, Efraim. *Studies in the Kabbalah Literature.* Ed. Joseph Hacker, Tel Aviv, 1976 [Hebrew].

——. *The Kabbalah at the End of the Thirteenth Century.* Jerusalem, 1969 [Hebrew].

Green, William M. "Augustine on the Teaching of History." *Univ. of California Publications in Classical Philology,* 12 (1944), 315–32.

Gregg, Robert C. and Dennis E. Groh. *Early Arianism: A View of Salvation.* Philadelphia, 1981.

Gribomont, J. "Les Hymnes de Saint Ephrem sur la Paques." *Melito,* 1–2 (1967), 147–82.

Grunder, Karlfried. *Figur und geschichte. Johann Georg Hamann's "Biblische Betrachtungen" als Ansatz einer geschichtsphilosophie.* Freiburg-Munich, 1958.

Guttman, Julius. *Philosophies of Judaism; the history of Jewish Philosophy from Biblical Times to Franz Rosenzweig.* Trans. David W. Silverman New York, 1964.

——. "Alexandre de Hales et le Judaïsme." *REJ,* 19 (1889) 224–34.

——. "Guillaume D'Auvergne et la Littérature Juive." *REJ,* 18 (1889) 291–55.

——. "John Spencer's Erklarung des Biblischen Gesetze in Ihrer Bezeihung Maimonides." *Festkrift i anleding af Professor David Simonsens.* 70-aavg todselsdag. Copenhagen, 1923.

——. "Das Problem der Kontingenz in der Philosophie des Maimonides." *MGWJ* 83 (1939), 406–430.

——. *Der Einfluss der maimonidischen Philosophie auf das christliche Abenland; Moses ber Maimon; sein Leben, seine Werke und sein Einfluss.* Eds. W. Backer, D. Brann, D. Simonsen (Leipzig, 1907), 175–204.

Hailperin, Herman. *Rashi and the Christian Scholars.* Pittsburgh, 1963.

Halperin, David J. *The Merkabah in Rabbinic Literature,* New Haven, 1980.

Hanson, R. P. C. *Allegory and Event: A Study of the Sources and Significance of Origen's Interpretation of Scripture.* Richmond, Va., 1959.

Harl, Marguerite. *Origène et la Fonction Révélatrice du Verbe Incarne. (Patristica Sorbonensia 2).* Paris, 1958.

Harnack, A. "Judentum und Judenchristentum in Justins Dialog mit Tryphon." *Texte und Untersuchungen zur geschichte der Altchristlichen Literature* 39 (1913), 47–98.

Harris, Jay. "The Image of Maimonides in Nineteenth-Century Jewish Historiography." *PAAJR* LIV (1987), 117–139.

Hartman, David, *Maimonides: Torah and Philosophic Quest.* Philadelphia, 1976.

Harvey, Warren Zev. "The Return of Maimonideanism." *Jewish Social Studies,* 42 (1980), 249–268.

———. "Political Philosophy and Halakhah in Maimonides." *Iyyun,* 29 (1980), 198–212. [Hebrew].

Hayward, Robert. *Divine Name and Presence: The Memra.* Totowa, N.J., 1981.

Heinemann, Isaak, *Ta'ame ha-Mitzvot be-Sifrut Yisra'el.* 2 vols. Jerusalem, 1958. [Hebrew].

———. "Scientific Allegorization During the Jewish Middle Ages." *Studies in Jewish Thought.* Ed. A. Jospe. Detroit, 1981, 247–269.

Heinemann, J. *Aggadah and its Development.* Jerusalem, 1974. [Hebrew].

Heschel, Abraham J. *Theology of Ancient Judaism.* 2 Vols. London, 1962. [Hebrew].

Hester, James D. "The 'Heir' and Heilsgeschichte: A Study of Galatians 4:1 ff." *Oikonomia.* Ed. Felix Christ. Hamburg-Bergstedt, 1967, 118–125.

Hillgarth, J. N. *The Conversion of Western Europe, 350–750.* Englewood Cliffs, N.J., 1969.

Hoffman, D. *Das Buch Leviticus.* Berlin, 1907 [Hebrew].

Hooykaas, Reijer. *Religion and the Rise of Modern Science.* Grand Rapids, 1972.

Hubbell, Harry M. "Chrysostom and Rhetoric." *Classical Philology* 19 (1943), 261–276.

Hundert, Gerson D. "Jewish Children and Childhood in Early Modern East Central Europe." *The Jewish Family: Metaphor and Memory.* Ed. David Kraemer, Oxford, 1989, 81–94.

Hyman, Arthur. "Maimonides' Thirteen Principles." *Jewish Medieval and Renaissance Studies.* Ed. Alexander Altmann. Cambridge, 1967, 119–144.

———. "Maimonides on Causality." *Maimonides and Philosophy.* Eds. Shlomo Pines and Yirmiyahu Yovel, Dordrecht, 1986, 157–171.

———. "A Note on Maimonides' Classification of Law." *PAAJR,* XLVI/XLVII (1979/80), 323–343.

Idel, Moshe, "Infinities of Torah in Kabbalah." *Midrash and Literature.* Eds. Gregory H. Hartmann and Sanford Budick, New Haven, 1986, 141–57.

Iggers, Georg G. *The German Conception of History.* Rev. ed. Middletown, 1983.

———. "The Dissolution of German Historicism." *Ideas in History Essays Presented to Luces Gottschalk by his Former Students.* Eds. Louis Richard Herr and Harold T. Parker. Durham, N.C. 1965, 288–329.

Ivry, Alfred. "Islamic and Greek Influences on Maimonides' Philosophy." *Maimonides and Philosophy.* Eds. Shlomo Pines and Yirmiyahu Yovel. Dordrecht, 1986, 139–156.

Jackson, Bernard S. "Legalism." *JJS* 30, (1979) 1–22.

Jackson, B. Darrell, "The Theory of Signs in St. Augustine's *De Doctrina Christiana.*" *REAug* 15 (1969), 9–49.

Jaeger, Werner Wilhelm, *Early Christianity and Greek Paideia.* Cambridge, 1961.

Jansma, T. "Narsai and Ephraem. Some Observations on Narsai's Homilies on Creation and Ephraem's Hymns on Faith." *Parole de l'Orient,* I (1970) 49–68.

Jedin, Hubert (ed.). *Handbook of Church History.* Vol. I, New York, 1965.

Jones, F. Stanley, "The Pseudo-Clementines: A History of Research." Part I and Part II, *The Second Century II.* 1982, 1–33, 63–96.

Kadushin, Max, *The Rabbinic Mind.* 3rd. ed. New York, 1972.

———. *A Conceptual Approach to the Mekilta.* New York, 1969.

Kasher, Hanna. "Commandments Between Man and God in the *Guide of the Perplexed.*" *Daat,* 12 (1984), 23–28 [Hebrew].

———. "Maimonides' Philosophical Division of the Laws." *HUCA* LVI (1985), 1–7 [Hebrew].

Kato, Takeshi. "Melodia Interior. Sur le traite *De Pulchro et Apto.*" *REAug* 12 (1966), 229–240.

Katz, David S. *Philo-Semitism and the Readmission of the Jews to England 1603–55.* Oxford, 1982.

Kelly, J. N. D. *A Commentary on the Apostle's Creed,* New York, 1954.

Kennan, M. E. "St. Gregory of Nazianzus and Early Byzantine Medicine." *Bulletin of the History of Medicine,* 9, (1941), 8–30.

Klein, M. L. "The Preposition KDM ("Before"); A Pseudo-Anthropomorphism in the Targums." *TS,* n.s. 20 (1979), 502–507.

Kluxen, Wolfgang. "Maimonides and Latin Scholasticism." *Maimonides and Philosophy.* Eds. Shlomo Pines and Yirmiyahu Yovel. Dordrecht, 1986, 224–231.

Konstantinou, Evangelos G. *Die Tugendlehre Gregors von Nyssa im Verhältnis zu der Antik-Philosophischen und Jüdisch-Christlichen Tradition (Das Ostliche Christentum.* Neue Folge, Heft 17). Wurzburg, 1966.

Kopp, Johanna. *Bruderliebe im Licht der Inkarnation.* (*Studia Salesiana*). Eichstatt and Vienna, 1963.

Koschorke, Klaus. *Die Polemik der Gnostiker gegen das kirchliche Christentum.* (*Nag Hammadi Studies 12)* Leiden, 1978.

Koukoules, P. *Basil, Gregory of Nazianzus and John Chrysostom as Educators.* Athens, 1951.

Kraft, R. A. "In Search of 'Jewish Christianity' and its 'Theology.' Problems of Definition and Methodology." *Judeo-Christianisme. Daniélou Festschrift.* Paris, 1972. 81–92.

Krieger, Leonard. *Kings and Philosophers, 1689–1789.* New York, 1970.

Krumbacher, Karl. *Geschichte der byzantinischen Litteratur von Justinian biz zum Ende des Ostromischen Reiches,* (527–1453). Munich, 1897.

Kustas, George L. "Saint Basil and the Rhetorical Tradition." *Basil of Caesarea Christian, Humanist, Ascetic: A Sixteen Hundreth Anniversary Symposium.* Ed. Paul Jonathan Fedwick, Toronto, 1981: I, 221–279.

Ladner, Gerhart B. *The Idea of Reform; its impact on Christian thought and action in the age of the Fathers.* New York, 1967.

———. "The Philosophical Anthropology of Saint Gregory of Nyssa." *DOP,* 12, 1958, 59–94.

Lamirande, E. "Étude bibliographique sur les Péres de l'Église et l'aggada." *VC,* 21 (1967), 1–11.

Lampe, G. W. H., ed. *The Cambridge History of the Bible, II.* Cambridge, 1969.

Lauerer, Don S. "Die Kondeszendez Gottes." *Das Erbe Martin Luthers und die gegenwartige theologische Forschung.* Ed. Robert Telke, Leipzig, 1928, 258–272.

Lessing, Gotthold Ephraim. *The Education of the Human Race.*Trans. F. W. Robertson, London, 1927.

Levenson, Joseph Richmond, *Confucian China and Its Modern Fate: A Trilogy,* Berkeley, Los Angeles, 1968.

Levinger, Yaakov. "Torato shel HaRebi Mi-Kotzk." *Tarbiz* 55 (1986), 101–121.

Liebermann, Saul. "Palestine in the Third and Fourth Centuries." *JQR* 36 (1946), 329–79; *JQR* 37 (1946), 31–54.

———. *Greek in Jewish Palestine: Studies in the Life and Manners of Jewish Palestine in the II–IV Centuries C.E.* New York, 1942.

———. "Rabbinic Polemics against Idolatry." in *Hellenism in Jewish Palestine: Studies in the Literary Transmission, Beliefs and Manners of Palestine in the I Century B.C.E.–IV Century C.E.* New York, 1962, 115–127.

———. "How Much Greek in Jewish Palestine?" *Biblical and Other Studies.* Ed. by A. Altman. Cambridge, MA, 1963, 123–141.

———. *Texts and Studies.* New York, 1974.

Liebeschutz, H. "Judaism and Jewry in the Social Doctrine of Thomas Aquinas." *JJS,* 13 (1962), 57–81.

Longsworth, Robert. *The Cornish Ordinalia: Religion and Dramaturgy.* Cambridge, MA, 1967.

Lowe, E. A. "The Script of the Farewell and Date Formulae in Early Papal Documents as Reflected in the Oldest Manuscripts of Bede's *Historia Ecclesiastica*." *RB,* 69 (1959), 22–31.

McClear, Ernest V. "The Fall of Man and Original Sin in the Theology of Gregory of Nyssa." *TS* 9, (1948), 175–212.

Maeyvaert, Paul, *Benedict, Gregory, Bede and Others.* London, 1977.

Manuel, Frank Edward. *The Eighteenth Century Confronts the Gods.* Cambridge, Ma., 1959.

———. *Shapes of Philosophical History.* Stanford, 1965.

———. *The Changing of the Gods.* Hanover, London, 1983.

Markus, R. A. *Saeculum: History and Society in the Theology of St. Augustine.* Cambridge, 1970.

———. "Trinitarian Theology and the Economy." *JThSt,* n.s. 9, (1958), 89–102.

———. "Pleroma and Fulfilment." *VC,* 8 (1954) 193–224.

———. " 'Imago' and 'similitudo' in Augustine." *REAug,* 10 (1964), 125–43.

———. "St. Augustine on Signs." *Phronesis* II (1957), 60–83.

Marrou, Henri Irenee. *A History of Education in Antiquity.* Trans. by G. Lamb. New York, 1956.

Maude, M. "Rhythmic Patterns in the Homilies of Aphraates." *AThR,* 17, (1935), 225–233.

Méridier, L. *L'influence de la seconde sophistique sur l'oeuvre de Grégoire de Nysse.* Rennes, 1906.

Meyvaert, Paul. *Benedict, Gregory, Bede and Others.* London, 1977.

Moore, George Foot. *Judaism in the First Centuries of the Christian Era: The Age of the Tannaim.* 2 vols. New York, 1971.

Morrison, Karl Frederick. *The Mimetic Tradition of Reform in the West.* Princeton, 1982.

Munk, Salomon. *Mélanges de Philosophie Juive et Arabe.* Paris, 1859.

Murray, Robert. *Symbols of Church and Kingdom: A Study of early Syriac Tradition.* London, 1975.

————. "A Hymn of St. Ephrem to Christ on the Incarnation, the Holy Spirit and the Sacraments." *Eastern Churches Review,* III, (1970), 142–150.

————. "St. Ephrem the Syrian on Church Unity." *ECQ,* XV, (1963), 164–176.

Musurillo, Herbert. "Some Textual Problems in the Editing of the Greek Fathers." *Studia Patristica III-Texte und Untersuchungen* 78. Berlin, 1961.

————. "History and Symbol: A Study of Form in Early Christian Literature." *TS,* 18 (1957), 357–87.

Nehorai, Michael, "Maimonides' System of the Commandments." *Daat,* 13 (1984), 29–42. [Hebrew].

Nemoy, Leon. *Karaite Anthology, Excerpts from the Early Literature.* New Haven, 1952.

————. "Al-Qirqisani's Account of the Jewish Sects and Christianity." *HUCA,* VII, (1931), 317–398.

Netanyahu, B. *Don Isaac Abravanel, Statesman and Philosopher.* Philadelphia, 1972.

Neusner, Jacob. *Aphrahat and Judaism: The Christian-Jewish Argument in Fourth-Century Iran.* Leiden, 1971.

Nuriel, Abraham. "Providence and Governance in *More Ha-Nevukhim.*" *Tarbiz* IL (1980), 346–355 [Hebrew].

————. "The Question of a Created or Primordial World in the Philosophy of Maimonides." *Tarbiz* XXXIII (1964), 372–387 (Hebrew).

Nwiya, Paul, *Exégèse Coranique et Langage Mystique: nouvel essai sur le lexique technique des mystiques musulmans. (Recherches publiees sous le direction de l'institut de lettres orientales de Beyrouth t.49 Serie 1: Pensée arabe et musulmanes).* Beyrouth, 1970.

Oberman, Heiko. *Forerunners of the Reformation: The Shape of Late Medieval Thought.* Philadelphia, 1981.

Oliver, James Henry. *The Civilizing Power: A Study of the Panathenaic Discourse of Aelius Aristides Against the Background of Literature and Cultural Conflict, with Text, Translation and Commentary.* {*Transactions of the American Philosophical Society,* N.S. Vol. 58, part 1}, Philadelphia, 1968.

O'Malley, John W. *Giles of Viterbo on Church and Reform. A Study in Renaissance Thought.* Leiden, 1968.

Orian, Meier. *Ha-Moreh le-Dorot.* Jerusalem, 1956.

Otis, Brooks. "Cappadocian Thought as a Coherent System." *DOP,* 12 (1958); 95–124.

———. "Gregory of Nyssa and the Cappadocian Conception of Time," *Studia Patristica,* 14 (1979), 327–57.

Ozment, Steven E. *The Age of Reform 1250–1550: an intellectual and religious history of late Medieval and Reformation Europe.* New Haven, 1980.

———. *Homo Spiritualis. A Comparative Study of the Anthropology of Johannes Tauler, Jean Gerson and Martin Luther (1509–16) in the Context of Their Theological Thought.* Leiden, 1969.

Pagels, Elaine H. *The Gnostic Gospels.* New York, 1981.

Paikarz, Mendel. *Biyemei Tzemikat Ha-Ḥasidut.* Jerusalem, 1978.

Pelikan, Jaroslav. "The Spiritual Sense of Scripture." *Basil of Caesarea Christian, Humanist, Ascetic: A Sixteen Hundreth Anniversary Symposium.* Ed. by Paul Jonathan Fedwick, Toronto, 1981: I, 337–360.

Pierre, H. "Économie ecclésiastique et réitération des sacrements." *Irenikon,* 37 (1937), 228–47.

Pinard, H. "Les Infiltrations Paiennes dans l'Ancienne Loi, D'après les Pères de l'Église." *RSR,* 9 (1919), 197–221.

Pines, Shlomo. "The Philosophical Purport of Maimonides' Halachic Works and the Purport of The Guide of the Perplexed." *Maimonides and Philosophy.* Eds. Shlomo Pines and Yirmiyahu Yovel. Dordrecht, 1986, 1–14.

———. " 'Israel, My Firstborn' and the Sonship of Jesus." *Studies in Mysticism and Religion Presented to Gershom G. Scholem on His Seventieth Birthday by Pupils, Colleagues and Friends.* Eds. E. E. Urbach, R. J. Z. Werblowsky and Ch. Wirszubski Jerusalem, 1967, 177–188.

———. "Ibn Khaldun and Maimonides." *Studia Islamica,* 32 (1970), 265–270.

Pocock, J. G. A. "The Origins of the Study of the Past: A Comparative Approach." *Comparative Studies in Society and History,* 4 (1961–62), 209–246.

Prestige, George Leonard. *God in Patristic Thought.* London, 1964.

Preus, James S. *From Shadow to Promise. Old Testament Interpretation from Augustine to the Young Luther.* Cambridge, MA, 1969.

Pruche, B. *Basile de Césarée, Traité du Saint-Esprit.* Ed. B. Pruche 2nd. ed. Paris, 1968.

Quasten, Johannes. *Patrology.* 3 Vols. Utrecht/Antwerp, 1950–60.

Quispel, G. "The Discussion of Judaic Christianity." *VC,* 22 (1968), 81–93.

Rawidowicz, Simon. "Saadya's Purification of the Idea of God." in *Studies in Jewish Thought.* Philadelphia, 1974, 246–68.

———. "She'elat mivnehu shel *Moreh Nevukhim.*" *Tarbiz,* VI (1935), 237–296. Reprinted in Simon Rawidowicz, *Iyyunim ba-Mahshevet Yisrael* I. Ed. B. C. I. Ravid (Jerusalem, 1969), 237–96.

Reines, Alvin Jay. "Maimonides' Concept of Mosaic Prophecy." *HUCA,* XL–XLI (1969–70), 325–61.

———. "Maimonides' Concepts of Providence and Theodicy." *HUCA,* XLIII (1977), 169–206.

———. "Maimonides' Concept of Miracles." *HUCA,* XLV (1979), 243–285.

Reumann, John. " 'Stewards of God'—Pre-Christian Religious Application of Oikonomos in Greek." *JBL,* 77 (1958), 339–49.

———. "Oikonomia = 'Covenant'; Terms for Heilsgeschichte in Early Christian Usage." *Novum Testamentum,* 3 (1959), 282–292.

———. "Oikonomia as 'Ethical Accommodation' in the Fathers and Its Pagan Backgrounds." *Studia Patristica,* 3, I (1961), 370–79.

Richards, Jeffery. *Consul of God: The Life and Times of Gregory the Great.* 1980.

Richter, G. "Uber die älteste Auseinandersetzung der syrischen Christen mit den Juden." *Zeitschrift fur die Neutestamentliche Wissenschaft,* 35 (1936), 101–114.

Rosenthal, E. I. J. "Torah and Nomos in Medieval Jewish Philosophy," *Studies in Rationalism, Judaism and Universalism: In Memory of Leon Roth.* Ed. Raphael Loewe. London, 1966, 215–230.

Rowbotham, Arnold H., *Missionary and Mandarin The Jesuits at the Court of China,* Berkeley, 1942.

Ruether, Rosemary Radford. *Gregory of Nazianzus, Rhetor and Philosopher.* Oxford, 1969.

Sailor, Danton B. "Moses and Atomism." *JHI*, 25 (1964), 3–16.

Saint-Simon, Claude Henri, comte de, *Introduction aux travaux scientifiques du dix-neuvième siècle, I* (Paris, 1808) in *Oeuvres Choisies*. (Bruxelles, 1859).

Sanders, E. P. *Paul, the Law and the Jewish People*. Philadelphia, 1983.

Santillana, Giorgio de. *The Crime of Galileo*. Chicago, 1955.

Saracheck, Joseph. *Faith and Reason: The Conflict over the Rationalism of Maimonides*. Williamsport, 1935.

Schechter, Solomon. *Aspects of Rabbinic Theology, Major Concepts of the Talmud*. New York, 1961.

———. *Studies in Judaism*. Philadelphia, 1960.

Scheops, Hans Joachim, *Theologie und Geschichte des Judenchristentums*. Tubingen, 1949.

———. *Jewish Christianity*. Trans. Douglas R. A. Hare, Philadelphia, 1969.

Schmitz, Fredrich Joseph. *The Problem of Individualism and the Crises in the Lives of Lessing and Hamann*. (*Univ. of California Publications in Modern Philology* V. 27), 1944, 125–48.

Scholem, Gershom. *Jewish Gnosticism, Merkabah Mysticism, and Talmudic Tradition*. New York, 1960.

———. *On the Kabbalah and Its Symbolism*. New York, 1969.

———. *Major Trends in Jewish Mysticism*. New York, 1974.

———. "The Name of God and the Linguistic Theory of the Kabbala." (trans. Simon Pleasance) *Diogenes*, 79 (1972), 59–81; 80 (1972), 164–94.

Schwartz, Edward. "Zur Geschichte des Athanasius." *Nachrichten der K. Geselleschaft der Wissenschaften zu Göettingen Philologische-Historische Klasse*, 1904, 333–356.

Schwen, Paul. *Afrahat: seine Person und sein Verstandnis des Christentums*. Berlin, 1907.

Sed, N. "Les hymnes sur le paradis de saint Ephrem et les traditions juives." *Le Muséon*, 81, (1968), 455–501.

Segal, Judah Benzion. *Edessa 'The Blessed City.'* Oxford, 1970.

Septimus, B. "Petrus Alfonsi on the Cult at Mecca." *Speculum*, 56, (1981), 517–33.

Sieben, Hermann Joseph. "Hermeneutique d' l'exégése dogmatique d'Athanase." *Politique et théologie chez Athanase d'Alexandrie Actes des Colloque de Chantilly, 23–25, Septembre 1973.* Ed. Charles Kannengiesser. Paris, 1974, 195–214.

Silver, Daniel Jeremy. *Maimonidean Criticism and the Maimonidean Controversy 1180–1240.* Leiden, 1965.

Simon, Marcel. "La polémique anti-juive de S. Jean Chrysostome et le mouvement judaïsant d'Antioche." *Annuaire de l'Institut de philologie et d'histoire orientales et slaves* IV, 1936 [*Mélanges Franz Cumont*] 403–421.

———. *Verus Israel: étude sur les relations entre chrétiens et juifs dans l'empire roman (135–425).* Paris, 1964.

Smalley, Beryl. *The Study of the Bible in the Middle Ages.* New York, 1950.

———. "William of Auvergne, John of La Rochelle, and St. Thomas Aquinas on the Old Law." *St. Thomas Aquinas Commemorative Studies,* Toronto, 1274–1974, I, 10–71.

———. *English Friars and Antiquity in the Early Fourteenth Century.* New York, 1960.

———. "Ralph of Flaix on Leviticus," *Recherches de théologie ancienne et médiévale,* 35 (1968), 35–82.

———. "An Early Twelfth-Century Commentator on the Literal Sense of Leviticus," *Recherches de théologie ancienne et médiévale,* 35 (1969), 78–99.

Smith, W. Robertson. *Lectures on the Religion of the Semites.* Edinburgh, 1889.

Smolar, Levy and Aberbach, Moshe. "The Golden Calf in Postbiblical Literature." *HUCA,* 39 (1968), 91–116.

Southern, Richard W. "Aspects of the European Tradition of Historical Writing: Hugh of St. Victor and the Idea of Historical Development." *TRHS* Series V, 21 (1971); 159–179.

Sowers, Sidney, "On the Reinterpretation of Biblical History in Hellenistic Judaism." *Oikonomia.* Ed. Felix Christ. Hamburg-Bergstedt, 1967, 18–25.

Spencer, John. *De Legibus Hebraeorum Ritualibus et Eorum Rationibus libri tres.* Cambridge, 1732.

Stead, G. Christopher, "Rhetorical Method in Athanasius," *VC,* 30 (1976) 121–37.

Stern, David. "Midrash and Indeterminancy." *Critical Inquiry* 15:1 (1988), 132–161.

Stern, Josef. "The Idea of a Hoq in Maimonides' Explanation of the Law." *Maimonides and Philosophy*. Eds. Shlomo Pines and Yirmiyahu Yovel. Dordrecht, 1986, 92–130.

Strack, H. L. *Introduction to the Talmud and Midrash*, New York, 1969.

Strauss, Leo. *Persecution and the Art of Writing*. Glencoe, 1952.

———. *Philosophy and Law: essays toward the understanding of Maimonides and his predecessors*. Trans. Fred Baumann, Philadelphia, 1987.

———. "How to Begin the Study of the *Guide of the Perplexed*" in *The Guide of the Perplexed*. Trans. S. Pines, Chicago, 1963.

———. "Notes on Maimonides' 'Book of Knowledge.' " *Studies in Mysticism and Religion Presented to Gershom G. Scholem on His Seventieth Birthday by Pupils, Colleagues and Friends*. Eds. E. E. Urbach, R. J. Z. Werblowsky and Ch. Wirszubski. Jerusalem, 1967, 269–283.

———. "Maimonides' Statement on Political Science." *PAAJR*, 22 (1953): 115–130.

Strecker, Geord. *Das Judenchristentum in den Pseudoklementin*. (*Texte und Untersuchungen zur Geschichte der altchristlichen Literatur*, Bd. 70). Berlin, 1958.

Stylianopoulos, Theodore G. *Justin Martyr and the Mosaic Law*. (*SBL Dissertation Series 20*). Missoula, Mont., 1975.

Talbert, Charles H. Ed. *Reimarus, Fragments*. Philadelphia, 1970.

Talmage, Frank E. *David Kimhi: the man and the commentaries*. Cambridge, 1975.

———. "Apples of Gold: The Inner Meaning of Sacred Texts in Medieval Judaism." *Jewish Spirituality*. Ed. Arthur Green. New York, 1986–1987, 312–355.

———. "David Kimhi and the Rationalist Tradition." *HUCA*, 39 (1968) 177–218.

———. "David Kimhi and the Rationalist Tradition. II: Literary Sources." *Studies in Jewish bibliography, history and literature in Honor of I. Kiev*. Ed. Charles Berlin. New York, 1972, 435–478.

———. "A Hebrew Polemical Treatise." *HThR*, 60 (1967), 323–348.

———. "R. David Kimhi as Polemicist." *HUCA*, 38 (1967), 213–35.

Tiele, C. P. *Histoire compareé des anciennes religions de l'Égypte et des peoples sémetiques*. Paris, 1882.

Tooley, Wilfred. "Stewards of God." *Scottish Journal of Theology*, 19 (1966), 74–86.

Touati, C. "Les Deux Théories de Maïmonide sur La Providence." *Studies in Jewish Religious and Intellectual History. Presented to Alexander Altmann on the occasion of his seventieth birthday.* Eds. Siegfried Stein and Raphael Loewe. University, Alabama, 1977, 331–343.

Twersky, Isadore. *Introduction to the Code of Maimonides. (Mishneh Torah).* New Haven, 1980.

————. "Concerning Maimonides' Rationalization of the Commandments; an Explication of Hilkhot Me'ilah, VIII:8." *Studies in the History of Jewish Society in the Middle Ages and in the Modern Period.* Eds. E. Etkes and Y. Salmon. Jerusalem, 1980, 24–33.

————. Ed. *A Maimonides Reader.* New York, 1972.

————. "Some Non-Halakic Aspects of the Mishneh Torah." *Jewish Medieval and Renaissance Studies.* Ed. Alexander Altmann. Cambridge, MA 1967, 95–119.

————. "Aspects of the Social and Cultural History of Provencal Jewry." *Journal of World History,* XI (1968), 185–208.

Urbach, Efraim Elimelich. "Homilies of the Rabbis on the Prophets of the Nations and the Balaam Stories." *Tarbiz,* XXV (1956) 272–289 [Hebrew].

————. "The Homiletical Interpretations of the Sages and the Expositions of Origen on Canticles, and the Jewish-Christian Disputation." *Tarbiz,* XXX (1960) 148–170. [Hebrew]. English translation in *Scripta Hierosolymitana* XXII (1971), 247–75.

————. "Rabbinic Exegesis and Origen's Commentaries on the Song of Songs and Jewish-Christian Polemics." *Tarbiz,* XXX (1960), 148–170 [Hebrew].

————. "The Rabbinic Laws of Idolatry in the Second and Third Centuries in the Light of Archaeological and Historical Facts. I–II." *Israel Exploration Journal,* 9, (1959–60) 149–165; 229–245.

————. *The Sages, Their Concepts and Beliefs.* Trans. I. Abrahams. 2 Vols. Jerusalem, 1979.

Vajda, G. "La Pensée religieuse de Moïse Maïmonide: unité ou dualité." *Cahiers de Civilisation Médiévale,* 9 (1966), 29–49.

Van Engen, John H. *Rupert of Deutz.* Berkeley, Los Angeles, London, 1983.

Van Lee, M. "Les idées d'Anselme de Havelberg sur le dévelopement des dogmes." *Analecta Praemonstratensia,* 14 (1938), 3–35.

von Campenhausen, H. F., *Greichische Kirchenväter,* Stuttgart, 1955.

Vööbus, Arthur. *History of the School of Nisibis.* CSCO 266, Louvain, 1965.

———. "Methodologisches zum Studium der Anweisungen Aphrahats." *OCh*, 46, (1962), 25–32.

———. *Peschitta und Targumim des Pentateuchs: neues Licht zur Frage der Herkunft der Peschitta aus dem altpalastenischen Targum.* Stockholm, 1962.

———. Ed. and trans. *The Statutes of the School of Nisibis.* Stockholm, 1961.

Vosté, J. M. "L'oeuvre exégétique de Théodore de Mopsueste au IIe concile de Constantinople." *RBibl* 38 (1929), 382–395, 542–554.

Wallace-Hadrill. D. S. *Eusebius of Caesarea.* London, 1960.

Walzer, Richard. *Galen on Jews and Christians.* Oxford, 1949.

Warburton, William. *The Divine Legation of Moses Demonstrated* 4 vols. *(British Philosophers and Theologians of the 17th and 18th Centuries).* Ed. René Wellek, New York and London, 1978.

Wellhausen, Julius. *Geschichte Israels.* Berlin, 1878.

White, Hayden V. *Metahistory: The Historical Imagination in Nineteenth Century Europe.* Baltimore, 1973.

———. "Romanticism, Historicism, Realism: Toward a Period Concept For Early 19th Century Intellectual History." In *The Uses of History.* Ed. Hayden V. White. Detroit, 1968: 45–58.

Wilensky, Sarah H. *The Philosophy of Isaac Arama in the Framework of Philonic Philosophy.* Jerusalem and Tel Aviv, 1956 [Hebrew].

Wilken, Robert Louis. *John Chrysostom and the Jews: Rhetoric and Reality in the late 4th century. (The Transformation of the Classical Heritage,* 4), Berkeley, Los Angeles, London, 1983.

———. *The Christians As The Romans Saw Them.* New Haven, 1984.

Willey, Basil. *The Seventeenth Century Background: Studies in the Thought of the Age in Relation to Poetry and Religion.* London, 1949.

———. *The Eighteenth Century Background: Studies on the Idea of Nature in the Thought of the Period.* London, 1949.

Williams, A. Lukyn. *Adversus Judaeos; A Bird's-eye View of Christian Apologiae until the Renaissance.* Cambridge, 1935.

Wolfson, Harry Austryn. "Extradeical and Intradeical Interpretations of Platonic Ideas" in *Religious Philosophy: A Group of Essays.* New York, 1965, 27–68; and *JHI,* 22 (1961), 3–32.

———. "Spinoza and the Religion of the Past." In *Religious Philosophy: A Group of Essays.* New York, 1965.

Yellin, David and Abrahams, Israel. *Maimonides.* Philadelphia, 1903.

Yerushalmi, Yosef. H. *From Spanish Court to Italian Ghetto Isaac Cardoso: A Study in Seventeenth-Century Marranism and Jewish Apologetics.* Seattle and London, 1981.

INDEX

317

INDEX OF BIBLICAL CITATIONS

New Testament